Fodor's EXPLORING

FRANCE

FODOR'S TRAVEL PUBLICATIONS
NEW YORK • TORONTO • LONDON • SYDNEY • AUCKLAND

WWW.FODORS.COM

Please note:
In January 2006, the French government transferred the administration and maintenance of approximately 18,000km (11,200 miles) of National roads to local authorities (*départements*), resulting in an extensive re-classification and re-numbering programme which will take several years to complete. You may find, therefore, that some of the road numbers used in this book do not match those appearing on current road signs.

Important Note
Time inevitably brings changes, so always confirm prices, travel facts, and other perishable information when it matters. Although Fodor's cannot accept responsibility for errors, you can use this guide in the confidence that we have taken every care to ensure its accuracy.

Published in the United States by Fodor's Travel, a division of Random House, Inc., and simultaneously in Canada by Random House of Canada Limited, Toronto. Published in the United Kingdom by AA Publishing.

ISBN: 978-1-4000-1833-8

Seventh Edition

Fodor's Exploring France

Author: **Adam Ruck**
Additional Writing and Research by: **Rosemary Bailey, Fiona Dunlop, Lindsay Hunt, Michael Ivory, Ingrid Morgan, Judith Samson, David Shepheard**
Revision Verifier: **Mike Gerrard**
Revision Editor: **Kathryn Glendenning**
Cartography: **The Automobile Association**
Cover Design: **Tigist Getachew; Fabrizio La Rocca**
Front Cover Silhouette: **Catherine Karnow**
Front Cover Photograph: **The Automobile Association**

Special Sales
This book is available for special discounts for bulk purchases for sales promotions or premiums. Special editions, including personalized covers, excerpts of existing books, and corporate imprints, can be created in large quantities for special needs. For more information, write to Special Markets/Premium Sales, 1745 Broadway, MD 6-2, New York, NY 10019 or e-mail specialmarkets@randomhouse.com.

A03259

Printed and bound in Italy by Printer Trento srl.
10 9 8 7 6 5 4 3 2 1

Boucherie
Charcuterie fine
H. SIEDEL
Fromage
DMC
mercerie

How to use this book

ORGANIZATION

France Is, France Was
Discusses aspects of life and culture in contemporary France and explores significant periods in its history.

A–Z
The book begins with sections on Paris, and is subsequently divided into geographical regions. Places of interest are listed alphabetically within each section, including suggested walks and drives. Within this section fall the Focus On articles, which consider a variety of subjects in greater detail.

Travel Facts
Contains the strictly practical information vital for a successful trip.

Hotels and Restaurants
Lists recommended establishments alphabetically by region, giving a brief summary of their attractions.

KEY TO ADMISSION CHARGES
Standard admission charges are categorized in this book as follows:

Inexpensive	under €3
Moderate	€3–€6
Expensive	over €6

ABOUT THE RATINGS
Most places described in this book have been given a separate rating. These are as follows:

▶▶▶	**Do not miss**
▶▶	**Highly recommended**
▶	**Worth seeing**

MAP REFERENCES
To make each particular location easier to find, every main entry in this book has a map reference to the right of its name. This comprises a number, followed by another number, such as 176B3. The first number (176) refers to the page on which the map can be found, the letter (B) and the second number (3) pinpoint the square in which the main entry is located. The maps on the inside front cover and inside back cover are referred to as IFC and IBC respectively.

Contents

My France

My first trip to France was unavoidable after a French boy, a little older than me, stayed with me and my family in England. A mulish 12-year-old, I went predisposed to have a bad time to prove myself right for not wanting to go. This was quite easy. Having driven from Paris to Provence via Lourdes, my hosts were delayed and reached Marseille airport four hours after I did. Minutes later we had a head-on collision with a truck, and I spent my first evening in France sitting outside Aix-en-Provence hospital.

The following two weeks seemed longer than a school term. Encouraged to drink wine in the evening, I found it helped me to sleep. The question was: to drink it neat (foul taste) or diluted (more of it)? Excursions were offered, but after the crash I was terrified of the car and said I was quite happy at the house. 'France and I do not agree,' I wrote pompously to my mother, delighting in my unhappiness.

The best part of the trip was when the Baron, my host, whose ribs had been broken in the accident, summoned me to his bedside in order to explain that owing to his incapacity I would have to take the train to Paris, where the last days of my stay were to be spent. Hooray! I was shown the Eiffel Tower but not allowed up. 'No true Parisian goes there,' said my friend with a sneer.

I was glad to get home but kept the language up, and came to love France through its literature. I soon developed an unhealthy interest in old buildings and discovered sightseeing as a good wet-weather alternative to tennis. After I left school I spent six months in Paris.

Once I could drive, I discovered the user-friendliness of France for a touring holiday, whether your budget confines you to *le camping municipal* or extends to the village hotel, and gradually my interest in the country broadened to include food, wine, landscape and even people. Slavishly devoted to guidebook star ratings, I would become furious when a long detour, or even a voyage, to a top-rated spot proved unrewarding. Sitting at the top of the Mont Beuvray, surveying one of the world's most boring views after a long drive through the only dull part of Burgundy, I almost exploded with rage. 'I could do better than this!' I shouted. 'Go on, then,' my passenger said. 'Since you seem to want to spend your whole life sightseeing, you might as well.'

Adam Ruck

Top: Pesmes on the River Ognon
Opposite: Beynac-et-Cazenac

France Is France Was

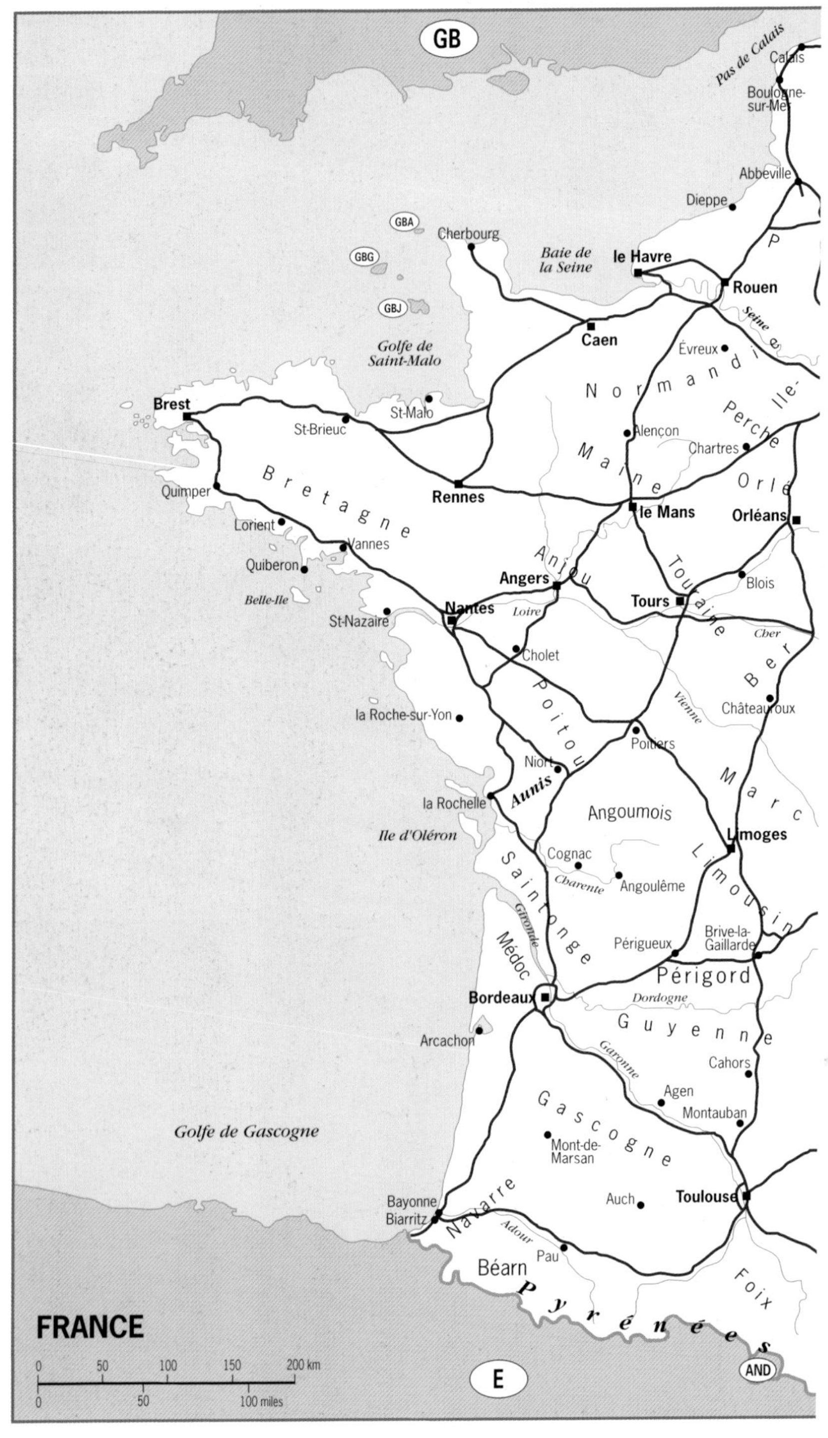
GB
Pas de Calais
Calais
Boulogne-sur-Mer
Abbeville
Dieppe
GBA
GBG
GBJ
Cherbourg
Baie de la Seine
le Havre
Rouen
Seine
Caen
Évreux
Golfe de Saint-Malo
Normandie
Brest
St-Malo
St-Brieuc
Alençon
Perche
Chartres
Maine
Bretagne
Rennes
Quimper
Orléans
le Mans
Lorient
Vannes
Quiberon
Anjou
Angers
Touraine
Blois
Tours
Belle-Ile
Nantes
Loire
St-Nazaire
Cher
Cholet
Berry
Poitou
Vienne
Châteauroux
la Roche-sur-Yon
Poitiers
Niort
Aunis
Marche
la Rochelle
Angoumois
Ile d'Oléron
Limoges
Cognac
Charente
Angoulême
Saintonge
Limousin
Gironde
Médoc
Périgueux
Brive-la-Gaillarde
Périgord
Bordeaux
Dordogne
Guyenne
Arcachon
Garonne
Cahors
Agen
Gascogne
Montauban
Golfe de Gascogne
Mont-de-Marsan
Bayonne
Biarritz
Navarre
Auch
Toulouse
Adour
Pau
Béarn
Foix
Pyrénées
FRANCE
0 50 100 150 200 km
0 50 100 miles
E
AND

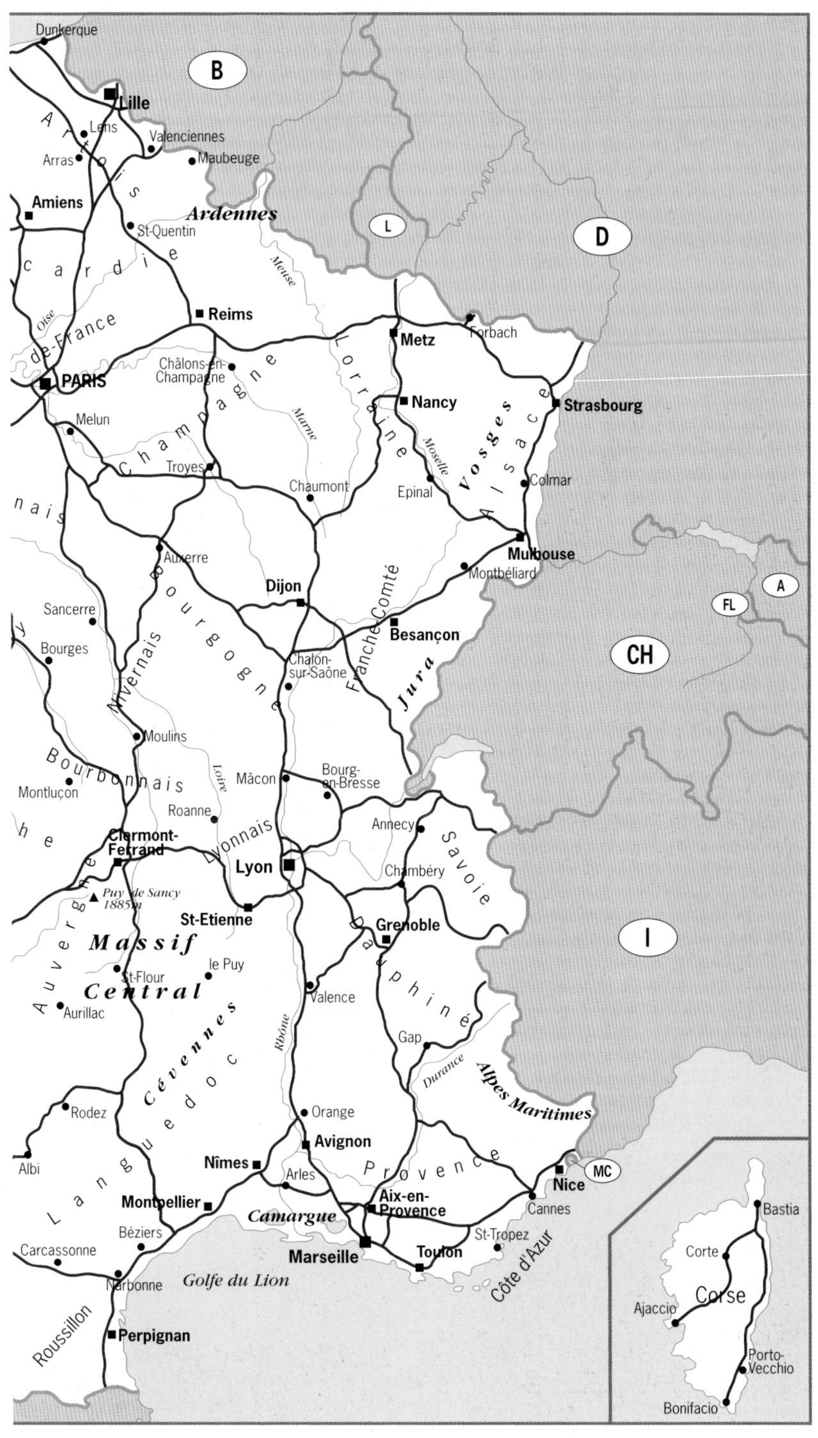
Dunkerque
B
Lille
Lens
Valenciennes
Arras
Maubeuge
Amiens
Ardennes
St-Quentin
L
D
Meuse
Reims
Oise
Metz
Forbach
Châlons-en-Champagne
PARIS
Nancy
Strasbourg
Melun
Marne
Moselle
Vosges
Alsace
Champagne
Lorraine
Troyes
Chaumont
Epinal
Colmar
Mulhouse
Auxerre
Montbéliard
Dijon
A
FL
Sancerre
Besançon
CH
Bourges
Franche Comté
Chalon-sur-Saône
Jura
Bourgogne
Nivernais
Moulins
Bourbonnais
Loire
Mâcon
Bourg-en-Bresse
Montluçon
Roanne
Annecy
Savoie
Clermont-Ferrand
Lyonnais
Lyon
Chambéry
Puy de Sancy 1885m
St-Etienne
Grenoble
Massif Central
Dauphiné
le Puy
I
St-Flour
Auvergne
Valence
Aurillac
Rhône
Gap
Cévennes
Durance
Alpes Maritimes
Rodez
Orange
Avignon
Languedoc
Nîmes
Provence
Albi
Arles
Nice
MC
Montpellier
Camargue
Aix-en-Provence
Cannes
Bastia
Béziers
St-Tropez
Corte
Carcassonne
Marseille
Toulon
Côte d'Azur
Narbonne
Golfe du Lion
Corse
Ajaccio
Roussillon
Perpignan
Porto-Vecchio
Bonifacio

Strongly individualistic, the French nature is such that their revolutions and uprisings once came and went as often as their governments. After two centuries of changing constitutions, political stability is only a recent phenomenon, introduced by De Gaulle with the Fifth Republic, relayed by the sphinx-like Mitterrand, and later steered by the more impulsive Chirac.

Monarchies, republics and empires have all had their turn over the last 150 years, interrupted by the traumatic four-year German occupation during World War II. Yet today France is regarded as one of the most powerful Western democracies, and a pivotal force within the European Union.

WHO GOVERNS? Far from being a mere figurehead, the French President in the Fifth Republic has considerable powers. Head of the army, responsible for nuclear force, and nominator of the Prime Minister, he can call referendums or dissolve Parliament. Strangely aloof in the gilded cage of the Elysée Palace, he is not allowed to set foot in the National Assembly and is only answerable to the Conseil Constitutionnel, an independent elected body that judges the validity of every law passed and guarantees the Rights of Man. The Prime Minister, who leads a Council of Ministers, answers to the National Assembly (lower house) and Senate (upper house), which together make up the body of Parliament.

Elected for seven years, the President's mandate can adversely cross the fortunes of Parliament, whose deputies are elected every five years. Twice during Mitterrand's reign (1986 and again in 1993) slumps in his Socialist Party's popularity forced him to 'cohabit' with right-wing prime ministers.

One of these, Jacques Chirac, was elected president in May 1995 after Parliament had radically swung to the right in 1993. Two years later, his popularity had plummeted, strikes and demonstrations were escalating. He dissolved Parliament and after the ensuing massive victory of the left, was left musing on the irony of having been the first right-wing prime minister to cohabit with a left-wing president, as well as the first right-wing president to cohabit with a left-wing prime minister.

Since then the 35-hour week has been introduced as a controversial way of fighting unemployment, and the French economy has slipped from fourth to fifth largest in the West. The euro was introduced in 2002, but outside the Elysée many aspects of European integration seem to be ignored.

In May 2007 the right-wing Nicolas Sarkozy was elected President.

Many worlds make up the Republic: a delightful rural idyll near Chartres

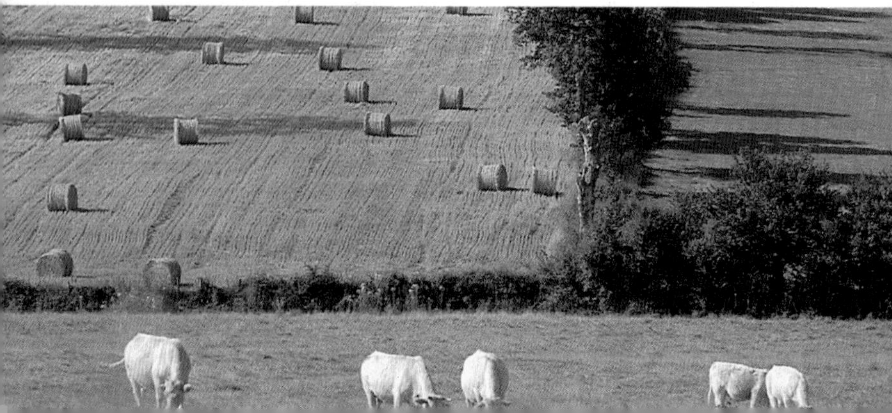

Of all Western European countries, France has possibly undergone the most radical social transformations since the 1950s. Previously a society and economy based on agriculture, and slowly undergoing industrialization, its top stratum was a highly intellectualized, cultivated middle class. The nobility had all but disappeared with the Revolution, but certain of their values had been adopted by the haute bourgeoisie, *one of which was an abhorrence of commercialism. This left the field open for the rise of the* petit bourgeoisie.

Property-owning, relatively well educated, the *petit bourgeoisie* had the reputation for great pride in its regional identity and a suspicion of intrusion. Since the 1950s, rural areas have lost both the lower middle classes and the land-working peasantry to the big cities. Today only some 4 per cent of the population is employed in agriculture (before the war the figure was 33 per cent). Moving into urban areas, the one-time country dwellers have renounced their historic individualism and become wage-earners. Strong on the virtues of family life, and maintaining their traditional keen eye on value, they have been a target for the National Front.

RELIGION AND MORALITY
Traditionally and still nominally a Catholic nation, France separated the Church from the State in 1905. Today maybe 14 per cent of the population goes to church, and religion is no longer a burning issue. However, the morality of the nation is still guided, at least officially, by Catholic values.

❑ More than 83 per cent of the population belongs to the Roman Catholic Church. Other major denominations include the Protestants (2 per cent), Jews (1 per cent) and Muslims (5–6 per cent), in urban areas. About 4 per cent claim no religion. ❑

EVER PLEASURE-LOVING The French were as influenced by the swinging '60s as the rest of the world. Although women obtained the vote only in 1946, their movement had its effect, legalizing the Pill and, in 1974, abortions. More than two-thirds of women work and many hold key posts in government and business, aided by a nursery school system that welcomes three-year-olds. Yet, unlike Anglo-American feminists, they cling to a feminine image while at the same time keeping pace with changes within society. Diane de Poitiers, Marie-Antoinette, Madame de Pompadour—the tradition is a long one. French morality is an individual's private business. While the nation may be aware that a public figure has a lover, strict privacy laws prevent media speculation.

Around four per cent of the population is employed in agriculture

The tapestry of France's population, which has always included regional identities (Bretons, Alsaciens, Corsicans) is becoming increasingly rich. Xenophobia and racism have come to the fore, as the immigration issue is tossed to and fro by political parties, each trying to win maximum electoral support. The 1999 census recorded a foreign population of 3.26 million (out of a total of 58.5 million), which does not include 1.8 million with French nationality and countless illegal immigrants. Some 10 per cent of the French population is of foreign origin—a proportion that demands attention.

As elsewhere in Europe, immigrants were brought in after World War II to cope with unwanted low-paid jobs. Portuguese, Italians and Spaniards were joined by people from the former colonies, particularly the Maghreb: Algeria, Tunisia and Morocco. Lesser numbers arrived from Central and West Africa, while French citizens from the DOM-TOM (overseas *départements* in the Caribbean, Indian Ocean and Pacific) also left their shores searching for work. The 1960s suburban *bidonvilles* of cheap prefabs were soon replaced by badly planned towerblocks, which in their turn became immigrant ghettos.

RACISM Today the situation has hardly improved, despite various government attempts to pour oil on troubled waters. Politicians of every party try to divert support from National Front leader Jean-Marie Le Pen and his overtly racist tirades, via Chirac's bungled sympathy for those 'driven crazy' by immigrants, or via Edith Cresson, as the then Socialist Prime Minister, talking of the need to 'fly planeloads home'. Phenomenally high unemployment, soulless suburbs, police harassment, attacks on immigrants, 1995's spate of terrorist bombs and endless tinkering with immigration and nationality laws has hardly cooled racial tensions.

❑ In January 2007, the French unemployment rate was 8.6 per cent; but it was around double that among North African immigrants. ❑

NO MAN'S LAND Rarely socially welcome, France's naturalized North Africans find themselves stranded between two cultures. Women, more than men, follow religious customs that can separate them from French society.

❑ In the 2002 Presidential elections, 16.86 per cent of the electorate voted for National Front candidate Jean-Marie Le Pen, who went through to the second round before losing to the eventual winner, Jacques Chirac. ❑

Support for the extreme right National Front runs high enough, particularly in the southeast. Immigrants feel understandably threatened. Assimilation, however, takes time and all is not negative: mixed marriages are on the increase and the third generation now speaks almost exclusively French. In the 1980s, *SOS Racisme* created a forceful lobby that led to a seriously increased awareness of the problems.

Young Algerians born in France in particular are also forging a new identity, calling themselves *les beurs* and successfully creating their own alternative music—*le Raï*. Full integration, though, is a long way off.

JEWISH COMMUNITIES Although France's oldest immigrant group, the Jewish population, has played a major role in French culture and politics over the last two centuries, it too suffers from racism. About 700,000 Jews (the largest community in Europe) originated from central Europe, and they were joined during the 1960s by an influx into France of Sephardic Jews from North Africa.

As well as revitalizing the Jewish community, the Sephards have underlined their distinct identity. Jewish sense of separation from 'mainstream' French history can only be heightened by the memory of the deportation of more than 117,000 Jews to concentration camps during World War II.

THE AMERICAN FACTOR Since World War II, the French have been at odds about the Americans. Some people rail against the Americans' insidious influence on French culture, their economic dominance and brash commercialism; but others admire and espouse many American commercial and cultural inventions (media styles, westerns, soap operas, rock 'n' roll, jazz, fast food and the Internet). However much French politicians may rant about the spread of American cultural hegemony and support the Académie Française in its unyielding crusade to keep all words purely French, only their unyielding stance against the 2003 Iraq war persuaded the public to turn away from American culture, albeit briefly.

❑ New President Nicolas Sarkozy has promised to try to mend relations with the United States, which have been somewhat strained of late due to France's non-support of the US stance on the Iraq War. ❑

Generally, the French welcome the advent of a high-tech society, and are ready to accept the 'winners'—whether they are foreign and speak a different language or not—but they

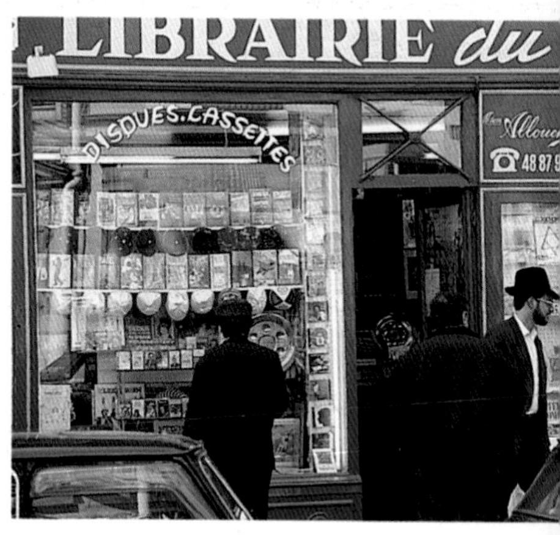

The well-known rue des Rosiers, in Le Marais, Paris...

❑ Sylvester Stallone and Sharon Stone figure among US citizens solemnly decorated by the French Minister of Culture in the last few years. ❑

are still just as ready as ever to exercise an intellectual judgement and to praise or criticize changes in society as they see fit.

The victory of France's football team in the 1998 World Cup may have helped, making heroes of its multicultural team, though defeat in 2006 diminished this effect.

...is the heart of the city's lively Jewish quarter, and is packed with Mediterranean-style restaurants and specialist shops

For France the 1970s and 1980s were decades of economic progress by leaps and bounds, reaping rewards from the near past and establishing a new, high-profile identity. State dirigisme *and centralized planning proved hard to maintain in the complexities of this newly wealthy society, despite the fact that the 1990s kicked off with a spate of nationalizations and rigorous controls.*

Yet the face of both society and the economy was transformed, bringing prosperity on most levels. In the early 1980s, industrial strategy was still tightly controlled by central government. Countless banks and mega-industries were nationalized, and the state share of industrial production rose from 15 to 30 per cent virtually overnight.

REVERSED POLICY After these initial steps, Mitterrand did a *volte face*, leading to tough fiscal and monetary policies, tax reductions, some privatizations (under Chirac's two-year government) and, above all, much financial deregulation. The French franc was locked into the Deutschmark, supported by an all-powerful Bundesbank.

A new breed of entrepreneurial French managers also appeared—a contrast to the old élitists of the Grandes Ecoles. Not least, modern high-tech industries benefited as much from government aid as from real market effectiveness.

FLUX It couldn't last. Recession (*la crise*) hit, deeply affecting the Gallic ego; unemployment soared to more than 12 per cent, with a lot more people depending in one way or another on state aid; corruption scandals rocked the higher echelons of industry and politics; the requirements to join the euro loomed larger and larger; social unrest and strikes broke out; and government went through a double flip from left to right and back again.

Nor could the gilded face of France conceal a widening rift between rich and poor: although the number of poor changed little in the 1990s, the poor got poorer and the rich got richer. Nor was the Socialist government's introduction of the 35-hour working week welcomed by industry. The compulsory minimum wage stands at around 50 per cent of the average wage but exorbitant social security charges discourage employers.

And yet, the recession seems to be easing, the introduction of the euro has passed without crisis, inflation is well under control at 1.2 per cent, unemployment has dropped slightly to 8.6 per cent, growth is patchy but respectable, France is still the fifth-largest industrial power in the West and the French are past masters at bouncing back.

France has had a rich and varied history, and now has one of the highest standards of living in Europe.

A nuclear power station at Civaux. Nuclear power now provides most of the energy which is required in France

FUTURE STRATEGIES Known today as much for the TGV, Minitel, Ariane and Concorde as for camembert and Château Margaux, France entered the 21st century with a vengeance. Moving to the forefront of modern technology—whether fast-breeder nuclear reactors or off-shore oil techniques—it has become a pace-setter in Europe.

Telecommunications, transport, biotechnology, computing and aerospace are fields where French know-how is recognized, although there is often a chasm between the world of pure research and its industrial applications. Less inspiring was France's obstinate insistence on perfecting nuclear war-heads through controversial tests in the Pacific in late 1995. Following the American example, French firms have invested heavily overseas. St-Gobain has factories in more than 40 countries, while Renault, Peugeot, Michelin, Total and Aerospatiale all have a strong overseas presence. By the end of 2006, however, France's trade deficit was €29.2 billion, a record. Falling car exports and rising energy costs were said to be prime reasons for the figures, not helped by problems faced by the Airbus company, based in Toulouse, with delays in delivering its flagship A380 super-jumbo jet.

❑ France's greatest industry is tourism: The country is the world's top tourist destination, with around 75 million visitors each year. This is about 50 per cent more than the country in second place, Spain. ❑

NEW ENERGY For years France depended on coal, gas, hydro-electricity and imported oil. When the oil crisis hit the country in 1973, it was importing nearly 75 per cent of its energy needs.

Home-grown nuclear power now accounts for three-quarters of France's national electricity requirements, and despite the ominous presence of more than 50 nuclear power stations throughout the country, there is little public outcry. Even after Chernobyl (when French authorities declared that the radioactive cloud dispersed at the French border), 70 per cent of the population agrees with the policy of continuing with nuclear power, though not, paradoxically, of building any new power stations.

Somehow, the EDF (French electricity board) public relations department convinces the public that French reactors are more sophisticated and less prone to accidents. Only time will tell whether or not they are right.

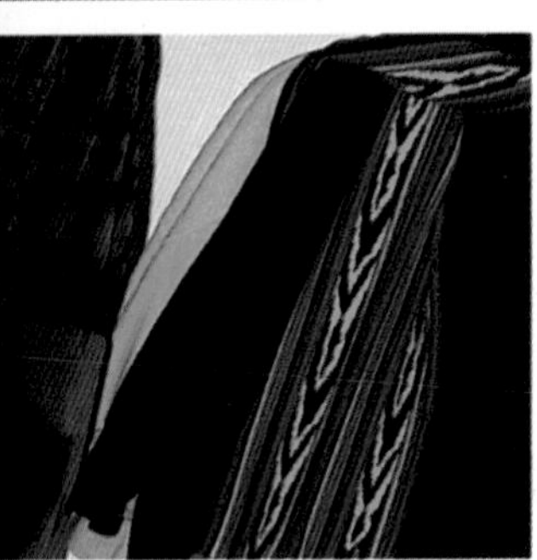

It was Christian Dior's 'new look' which set the tone for post-war Paris fashion hegemony: Women all over the world threw away the masculine, practical clothes that had dominated the war years and bowed to Dior's new feminine style. Despite repeated offensives from Milan, New York, London and Tokyo, high French style still maintains a firm grip on the successful marketing of thousands of signed accessories —the bread and butter of every top couturier. And the French remain leaders in street chic.

In France the term 'haute couture' is defined and protected by law, and in 2007 there were only eight official haute couture houses in the country. The often outrageous catwalk designs that fill the fashion pages of the world, which bring the A-list like homing pigeons to the collections, are only an extravagant marketing ploy, the necessary draw to help sell you the more mundane pret-à-porter collections and, even more profitably, perfumes. Chloë, Kenzo, Montana, Gaultier, Mugler, Chantal Thomass and Cerruti are names whose fame is often greater than that of the more obscure couturiers.Today, it is the more accessible *créateurs de mode* who really drive the industry. Wilder, racier, younger, the fashion creators' style can be outrageous, but when their twice-yearly collections are presented in the Carrousel du Louvre (a specially designed space beneath the Louvre pyramid (see page 52), Parisian hotels are taken by force.

MIXED INFLUENCE French shrewdness in realizing the scope and power of fashion extends to the acceptance of talented foreigners into their midst. Among the *grands couturiers* are four Italians, one Spaniard, one Japanese and one Norwegian, not to mention the ubiquitous Karl Lagerfeld, of German origin. The fashion creators include the Japanese Kenzo, influential Issey Miyake, several Italians and the English Stella McCartney, Alexander McQueen and John Galliano. Strict rules govern production and marketing, and only those fashion houses with strong financial backing succeed. Yves St-Laurent would never have survived without the astute Pierre Bergé, nor Dior without the textile giant Boussac.

In total, the prestigious French fashion and luxury goods industry manages to generate an annual turnover of around 31 billion euros, though the number of regular haute couture customers is estimated at only 3,000 worldwide. Skilled craftsmen and women dedicated to the creation of luxury can be found only in Paris. But as their ages advance, fewer young people choose to come forward to replace them in a laborious and traditional field.

You'll see all sorts of fashion styles in Paris

CUT OF THE CLOTH The rest of French fashion is heavily dependent on impetus and inspiration from the upper echelons. No designer can exist outside Paris, but textile manufacturers are scattered all over the country. Much of French elegance depends on the fine quality of fabrics and the 'backward' French textile industry specialized for years in producing small runs of divine, costly cloths. Lyon was until relatively recently the hub of the silk industry, though cheaper foreign suppliers are now stepping in.

The chic displayed by the average Frenchman or woman seems to emanate from a high degree of self-confidence. Posture and careful toilette can clearly pay dividends—one only has to look at the result.

❑ Denim actually originated in Nîmes (hence the name 'de Nîmes'). The denim trousers worn by Genoese sailors were taken to America by Levi Strauss, who added rivets and sold them to cowboys. ❑

Keeping up with the latest trends is an expensive affair, but most French people manage to acquire the latest accessories. It is this innate sense of what is suitable and an eternal desire to please that ensures an impeccable turn-out.

Good to look at, but it might break the budget: a stylish display in the Boutique Christian Dior

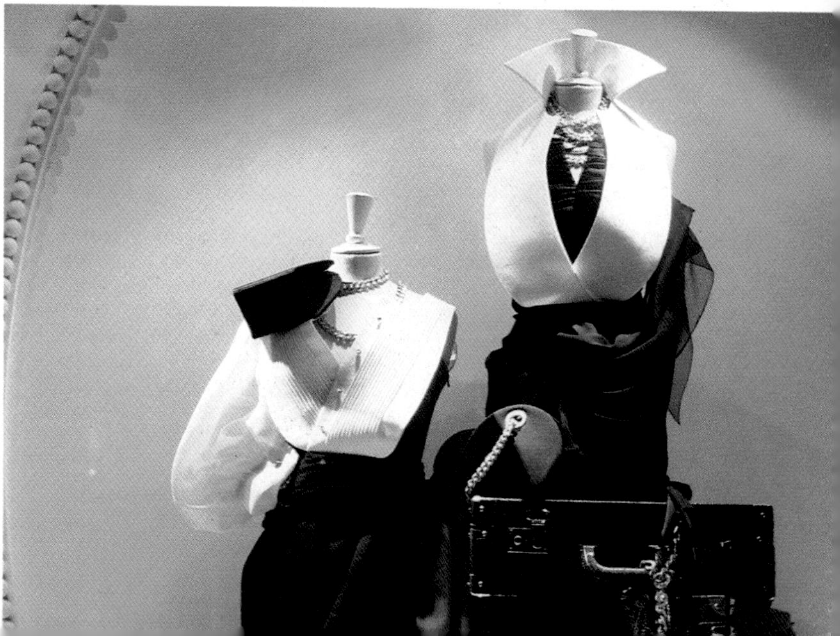

'France is the most brilliant and dangerous nation in Europe, best suited to become in turn an object of admiration, hatred, pity, terror, but never of indifference.' The words were those of Alexis de Toqueville from the 19th century, but the thought is still relevant today. Student idealism is as potent in France as it was in the 1960s, as this nation spawns thinkers from generation to generation, most of whom end up in Paris and on the Left Bank. Joined by artists, film directors and diverse literati, they should be providing some hot discussion in the new millennium... but are they?

Ever fashion conscious, the French are drawn to new abstract ideas like moths to flames; the national passion for debate starts at school, where verbal dexterity is encouraged. Post-war thought was governed by the existentialism of Camus and Sartre.

Shakespeare and Company: English words for sale in the Latin Quarter of Paris

Most intellectuals were strongly influenced by their disenchanted voices and expressions of man's freedom to choose his destiny. But by the late 1960s a new approach began to take over, broadly called structuralism, bringing to the fore theorists such as Barthes, Foucault, Lacan and Lévi-Strauss, all of whom rejected the bourgeois view of history and saw man as the prisoner of a determined system. Philosophers such as Derrida, Kristeva, Deleuze and Lyotard relayed this rationalist approach, exploring the concept of 'post-structuralism', but remain well beyond the bounds of general understanding and concerns.

FIN DE SIECLE After Glucksmann and Bernard-Henri Lévy in the late 1970s, no new figures emerged during the 1980s and 1990s, creating a gaping void, linked with a general mental apathy and the erosion of left-wing ideology: After all, world economic crises were monopolizing attention and communism was dead. Meanwhile, historians, economists and sociologists, such as the hugely influential Pierre Bourdieu, filled the void. Philosophy, however, did not die. A scattering of disparate names is starting to appear: Debray with his *médiologie*, Honfray with 'new hedonism', Roméro, young and brilliant, and Finkelkraut, steady and serious. New millennia, apparently, concentrate the mind.

❑ Intellectuals in France still have clout, though. During the 1994 European elections, an *ad hoc* group led by Bernard-Henri Lévy managed to drag Bosnia onto the political agenda; and in 1987, a group of 100 film-makers and intellectuals forced the government to water down its proposed immigration reforms. ❑

LITERARY LOW The world of literature has followed a similar pattern. The famous old literary reviews, through which you could hear the rattle of gun-fire between intellectuals, have given way to fact-based news magazines. Authors with the universal appeal of Flaubert, Zola, Maupassant, Proust, Camus, Colette or Sartre have not been replaced, and the exponents of the *nouveau roman* of the 1960s have virtually retired.

Publishing is monopolized by three major companies, which also control the juries of the main literary prizes. Despite this, the influence of *Les Editions de Minuit*, who refuse to publish anything other than new, intellectual, original and avant-garde books, continues to grow.

CINEMA is still going strong and channels much of French creative talent. Since Louis Lumière directed the first moving pictures in the 1890s, the French have maintained their predominance in a specific genre: poetic, intimate, intelligent and sensitive, they focus on human relations and life. Although the heyday of recognizable styles such as the 1960s *nouvelle vague* is over, the *cinéma d'auteur* is still buoyant. Godard, Chabrol, Rohmer, Resnais and Malle have all left their indelible stamp, while more recently, Besson, Berri, Serreau, Annaud, Corneau and Téchiné continue to innovate. On screen, Gérard Depardieu, Catherine Deneuve and Juliette Binoche have achieved international status. Benefiting from substantial state subsidy, French cinema retains a strong sense of the Gallic despite inroads from Hollywood, and is still the third-largest producer in the world.

Cinema is still big business

ART IN CRISIS After dominating the world, Paris lost to New York when World War II broke out. Since then the hoped-for comeback has never quite happened, despite public interest and government backing. Galleries and museums carpet the country but there is a crisis of creativity and few contemporary French artists have achieved world renown. Buren? César? Boltanski? Garouste? Although big at home they mean little abroad. As in literature, it is almost as if the French have been waiting for the 21st century.

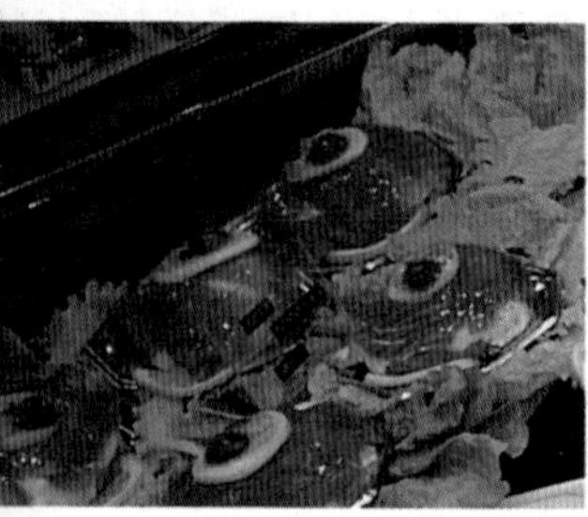

French cuisine epitomizes the complexities of the national character. Science, sensuality and creativity combine to produce, at its best, food fit for the gods. Every region of France has its special dishes, proudly refined from generation to generation, and by the 1990s these were being revived by chefs weary of the two-carrot nouvelle cuisine. *Hearty, so-called 'peasant' dishes are now widely available.*

Twenty years of invasion by a lighter, fresher diet has left its mark: The *nouvelle cuisine* school has been assimilated into a new approach to cooking which puts as much emphasis on nutrition as on inventive tastes and presentation.

QUICK CUISINE Don't believe that every French family sits down to a gastronomic orgy every evening. The advance of the 20th century brought with it a rushed lifestyle and the French adopted convenience foods like every other Western nation. Food is no longer the priority it once was.

Since the 1990s fast food joints have invaded every town and the young, ever attracted to all things American, now—unlike their parents' generation—generally accept fast food as a way of life.

French bread comes in many delicious varieties

Old habits of lengthy, elaborate preparation do survive, but these days many people, especially wealthy town dwellers, if not eating in a restaurant, are more likely to dine on some pasta and a salad than indulge in preparing a *blanquette de veau*.

DINNER TALK Food and wine are still serious topics, talked about at length and with at least 15 national magazines devoted to them. Diners are choosy about the restaurants they frequent, whether the world-famous havens of top chefs like Alain Ducasse, Paul Bocuse, Guy Savoy and Michel Guérard, or a local bistro.

Foreign influences have made themselves felt, too, and the recent assimilation of *nouvelle cuisine* has led to a boom in Japanese restaurants, and avant-garde treatments of seaweed. A new consciousness of ecology and dietetics in the 1960s and 1970s nurtured Michel Guérard's famous *cuisine minceur*, but countless Japanese apprentice chefs in the top Paris kitchens emphasized texture and meticulous presentation. The largest cookery school in the world is now in Tokyo.

❑ France produces about 10 billion bottles of wine per year, and 95 per cent of it is drunk in France. Consumption averages 90 litres a year per person. ❑

FOODIES' NEWS However easily this new style of cooking was adopted by France's most famous chefs, it would not have been so widespread without the influential gastronomic magazine and guide the *Gault Millau,* launched in the 1970s. Daring to confront on its own terrain the long-standing little red book, the *Michelin Guide,* the innovative *Gault Millau* preached and praised an innovative approach, setting the pace with its own journalistic style. Chefs were encouraged to sweep away old rituals and prejudices, take risks and marry the unmarriageable. Thus a new generation of diners was brought up on flourless sauces, fish, delicate vegetable mousses and harmoniously arranged plates. Classic table service disappeared and a more balanced, nutritious gastronomy shifted into top gear.

GOOD OLD DAYS Some may look back with nostalgia to the last days of *grande cuisine,* which really ended with World War I. But who has time these days to sit down to a five-hour, 16-course lunch? The line of illustrious historic chefs is long, from Taillevent (who wrote the first treatise on cooking) to Beauvilliers and the master of modern French cooking, Carême, author of five volumes about 19th-century French cuisine. Today's masters can no longer doggedly follow tradition: they must invent and personalize, while returning to products and techniques born from regional cooking.

HOME GROUND Paul Bocuse, unofficial French gastronomic ambassador, is himself descended from a line of chefs going back to 1765. After the necessary apprenticeship at Paris's top restaurants he returned to Collonges-au-Mont-d'Or, just outside Lyon, where diners still lap up his black truffle soup. France's gastronomic capital, Lyon, has the most varied supply of fresh produce at its doorstep. As the French couturier uses the richest fabrics, so the chef's priority is to show off the fresh, mouthwatering, perfectly ripe ingredients of his region.

La nouvelle cuisine de terroir (regional nouvelle cuisine) led by Roger Vergé, Jacques Maximin, André Daguin or Lucien Vanal is to be found scattered all over this varied country and with outposts in Paris too, and even if your purse doesn't stretch to the greats, there's little to beat a traditional regional dish in a family restaurant.

Eating at a bistro: not necessarily a very intimate affair

'Work hard, play hard' seems to be the maxim for every French family. The French are a hard-working nation. The working week is now only 35 hours long, and there are five weeks' holiday a year (the longest in Europe), as well as 11 days of public holidays, but executives often start work at 8am and don't finish until 12 hours later. Weekends have thus become sacrosanct, often spent at a weekend home, and holidays are seemingly calculated to the minute. A national enthusiasm for sport, which the French take as seriously as their other occupations, is evident everywhere you go.

It was not until the 1936 Front Populaire government that social reforms were made stipulating two weeks' annual paid holiday, a 40-hour week and compulsory collective bargaining. The new *congés payés* changed the face of the nation and, when extended after the war, led to that familiar sight of entire cities closed down for August with main roads taken by storm on the 1st and 31st. Changes in school holidays and state encouragement have now spread holidays over July and August and the traditional month's duration is often reduced to allow for an increasing number of shorter breaks, such as skiing holidays in February and/or a break over the Christmas period.

Further short holidays are astutely concocted by bridging a public holiday with a nearby weekend (*faire le pont*). This means that May, which carries three separate holidays, becomes a complete wipe-out in terms of economic productivity.

HOMELY HOLIDAYS The majority of French families still take their holidays at home. Although surprisingly few travel abroad, small but growing numbers cross the border to Spain, Italy or Britain. Faster growing groups, the more affluent classes in particular, are opting for more exotic destinations.

Begun in 1950, the Club Méditerranée holiday villages have been influential in opening up destinations where previously few Frenchmen dared to tread. This formula of controlled individualism suits French needs: once a year they let their hair down in some exotic spot without experiencing undue risk.

And more recently, the charter company Nouvelles Frontières has escorted groups of French people round Indian temples or paddled them up the Amazon.

SPORTS HOLIDAYS are increasingly popular. Cycling has always been a popular French sport, followed closely by football and, in the southwest, rugby. But along with the rise in leisure time and spending power, the French have taken up tennis—inspired by idols Yannick Noah, Henri Leconte and Cedric Pioline—horse-riding, sailing, golf and the ubiquitous urban gyms. Previously the only national sports had been *boules* and fishing—and leisure time was spent mainly over long voluble meals, in dance-halls, at the cinema, or chatting at a local café.

Cinema attendance is back on the increase but elsewhere TV continues its relentless rise: *boules* is now more a retirement sport, nightclubs attract only a very young urban crowd and even cafés are losing their clientele and being forced to close.

LE WEEKEND Conversely, with one family in nine owning a weekend home, the French are returning to their rural origins and the joys of nature. But not to church: Even before the war, many French people were losing their faith and finding interests unrelated to the Church. Although 75 per cent still describe themselves as Catholic, the majority of French people now spend their Sundays, and Saturdays, hiking, gardening, eating, of course, and indulging in the new national pastime of *bricolage* (DIY), filling sleepy little villages with the happy sounds of hammers and drills.

FOLLOWING THE RULES Back at work the French are industrious and not usually prone to strike. The number of days lost to strikes is low and, at 9 per cent, union membership is the lowest in Europe. But, as union membership is concentrated in the public sector, it does not stop even token strikes severely disrupting the transport, tax or education systems.

When this fails, the French revert to the spirit of 1789 and take to the streets. Doctors, nurses, students and car workers demonstrate; farmers have been known to burn British lamb, fling chickens at politicians and tip Spanish wine onto motorways; fishermen have delivered tonnes of fish to elected representatives; and lorry drivers have brought the whole country to a grinding halt for weeks on end.

Weekend leisure: punting on the Charente river

The French may grumble, but they rarely complain, viewing their right to demonstrate as absolute. The government usually intervenes with an amendment or a hand-out and then everything returns to normal once more.

After two post-war decades of frenetic growth and mindless modernization, France has finally developed a more rational approach to town planning and, above all, consideration for the 'quality of life'. Since the 1970s, numerous town councils have switched their emphasis from building monolithic housing estates to concentrating on schemes of a more ecological or aesthetic nature.

With more power in the hands of local authorities, architecture and urbanism have become political status symbols: Throughout France towns vie with each other to design the most avant-garde pedestrian zone, museum or conference hall, or to carry out the most ambitious restoration scheme.

CHANGING CONDITIONS Somewhat belatedly, the French have recognized the importance of welfare and leisure amenities and the dangers of tower-block ghettos. Early in the 20th century millions moved from the land to embrace city life, but very often their housing conditions were basic: In 1954, for example, only 10 per cent of French homes had a bath or shower and only 27 per cent had flushing lavatories. But a crash public housing scheme (called HLM, *habitation à loyer modéré*), which by 1975 peaked at 550,000 homes a year, soon encircled every French town with modern blocks. The *nouvelles villes* (new towns) around Paris pursued the same policy on a larger scale. Today basic home comforts are available in nearly all houses: By the mid-1980s only 12 per cent were without a bath or shower. Public housing now looks to individual houses springing up on the outskirts of every town, and to more intelligent inner-city projects, while some of the early blocks have been unceremoniously dynamited.

CHANGING TASTES It was really in the 1980s under President Mitterrand that public awareness of architecture blossomed. Visitors to Paris are unlikely to miss seeing what has become the granddaddy of them all: the controversial Centre Pompidou. Built in 1977, of British/Italian design, its polychromatic high-tech style upset many. But it set the tone for a new generation of architects and a new attitude to public building, and, newly restored, it today attracts more visitors than the Eiffel Tower.

BIG IDEAS At his election Mitterrand immediately announced plans for his *grands projets,* while completing others initiated by Giscard d'Estaing (La Villette, Musée d'Orsay). As Paris became a building site and a new billion-franc project seemed to hit the drawing board daily, the French realized that 'modern architecture' was not just a rectangular block.
It was becoming more subtle, as were its implications. Accused of having a 'Louis XIV complex', Mitterrand commissioned monument after prestigious monument, while his arch-rival, Jacques Chirac, as Mayor of Paris, played a vanguard action with less visible urban projects, many of which are finally bringing some green to the city.

As a result, Paris has become a window of contemporary design—not only by French architects. La Grande Arche looms in the west; Dominique Perrault's Bibliothèque de France rises over eastern Paris. At the same time, behind the scenes, gentrification continues, as districts like Le Marais and Bastille are renovated, rents rise and Paris becomes an increasingly sophisticated city. But will this activity turn it into a stultified museum and strip it of its essential local vibrancy?

REGIONAL STYLE Not slow to follow the capital's example, the provinces have also scrubbed their façades and invested heavily in presenting a modernized image to the rest of Europe. Since the autonomy of the 22 regions was increased in the 1980s, their self-consciousness and individual ambitions have rocketed.

Obsessed by city status, towns such as Montpellier, St-Etienne or Bordeaux compete with each other in attracting foreign investment and in exporting a contemporary image. Every city seems to have its *technopole*, or its 'international' airport, while modern art museums mushroom everywhere.

Apart from massive rebuilding of city central areas, many places throughout France were spruced up for the 1993 European ball and the Millennium celebrations in 2000.

❑ The most extraordinary city project to be found in France is that of Montpellier, where the Catalan architect Ricardo Bofill has designed neoclassical medium-rent social housing that is, in the local mayor's words, 'the Rome of tomorrow'. ❑

Rouen has been superbly restored, with the omnipresent pedestrian precinct, while the medieval streets of Rodez are gentrified to an almost absurd degree. However, this is the danger: If renovation and rebuilding continue at such a rate, France risks losing much of its unique character for the sake of a bland, pristine and uniform Euro-face.

La Géode, the spherical cinema in the Parc de la Villette, Paris

If Napoleon, let alone Louis XIV's minister Colbert, could see the political structure of France today, he would certainly turn in his grave. Decentralization gathers momentum and devolution is a reality in a nation that was once the most centralized of all. This policy really came to fruition in 1982 when Mitterrand's administration granted far greater autonomy to the restructured 22 regions, further increased by direct elections for regional councils in 1986. At the same time, the reorganization cut across traditional and cultural boundaries, causing bitter controversy throughout the country but particularly in rural areas.

CITY SCENE Today, France has a handful of burgeoning cities that are able to stand on a par with their European equivalents, from Barcelona to Turin, while at the same time managing to contain any separatist sentiments.

The French provinces were long seen as sleepy, narrow-minded, bourgeois backwaters, where only the priest or *boule*-playing mayor had any importance. Inhabitants of any intelligence were destined for instant intellectual death in what was known as *le désert français*. Anyone with ambitions or initiative headed straight for Paris, leaving the claustrophobic provinces to Madame Bovary and her kind.

INDUSTRIAL MAGNETS The rural exodus continued until World War II and well into the 1950s, leaving behind an already underpopulated countryside, as people flocked to the growing industrial hubs and, of course, to the cultural and economic metropolis of Paris.

But the tide had started to turn under German occupation, when the government was moved to Vichy and the southern provinces, cut off from the north, were forced to act for themselves. This was also the chance for the provincial press to play a role in daily life. Post-war policies concentrated on catching up and gearing up a backward industrialization. Communications were one of France's greatest drawbacks: even in 1970 the country had fewer telephone lines than Greece and half as many as the UK or Germany.

Tunnels (Mont Blanc), bridges, motorways and railways were built, which opened up new investment possibilities and increased mobility. Today nearly all French households have not only a phone but a Minitel (computerized telephone directory) and increasingly the Internet as well. The railway system is one of the most technologically advanced in the world and motorways, though expensive for the user, radiate across the former *désert*.

A new look: modern civic buildings in Carnac

❑ In 1992 Strasbourg set an example of new 'clean city living' by creating a car-free central zone and, two years later, by introducing trams. ❑

ABOUT TURN Thus the pattern has changed and even Parisians are moving to the provinces. Increasing inner-city congestion, urban tensions, pollution and a high cost of living have lessened the appeal of the big cities. Looking for a calmer, less neurotic rhythm and more living space at a lower cost, the French are transferring to Montpellier, Lyon, Bordeaux, Toulouse or Grenoble.

Government schemes initially showed the way for the post-war shift: atomic and space research stations were set up in Brittany, mass tourist projects in the Languedoc, Aérospatiale was a partner in the development of the Concorde and Airbus in Toulouse and France's own 'silicon valley', Sophia Antipolis, grew up out of the lavender fields of Provence. Aid often came from the government agency DATAR, created in 1963 to stimulate new economic ventures and help with the infrastructure for these emerging regions. In La Rochelle, an experiment started in 1995 enables you to rent an electric car to take you round in an eco-friendly way. It has been a great success, and is now a municipal service. For information, call Info Auto Plus, tel: 05 04 34 02 22.

LIVING OPTIONS However rich the economic life of a town may be, few people want to live there without a reasonable choice of leisure activities. Here, again, the map of France has been radically transformed, first with Malraux's famous Maisons de la Culture in the 1960s and more recently with a flood of prestigious new museums, concert halls and cultural venues.

Jack Lang, Socialist Minister of Culture throughout most of the 1980s, stimulated local decision-making and created specialized schools and major arts festivals throughout the country. Montpellier is now seen as the place for contemporary dance, Arles and Lyon for photography, Montbéliard for video, Grenoble and Bordeaux for contemporary art. Even so, every artist has to come to Paris for the ultimate consecration.

REGIONAL REDISCOVERY Provincial towns have thrown off the cloak of central state influence and in some cases their populations have trebled since the 1970s. As the government transfers entire departments of civil servants to the regions and exorbitant rents create a surfeit of empty office space in Paris, the relationship between capital and regions continues to adjust.

ANGLIAE
PARS
London
Douer
Duyncke
Calis
Picar
die
Roan
Caen
Alencon
Paris
Fra
nce
S. Malo
Vendosme
Mans
Bretaigne
Orleans
Anjou
Tours
Loire flu
Bourges
Angiers
Nantes
Poictou
Poictiers
Molin
Rachelle
Limog
Saintes
Clermon
Limosin
Bordeaulx
Guien
Agen
Cahors
Montauban
Monreal
Bayona
Toulouse
Carcassone
Gualcoigne
Narb

The first evidence of human life in the area now known as France goes back nearly half a million years, to a time when the ancestors of modern man left traces of their occupation in the form of stone tools and weapons. Eventually, these people were replaced by the first Neanderthals.

Neanderthals were skilled hunters and workers in stone, but they were unsophisticated in comparison with the next wave of migrants, known now as 'Cro-Magnon' people after the cave where a skeleton was excavated in 1868. The subtlety of Cro-Magnon culture is revealed in the still vibrant wall paintings of the Lascaux caves in Dordogne. This society was gradually subsumed into an age known as Mesolithic, when the nomadic way of life probably gave way to permanent settlements. Some time around 4500BC, people began to grow food rather than gather it, and to enclose and tame animals rather than manage wild herds. All of this was made possible by the cultivation of grains to feed humans and animals all year. This, the Neolithic Revolution, led to the transformation of the landscape into something approaching the one we know today. The most obvious legacies of the Neolithic era are the complex ceremonial sites such as Carnac, in Brittany.

These monuments were developed by Bronze Age settlers, who introduced metalworking skills. The Neolithic and Bronze Ages spanned nearly 5,000 years, and much of that time was peaceful: The bronze weapons that remain may only have been ceremonial.

The disruption of this peaceful society seems to coincide with the arrival of Celtic tribes. Their culture and ironworking skills mark the beginning of a much more fully documented period of history—due largely to the written records of a new wave of invaders: the Romans.

ROMAN VS GAUL The Celts became known as Gauls to the Romans, who set out to halt their advance into northern Italy. In 190BC, the Romans came to defend the then Greek-owned port of Marseille, and advanced to Narbonne, Aix, Arles and Nîmes. In 58BC, Julius Caesar finally crushed the Gauls.

❑ A famous Gallic uprising against the Romans was led by the chieftain Vercingetorix, who in 52BC was captured at Alesia, and taken to Rome and executed. Caesar came to be both ally and conqueror of the Gauls, at once helping them to defend themselves in their turn against invaders from across the Rhine and enabling Rome to exploit new territory with trade and taxation. ❑

Carved megaliths at Locmariaquer

In 43BC, the Romans established their central government at Lyon, and trade to the north, with Britain, and to the south, with Spain and Italy, flourished. The new conquerors built stables (Arles), amphitheatres (Nîmes), circuses (in the Latin Quarter in Paris), baths, aqueducts (Pont du Gard), and founded schools (Autun and Reims). The whole of the country was also criss-crossed by an efficient network of roads.

The Gauls themselves became increasingly Romanized, benefiting from the new political and economic stability. Many educated Gauls, now speaking a form of Latin, were assimilated into the Roman Empire, and held positions of power within the imperial administration, later being entitled to Roman citizenship.

CHRISTIANITY It was during the Roman period that Christianity was first introduced into France, from the second century AD. Early Christians were persecuted: The great Saint Denis of Paris was beheaded at Montmartre (Martyr's Hill) in AD262. The turning point came, however, with the conversion of the Emperor Constantine in the year AD312, when Christianity became the official state religion. Priests such as Martin of Tours were then eager to drive out the old pagan ways of the Celts, and many monasteries and churches were founded. By the year AD500, the Church had established itself as a powerful presence alongside the state, and exerted an influence which has continued to the present day.

BARBARIAN INVASIONS From AD300, the Roman Empire was in decline, and successive emperors were hard pushed to secure Gaul against the incursions of the Barbarian tribes from Germany. The Romans repeatedly fought back, but when, after AD400, the great invasions of the Vandals began, the collapse of the empire was inevitable.

Attila the Hun advanced into eastern France and the Romans withdrew to Orléans, Tours and Bordeaux, so that when Rome itself was sacked and finally overrun in AD455, Gaul was abandoned to the conquering tribes of Visigoths, Burgundians, Alemanni and Franks. In AD481, Clovis became the first Merovingian king of the Salian Franks, who ruled the area between the Rhine and the Seine, and the foundations were laid of a recognizably modern France.

❑ The Vandals overwhelmed the Romans with their brilliant horsemanship; they fought with bow and arrow from horseback—but according to Saint Jerome they 'could not walk on foot, and once dismounted, count themselves dead'. ❑

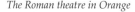

The Roman theatre in Orange

During the 500 years of Frankish rule, there was a constant struggle to expand territorial control. The south remained Romanized, with local aristocrats holding most of the land. The walled cities were governed by bishops, and religious schisms showed Christianity's hold was only skin-deep until Charlemagne was crowned in Rome by the Pope in 800.

Clovis' own conversion to Christianity and his political marriage to Clotilda, a Burgundian princess, helped to secure Frankish power over a broader area. This power was under the feudal regime, in which vassals pledged allegiance to their overlords and provided services, taxes and military support in return for protection and benefices. After Clovis, civil strife between warring robber barons was rampant, and successive Merovingian kings, like Dagobert I (628–37), tried in vain to impose law and order. The Frankish kings became *rois fainéants* ('do-nothing kings') as power was effectively passed to their administrators, the so-called 'mayors of the palace'.

THE CAROLINGIANS In 732, one of these mayors, Charles Martel, usurped royal power, and became the first of the Carolingian kings. Martel led forays against the Arabs, the Burgundians, the Aquitanians and the Saxons. By confiscating lands and giving these out as fiefs to his followers, he managed to establish a wide influence.

The long-term project of uniting Gaul was virtually realized by Martel's grandson, Charlemagne, who was crowned in Rome by the Pope on Christmas Day 800, and became the founder of the Holy Roman Empire, an entity which was to last officially for 1,000 years.

Charlemagne was a great warrior and cunning politician, and it was his own personal energy and frequent ruthlessness that held together a vast amalgam of lands in central and western Europe. His capital at Aix-la-Chapelle became the hub of a cultural Renaissance, whose reputation attracted scholars from many lands.

DIVISION OF EMPIRE The feudal cohesion that Charlemagne imposed on Gaul, with a set of counties and marches, was short-lived. On his death in 808, the empire was divided among his sons, and the western section, Francia, fell prey to the ambitions of nearby dukes.

Meanwhile, a flourishing civilization had arisen in the Languedoc, around the counts of Toulouse. In the north, Viking Norsemen, or Normans, as they became known, established themselves at Rouen. The Church had also acquired tremendous authority and great wealth, often using its assets to thwart the policies of the kings. A state of aristocratic anarchy prevailed, and only lip-service was paid to the sovereignty of the Carolingians.

In 987, Hugh Capet was anointed King of France, founding a new dynasty of Capetian kings. Like his predecessors, his range of influence was largely confined to the Ile de France, and for three centuries, royal power was relatively limited. The Church, meanwhile, came under pressure to put an end to corruption. The order of Benedictine monks at Cluny, founded in 909, tried to provide a new moral discipline, claiming a direct link to the Pope in a bid to side-step the powerful bishops.

The Papacy itself had reformed and in 1095 Pope Urban II launched the first Crusade to 'liberate' Palestine from the domination of the Saracens. The Crusades galvanized thousands of French men and women from all classes in a renewal of faith and devotion, in which princes and kings often participated for a mixture of religious and political purposes. Louis IX (1226–70), later canonized, was himself taken captive in Egypt on a crusading expedition and ransomed at an exorbitant fee.

AGE OF LEARNING The Church also promoted learning and scholarship in the new schools and universities. The University of Paris was set up around the year 1200, and soon became the intellectual hub of Europe, attracting famous teachers and scholars, including Peter Abelard and Thomas Aquinas. And it was during the Middle Ages that Gothic architecture came into its own in superb cathedrals like those at Reims, Amiens, Chartres and Notre-Dame in Paris.

HARD TIMES In the 10th and 11th centuries, although trade and commerce had blossomed, the costs of war at home and abroad forced princes to raise taxes. In the early

❑ The Holy Order of the Knights Templar, founded in 1120, had its headquarters in Paris. The Templars' wealth was a coveted prize, and Philip IV brutally suppressed them in 1307 with appalling torture and execution, and seized their assets for himself. ❑

Tapestry depicting Joan of Arc at the château of Chinon in 1428

14th century, poor harvests led to famine and disease. Meanwhile, a new class of mercenary knights emerged, regularly switching allegiances between lords.

STRUGGLE FOR SUPREMACY Philip Augustus (1180–1223) consolidated royal power, driving the English out of their Angevin Empire, which had grown up in Aquitania, Brittany, Gascony and Normandy. The King strengthened Paris as his capital city and backed the Church against the Albigensian heretics (Cathars) in the Languedoc. When, in 1245, under Saint Louis, the siege of the hilltop fortress at Montségur ended in the burning of hundreds of Cathars, the independence of the south was broken. From 1309, the popes were in exile at Avignon, a city under the control of the French king. So the Capetians were looking strong at the start of the 14th century. But in 1328, Charles VI died with no male heir. At first the crown passed to Philip IV of Valois, but soon the young King Edward III of England, a grandson of Philip IV, also laid claim to the throne. This dispute led to the devastating Hundred Years' War.

THE HUNDRED YEARS' WAR The war had three main phases. In 1338, Edward seized back lands in Gascony. The English advanced into Poitou, took Caen, and won the historic battle of Crécy in 1346. To add to French misfortunes, the Black Death now swept the land, killing nearly a third of the population and leading in turn to peasant uprisings, or *jacqueries*. In 1360, the new king, John II, was captured at Poitiers, and the French were forced to cede Aquitania and Calais to the English.

The second phase of the war followed the death of Edward III and his son the Black Prince, when the English position had begun to weaken. In 1415, Henry V returned to defeat the French at Harfleur and Agincourt. Aquitania, Normandy, Brittany and Anjou became English territories and Henry married the French king's daughter. Both he and his wife died in 1421, and the quarrel over the throne passed to their infant son, the future Henry VI, and the Dauphin, the future Charles VII.

The third phase of the war brought the shepherdess and saint Joan of Arc, to raise the siege of Orléans and help Charles to be crowned in the cathedral at Reims. Soon after this, Joan was captured and burned at the stake in Rouen in 1431, but Charles went on to win decisive victories over the English. When the English eventually withdrew from Normandy in 1453, the Hundred Years' War was finally over.

THE AFTERMATH War and disease had shaken the foundations of feudalism. Aided by a civil service drawn from the emerging bourgeoisie, Louis XI was now able to end the factionalism of the Middle Ages. When he died in 1483, Burgundy, Normandy, Brittany, Picardy, Anjou, Provence and Roussillon were all subdued, and France had begun to develop into a modern nation-state.

The Renaissance was the time of an explosion of tremendous creative energy in the arts, literature, philosophy and science. The city-states of 15th-century Italy had been its birthplace, but the revived knowledge of the ancients and the developing concerns of humanism, together with a new consciousness of exploration and experiment, spread across the whole of Europe.

François I (1515–47) presided over the patronage of the arts in France. Many of the beautiful châteaux of the Loire Valley, like those at Chambord, Chenonceau and Azay-le-Rideau, were built at this time. Art collections and libraries were expanded and artists were attracted to the court, including the Italians Benvenuto Cellini and Leonardo da Vinci (who spent the last years of his life working in France and is buried at Amboise). Literature also flourished, under a group of poets known as the Pleiade; the love poetry of Ronsard and Du Bellay is among the most beautiful in the French language. Rabelais wrote his farcical novels *Pantagruel* and *Gargantua* during this period, and the retired mayor of Bordeaux, Michel de Montaigne, composed his essays on knowledge and the enigmas of the human condition.

THE WARS OF RELIGION François built France into the new system of European diplomacy, and negotiated a set of carefully arranged marriages to check the age-old rivalries with England and the powerful Habsburg dynasty which ruled Spain, the Netherlands and the Holy Roman Empire. The picture became more complicated, however, once the Reformation in Germany gained momentum. When, in 1517, Martin Luther was excommunicated, the many German princes took sides in theological debates on transsubstantiation and Papal authority—by championing the Protestant cause. For political reasons, many opposed the Habsburg Emperor, Charles V, who was a Catholic Spaniard.

This political dimension was slow to emerge in France because of the tradition of Gallicanism, which meant that the clergy were more directly linked to the king than to the Pope. Nevertheless, in 1523, the *Parlement* of Paris seized and burned Luther's books, and, after some hesitation, the king decided that the Lutheran heretics were a threat to be stamped out.

REPRESSION of the Protestant Huguenots remained ineffectual, however. In 1536, Jean Calvin published his *Institutions of the Christian Religion*, and many Frenchmen sought instruction in his teachings in the independent Swiss state of Geneva. Protestant churches continued to spring up throughout France, and in 1560, Charles IX went so far as to issue an amnesty against religious persecution.

However, civil war eventually broke out as the members of the royal household divided between the two faiths in a fight for power. The Prince de Condé headed the Huguenot Montmorency faction against the Duc de Guise, who defended the royalist Catholic cause. The war was fought at different levels, with some full-scale military engagements (at Dreux and Jarnac), and a terrorist campaign of political murders (the Duc de Guise, the Prince de Condé and Henry III were assassinated). But the frequent outbreaks of crowd violence were the most horrifying; on 24 August 1572, thousands of Huguenots were murdered in riots in what became known as the Saint Bartholomew's Day Massacre.

Cardinal Richelieu by R. Woodman

HENRY IV Supported by the traditionalist Catholic League, Henry of Navarre became the first Bourbon king (1589–1610). He was an ex-Huguenot turned Catholic, and, with his chief administrator Sully, he tried to restore political and social harmony. In 1598, he issued the Edict of Nantes, which guaranteed the right of worship to the Protestants. Although this helped to heal the wounds of civil strife, Henry was himself assassinated by a Catholic extremist one day while in his carriage.

The reign of Louis XIII (1610–43) saw the rise to power of the great Cardinal Richelieu. Richelieu was a wise and wily statesman, whose strength lay in a dedication to the French national interest. Richelieu set about creating a complex balance of power in Europe, negotiating often secret treaties with different heads of state, playing off the German Protestants against the Catholic Habsburgs during the Thirty Years' War, and contracting alliances via royal marriages, including Charles I of England. At home, he helped Louis cultivate the patronage of dukes and princes, overrode the various *parlements* and sent out his *intendants*, or agents of the crown, to collect taxes and manage the fiscal affairs of the state. Richelieu was a prime mover in assuring a strong central government, and did much to resolve the centuries-old antagonism between the nobility and the crown by paving the way for absolute monarchy.

Louis XIV (1643–1715) was France's most glorious and longest-reigning king. Only five years old when he ascended the throne, his first task was to secure his position against La Fronde, an alliance of discontented nobles who sought to overthrow him. Louis successfully broke down the opposition and from 1661 he was determined to exercise absolute power. He believed in his God-given right to govern the country and saw the welfare of the state as embodied in his own person: L'Etat, c'est moi *became the motto which characterized the Sun King's attitude to his role and to his country.*

Under Louis XIV's rule, France rose to new heights of prosperity and glory. The rise of mercantilism, masterminded by his minister of finance and loyal supporter Colbert, saw new industries grow up, and imports from the colonies in Canada, Louisiana (named after the king) and India brought massive wealth to the country. By contrast, however, much of this affluence was squandered by the lavish lifestyle of the royal household and by the wars which Louis waged against other European countries.

In the 1670s, work began on the construction of the huge and magnificent palace at Versailles. This became the new seat of the court and a symbol of national unity. Everyone jostled to take up residence there and enjoy the endless round of feasts, balls and concerts, the elaborate rules of etiquette and social frivolities which Louis staged to divert the aristocratic families from more serious political concerns. Everything good, it seemed, emanated from the Sun King.

WARRIOR KING Louis also headed an impressive war machine, built up by General Vauban, which he launched into several ill-fated campaigns. In 1672 Louis declared war on the Netherlands, and in 1685 he revoked the Edict of Nantes. These actions incensed the Europeans. The Germans rose up at the hostility which Louis, a staunch Catholic, had shown to Protestants. In 1688, William of Orange, himself a Dutch Protestant, became king of England, and soon most of Europe was ranged against France. Yet, in 1689, Louis invaded the Rhineland, and many years of war ensued, in which France suffered eventual defeat.

Undeterred, Louis sparked the War of the Spanish Succession, by insisting that his grandson be settled on the throne of Spain as Philip VI. The Europeans again objected, and after a series of humiliating defeats in the years 1701–13, notably at Blenheim, the French were forced to retreat. The terms of the Treaty of Utrecht involved both the permanent renunciation of Bourbon claims to rule Spain and the loss of France's main colonies in the Americas.

AGE OF ORDER Louis's reign saw the rise of classicism, in which order, reason and elegance were major features. René Descartes, in his *Discourse on Method* (1637), had laid the foundations for modern science by emphasizing the importance of rational argument from observable facts. Love of order is reflected in all the arts of the period, whether in the architectural symmetries of baroque *hôtels* and *châteaux*, in the layout of parks and ornamental gardens, in Pascal's mechanical 'computers', or in the harrowing precision and logic of Racine's tragedies.

THE ENLIGHTENMENT These trends in science, culture and the life of the mind led, in the 18th century, to the Age of Enlightenment. French philosophers such as Voltaire, Diderot and Rousseau turned their thoughts to the practical applications of knowledge and the possibilities of social change. The absolutism of the monarchy had grown out of the 1,000-year-old traditions of feudalism, but now its structures were outliving their usefulness. The established *Ancien Régime* of kings and princes was increasingly alarmed by the spread of revolutionary ideas.

But the storm was brewing. Under Louis XV (1715–74), France was brought closer to the brink of chaos. Rivalries between noble families, the corruption of officials, the widespread abuse of privileges, the division between Paris and the provinces, the incompetent management of the economy, all contributed to the widening gap between rich and poor. Taxation was high, famine and squalor were rife across the land, while a privileged minority lived in the lap of luxury.

In the early years of the reign of Louis XVI (1774–93), food riots were commonplace, the monarchy was bankrupt, the financial and bureaucratic institutions were becoming increasingly rickety and ineffectual, and the time was ripe for a massive social and political upheaval.

❑ One of the most unpopular of the many taxes in the 17th century was the salt tax, *la gabelle*. In some provinces, where salt was a government monopoly, it was compulsory to buy a fixed amount. ❑

The Sun King: a miniature of Louis XIV, the longest-reigning French king

In 1789 began one of the most dramatic episodes in France's history. In a last-ditch effort to resolve the country's pressing problems, Louis XVI summoned the Estates General, representing the three states of the nobility, the clergy and 'the rest'. The Estates had no real political power, and had not convened since 1614, so their negotiations soon got bogged down over questions of procedure. The Third Estate, representing more than 95 per cent of the 20-odd million people of the country, decided to form a breakaway National Assembly.

One morning, finding the door to the meeting hall inexplicably locked, the Third Estate withdrew to a nearby tennis court and swore an oath not to disperse until they had founded a new constitution. The King, in a panic, dismissed them, and in the ensuing unrest the crowds in Paris, fearing a military crackdown, stormed the prison of the Bastille on 14 July.

THE REVOLUTION The National Assembly, composed mainly of liberal Girondins and radical Jacobins, issued the Universal Declaration of the Rights of Man. France was divided into a set of administrative *départements*, and feudal duties and hereditary titles were abolished. At first, the King went along with this new order of things, but in June 1791, he foolishly tried to escape.

❑ Legend has it that Louis XVI was captured at Varennes because he was recognized from his likeness on a coin. ❑

In September 1791, a constitutional monarchy was officially declared, but there was a growing fear that the *émigrés* (exiled aristocrats), helped by European heads of state, were going to invade. To pre-empt this, France declared war, and won an immediate, astounding victory at Valmy against the Austrians and Prussians.

FIRST REPUBLIC The imprisoned Louis could no longer be trusted. A new Convention abolished the monarchy and proclaimed the First Republic. In 1793, Louis was put on trial for treason, convicted and guillotined. Unfortunately, none of this revolutionary activity had really helped to solve the severe domestic problems of food shortages and money. In April 1793, a Committee of Public Safety was created to impose social reforms, ensure law and order and protect the Revolution. A power struggle among the Revolutionary leaders led to the Jacobins ousting the Girondins. Robespierre, who emerged as virtual dictator, unleashed a Reign of Terror.

The Revolution now spun out of control and turned into a bloodbath of executions, wiping out thousands of former nobles, clergy and ordinary 'citizens'. Even the original leaders, Desmoulins, Danton, Saint-Just and the incorruptible Robespierre himself, were sent to the guillotine. In 1795 a Directory, politically conservative and backed by the army, attempted to restore order, but its efforts remained futile, until an opportunistic Corsican, General Napoleon Bonaparte, mounted a surprise *coup d'état* in 1799.

NAPOLEON AND EMPIRE Napoleon immediately established his own brand of personal dictatorship. He was immensely successful. At home, he reformed taxation, confirmed the

post-Revolutionary property rights, set up a Bank of France to help the economy, developed the *Code Napoléon* to administer the law of the land, and restored the Church. He then launched into a series of brilliant military campaigns which swept across Europe. In the decade 1800–10, the French won victories at the battles of Marengo, Austerlitz, Jena and Wagram, and gained control over Italy, Spain, Germany and Poland. In 1804, Napoleon had himself crowned Emperor in Rome.

The Emperor Napoleon

Europe fought back. Britain and Spain counter-attacked in the Iberian Peninsula, while a sea blockade starved France of important trade and supplies. In 1812, Napoleon launched an ill-fated Russian campaign, prevailing at the hard-fought battle of Borodino and marching into a tactically deserted Moscow. The severe Russian winter proved fatal. Napoleon's lines of communication and supplies were badly overstretched, and the *Grande Armée* was forced into ignominious retreat. Thousands of soldiers perished in the snow. At Leipzig, the French suffered a crushing defeat, and eventually, in March 1814, Napoleon abdicated.

EXILE Even this was not the end of the irrepressible *petit caporal*. In 1815, Napoleon escaped from exile on the Mediterranean island of Elba, and staged a brief comeback, only to be conclusively overcome at the Battle of Waterloo. This time, his captors banished him to remote St. Helena in the south Atlantic, where he died in 1821. The man was dead, but the Napoleonic legend, and the legacy, lives on.

❑ During his crowning ceremony, Napoleon seized the imperial crown from the hands of the Pope and placed it on his own head. ❑

After Napoleon, the Bourbon monarchy was restored. Under Louis XVIII (1814–24) France settled into a period of much-needed peace, while Charles X (1824–30) tried to turn the political clock back to reinstate the old ways. Such reaction was in vain, however, for the bourgeoisie were hungry for power, and the momentum of industrialization created new aspirations which backward-looking policies could not hope to fulfil. In the summer of 1830, the barricades went up in Paris, the King abdicated, and Louis-Philippe was made head of the 'July monarchy'.

Now a rapid industrial revolution took place. Output in coal, iron and textiles multiplied, and a national railway system was developed. As the money-grabbing bourgeoisie grew rich, however, the workers felt increasingly oppressed. Romanticism gave expression to the complex feelings of dislocation France was experiencing. Writers such as Châteaubriand, Vigny and Hugo evoked a nostalgia for the past, and the value of individual imagination and emotion was invoked against the constraints of reason and routine. Socialist philosophies also sprang up, with thinkers like Saint-Simon and Fourier offering visions of an alternative social order often prefiguring much in Marxism.

THE 1848 REVOLUTION By 1848, the ghost of revolution again haunted Europe. Food shortages and a recession had starving peasants on the rampage in the countryside, and the crowds in Paris again took to the barricades. Armed insurrection forced Louis-Philippe to abandon his throne, and the Second Republic was proclaimed. Once again, heady idealism failed to effect any substantial changes; then out of the turmoil emerged Louis-Napoléon, the emperor's nephew, who managed to get himself elected France's first president. He first took steps to enhance his popularity, and then, in 1851, seized his chance to mount his own *coup d'état* and crowned himself Emperor.

Napoleon III, as he now was, steered a course between competing political factions and enabled France to prosper. The right to vote was extended, trade unions were made legal and schools educated more of the young. In 1869, the Suez Canal, a vast engineering project backed by the French, opened the way to increased trade with the Far East. Baron Haussmann undertook the systematic modernization of the capital, clearing slums and laying out the boulevards, squares and gardens which have made Paris so renowned a metropolis.

TIPPING THE BALANCE Across the Rhine, Chancellor Bismarck was busy unifying Germany and

Henri Toulouse-Lautrec...

destabilizing the balance of power. In 1870, diplomatic provocation gave way to war. France lost battles at Metz and Sedan, and Napoleon III was himself taken prisoner. Paris fell to the advancing Prussian army. After the calamity of defeat, a new National Assembly clung to nervous conservative policies. In March 1871, a more radical municipal council was elected in Paris; the 'Commune' rose up against the national government, who sent in troops to besiege the capital. After six weeks of fierce guerrilla-style urban warfare, the uprising was crushed, and some 20,000 communards were either summarily shot or deported.

FIN DE SIECLE In 1875, France made a new start with the Third Republic. The political division between left and right persisted. Socialism gained ground, with a growing left-wing movement led by Jaurès, and for a time it was feared that the conservatives, under General Boulanger, might try another coup.

Meanwhile, investment abroad brought great wealth from the colonies in Indo-China, northern and Black Africa, and the Near East. France boasted an empire second only to that of Great Britain.

Deep social divisions became manifest in the Dreyfus affair. In 1896, Captain Dreyfus, a Jewish army officer, was accused of espionage. On forged evidence, he was deported to the notorious penal colony at Devil's Island. The whole of France split into two camps over the question of his innocence. Among the traditionalist Catholics, anti-semitic feelings ran high, while Emile Zola, in his famous article *J'accuse*, denounced a miscarriage of justice. Eventually, Dreyfus was acquitted, but the bitterness the affair aroused was long-lived.

REVOLUTIONS IN ART During this time, a wave of experimentation broke out in the arts. In literature, the realism of the great novelists, Balzac and Flaubert, gave way to Proust's meditations on time and memory, while the sensual poetry of Baudelaire was followed by the ethereal symbolism of Mallarmé's sonnets. In the visual arts, Impressionism outraged the traditional salons, as new techniques in composition, tone and texture were developed by Manet, Monet, Cézanne, Gauguin, Pissarro, Renoir and Van Gogh.

In music, too, new textures of sound and tonal harmony were introduced by Debussy, Satie and Saint-Saëns; and the new arts of photography, developed by Daguerre, the cinema, developed by the Lumière brothers, and the commercial poster-art of Toulouse-Lautrec, captured the imagination as the century moved into a mood of *fin-de-siècle* decadence.

Meanwhile, great-power rivalries loomed large. Germany's attempts to isolate France were thwarted by an alliance with the Czar and the entente cordiale with Britain. Austria–Hungary's interventions in the Balkans threatened access to Suez, and to supplies of oil. The spiral of the arms race brought the European imperialists to an unavoidable showdown.

...and Vincent Van Gogh: celebrating a new age in French art and decadence

The assassination of the Archduke Franz Ferdinand of Austria, in Sarajevo in June 1914, was the trip-wire which plunged Europe into war. Austria declared war on Russia; and when Russia responded, Germany in turn declared war on Russia, and then Britain and France declared war on Germany. The Schlieffen Plan allowed German forces to move swiftly through Belgium and penetrate into north-eastern France.

The battle of the Marne halted the German advance, and years of trench warfare followed. Thousands fell, at Ypres, at Passchendaele, defending a few yards of mud in fields where once poppies blossomed. In 1916, Marshal Pétain held the symbolic stronghold of Verdun against persistent attack, before launching a counter-offensive on the Somme. The stalemate was only broken by the intervention of the Americans, who entered the war in 1917, finally forcing the Germans to capitulate in November 1918.

THE COST OF THE WAR

A generation of young French men had been sacrificed, with more than a million dead and 3 million wounded. Large areas of Flanders and the Ardennes were devastated. Inflation and the national debt had rocketed. The gains were comparatively slight: Alsace and Lorraine were returned to France, and the Treaty of Versailles, which was signed in 1919, imposed massive war reparations on the Germans.

After the horrors of the trenches, many Frenchmen turned to promoting the cause of peace, and France contributed significantly to the newly created League of Nations and international conferences on disarmament. In the 1920s, reconstruction was initially paid for out of the reparation money from Germany; when the Germans stopped paying, French troops were sent to occupy the Ruhr. In spite of a series of unstable governments, things were relatively buoyant, until the Wall Street crash of 1929 provoked a world recession. In the 1930s, unemployment rose, and the French economy nosedived. Some feared, and others hoped, that there would be a Communist takeover, but the socialist Front Populaire, elected in 1936 under Léon Blum, was in the event shortlived.

APPEASEMENT AND WAR

Meanwhile, the Nazis were gaining strength in Germany. In 1935, Hitler broke the terms of the peace and ordered German rearmament. The French, fearing a collision course, sought to contain Germany with a series of fragile alliances, and even agreed to German expansion in the east. In 1938, Hitler annexed Austria

Greed, Revenge and other devils sign the Treaty of Versailles, 1919

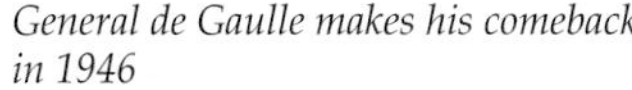

General de Gaulle makes his comeback in 1946

and the Sudetenland in Czechoslovakia, and, signing a non-aggression pact with the Soviet Union, invaded Poland. Finally, both Britain and France abandoned their policy of appeasement and declared war.

WORLD WAR II The quiet months of the so-called 'phoney war' were shattered by the Blitzkrieg of April 1940: Hitler invaded Belgium, Denmark and the Netherlands, and dodged the Maginot Line, in which France had invested heavily after 1918 to prevent another German attack. After the panic evacuation of Allied troops from the beaches of Dunkerque, Nazi stormtroopers marched into Paris.

❑ 'The French will only be united under the threat of danger. Nobody can simply bring together a country that has 265 kinds of cheese.'—Charles de Gaulle ❑

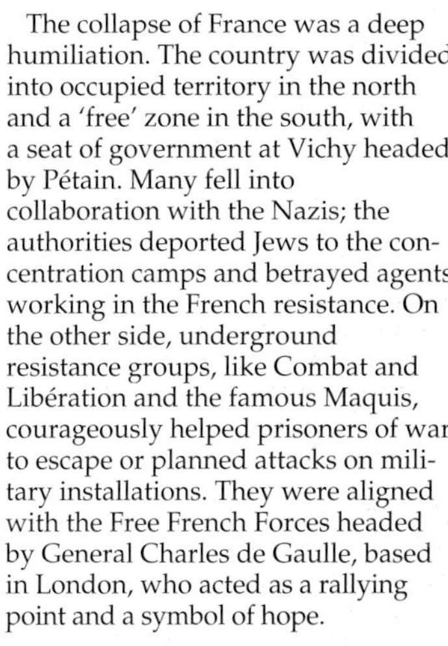

The collapse of France was a deep humiliation. The country was divided into occupied territory in the north and a 'free' zone in the south, with a seat of government at Vichy headed by Pétain. Many fell into collaboration with the Nazis; the authorities deported Jews to the concentration camps and betrayed agents working in the French resistance. On the other side, underground resistance groups, like Combat and Libération and the famous Maquis, courageously helped prisoners of war to escape or planned attacks on military installations. They were aligned with the Free French Forces headed by General Charles de Gaulle, based in London, who acted as a rallying point and a symbol of hope.

LIBERATION As the war progressed, Hitler's forces were worn down on the eastern front, and the Allies united to prepare an invasion. In June 1944, the first landings of Allied troops on the beaches of Normandy were launched and the Nazis were steadily driven back out of France.

In August, Paris was liberated, and de Gaulle led a victory parade along the Champs-Elysées. Former collaborators were shot or publicly humiliated or, like Pétain, sentenced to prison. De Gaulle founded a provisional government to bring back to life a country once more ravaged by war. A national referendum opted for the creation of a new state, and in May 1946 the constitution of the Fourth Republic was declared. After 40 years of strife, France was ready to set itself on the road to reconciliation and recovery.

In the aftermath of war, France had to rebuild its infrastructure but also its entire economy and a new national identity. This involved a constant tension between the desire for traditional independence and the harsh realities of the modern world. It was with the aid of the Marshall Plan that Jean Monnet's Four Year Plans were able to relaunch French industry.

In 1951, the European Coal and Steel Community linked France to West Germany, Italy and the Benelux countries, and this formed the basis of the European Economic Community. In the realm of defence, French wishes for a European 'column' were overridden by the American-led NATO, which held sway as the Cold War began to develop.

OVERSEAS France now entered the traumatic era of decolonialization. French paratroopers were routed at Dien Bien Phu in 1954, which dealt a severe blow to the nation's morale. In 1956, Egypt seized the Suez Canal. Britain and France invaded to protect navigation rights, but this turned into a fiasco after American intervention and Soviet threats persuaded them to withdraw. And then there was the Algerian situation.

ALGERIA Although Syria, Lebanon, Tunisia and Morocco were all granted independence peacefully, it was Algeria which focused political tensions. Since 1945, the Algerian National Liberation Front had kept up a campaign of terrorism, but the large number of settled French colonists were unwilling to relinquish power. More and more troops were despatched to keep law and order, though there were sinister reports of unlawful torture and bombings. The generals commanding the army in Algeria threatened rebellion, and even a coup, and for a time seized Corsica. The crisis caused the collapse of the government, and with it the Fourth Republic.

THE FIFTH REPUBLIC General de Gaulle was recalled from retirement to help solve the dilemma. He instituted the Fifth Republic, giving him, as president, increased powers, and opted first for a version of Algerian 'self-determination'. His decision proved unpopular among the members of the *Organisation de l'Armée Secrète*, which was composed of disgruntled officers and colonists. They mounted a terrorist campaign of their own, but de Gaulle stood his ground and in 1962 Algeria was granted independence.

Under de Gaulle, the 1960s became a time of rapid modernization. A wilting economy was boosted as France espoused consumerism. De Gaulle himself was all for traditional grandeur. His dream was for a united Europe stretching 'from the Atlantic to the Urals'. He resented American influence, and in 1966 he withdrew from NATO and forged ahead with the development of the independent nuclear *force de frappe*. He ensured that France would continue to play a leading role in the Common Market by twice saying *Non!* to entry by the United Kingdom.

UPRISINGS For all his experience and political astuteness, de Gaulle was unprepared for *les événements* of May 1968. Students and workers took to the streets to protest against the Vietnam War, wage settlements and the 'system'; riot police stormed the barricades with tear gas and truncheon charges, and within days a general strike brought the whole country to a standstill. Somewhat at a loss, de Gaulle called for fresh elections, but when his proposals for reform were rejected in a national referendum, he retired from the stage.

François Mitterrand addresses the Socialists in 1973

In the 1970s, both presidents Georges Pompidou and Valéry Giscard d'Estaing continued to pursue broadly Gaullist policies. The oil crisis of 1973 brought inflation and recession, and the alliance between the socialists and the communists gained ground. In 1981, finally, the Socialist François Mitterrand was elected to the presidency. Sweeping social changes were expected, and new legislation provided for more nationalization, ensured a minimum wage, and ended capital punishment. But harsh economic realities forced the government to backtrack into a policy of austerity, and disillusionment set in. In 1986, France weathered another constitutional crisis when a conservative prime minister, Jacques Chirac, was appointed to 'cohabit' with a socialist president. In 1988, Mitterrand was elected to a second term. In 1993 the electorate swung to the right, with Chirac elected to be President in 1995. In 2002, despite popularity for a far-right candidate, France rallied to give Chirac a landslide victory. In 2007, the right-wing Nicolas Sarkozy became President.

Meantime, with the adoption of the euro in 2002, France is leading the way to an integrated Europe. In May 2003, former President Giscard d'Estaing revealed his blueprint for a new European Constitution, creating a superpower to rival the USA. Together with France's opposition to the Iraq war this led to icy relations between the USA, UK and France, which may take a while to thaw.

Part-Dieu station, Lyon. The national rail network symbolizes modern France

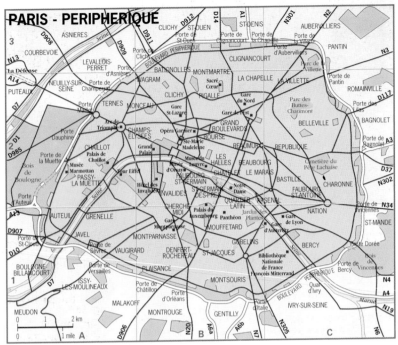

PARIS - PERIPHERIQUE

PARISIANS are a country if not a race unto themselves, notorious for their love of good food and high fashion, their radical intellectualism and their speedy approach to life. Paris is certainly not where the expression *douceur de vivre* originated. But it is an intellectual and artistic hotbed that has always enjoyed exporting its ideas, while happily importing and absorbing those of visiting foreigners. Although long vilified for their offhand attitude to tourists, Parisians have become much more approachable.

And the face of the city itself is also being transformed: scrubbed, renovated, relandscaped, rebuilt, it has hardly stopped to breathe since the 1980s and looks ambitiously to the future.

Opposite: the Arc de Triomphe is spectacular at night Below: Notre-Dame, one of the world's most famous cathedrals

CHARMED CIRCLE Nestling in the thickly forested saucer of the Ile de France, the intramuros population of Paris is just over 2 million; but if you count a growing number of satellite towns and the suburbs of the Ile de France it exceeds 11 million. Yet however accessible the suburbs become, the 'true Parisian' lives inside the circle of 19th-century *portes* that contain its 20 *arrondissements*. Outside that limit are the *banlieusards*, the suburbanites, commuting into central Paris by RER.

More than 75 per cent of suburban dwellers use cars, since their local transport, excluding the limited RER network, is totally abysmal and there is no other choice. Monstrous traffic jams build up in Paris, and on the *périphérique* (ring road) these are part of daily life—sometimes stretching the 25km (16 miles) as far as Roissy airport. Efforts are now being made to control traffic and pollution; these efforts include the introduction of

A-Z Paris

car-free days. Amenities are still being developed and much thoughtless suburban planning of the 1960s and 1970s has left a generation of lost souls and a few delinquents. Many of France's North African immigrants live in these characterless areas and have become targets for increasingly frequent racist attacks.

THE NEW LOOK At the same time, some of the most controversial architecture of Paris is appearing in satellite towns such as Noisy-le-Grand, St-Quentin-en-Yvelines or Cergy-Pontoise. Cultural facilities have grown from the days of Malraux's famous Maisons de Culture, and inner suburbs such as Bobigny or St-Denis now boast modern venues staging international productions.

For visitors driving around the Ile de France and coming into Paris, the landscape is not always as expected. Often peppered with an unplanned array of hoardings and advertisements, the *routes nationales* can be a shock. But turn off suddenly to follow the road to a château and you may find yourself in rolling, forested terrain. When not a spread of instant bungalows, villages are spruce and it is more than likely half the houses belong to Parisian weekenders. Avoid routes entering Paris on a Sunday night: Traffic jams are guaranteed.

PARIS LIFE In the heart of Paris getting about is easy if you stick to the excellent public transport system or your own two feet. Distances are not great and by Métro it is unlikely to take more than 30 minutes from one end of a line to the other.

Parisians lead fast lives, spending freely, and in consequence have to earn well to keep up. Time is valuable, and at the end of the day they like nothing better than strolling along the boulevards or sitting in a café nursing a drink as they watch the passersby and put the world to rights. From early evening to the small hours Paris vibrates with life.

Join in the Parisian way of life in the cafés of St-Germain or the new haunts of the Bastille; dine in animated brasseries or bistros where shared tables give an opportunity to chat with fellow diners. The spirit of Paris, as well as its illuminated monuments, well deserves the description 'city of light'.

▶▶▶ CITY HIGHLIGHTS

Arc de Triomphe *page 52*

Centre National d'Art et de Culture Georges Pompidou *page 56*

Louvre *page 52*

Montmartre and Sacré-Cœur *page 59*

Musée d'Orsay *page 54*

Notre-Dame *page 57*

La Sainte-Chapelle *page 57*

Tour Eiffel *page 55*

Versailles *page 65*

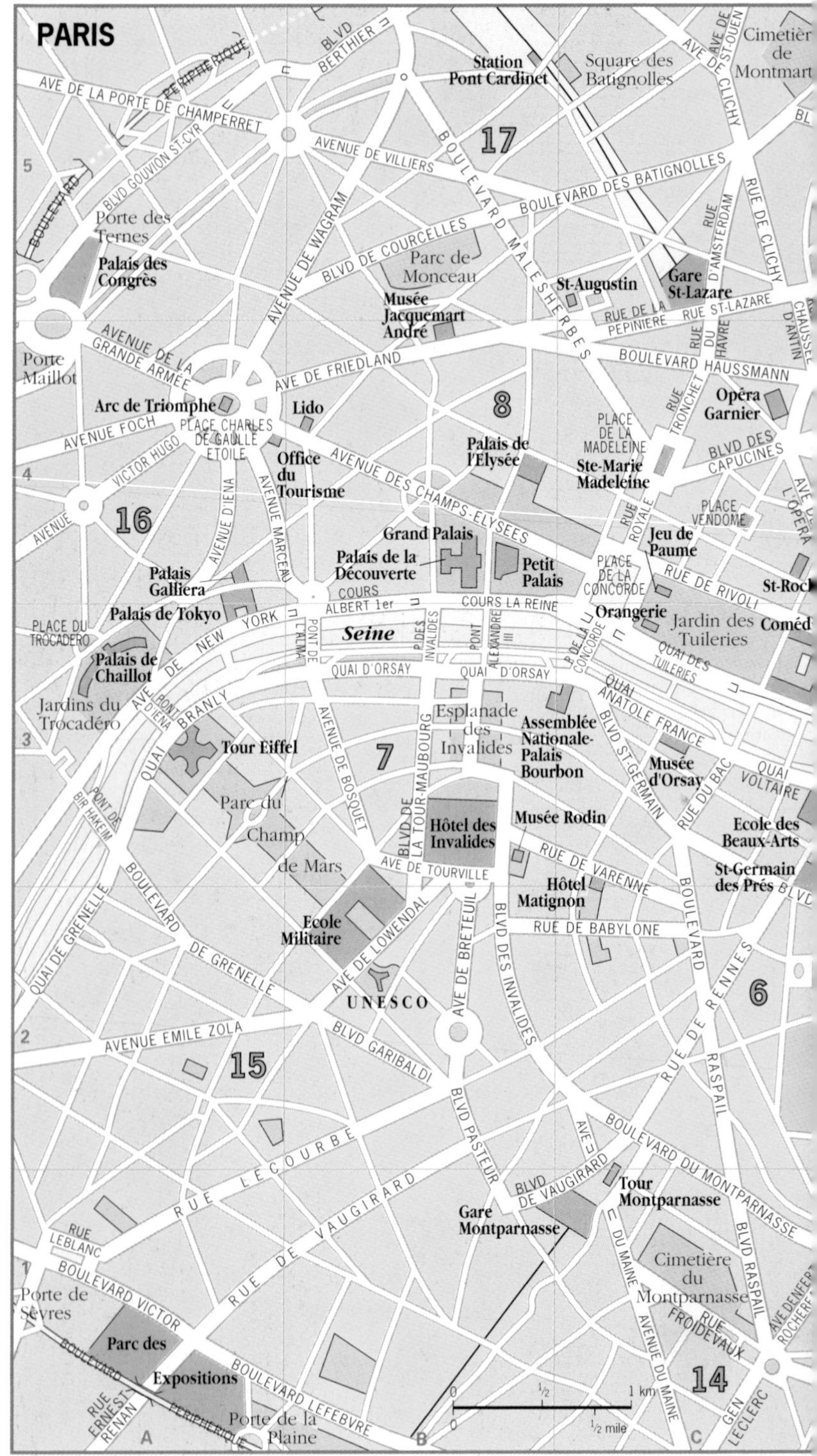
PARIS
Station Pont Cardinet
Square des Batignolles
Cimetière de Montmartre
17
Porte des Ternes
Palais des Congrès
Parc de Monceau
Musée Jacquemart André
St-Augustin
Gare St-Lazare
Porte Maillot
Arc de Triomphe
Lido
8
Opéra Garnier
PLACE CHARLES DE GAULLE ETOILE
Office du Tourisme
Palais de l'Elysée
PLACE DE LA MADELEINE
Ste-Marie Madeleine
PLACE VENDOME
16
Grand Palais
Palais de la Découverte
Petit Palais
Jeu de Paume
PLACE DE LA CONCORDE
Palais Galliera
Palais de Tokyo
Orangerie
Jardin des Tuileries
PLACE DU TROCADERO
Seine
Palais de Chaillot
Jardins du Trocadéro
Esplanade des Invalides
Assemblée Nationale-Palais Bourbon
Tour Eiffel
7
Musée d'Orsay
Parc du Champ de Mars
Hôtel des Invalides
Musée Rodin
Ecole des Beaux-Arts
St-Germain des Prés
Hôtel Matignon
Ecole Militaire
UNESCO
6
15
Tour Montparnasse
Gare Montparnasse
Cimetière du Montparnasse
Porte de Sèvres
Parc des Expositions
Porte de la Plaine
14
0 1/2 1 km
0 1/2 mile
AVENUE DES CHAMPS-ELYSEES
BOULEVARD HAUSSMANN
AVENUE DE WAGRAM
BOULEVARD MALESHERBES
BOULEVARD DES BATIGNOLLES
AVENUE FOCH
AVENUE DE LA GRANDE ARMÉE
AVE DE FRIEDLAND
QUAI D'ORSAY
COURS LA REINE
RUE DE RIVOLI
BOULEVARD DE GRENELLE
AVENUE EMILE ZOLA
RUE LECOURBE
RUE DE VAUGIRARD
BOULEVARD DU MONTPARNASSE
BOULEVARD VICTOR
BOULEVARD LEFEBVRE
BOULEVARD PERIPHERIQUE

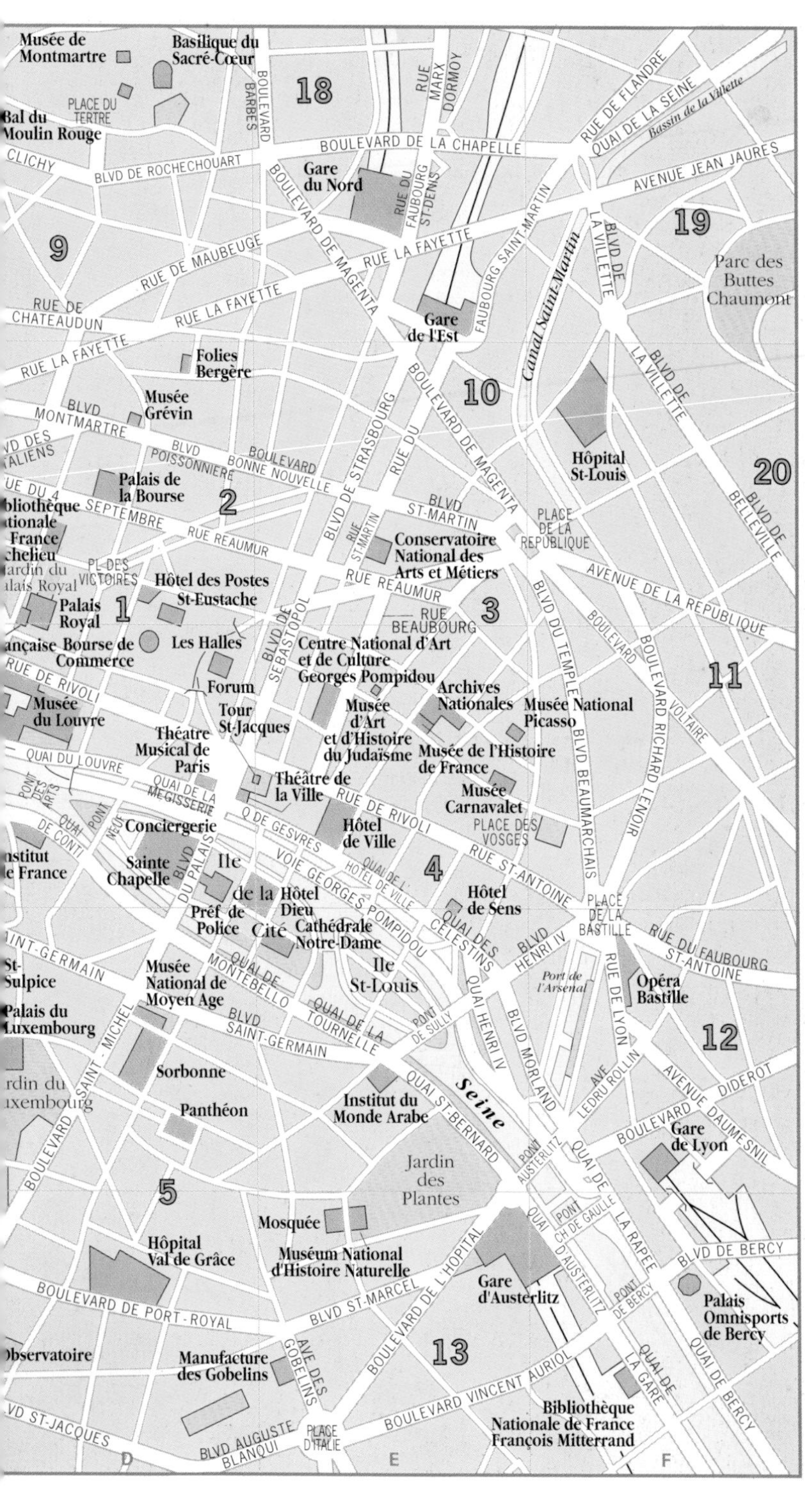

Musée de Montmartre
Basilique du Sacré-Cœur
Place du Tertre
Bal du Moulin Rouge
Boulevard Barbès
18
Rue Marx Dormoy
Rue de Flandre
Quai de la Seine
Bassin de la Villette
Boulevard de la Chapelle
Clichy
Blvd de Rochechouart
Gare du Nord
Rue du Faubourg St-Denis
Avenue Jean Jaurès
19
Parc des Buttes Chaumont
9
Rue de Maubeuge
Boulevard de Magenta
Rue La Fayette
Faubourg Saint-Martin
Canal Saint-Martin
Blvd de la Villette
Rue de Chateaudun
Gare de l'Est
Folies Bergère
Musée Grévin
Blvd Montmartre
10
Boulevard de Strasbourg
Rue du
Hôpital St-Louis
20
Blvd des Italiens
Blvd Poissonnière
Boulevard Bonne Nouvelle
Palais de la Bourse
2
Rue du 4 Septembre
Bibliothèque Nationale de France Richelieu
Blvd St-Martin
Place de la République
Blvd de Belleville
Rue Reaumur
Rue St-Martin
Conservatoire National des Arts et Métiers
Jardin du Palais Royal
Pl des Victoires
Hôtel des Postes
St-Eustache
Avenue de la République
Palais Royal
1
Blvd de Sebastopol
Rue Beaubourg
3
Les Halles
Bourse de Commerce
Centre National d'Art et de Culture Georges Pompidou
Boulevard Voltaire
Boulevard Richard Lenoir
Blvd du Temple
11
Rue de Rivoli
Musée du Louvre
Forum
Tour St-Jacques
Archives Nationales
Musée National Picasso
Théâtre Musical de Paris
Musée d'Art et d'Histoire du Judaïsme
Musée de l'Histoire de France
Blvd Beaumarchais
Quai du Louvre
Quai de la Mégisserie
Théâtre de la Ville
Musée Carnavalet
Pont des Arts
Pont Neuf
Quai de Conti
Conciergerie
Q de Gesvres
Hôtel de Ville
Place des Vosges
Institut de France
Sainte Chapelle
Blvd du Palais
Ile de la Cité
Voie Georges Pompidou
Quai de l'Hôtel de Ville
4
Rue St-Antoine
Hôtel Dieu
Préf de Police
Cathédrale Notre-Dame
Hôtel de Sens
Place de la Bastille
Rue du Faubourg St-Antoine
Blvd St-Germain
Quai des Célestins
Blvd Henri IV
Port de l'Arsenal
Opéra Bastille
St-Sulpice
Musée National de Moyen Age
Quai de Montebello
Ile St-Louis
Rue de Lyon
Palais du Luxembourg
Blvd Saint-Germain
Quai de la Tournelle
Pont de Sully
Quai Henri IV
Blvd Morland
12
Boulevard Saint-Michel
Sorbonne
Jardin du Luxembourg
Institut du Monde Arabe
Quai St-Bernard
Seine
Ave Ledru Rollin
Avenue Daumesnil
Diderot
Panthéon
Pont Austerlitz
Boulevard
Gare de Lyon
Jardin des Plantes
5
Quai de la Rapée
Mosquée
Pont Ch de Gaulle
Quai d'Austerlitz
Hôpital Val de Grâce
Muséum National d'Histoire Naturelle
Boulevard de l'Hôpital
Gare d'Austerlitz
Blvd de Bercy
Palais Omnisports de Bercy
Boulevard de Port-Royal
Blvd St-Marcel
Pont de Bercy
Observatoire
Manufacture des Gobelins
Ave des Gobelins
13
Quai de la Gare
Quai de Bercy
Boulevard Vincent Auriol
Bibliothèque Nationale de France François Mitterrand
Blvd St-Jacques
Blvd Auguste Blanqui
Place d'Italie
D
E
F

Viewing one of the 30,000 works of art in the Louvre...

Beat the queues at the Louvre by booking your entrance ticket in advance at any FNAC store in France (tel: 08 92 68 36 22) or through Ticketnet (tel: 08 92 39 01 00; www.ticketnet.fr) or through the museum's website, www.louvre.fr

...and recovering near the Arc de Triomphe

Rive Droite

Covering a much greater area than the Rive Gauche, the Right Bank governs the north, east and west of Paris in a curved sweep north of the Seine. This is where most museums and monuments are concentrated, as well as regal squares and boulevards, often the results of Baron Haussmann's frenetic urban transformations in the mid-19th century. Less intimate in scale, more disparate in style, it ranges from tackiness to high luxury.

The Louvre▶▶▶ Cour Napoleon, 99 rue de Rivoli (*Open* Thu–Mon 9–6, Wed 9am–10pm. *Closed* Tue. *Admission: expensive*). Hard to miss in its central riverside location is the Louvre, now face-lifted and expanded to be the world's largest museum and entered through I. M. Peï's controversial glass pyramid (or the Porte des Lions entrance if you have a ticket). Symbol of seven centuries and 17 rulers, the Louvre developed from 12th-century fortress origins, and was rebuilt and extended in Renaissance style by François I and classical style by Louis XIV, who completed the awesome Cour Carrée. The royal art collection was first displayed to the public during the Revolutionary period; today 30,000 works are exhibited, while many more remain in storage. Archaeological treasures found during recent excavations have added to the permanent display. The marble entrance under the pyramid skylight leads to the three wings, with categories and 'hit' exhibits (*Venus de Milo, Mona Lisa*, etc) well signposted.

Further along the rue de Rivoli are the **Musée de la Mode et du Textile▶**, the **Musée de la Publicité▶** and the **Musée des Arts Décoratifs▶▶**—all Palais du Louvre, 107 rue de Rivoli (*Open* Tue–Sun 10–6. *Admission: moderate*). The latter has furniture, decorative objects and period rooms from the Middle Ages to the present.

Unique Viewpoint Looking through Napoleon's **Arc du Carrousel** due west, you see one of the city's great perspectives: through the **Jardin des Tuileries▶▶** to the place de la Concorde, up the Champs-Elysées to the Arc de Triomphe and beyond to the office blocks of La Défense and the Grande Arche. The Tuileries houses the recently renovated **Orangerie▶▶**, with Monet's spectacular series of *Nymphéas*, and the **Jeu de Paume▶**, 1 place de la Concorde (*Open* Tue 12–9, Wed–Fri 12–7, Sat, Sun 10–7. *Admission: moderate*), a contemporary art exhibition. The terrace provides a superb view across the **place de la Concorde▶▶**, with its Egyptian obelisk and neoclassical mansions, and across the Seine to the **Palais Bourbon**, home of the National Assembly, while in the distance looms the Tour Eiffel and the glass domes of the Grand Palais. A footbridge links the Tuileries to the Rive Gauche.

The Grand Palais▶▶ (*Open* Tue–Sun 10–8, Wed 10–10. *Admission: moderate*) was built for the 1900 Exposition Universelle, and epitomizes the soaring domed iron and glass architectural style, while the **Petit Palais** opposite is more baroque in style. The sheer scale of the Grand Palais accommodates a science museum, the **Palais de la Découverte▶**.

Walk

Concorde to the Palais Royal

Starting at the Concorde, walk up to the Jeu de Paume, then back to the terrace, where steps lead to road level. Turn left off the rue de Rivoli up the rue de Castiglione to the place Vendôme. Cross the square and turn right down the rue Casanova, which becomes the rue des Petits-Champs. After the Bibliothèque Nationale, turn right to the rue de Beaujolais, which leads to the Palais Royal; pass the 1806 restaurant Le Grand Véfour. Walk through the gardens, past the back of the Comédie Française. Emerging on the place du Palais Royal, either enter the Louvre or turn left along the rue St-Honoré to Les Halles.

The **Champs-Elysées▶▶** is again the focus for Paris, recovered from its decline with an influx of new hotels, restaurants and luxury shops. A main attraction is the **Arc de Triomphe▶▶▶**, crowning the crossroads, L'Etoile. There are great views from its summit platform. Just north of the Louvre, on the place du Palais Royal, stands the famous theatre, the **Comédie Française**, and behind this is the **Jardin du Palais Royal▶▶**. The palace was built in 1642 and the adjacent apartments in 1780, their arcades soon sheltering fashionable cafés. In the front courtyard are Daniel Buren's controversial 1986 striped columns.

Running northwest from the Palais Royal, the avenue de l'Opéra culminates in the **Opéra Garnier▶▶**, Palais Garnier, place de l'Opéra (www.opera-de-paris.fr *Open* Mon–Sat 11–6.30. Guided visits possible. *Admission: moderate*). Garnier's lavish design, completed in 1875, comes into its own inside, with a magnificent *grand escalier*. Leading off the place de l'Opéra is the **rue de la Paix**, lined with top jewellers; this runs into the **place Vendôme▶▶** (1715), home to the Ritz and crowned by a column commemorating Napoleon's victories. The nearby **rue St-Honoré** epitomizes the Rive Droite: Its western end, the Faubourg, boasts luxury boutiques, while to the east are **Les Halles**, a meeting point for itinerant youth.

Above: the skylit Forum des Halles was part of a controversial 1970s redevelopment of the old central market of Les Halles

60,000 BULLOCKS

In pre-Revolutionary days the Parisian population was 600,000. Its annual consumption was the following: 60,000 bullocks, 15–20,000 cows, 200,000 calves, 420,000 sheep: an estimated total of 42 million kg (93 million lb) of meat.

Rive Gauche

Stretching from the **Quartier Latin▶▶** (5th) in the east across the increasingly bourgeois hub of **St-Germain-des-Prés▶▶** (6th) to the sedate 7th *arrondissement* and its pinnacle, the Tour Eiffel, the heart of the Left Bank is part officialdom, part academia, part bohemia and part aesthetics. Narrow streets lined with shops, cinemas, galleries and inviting bistros combine to create an atmosphere more of *far niente* than of a hectic capital city.

The Sorbonne Students have monopolized the 5th since the Sorbonne's foundation in 1257. Now joined by other colleges, it seems impervious to time: twisting streets full of bookshops, inexpensive eateries and historic churches, culminating in the **Panthéon▶** (*Open* daily 10–6; Apr–Sep 10–6.30. *Admission: moderate*) at the summit of the Montagne Ste-Geneviève. To the east lies Jean Nouvel's striking **Institut du Monde Arabe▶**, 1 rue des Fossés Saint-Bernard (*Open* Tue–Sun 10–6. *Admission: free; museum moderate*), and the **Jardin des Plantes▶**, home to botanical gardens and the superbly renovated **Musée Nationale d'Histoire Naturelle▶▶** (*Open* Wed–Mon 10–5.15. *Closed* Tue. *Admission: moderate*).

A popular Left Bank restaurant

On the crossroads of boulevards St-Michel and St-Germain, the **Musée Nationale du Moyen Age/Thermes de Cluny▶▶**, 6 place Paul-Painlevé (*Open* Wed–Mon 9.15–5.45. *Admission: moderate*), the former Musée Cluny, represents the span of the Latin Quarter's early history: Don't miss the Roman baths integrated into this Gothic mansion. The museum's collections include the *Dame à la Licorne*, a series of six allegorical 15th-century tapestries.

St-Germain Beyond boulevard St-Michel, the atmosphere changes as the 6th *arrondissement* begins. Rising above the central crossroads of the rue de Rennes and the boulevard St-Germain is the Romanesque tower of the 1163 church of **St-Germain-des-Prés▶▶**, worth visiting for its architecture and evening concerts. Once a powerful Benedictine monastery, its fortifications disappeared in the late 17th century to make way for the residential Faubourg St-Germain. Close by are the **Brasserie Lipp**, the **Café de Flore** and the **Deux Magots**, all intellectual havens. Beyond streets of boutiques is the church of **St-Sulpice**, famous for its gigantic 6,588-pipe organ.

Ideal for promenading, jogging or sunbathing, the **Jardin du Luxembourg▶▶**, redolent of *nouvelle vague* films, stretches south from Marie de Médicis' **Palais du Luxembourg**, now home to the Senate, as far as the boulevard du Montparnasse.

Musée d'Orsay Back down at the Seine, linking the 6th and 7th *arrondissements*, is the **Musée d'Orsay▶▶▶**, 1 rue de la Légion d'Honneur (*Open* Tue–Sun 9.30–6, Thu 9.30am–9.45pm. *Closed* Mon. *Admission: expensive*). Once a hotel and railway station, it is now a renovated museum devoted to art and applied arts 1848–1914. Beneath Laloux's 1900 shell are galleries taking you from Romanticism through academic works to Symbolism, the Ecole de Barbizon and finally to the jewel in the Orsay's crown—the Impressionists.

The sculptor Auguste Rodin (1840–1917) has his own museum, south of the boulevard St-Germain. Set in one of the 7th *arrondissement's* loveliest gardens, the **Musée Rodin▶▶**, Hotel Biron, 77 rue de Varenne (*Open* Apr–Sep Tue–Sun 9.30–5.45; Oct–Mar 9.30–4.45. *Closed* public holidays. *Admission: moderate*), has a collection of bronzes and marble works. The **Assemblée Nationale** lies to the north, glowering across the bridge at the Concorde.

Les Invalides The most impressively scaled monument of the Rive Gauche was built under Louis XIV to house 6,000 invalid soldiers—hence its name. Inside this vast group of buildings is the vast military collection of the **Musée de l'Armée▶**, while towering over it all is the magnificent baroque church **l'Eglise du Dôme▶▶** (*Open* daily 10–5; 10–7 in summer. *Admission: expensive*). Some of France's greatest soldiers are entombed here, including Napoleon. Leading elegantly west from the military academy are the formal gardens of the **Champ-de-Mars**, crowned at their end with the **Tour Eiffel▶▶▶**, Champ de Mars (*Open* daily 9.30am–11pm; summer 9am–midnight. *Admission: expensive*). Walk below it, climb it, dine at it: It's an unforgettable experience.

Inside the Musée d'Orsay

Walk

Pont des Arts to rue Soufflot

Starting from the Pont des Arts, walk east along the Quai de Conti, past the Institut de France, home to the Académie Française, and turn right at the Hôtel de la Monnaie. The narrow rue Guénégaud leads past galleries to the rue Mazarine. Turn left here, following it to the boulevard St-Germain, passing Paris's first café, Le Procope. At the three-pronged fork leading south from Odéon, take the left street, the rue Monsieur-le-Prince, which winds uphill to the rue Racine. Turn right here to arrive at the Théâtre de l'Odéon, behind which unfolds the Jardin du Luxembourg. Return to the northeast corner and emerge onto the boulevard St-Michel. Straight ahead is the rue Soufflot, which conceals a Gallo-Roman forum and ends at the Panthéon.

Floor-level shopping at Les Halles

Bateaux-mouches *ply the Seine day and night, taking in Notre-Dame on the circuit*

Le Marais and the Ile de la Cité

The transformation of Les Halles and Le Marais is a modern phenomenon. Stretching from Les Halles east to the Bastille, the renovated Marais has almost completely recovered the fashionable identity of its mainly 17th-century origins. Although geographically bordered to the south by the Seine, its historic character spills over onto the Ile St-Louis. The other, larger island, the Ile de la Cité, is the historic heart of Paris.

Centre National d'Art et de Culture Georges Pompidou ▶▶▶, rue St-Martin (*Open* Wed–Mon 11am–10pm; exhibitions close at 9pm. *Admission: moderate; free first Sun each month*). After two years' work, the Centre Pompidou re-opened in 2000, its multi-hued high-tech architecture intact, reigning over the renovated quarter that surrounds it. Within, the galleries of the Musée d'Art Moderne have been enlarged and restored and follow a more logical route from contemporary art to early moderns, Surrealists and Abstract Expressionists. There are also underground performance spaces, innovative new restaurants and, of course, the magnificent view from the top floor (you have to pay for the escalator), while the precint below buzzes with crowds.

Le Marais Immediately east, **Le Marais▶▶** bristles with trendy restaurants and bars, art galleries and boutiques, replacing traditional craftsmen. The lively Jewish quarter, dating from the 13th century, focuses on the **rue des Rosiers**. The **Musée d'Art et d'Histoire du Judaïsme▶** in the Hôtel de Saint-Aignan, 71 rue du Temple (*Open* Mon–Fri 11–6, Sun 10–6. *Closed* Sat. *Admission: inexpensive),* is fascinating, as is the **Maison Européene de la Photographie▶**, Hotel Hénault de Cantobre (*Open* Wed–Sun 11–8. *Admission: moderate).* The **rue Rambuteau**, leading into the **rue des Francs-Bourgeois**, is the main east–west axis along which are located monuments such as the **Musée Carnavalet▶▶**, 23 rue de Sévigné (*Open* Tue–Sun 10–6. *Closed* Mon. *Admission: moderate*), which contains a museum covering the history of Paris, as well as superb period rooms, including those of Madame de Sévigné. One block north stands the beautifully renovated Hôtel Salé, home to the **Musée National Picasso▶▶**, Hôtel Salé, 5 rue de Thorigny (*Open* Wed–Mon 9.30–5.30; also 9.30–6 in summer. *Admission: moderate*).

Place des Vosges Le Marais culminates in the east with the **place des Vosges▶▶**, completed in 1612. Once the site of a royal palace, its 36 red-brick mansions soon housed the *crème de la crème* of Parisian aristocracy and literati, today replaced by designers and artists. Former resident Victor Hugo has left a museum well worth a visit. Across rue St-Antoine, Le Marais also contains the medieval **Hôtel de Sens**, the **Hôtel de Sully** and, behind the **Hôtel de Ville**, the church of **St-Gervais-St-Protais**.

Bastille Indelibly marked as a Revolutionary symbol, the **Bastille▶** is today an animated district dedicated to a youthful avant-garde, whether in its galleries, nightclubs or philosophy cafés. As recently as the 1980s it was

Walk

Beaubourg to the place des Vosges

Starting from the Centre Georges Pompidou, take the rue Rambuteau and cross the rue des Archives. On your left is the vast courtyard of the Hôtel de Soubise. Continue along rue des Francs-Bourgeois past the 1510 turret of the Maison de Jean Hérouët before turning left into the rue Payenne, by the Musée Carnavalet. Walk past some typical Marais gardens and the Parc Royal. Turn left, then right to enter the rue de Thorigny and pass the Hôtel Salé (Musée National Picasso). Walk round to the garden at the back, turn left down rue Vieille du Temple as far as the rue des Rosiers on your left. Walk to the end, turning left up rue Pavée and right back into the rue des Francs-Bourgeois. Continue to the end of the street and the place des Vosges.

resolutely home to furniture craftsmen, but its identity changed as artists moved into abandoned workshops and the new 'people's opera' opened in 1990. A marina, the Port de l'Arsenal, terminates the canal St-Martin.

The islands Floating mid-stream between the Rive Gauche and Rive Droite, the Iles are very different in character. The village-like **Ile St-Louis▶▶** grew up as a successful property development in the 17th century. The adjoining **Ile de la Cité▶▶**, famous for Notre-Dame, Sainte-Chapelle and the **Conciergerie▶**, is a bizarre mixture of the sublime and the banal. Alongside its medieval monuments stand government symbols such as the **Palais de Justice**, the **Hôtel Dieu** (a massive hospital) and the **Préfecture**, the central police station. The stained-glass windows of the 13th-century **La Sainte-Chapelle▶▶▶**, 4 boulevard du Palais (*Open* daily 9.30–6.30; 10–5 in winter. *Admission: moderate*), and the intricate sculptures and rose windows of the **Cathédrale Notre-Dame de Paris▶▶▶**, place du Parvis-Notre-Dame (*Open* daily 8–6.45. *Closed* during services. *Admission free*), attract millions every year.

FORMER PRISON
Monopolizing the northern stretch of the Ile de la Cité, the turreted walls of the Conciergerie are a grim reminder of the Revolution, when more than 4,000 citizens, including Marie-Antoinette, were imprisoned there.

Beyond the central area

The winding path of the Seine, lined with blissfully shady *quais* and massive monuments, tends to monopolize visitors' attention. But don't forget that there is more to Paris than the Louvre and Notre-Dame. Today's city gates, encircling the 20 *arrondissements*, were built in the mid-19th century, while Haussmann was still busy laying out a modern city, and included what were then outlying districts such as **Montmartre**, **Montparnasse** and **Père-Lachaise**. As the years pass, Paris spreads farther. Urban developments have provided new poles of attraction at **La Villette** and **La Défense**. Meanwhile, **Vincennes** and **Boulogne**, former royal hunting grounds, are lungs for the east and west of the city.

Grandeur, 1930s-style—the Palais de Chaillot is home to the brand new Cité de l'Architecture et du Patrimoine (Open Mon, Wed–Fri 12–8, Sat, Sun 11–7), which includes changing exhibitions on architectural and cultural themes.

Palais de Chaillot Built for the Paris Exhibition of 1937, the grandiose Chaillot completes a monumental axis sweeping across from the Ecole Militaire, down the Champ-de-Mars, under or over the Tour Eiffel and across the Seine to the gardens below. Its other façade dominates the **place du Trocadéro**, a famous haunt for well-heeled local residents. Following a fire in 1997, the building was redeveloped and now includes the Cité de l'Architecture et du Patrimoine. Nearby are the twinned forms of the **Palais de Tokyo**, home to Paris' excellent **Centre d'Art Contemporain▶** (*Open* Tue–Sun 12–12. *Admission: moderate*), dedicated to modern design.

Bois de Boulogne Immediately to the west, through Passy, beyond the wonderful Impressionists of the **Musée Marmottan-Monet▶▶**, 2 rue Louis-Boilly (*Open* Tue–Sun 10–6. *Admission: moderate*), is one of the many entrances to the extensive **Bois de Boulogne**. Donated to the city by Napoleon III, it was redesigned by Haussmann to resemble London's Hyde Park. Rent bicycles or rowing-boats, wander in the rose gardens of the **Jardin de Bagatelle▶▶**, or recuperate in the luxurious restaurant of the pretty Pré Catalan.

La Défense Western Paris no longer ends here. Since the late 1950s the business hub of **La Défense** has sprouted anarchically skywards, leaving as many architectural horrors as marvels. Otto von Spreckelson's monumental **Grande Arche▶** (*Open* daily 10–7; 10–8 in summer. *Admission: moderate*), completed in 1989, has at last given a focus to the high-rises and its roof views are superb.

Montparnasse Another tower dominating Paris' skyline is the Tour Montparnasse, a 1970s hiccup, which was part of a massive urban development, signifying the birth of an entirely renovated *quartier* which includes the city's most confusing railway station. Although no longer the artists' mecca that it was in the 1920s, it retains a few symbols, particularly the rebuilt bar and brasserie of **La Coupole**. Side streets like the **rue Vavin** or **rue de la Gaieté** are essential relics of this epoch.

La Villette Attempts at creating another cultural island have been concentrated in the northeastern corner of Paris at **La Villette**, avenue Corentin-Cariou, with its **Cité des Sciences et de l'Industrie** (*Open* Tue–Sat 10–6, Sun 10–7.

Closed Mon. *Admission: expensive*). Completed in 1993, this multicultural park complex contains an impressive museum of science and technology, a spherical cinema (**La Géode**), the renovated 19th-century cattle market christened **La Grande Halle** (used for concerts and exhibitions), a music academy and concert halls.

Eastern Paris Here are two more popular promenading areas: the cemetery of **Père-Lachaise▶▶** and the Bois de Vincennes. The former, spreading over a hillside, must contain the greatest density of celebrated writers, musicians and artists in the world. Armed with a plan, visitors set off in search of the tombs of Edith Piaf, Jim Morrison, Modigliani, Chopin or Oscar Wilde. More mundane, the **Bois de Vincennes▶** is the eastern equivalent to Boulogne, and is similarly equipped with lakes, woods (severely damaged by the storm of 1999), rose gardens, a zoo and, its pride and glory, a severe medieval fortress once home to French kings. Vincennes will no doubt regain popularity with the urban developments currently taking place in nearby Bercy and Tolbiac, where Dominique Perrault's controversial **Bibliothèque Nationale de France** now stands.

Montmartre▶▶ Montmartre's winding streets and steps climb up to the white Roman–Byzantine cupolas of **Sacré-Cœur▶▶**, 36 rue du Chevalier-de-la-Barre (*Open* daily 6.45am–11pm. *Admission: free.* Dome and Crypt *open* 9–6. *Admission: inexpensive*). Built as atonement for the massacred victims of the 1871 Franco-Prussian War, it attracts millions for its **spectacular view▶▶▶** across Paris. Montmartre also means throngs of fake artists, but its leafy backstreets and vineyard cannot shake off a unique, peaceful character. Here, too, the Moulin Rouge is a reminder that more than 30 windmills once ground silex from quarries—almost causing the hill to collapse.

VIADUC DES ARTS

Running the full 4.5km (3 miles) between the Bastille and the Bois de Vincennes is a walkway-cum-garden with cycle path, the Promenade Plantée. For 1.5km (1 mile) it runs along a viaduct whose converted red-brick archways below house workshops for numerous craftspeople and restorers, as well as providing a showcase for contemporary artists. This is the trendy end of the vast developments changing the face of eastern Paris.

Montmartre lights up at night with bars and cafés spilling onto the cobbled streets

TUMBLING SPIRE
Building started on Beauvais Cathedral in 1227 but the choir collapsed a few days after completion under the weight of its ambitious design. A replacement was completed in the late 14th century, but remained roofless for two centuries. More disaster struck in 1573 when the new 153m (502ft) spire tumbled, leading to the closure of the cathedral in 1605.

The Temple of Love, one of the ornaments to be found in Le Nôtre's grounds of the Château de Chantilly

Ile de France

►► Chateau d'Anet *240A2*

Ile-de-France (Open: Apr–Oct Wed–Mon 2–6.30; Nov–Mar Sat, Sun 2–6. Admission: moderate). No direct train line

In 1548, Diane de Poitiers, Henri II's ambitious mistress, commissioned the architect Philibert Delorme to expand and rebuild Anet. Some of the greatest Renaissance artists, Jean Goujon, Germain Pilon and Cellini, created a magnificent home for this powerful woman. She later moved to the fabulous Loire château of Chenonceaux, but after Henri's death in 1559 she was ousted by his widow, Catherine de Médicis, and returned to Anet. An extravagantly decorated chapel containing her tomb is one of the few remaining features alongside one wing, the beautifully sculpted front entrance and a lovely park.

► Parc Astérix *240B2*

Plaily (Open: Apr–Nov either 10–6 or 9.30–7, depending on day of week or season. Closed some days, so call to confirm: 08 26 30 10 40. Admission: expensive)

Only 35km (22 miles) north of Paris, this park, a rival to Disneyland, based on the antics of the Gallic cartoon hero Astérix, created by Albert Uderzo, is packed with replica Roman monuments, gladiators, slaves and an imaginative range of related games, fun-fair rides including the Zeus Thunder rollercoaster and gastronomy. Nor is his fat, devoted friend Obélix forgotten. It is well organized and very popular on weekends, so be prepared for a long wait for attractions.

► Beauvais *240A3*

In the flat Picardy landscape, the bulky medieval cathedral of Beauvais rises above the surrounding roofs. Apart from the incredible scale of the choir, its most astonishing features are the stained glass, the sculpted stone portals and the remains of the 'Basse Oeuvre', a rare 10th-century Carolingian church incorporated into the cathedral. Beside the cathedral, the old bishop's palace houses the renovated and expanded collections of the Musée Départemental de l'Oise, the principal museum of the Oise *département*.

►►Chateau de Chantilly (Chateau/Musée Condé) *240A2*

(Open: Apr–Oct Wed–Mon 10–6; Nov–Mar Wed–Mon 10.30–5. Admission: moderate)

Rail: Chantilly

Famous for its forests, racecourses and whipped cream, Chantilly also boasts a château. Its attractive and mixed architectural styles reflect a lively history, from Renaissance origins through destruction in the Revolution to rebuilding in the 19th century. The magnificent grounds were transformed by Le Nôtre, who added lakes and canals. Inside the château, the **Musée Condé** displays Italian and French Renaissance furnishings, a remarkable art collection ranging from Raphael to Delacroix and a facsimile of the illuminated medieval manuscript the *Très Riches Heures du Duc de Berry* (original not on view).

►► Cathédrale de Chartres 240A2

place de la Cathédrale (Open: daily 8.30–7.30. Admission free) A11 southwest of Paris. Rail: Chartres

'The acropolis of France' (Rodin), Notre-Dame de Chartres, replaces five successive churches, the last built in 1021 to house the relics of the Virgin Mary. Numerous fires culminated in the devastating flames of 1194, which inspired the community to build a new cathedral—a task that was accomplished in 25 years. The lower half of the façade remains pure 11th-century Romanesque, while the rest of the cathedral represents the transition to Gothic. Inside the cathedral, 176 luminous stained-glass windows of classical and modern designs attest to the talents of the Chartres craftsmen. The crypt dates mainly from the 11th century and is the largest in France (there is an entry charge).

The mismatched towers of Notre-Dame de Chartres are a result of lightning striking the north tower in the 16th century, decapitating its spire

► Château de Compiègne 240B2

5 place du Générale-de-Gaulle, 60200 Compiègne (Open: Wed–Mon 10–6. Admission: moderate) Rail: Compiègne

Surrounded by the glorious Forêt de Compiègne, the elegant town of Compiègne was a preferred retreat for French kings from the 14th century onwards. Louis XIV gave some spectacular parties there; both Louis XV and XVI extended the château and Napoleons I and III also enjoyed its grandeur. The lavish rooms are arranged according to period, the most impressive being Empress Josephine's bedroom, the Grand Salon and the ballroom.

►► Disneyland Paris 240B2

Marne-la-Vallée (Open: daily 9–8; open later some weekends and holidays. Admission: expensive). RER: Line A from central Paris

The fourth Disney theme park opened its doors in 1992, an American paradise in the heart of Europe. Hotels grouped round a lake allow visitors to explore the Disneyland Park, its attractions ranging from the vaguely medieval castle of Sleeping Beauty to a science fiction environment à la Jules Verne. Next to Disneyland is the film- and TV-based Walt Disney Studios Park, with rides based on popular films—real and animated.

► Dreux 240A2

Its forest long preserved as hunting ground, Dreux became the personal property of the royal family in the 16th century and still has strong royalist connections. In recent years it has controversially supported the extreme right party, the Front National. The main monument of this market town is a hilltop chapel built by Louis-Philippe's mother as the mausoleum for the Orléans family, still the French pretenders to the throne.

►► Chateau d'Ecouen 240A2

(Open: Apr–Sep Wed–Mon 9.30–12.45, 2–5.45; Oct–Mar Wed–Mon 9.30–12.45, 2–5.15. Admission: inexpensive)

This superb château, on the edge of the Parisian suburbs, was built in the mid-16th century for the Constable Anne de Montmorency. Today it houses a museum devoted to the Renaissance period.

MONSIEUR PLATE-SNATCHER

In the outskirts of Chartres lies an extraordinary house and garden, created by an eccentric. Using thousands of multi-hued fragments of smashed plates, glass, mirror and ceramic, he plastered the walls and even his wife's sewing machine with mosaic murals. The garden even contains a mosaic throne. The Maison Picassiette (literally plate-snatcher) is at 22 rue du Repos (*Open:* Apr–Oct Mon, Wed–Sat 10–12, 2–6, Sun 2–6. *Closed* Tue).

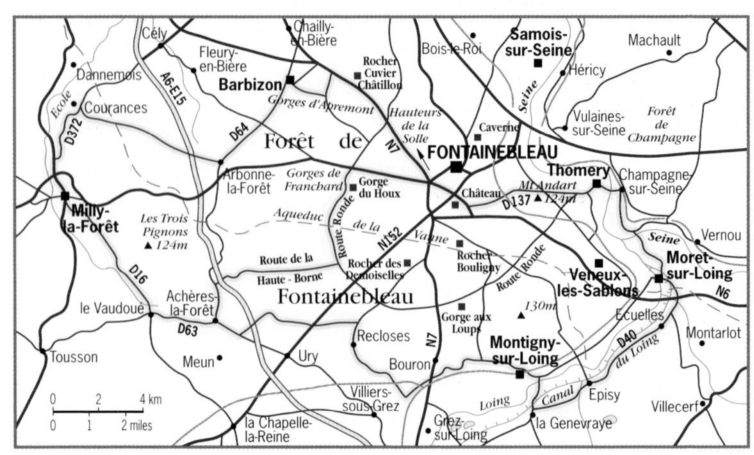

Drive

The Forest of Fontainebleau

Start your tour at the sprawling Château de Fontainebleau.
The largest forest in the Ile de France is that of **Fontainebleau** (*Open* Jun–Sep Wed–Mon 9.30–6, Oct–May Wed–Mon 9.30–5. *Admission: moderate*). Rich in natural wonders (6,000 species of insects, 200 birds), as well as a wide variety of flora and fauna, it was originally a 12th-century hunting lodge. The forest was much damaged during the violent storms in 1999. The château was transformed in the 16th century by François I and later used by Napoleon. The lovely gardens, which were re-landscaped by Le Nôtre in the mid-17th century, are criss-crossed by canals.

Leave Fontainebleau by the N7, which takes you to Barbizon.
On your left are the Gorges d'Apremont, which invite you to stop to climb up. Barbizon itself was home between 1825 and 1870 to landscape painters who created their own movement. Corot, Millet, Rousseau and Daubigny all worked here, painting in the open air and spending their evenings at the Auberge du Père Ganne. Today it is full of commercial galleries, but remains pretty; and there are items of memorabilia in the houses of Millet and Rousseau.

From Barbizon follow the D64 to Arbonne-la-Forêt. Take a tiny road on the right to reach Courances.
The château is sometimes open to the public, and the pure classical gardens and canals are exceptional (*Open* Apr–Oct, on demand 2–6.30).

Drive south to Milly-la-Forêt.
Milly-la-Forêt was once the home of Jean Cocteau; he is buried in the 12th-century church. The enormous beamed wooden market hall in the main square is 15th-century.

Leave Milly, passing the church, via the D16 and drive to Le Vaudoué.
On your left is the 124m (407ft) hill of Les Trois Pignons, one of the most beautiful parts of the forest.

Continue to Achères-la-Forêt, from where you can either circle back to Fontainebleau via the Gorges de Franchard, another notable climbing and panoramic spot, or continue to the very pretty River Loing. Drive south of the Loing on the D40 to Moret.
This fortified medieval town was once home to the Impressionist painter Sisley. Its Grande Rue is lined with medieval and Renaissance houses.

Return to Fontainebleau via Champagne-sur-Seine.

►► Rambouillet, Château de 240A2

Yvelines (Open: Apr–Sep Wed–Mon 10–11.50, 2–5.30; Oct–Mar 10–11.45, 2–4.30. Closed: public holidays and when the President is in residence. Admission: moderate).
Lying about 55km (34 miles) southwest of Paris, the Château de Rambouillet has been the country retreat for French presidents since 1897. Dating from the 14th century, it really came into its own when François I died there after becoming ill while hunting in the forest. It was later much appreciated by Louis XVI. Marie-Antoinette was less impressed and described the château as a 'toad-pond'; to appease her a dairy was built inside an English-style garden. The magnificent park has been landscaped over several centuries.

►► St-Denis 240A2

(basilique) 2 rue du Strasbourg, Seine-St-Denis (Open: Apr–Sep Mon–Sat 10–6.15, Sun 12–6.15; Oct–Mar Mon–Sat 10–5.15, Sun noon–5.15. Closed: public holidays. Admission: moderate).
The daunting necropolis of French kings, a Métro ride from central Paris, is often overlooked by visitors. The Christian martyr St. Denis, who was decapitated at Montmartre, is said to have staggered to the north carrying his head to a rural burial. A church rose on this site in the 5th century, but today's basilica was built by the leading churchman and royal official Suger in the early 12th century. Its Gothic beauty inspired similar edifices at Chartres, Meaux, Senlis and Notre-Dame. Following the example of the seventh-century Dagobert, St-Denis was for more than 12 centuries the royal burial ground. Restored from Revolutionary pillaging, it remains an incredible museum of funerary sculpture. St-Denis also boasts the new flying-saucer Stade de France, built for the 1998 football World Cup.

► St-Germain-en-Laye 240A2

The main interest of this chic Parisian suburb lies in its medieval fortress, much rebuilt by François I in the 16th century. The château now houses the **Musée des Antiquités Nationales►** (*Open* Wed–Mon 9–5.15. *Admission: inexpensive*), a showcase of archaeological artefacts. The home of the late 19th-century artist Maurice Denis is now a museum with a superb collection of works of art.

LIKE A WOMAN
'Many men, not all of them French, have loved France like a woman, seeing in it, according to each context, their mother, their mistress or the woman of their dreams.'—
André Fontaine,
Le Monde, 1982.

The Grande Terrasse of St-Germain-en-Laye's fortress was designed by Le Nôtre in 1668–73 and stretches for 2.4km (1.5 miles). The view from the terrace across the valley of the Seine inspired the Impressionist painter Sisley

The Musée National de Céramique in Sèvres displays valuable examples of porcelain from Sèvres, Vincennes and Dresden, and copies of Oriental pieces, Italian majolica and Islamic ceramics

VAUX'S HIGHLIGHTS
Inside Vaux, don't miss the Salon des Muses, with ceiling paintings by Le Brun of nine different muses. Here Molière and his troupe first staged *L'Ecole des Maris* with Queen Henrietta-Maria of England and Fouquet as audience. Upstairs, the superb Chambre du Roi was subsequently copied at Versailles and throughout Europe.

► Sceaux *240A2*

The well-tended park at Sceaux once surrounded a 1677 château that was used for receptions and has become popular for promenading or picnicking Parisians today. Those early days ended with the Revolution when the original château was destroyed. Today's château was built in 1856; the grounds were restored to Le Nôtre's design in the 20th century. Inside, the **Musée de l'Ile de France** (*Open* summer Wed–Mon 10–6; winter daily 10–5. *Admission: inexpensive*) has paintings, costumes, royal porcelain and other objects relevant to this region's history. The park is open from dawn to dusk. The Orangerie has touring exhibitions and cultural events.

►► Senlis *240B2*

Formerly a Roman settlement, Senlis became home to a remarkable Gothic cathedral in 1153; building was not completed until 1560. The sculptures of the main entrance are devoted to the Virgin Mary and the lateral porches are typical of the Flamboyant Gothic style. The town is full of Renaissance houses and 17th- to 18th-century town houses. It is devoid of a railway thanks to local lobbying in the 19th century. Many Gallo-Roman ruins remain too. Some have been integrated into the remains of the medieval castle (Musée de la Venerie, Château Royal, place du Parvis-Notre-Dame; *open* summer Mon, Thu, Fri 10–12, 2–6; winter Sat, Sun 11–1, 2–6, Wed 2–6 or 2–5. *Closed* public holidays. *Admission: inexpensive*); others are still visible: 16 towers have survived from this period.

► Sèvres *240A2*

Between Versailles and Paris lies the pretty old suburb of Sèvres (the baroque composer Lully lived here, as did Balzac), which borders on the 392ha (970-acre) park of St-Cloud, with its Le Nôtre-designed waterways and views over Paris. Home to the royal porcelain factory, moved from Vincennes in 1756 by Madame de Pompadour, Sèvres has become synonymous with French craftsmanship, examples of which can be seen in its **museum►**, in place de la Manufacture (*Open* Wed–Mon 10–5).

►► Vaux-le-Vicomte, Château de *240B2*

77950 Mancy (Open: late-Mar to mid-Nov daily 10–6 (house closed 1–2); also Jul–Aug Fri 8–midnight; candlelit musical evenings May to mid-Oct, Sat; fountain displays 2nd and last Sat of month, 3–6. Admission: expensive)

Without Vaux, Versailles would never have happened. It was here that Louis XIV's shrewd, power-hungry Minister of Finance, Fouquet, decided to build a monument to the artists of the epoch—and to himself. Between the architect Le Vau, the painter Le Brun and landscape gardener Le Nôtre, a château and park of unsurpassed extravagance and beauty were built between 1656 and 1661. Unfortunately for Fouquet, Louis XIV was only too aware of its value and soon clapped his minister into prison, then proceeded to build Versailles. A victim of the vagaries of French history, Vaux-le-Vicomte was saved by an industrialist and has undergone extensive restoration over the last century. The formal gardens are a masterpiece of French style, with terraces, fountains, statues and ponds.

The Water Gardens in Versailles are best seen in full action ('les grandes eaux') *from early May to early October on Sunday at 3pm*

►►► Versailles 240A2

(Open: (château) Apr–Oct Tue–Sun 9–6.30; Nov–Mar Tue–Sun 9–5.30; (Les Trianons) Apr–Sep daily 12–6; Oct–Mar 12–5. Admission: expensive. Open: (gardens) daily dawn–dusk, except during bad weather. Admission free, except for les grand eaux *(fountain display): moderate)*

Every imposing avenue of Versailles converges on the palace, the town's *raison d'être*, Louis XIV's greatest creation and a world unto itself. In 1661, Louis decided to move his court and government to this swampy area, an astute way of isolating them but also of marking the flowering of French baroque in an area with unlimited space for expansion.

The garden façade best epitomizes the Sun King's ambitions. Faced in stone, lined with Ionic columns and capped with ornamental balustrades and carved trophies, the central section is part of the 'envelope' Le Vau designed around the original hunting lodge.

The Royal Apartments are divided into the 'Grands' and 'Petits'. The 'Grands', laid out in the 1670s by the King's chief painter, Le Brun, were the luxurious public rooms. The jewel of this stretch is the Galerie des Glaces, the largest, most magnificent and last public room to be completed. Le Brun's painted ceilings depict the King himself, while the 17 great mirrors once reflected candelabra, damask and precious furniture. Beyond is the Queen's Apartment and a series of dull picture galleries built later by Louis-Philippe. Before entering the 'Grands', don't miss the **Royal Chapel**, a perfect combination of elegance and grandeur, laid out on two levels. The 'Petits Appartements' can be seen only with a guided tour. These were the royal family's real living quarters.

The gardens The severe symmetry of the largest palace gardens in Europe, another of Le Nôtre's masterpieces, is relieved by hundreds of statues, 'follies' and fountains, not to mention the canals. If your time is limited, a small train will take you through the park (*Open* dawn–dusk) to the **Trianons**, two more modest kingly residences. The 'Grand Trianon' was built for Louis XIV to escape from the palace routine; the neoclassical 'Petit Trianon' was built by Gabriel for Louis XV. Its grounds were later entirely transformed for Marie-Antoinette to play at milkmaid in a theatrical village, the *hameau*. For visitors similarly wanting to escape palace tedium, bicycles and rowing boats are for rent at the Grand Canal.

EUROPE'S LONGEST

In 1678, Hardouin-Mansart filled in the terrace to create the almighty Galerie des Glaces (Hall of Mirrors), the most famous room in the palace, and added two blocks north and south to make the garden façade of Versailles the longest (570m/625yd) in Europe.

LE POTAGER DU ROI

A stone's throw from the château lie 9ha (22 acres) of impeccable kitchen gardens-cum-orchards, virtually unchanged since their creation by La Quintaye between 1679 and 1683. Micro-climates within the 29 walled gardens surrounding the central sunken gardens and terraces enabled La Quintaye to develop methods of growing produce out of season, as well as new pruning techniques still used for the 5,000-odd fruit trees. Unusual vegetables flourish such as blue Hungarian pumpkins, 50 varieties each of apple and pear—such was the choice set at the king's table (now sold to the public).

NO LIMITS
'Paris is complete, Paris is the ceiling of human kind...It has no limits, Paris does more than make the law, it makes fashion. Paris can be stupid if it wants, it sometimes allows itself this luxury. The clouds of smoke from its chimneys are ideas of the Universe. A pile of mud and stone if you like but, above all, a moral being. It is more than great, it is immense. Why? Because it dares.'—Victor Hugo, *Les Misérables*.

Shopping

The perennial problem of Paris is how to escape without running up an almighty overdraft. Temptations lie in wait round every corner, many outrageously expensive but some just within a normal budget.

Markets For food and wine, go straight to the main market streets (closed on Mondays), which have a vast array of fresh produce and clusters of specialized shops. The most touristy, the **rue de Buci** (6th *arrondissement*), is the least impressive. Go instead to the **rue Montorgueil** (1st), traditionally part of Les Halles; the popular **rue Mouffetard** (5th); the **rue Poncelet** (17th); the picturesque **rue du Poteau** (18th); or the **rue Lepic** in Montmartre (18th). For North African produce, head for the back streets of Belleville or try the vibrant **Marché d'Aligre** (12th). Nearby, at the **Bastille**, an immense, generous Sunday morning market is held. Lovers of Asiatic delicacies should go to **Chinatown** (13th), where numerous shops and supermarkets are concentrated among the restaurants south of the place d'Italie.

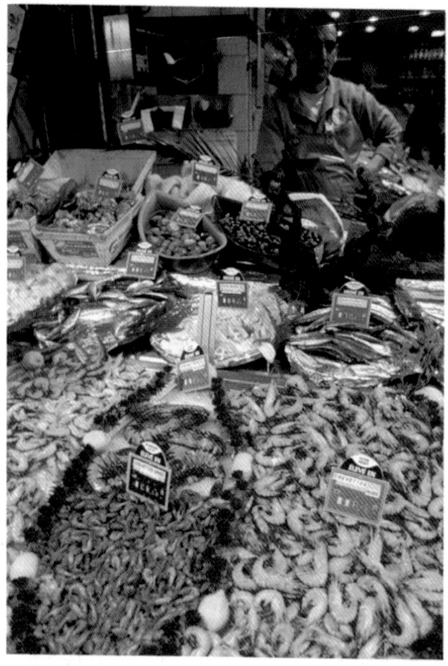

For the best in fresh food, go to market

Fashion For cheap but stylish clothes head for the boutiques on **rue de Rennes**, and **boulevard St-Michel**, popular with students. Slightly more stylish, the boutiques of the **boulevard St-Germain** and **Les Halles** always stock the latest crazes. L'Espace Créateurs in Les Halles stocks 50 young designers. Designer *prêt-à-porter*, from Kenzo to Mugler, is best chased around the **rue Etienne-Marcel** and the **place des Victoires** (1st). Top shoe designers such as Stephane Kélian are also here. And for the very top end of the market go to the **Faubourg St-Honoré** and the **avenue Montaigne**. But don't miss **Galeries Lafayette** on boulevard Haussmann. **TATI,** boulevard de Rochechouant, is a bargain basement department store, while **Le Mouton à Cinq Pattes,** rue Saint-Placide, and **L'Habilleur,** rue de Poitou, sell discount designer wear.

Bric-à-brac and antiques are relegated to the flea markets, from the **Porte de Clignancourt** (*Open* Sat–Mon) to the **Porte de Vanves** (weekends only) or the daily auctions held at **Drouot**. Valuable pieces can be seen at the enormous **Louvre des Antiquaires** (Métro: Palais-Royal) or in the world-famous **Carré Rive Gauche**, a grid of streets behind the Quai Voltaire (7th) chock-a-block with priceless objects and paintings. Antiquarian book- and print-lovers could spend a lifetime exploring the backstreets of the **Quartier Latin** and the *bouquinistes* lining the *quais*.

Food and drink

The choice of eating places in Paris is almost disarming—where to start? All depends on your budget: you could spend every evening in the 3-Michelin-star restaurants of the 8th *arrondissement*—**Taillevent, Alain Ducasse** and **Pierre Gagnaire**—or just head straight for the smokey bistros of the Quartier Latin and St-Germain.

Even if your pocket does not stretch to **Michel Rostang** or **Guy Savoy's** establishments, you can try their more affordable bistros, both near the Etoile. There is a gamut of famous brasseries, from **Flo, Julien** and **Terminus Nord** in the 10th to the **Vaudeville** or the **Grand Colbert**, both near the Bourse in the 2nd, **Bofinger** at the Bastille, the art deco artists' monument in Montparnasse, **La Coupole**, or the **Brasserie Lipp** in boulevard St-Germain.

If your aim is for a more intimate tête-à-tête that is not ruinous, go straight to **Marais**, where trendy but moderate bistros and restaurants offer acceptable cuisine. The side-streets of **St-Germain-des-Prés** have equally inviting pickings, particularly near the Métro Mabillon. For limited budgets try the **rue de l'Echaudé**, the **rue St-Benoît** and the **rue Monsieur-le-Prince**. In the 5th, low-budget visitors should go to the **rue des Boulangers**, while the **rue St-Séverin** and **rue de la Huchette** have lots of Greek, middle-eastern and, strangely, Savoyard restaurants.

Night food The Bastille area has become a nocturnal haunt for trendy young Parisians (20 to 30 age group). Small restaurants and bars abound along the **rue de la Roquette**, the **rue de Lappe** and the **rue de Charonne**. Les Halles is more downmarket but very vibrant. Other age groups may prefer the **boulevard St-Germain** and its side streets.

Ethnic food enthusiasts should go for Asiatic food to the 13th (**Chinatown**) or 20th (**Belleville**), for Japanese the **rue Ste-Anne** (2nd) and for North African any of the couscous restaurants scattered all over the capital. See also **Hotels and Restaurants**, page 283.

FRENCH TASTES
In 1991, 63 per cent of French people thought they ate too much compared with only 50 per cent in 1971. Today, 66 per cent think they drink too much. Of all foreign cooking, 66 per cent of the French particularly enjoy Italian, 51 per cent North African, 35 per cent Chinese, 32 per cent Vietnamese, 20 per cent Greek, 17 per cent Indian, 16 per cent Japanese and a mere 6 per cent English cooking.

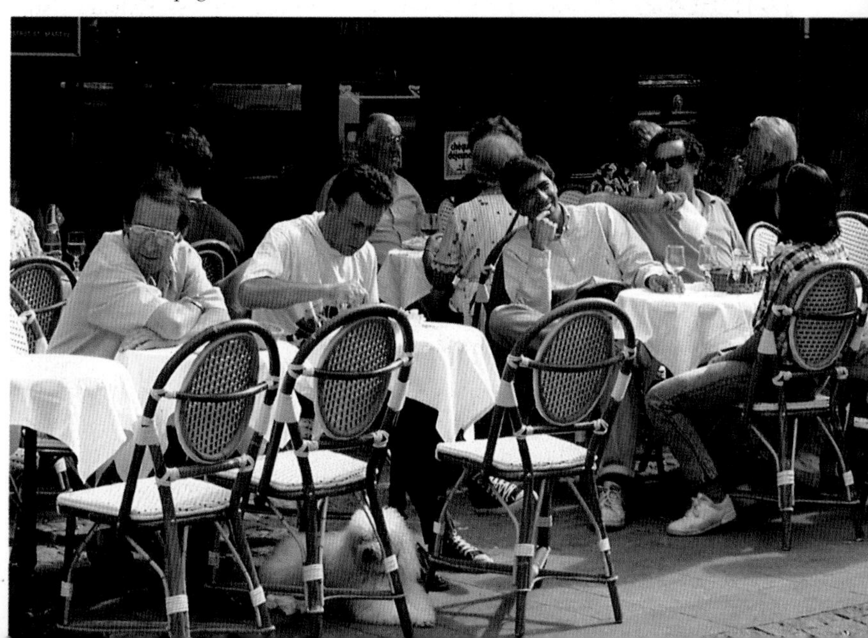

Café-terraces are the ultimate Parisian institution, ideal for people-watching, penning a novel or a discreet rendezvous

Nightlife

It is unavoidable: when in Paris you have to partake of the nocturnal forbidden fruits. Part of the myth and part of the fun, there are haunts for all generations and tastes.

Pigalle is still hot, still changing since the days of Toulouse-Lautrec. Around the **place Blanche** and the **place Pigalle** is a multitude of haunts, from the classic **Moulin Rouge** to drag clubs like **Folies Pigalle**, trendy bars like **Le Moloko** or **Divan du Monde**. Try the kitsch of **Lili La Tigresse** followed by a more leisurely belly-dance at **Shéhérazade**. Ballroom dancing (without the dress) is back in style at **Le Bal Elysée Montmartre,** with big bands, and a varied list of events for all types and ages.

Late night Les Halles offers plenty of jazz bars and late-night haunts. For peep-shows and tackiness the northern section of the **rue St-Denis** has it all, but for a late drink with good live or recorded music go to the **rue des Lombards**: **Au Duc des Lombards** is always buzzing, as is **Sunset**, a few doors away. **Le Petit Opportun**, round the corner, is still hot for jazz if you can find a seat. The rue Berger has another stretch of popular music bars: **Eustache** at No. 37 is cheap and friendly. Then there's always the long-standing, ultra-trendy nightclub, **Les Bains**.

Another nocturnal zone circles around **Le Palace**, the notorious theatrical disco in the Faubourg Montmartre, and downstairs is the more select **Privilège**. The **Rex** pulls in crowds for its techno and house, while jazz enthusiasts track down the **New Morning** live jazz bar or swing to Dixieland at **Le Petit Journal** in St-Michel.

Light fantastic Concentrated around the **rue de la Roquette** and the **rue de Lappe** at the Bastille are renovated old dance halls (**Le Balajo**) and busy bars that are open till the early hours. Gentrification of the area has moved some of these bars north to the **Oberkampf** area: same crowd, different place. Try **Cithéa** on the rue Oberkampf itself. For more mature visitors the **Champs-Elysées** area has several rather select nightclubs, including **Régines**, **Villa Barclay, Le Queen** and the stylish **L'Arc** (with garden), as well as smart cocktail bars away from the flashing lights that guide tourists into the **Lido** and the **Crazy Horse Saloon**.

HAIR OF THE *CHIEN*
It's six in the morning, you've been dancing all night: It's time for breakfast. Try the freshly baked goodies at Chez Jean-Mi, rue de d'Ancienne Comédie (6th); La Maison d'Alsace, avenue des Champs-Elysées (8th), for a dozen oysters; the Mustang Café (until 5am only), boulevard du Montparnasse (14th), for tacos; Le Dépanneur, rue Fontaine (9th), for a follow-up tequila; some onion soup, tripe or a pig's trotter at the aptly named Au Pied de Cochon, rue Coquillière (1st).

CELLAR RATS
The rhythms of 'be-bop' started in post-war St-Germain at the Tabou Club in rue Dauphine, which opened in 1947 with Juliette Greco, Boris Vian and Jacques Prévert. Sacrilegious in tone, exuberant in expression, these infamous night-owls were reacting to the severe restrictions of the war years. They were soon named the 'cellar rats'.

Parisian nocturnal fidelities may be fickle, but the Moulin Rouge survives—thanks to tourists

Hotels

With more than 2,000 hotels and up to 28 million tourists spread between them annually, Paris caters for all tastes and budgets. It is one of the rare European capitals that offers quite acceptable and affordable hotels in central areas, while a dozen or so establishments maintain standards of luxury straight out of another epoch. Unfortunately, France has the smallest minimum legal size of bathrooms and bedrooms in Europe, and in Paris, where real estate does not come cheap, many hoteliers exploit this standard to the full.

High style The 8th *arrondissement* (**Champs-Elysées, avenue George V**, **avenue Montaigne**, **Faubourg St-Honoré** and surrounding streets) is by far the most chic locality, with a high concentration of luxury and 4-star hotels. This is where you stay if you need to pop out for another fitting at Dior's or to shop at Hermès.

Following closely in the luxury stakes is the 1st *arrondissement* (**Tuileries, Louvre, place Vendôme**), convenient for high-class accessories and for culture, yet whose backstreets have a sprinkling of affordable 2- and 3-star hotels. The adjacent 9th (**Opéra**, **Grands Boulevards**) has the densest concentration of hotels, more than half of which are budget 2-star establishments. The **Faubourg Montmartre** claims the majority; many are used by tour operators, but farther north near to **Pigalle** and **Montmartre** are some characteristic family-run hotels.

What's Left? The area most visitors should and do head for is the Rive Gauche, the 5th, 6th and even 7th *arrondissements*. Less business-like in atmosphere than the Right Bank, the **Quartier Latin** and **St-Germain-des-Prés** house a host of reasonable 1-, 2-star and some very attractive 3-star hotels. In general, prices are lower on this side of the Seine.

Becoming increasingly similar in style is the Rive Droite's **Marais** district (3rd and 4th): lively, full of history, restaurants, galleries, boutiques and bars, and within easy reach of other *quartiers*. More youthful in temperament, it also borders the **Bastille**, where new hotels are opening yearly.

May, June, September and October are the hardest months to find rooms—be warned! It would be sensible to book hotels in advance.

See also **Hotels and Restaurants**, pages 274–276.

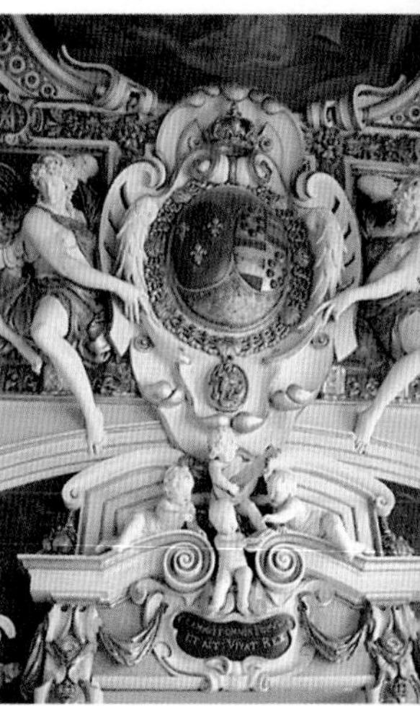

Visitors with fat wallets will head for a handful of the world's most luxurious and historic hotels—from the Ritz to the Crillon and George V

A TERRIBLE PLACE

'Paris is a vast studio of putrefaction where misery, plague and disease work together, where neither air nor sun penetrates. Paris is a terrible place where plants wilt and perish, where out of seven children, four die within the year.' — Victor Considérant, 1848.

1- and 2-star hotel comforts can be surprising but are unlikely to include Van Gogh originals

Practical points

Air Paris has two international airports: **Orly** (14km/ 9 miles south) and **Roissy/Charles-de-Gaulle** (23km/ 14 miles north). Both are served by international and domestic airlines. The terminals of **Orly-Sud**, for international flights, and **Orly-Ouest**, for domestic flights, can be reached by Air France bus from the Invalides or Montparnasse; by Orly-bus from Denfert-Rochereau; by RER line C from Austerlitz; or by Orlyrail from Châtelet. **Roissy I** (foreign airlines) and **Roissy II** (Air France) can be reached by Air France bus from Etoile or Montparnasse; by Roissybus from behind the Opéra; or by RER line B (Roissy-Rail) from Gare du Nord.

Car If you arrive in Paris by car you will eventually end up on the *boulevard périphérique*. This ring road encircles central Paris with exits at each of the gates—the *portes*—and avoids crossing unnecessary stretches of the central area. However, it can get disastrously jammed up, particularly during the evening rush hour (between 6 and 7). If arriving from the west of Paris follow signs for *voie express Georges Pompidou*: this expressway is what you should follow to be spirited along beside the Seine into the heart of Paris.

Driving in Paris is not advisable, nor will it save you time. Parking has become a real problem and even if you imitate Parisian on-street parking, it is still difficult. There is an increasing number of central underground car parks where you can safely leave your car for a few days while touring the city by public transport. If you insist on driving, keep out of the bus lanes and remember to give priority to the right.

Train Paris is served by six mainline stations, each covering a different part of France or Europe. The **Gare du Nord** is for northern France, Belgium, the Netherlands, Germany, Scandinavia and Britain; the smaller **Gare St-Lazare** serves Normandy and its channel ports. For eastern France, Germany, Austria, Switzerland and eastern Europe, the **Gare de l'Est** will be your destination. The **Gare de Lyon** speeds you south to the Côte d'Azur and southeast to Italy and Switzerland. Trains for southwest France, Spain and Portugal leave from the **Gare d'Austerlitz**, but not the TGV services; these leave from the **Gare Montparnasse**, a modernized station seemingly without any logic, along with trains to western France, Brittany and the Atlantic coast. All are on the Paris Métro. Be careful about choosing the correct section of the station: *banlieue* means suburbs; *grandes lignes* designates mainline trains. And always validate (*composter*) your ticket before boarding.

Inside Paris Finding your way around Paris is not complicated. The *arrondissement* system starts at the heart (Louvre, Châtelet) and curls outward, snail-like, to end in the 20th, the eastern *quartier* of Belleville. Street numbers start at the Seine, working outward. Walking around Paris is a pleasure, and safe; for longer distances the Métro is easily mastered. Buy a *carnet* of 10 tickets or a *Paris-Visite*, valid for three or five days, which also

CANAL TRIPS
Take a three-hour trip along Paris' Canal Saint-Martin, above and below ground and through a couple of locks. Boats run between the Bastille's Port de l'Arsenal or the Musée d'Orsay and La Villette, taking you along a leafy partly underground itinerary in eastern Paris, past the famous Hôtel de Nord and around the Parc de la Villette (from Port de l'Arsenal, daily, tel: 01 42 39 15 00; or from Musée d'Orsay, Apr–Nov daily at 9.30 and Sundays in winter, tel: 01 42 40 96 97).

BATOBUS
Re-launched in 1997, this boat service plies the Seine between Easter and mid-October, providing a quick and pleasant way of getting around Paris, while enjoying its riverside architecture. Three boats operate daily services between the six docking points at the Tour Eiffel, the Musée d'Orsay, St-Germain-des-Prés, Notre Dame, l'Hôtel de Ville and the Louvre (departures every 25 minutes, 1- or 2-day passes available).

MUSEUM PASS
Museum and monument admission charges can mount up dramatically, as do the numbers of people waiting to be admitted, so if you are planning intense cultural sightseeing it is worth investing in a *Carte Musée et Monuments*. This is available at major museums and Métro stations, valid for 1, 3 or 5 consecutive days and covers 70 destinations in the Paris region.

gives discounts at many sights. *Mobilis* is an alternative one-day pass across different zones. Métro tickets are also valid for central sections of the *RER* (local trains) and for buses; validate (*composter*) them as you board. Most buses stop at 8 or 9pm, but Noctambus night buses run 1–6am. The Métro runs from about 5.30am to around 12.30am. Lines are named after the last stop in each direction. To change lines look for *Correspondance* signs.

Taxis are not Paris's greatest asset. Be prepared for extras to be added to any fare from stations or airports and don't be surprised if they refuse to take four passengers. Several radio-taxi firms exist (**Taxis Bleus**: tel: 01 49 36 10 10; **G7**: tel: 01 47 39 47 39; **Alpha**: tel: 01 45 85 85 85) but this makes for a more expensive ride.

Emergency purchases Very useful is the network of drugstores, hardly changed since the 1960s. Open till 2am daily, they sell items ranging from newspapers, books and CDs to medicine, camera equipment, gifts, wine, cigarettes, a snack or a meal. You can find them at the top and bottom of the Champs-Elysées, and at l'Opéra.

Few of Hector Guimard's original art nouveau Métro entrances remain: The best are at Abbesses and Porte Dauphine

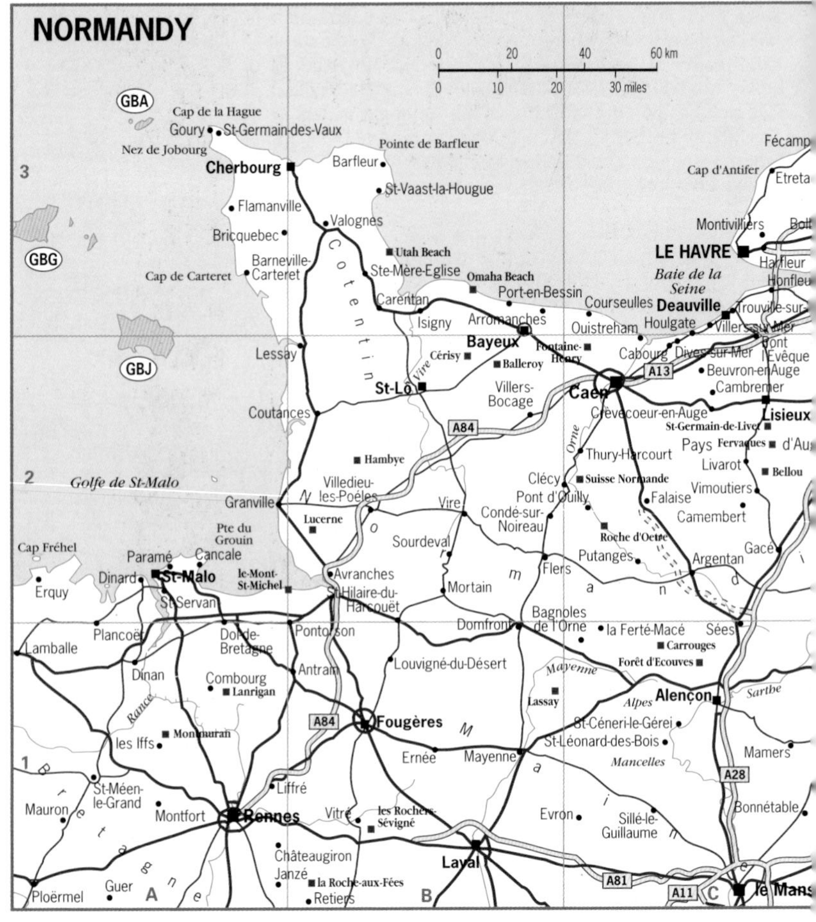

▶▶▶ REGION HIGHLIGHTS

Bayeux *pages 75*

Deauville *page 76*

Etretat *page 74*

Honfleur *page 76*

Mont-St-Michel *page 83*

Pays d'Auge *page 84*

Rouen *page 86*

NORMANDY emerged from a long era of conflict and invasion. Viking invaders sailed up the Seine in the ninth century, wreaked their usual havoc and won themselves a handsome duchy, from which their vigorous descendants exported well-ordered Norman rule and striking architecture to England and the Mediterranean.

After William the Conqueror's invasion of England in 1066, Normandy was passed to and fro between English and French rulers. More recently, Normandy was the setting for the 'D-Day' landings in 1944. The Battle of Normandy inflicted terrible damage on many old towns and villages.

ART AND BEAUTY Northwest of Paris, the Seine meanders through the heart of Normandy past fortresses, abbey ruins and the beautiful old city of Rouen. This is a region rich in artistic associations (Impressionists, Flaubert, Proust) from the period when the Normandy coast, easily accessible by train from Paris, was the height of fashion. To the west of the mouth of the Seine, the resorts of the Côte Fleurie still have plenty of chic, especially Deauville, with its

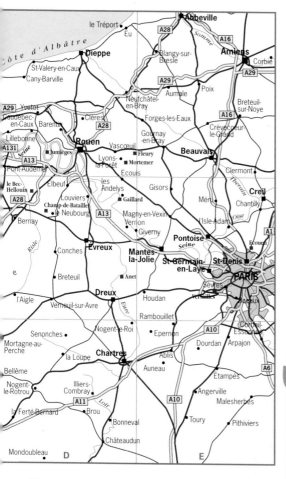

golf and horses. Inland, the Pays d'Auge is Normandy at its most fruitful: Camembert and Calvados territory, with timbered manor houses, fat cows in the orchard, and a diet of cream and butter. Sadly, many of Normandy's forests were damaged in the 1999 storm, and it will be many years before they are restored.

POORER COUNTRY Western or Lower Normandy is poorer, more rugged land, geologically of a piece with Brittany. It keeps its quiet charms to itself—fortunately for those who love it.

ETRETAT
This fashionable seaside resort was popular in the 19th century with writers such as Dumas, Gide and Maupassant. Two Spanish queens stayed at Château Les Aygues and Etretat was painted by Boudin, Corot, Courbet, Delacroix and Monet. Etretat's 'pilgrims' today are mainly hikers (the tourist office provides maps and further details).

BENEDICTINE
Benedictine is still made to the original recipe first concocted by a monk in 1510. The Palais Bénédictine was purpose-built in the 1880s, five minutes from the abbey, by Alexandre Le Grand, a wine wholesaler, for the commercial production of the liqueur. Visitors can see the distillery and cellars where it matures in oak casks, as well as tasting it (*Open* daily).

The Benedictine distillery (right)

▶ Albâtre, Côte d' *73D3*

This 100km (60-mile) stretch of once fashionable coastline between Dieppe and Etretat was named after its chalky cliffs and milky waves. **Etretat▶▶▶** is the best place for cliff walks, set beautifully on a shingle beach and immortalized by Monet. A small museum commemorates the fatal first attempt to fly the Atlantic by two French aviators in 1927. **Fécamp** is a larger town and busy commercial port, famous for the Benedictine liqueur based on an elixir made by the monks of its abbey. The drink has a museum to itself and the great abbey church (La Trinité) contains works of art. Pilgrims venerate a marble tabernacle said to contain the blood of Christ (behind the altar).

▶ Alençon *72C1*

A handsomely restored old market town, north of Le Mans, Alençon's Gothic buildings include a fat fortress with bulging towers, now a prison; the 14th- to 15th-century church of Notre-Dame, and the 15th-century merchant's town house Maison d'Ozé, now the Tourist Office. But Alençon's great fame is its lace industry, by appointment to Louis XIV. Both the **art museum Cour Courée de la Dentelle** and the **Musée de la Dentelle au Pont d'Alençon▶▶**, 33 rue du Pont-Neuf, Alençon (*Open* summer Tue–Sun 10–12, 2–6; winter Tue–Sun 10.30–12, 2–5.30. *Admission: moderate*) have superb collections. Musée Général Leclerc, rue de Pont Neuf, focuses on World War II.

▶ Alpes Mancelles *72C1*

Considering no summit rises higher than 417m (1,368ft), 'Alpes' overstates the mountainous nature of this part of the Normandy/Maine Regional Nature Park, southwest of Alençon around the Sarthe Valley. But it is a picturesque region of fast-flowing streams, rocky gorges and slopes covered in heather and broom. **St-Léonard-des-Bois** is the best base: an attractive village with places to stay. Interesting frescos can be seen at the former hermitage of Ste-Céneri-le-Gérei.

▶ Balleroy, Château de *72B2*

This elegant low 17th-century château remained in the family for three centuries until bought by an American multi-millionaire, the late Malcolm Forbes. It has a sumptuous interior and contents, and a hot-air balloon museum (*Open* mid-Mar to Jun, Sep to mid-Oct Wed–Mon 10–6; Jul–Aug daily 10–6. *Admission: expensive*).

Bayeux ▶▶▶ see page 75

Having beaten off French invaders in 1054 and 1058, William, Duke of Normandy, turned his attentions to lands across the Channel. In 1066, England's new king, Harold, was crowned; in the same year he was defeated and killed by William's forces at the Battle of Hastings. On Christmas Day 1066, William the Conqueror was crowned King of England.

A few years after the conquest of England, Bishop Odo of Bayeux commissioned a work of embroidery to adorn the choir of the cathedral on feast days, illustrating the Battle of Hastings and events leading up to it: a moral tale of Harold's perfidy punished. Traditionally known as Queen Matilda's Tapestry, the 70m (230ft)-long work (wool on linen) was in fact produced in 10 years (1070–80) by English nuns.

Touring tapestry The story is told in 58 scenes bordered by friezes of mythical beasts and enlivened by a wealth of incidental detail, with captions and names of the main actors in Latin. Napoleon so appreciated the story, with its stylized depiction of the English as long-haired villains and the Normans as clean-cut heroes, that he took the tapestry on a tour of France as part of the marketing for his planned invasion of England.

Bayeux itself, inland from the 'invasion beaches' of the Calvados coast, was the first town to be liberated in 1944 and came through World War II unscathed. The central area is correspondingly pretty and a popular holiday base, with good hotels and old timbered houses. The tourist office is in the old fish market, Pont St-Jean. The beautiful cathedral is mostly 13th-century Gothic, but has Romanesque towers and arches in the nave, decorated with splendid reliefs. The carvings over the south doorway tell the story of the murder, by the English King Henry II's soldiers, of Thomas à Becket, Archbishop of Canterbury, in 1170.

THE TAPESTRY
Political propaganda or a valuable historical document: The tapestry can be enjoyed on many levels. The strip of linen is surprisingly narrow (only 50cm/20in wide) and although it is well displayed, the number of people waiting to see it is often a problem. But there is an excellent slide show, audio guides and a photographic replica. **Tapisserie de Bayeux▶▶▶**, Centre Guillaume-le-Conquérant, Rue de Nesmond, Bayeux (*Open* May–Aug daily 9–7; Sep–Apr daily 9.30–12.30, 2–6. *Admission: expensive*).

Harold's brothers Lewine and Gyrd are killed during the Battle of Hastings—as depicted in the Bayeux Tapestry

The short stretch of coast from Honfleur at the mouth of the Seine to Cabourg at the mouth of the Dives is the smartest, indeed about the only remotely fashionable, section of the north coast of France. The landscape is less rugged than to the north of the Seine, with long sandy beaches briefly interrupted by mini cliffs, and a lush hinterland of orchards, thatch and timbered manor houses (the pays d'Auge).

MONET'S MENTOR
The son of an Honfleur ferryman, Eugène Boudin (1824–98) was the young Monet's mentor at Le Havre, and influenced Impressionism through his methods (painting outside and often recording the date, time and wind speed) and subject matter: bright, breezy Normandy seascapes, with a foreground of doll-like figures, indulging the new taste for seaside leisure. Boudin's use of paint remained more traditional.

Apart from the view of Le Havre across the estuary, now spanned by the magnificent new Pont de Normandie, **Honfleur▶▶▶** is at heart a picturesque fishing port and artists' colony, with tall slate-hung houses overlooking the old port. Ste-Cathérine is an unusual 15th-century wooden church built by shipbuilders (it shows); and there are several good museums, one devoted to Boudin and other local marine artists, who got together at the Ferme St-Siméon (now an exclusive hotel). The sea has receded and Honfleur now has gardens where once was a beach.

Different styles Separated only by the waters of the Touques, Trouville and Deauville lie at the heart of the Côte Fleurie. Both have big sandy beaches with duckboard promenades and ornate turreted villas, but there is a marked difference of style. **Trouville**, the first to become fashionable (in the 1850s), is now the poor relation, but does have a year-round community. **Deauville▶▶▶** grew from nothing in the last quarter of the century, an affluent sprawl of big hotels in typically Norman timbered style, with a casino, spa, airport and other trappings of high society. It likes to be known as the Monte Carlo of the north, but bears a closer resemblance to Biarritz.

Quieter scene West of Deauville lies a series of quieter resorts, all with good beaches: **Blonville**, **Villers-sur-Mer** and **Houlgate**, the last two separated by cliffs which force the road inland. The former port of **Dives-sur-Mer**, where William the Conqueror set sail, has kept its 15th-century wooden market hall near the Guillaume le Conquérant shopping mall. On the opposite bank lies **Cabourg**, a stiflingly pretentious resort where most things are dedicated to the memory of Marcel Proust, who stayed often at the Grand Hotel, and wrote about Cabourg (as Balbec). At the Grand, time is not lost, merely arrested.

Fishing boats in the old port of Honfleur

►► Caen *72C2*

A big city and river port, mostly rebuilt after intense bombardment in 1944, Caen is not an obvious tourist magnet. It has its appeal, however: great churches and excellent museums, including **Le Mémorial (Musée de la Paix)►►**, Esplanade Eisenhower (*Open* summer daily 9–7; 13 Jul–26 Aug 9–8; winter 9–6. *Closed* first two weeks Jan. Guided visits Apr–Sep. *Admission: expensive*; northwest of town, near the D22 exit to Creully), a presentation of life during World War II and the Cold War.

Town sights Caen owes its importance to William the Conqueror and his wife Matilda, who made it their base. William and Matilda were cousins, and their marriage led to excommunication, lifted only when they founded an abbey each, one for men and one for women, at Caen. The two churches, St-Etienne (gentlemen) and La Trinité (ladies), survive, sited to the east and west of the central fortress. Both show Norman Romanesque architecture at its most severe. A plaque marks William's empty tomb at St-Etienne. Both buildings offer daily tours.

Between the abbeys, reconstructed fortress ramparts with a walkway now enclose the **Musée des Beaux Arts►►** (*Open* Wed–Mon 9.30–6. *Admission: free*). Outside the walls (via the porte sur la Ville) the 15th- to 16th-century church of **St-Pierre►** contrasts sharply with the abbey churches, with their Renaissance ornament. A few old timbered houses survived the war, as did much of the 18th-century place St-Sauveur, near St-Etienne.

MEDIEVAL MANNERS
Originally reluctant to accept a bastard's suit, Matilda was persuaded to change her mind when William dragged her round Lille by the hair, a wooing tactic that even then must have seemed primitive.

Carrouges, Château de *72C1*

This vast brick château of many periods seems like a moated village turning its back on intruders. As well as the guided tour, there is an information point for the Normandy/Maine Regional Nature Park and a crafts showroom. The gardens are under restoration (*Open* Apr to mid-Jun, Sep daily 10–12, 2–6; mid-Jun to Aug 9.30–12, 2–6.30; Oct–Mar 10–12, 2–4.30. *Admission: moderate*).

► Champ-de-Bataille, Château de *73D2*

This magnificent late-17th-century château has twin symmetrical brick and stone wings—one for the duke, the other for guests. There is varied decoration and contents, and a fine park (*Open* May, Jun, Sep daily 2–6; Jul, Aug 10–6. *Admission: moderate*).

CAEN STONE
The creamy whiteness of Caen limestone gives it the appearance of being too soft for building material, yet it has created magnificent monuments, not just in France but also in England. The stone was taken down the River Orne and across the English Channel for use in the cathedrals of Canterbury and Winchester, as well as Westminster Abbey.

Dieppe's attractive fishing port flourished in the Middle Ages before being overtaken by Le Havre

LES MOUTIERS
Five kilometres (3 miles) west of Dieppe at Varengeville-sur-Mer lies one of France's most beautiful private gardens. It was landscaped at the turn of the 20th century by the English architect Sir Edwin Lutyens, in consultation with the great garden designer Gertrude Jekyll. It is open to the public daily, mid-March to mid-November (tel: 02 35 85 10 02).

LA CITÉ DE LA MER
This has taken over half of Cherbourg's fine art deco trans-Atlantic passenger terminal and is an excellent introduction to human exploration of the ocean: from the earliest bathyspheres to France's first nuclear submarine. The submarine and aquarium are open for tours.

► Cherbourg *72B3*

A vast port for naval and passenger ships, this town was destroyed under German occupation in 1944, but remained a vital supply line for the Allied forces. Buildings and setting are equally uninspiring but respite is offered at the century-old **Parc Emmanuel Liais►**.

► Cotentin *72B3*

The rocky head of this anvil-shaped peninsula is at its most impressive in the west, with granite cliffs at **Cap de la Hague** and **Nez de Jobourg** and a sandy bay between them; there are hotels at **St-Germain-des-Vaux** and tiny **Port Racine**. In the sheltered northeast, **Barfleur** and **St-Vaast-la-Hougue** are fishing ports with some charm. To the south stretch the dunes of Utah Beach (see opposite).

There is better bathing on the peninsula's west coast, between the Flamanville nuclear power station and Le Cogena nuclear reprocessing plant. The best base is **Barneville-Carteret►**, a merger of villages on an estuary sheltered by the Cap de Carteret, with good cliff walks, beaches and excursions to the British island of Jersey. Nearby the former homes of Jacques Prévert and Millet are both open daily. The best thing about the Cotentin interior is the town of **Bricquebec►**—unpretentious, unspoiled and with an excellent market on Saturdays.

► Dieppe *73D3*

A Roman sea-water spa and the top port of Renaissance France, Dieppe developed into a seaside resort in the 19th century. Today it is a busy fishing port, with an excellent Saturday market and good shopping. A free bus service runs the 2km (1 mile) from the cross-channel (*Transmanche*) ferry terminal to the old town, near the pedestrianized Grande Rue. The long pebble beach is overlooked by the 15th-century **Musée de Dieppe,** rue de Chastes, Vieux Chateau (*Open* Wed–Mon 10–noon, 2–5; also Jul–Aug 5–6. *Admission: inexpensive*), illustrating Dieppe's seafaring history. There is more marine interest at the **Cité de la Mer** (*Open* daily 10–12, 2–6. *Admission: moderate*). The Square du Canada has memorials to the Canadians who died in the Operation Jubilee raid of 1942.

► Domfront *72B1*

This former fortress town in Lower Normandy commands a river gorge. Castle ruins stand in public gardens at the top of the town. There are remains of old ramparts, and picturesque streets around the modern church (St-Julien). Across the river stands the truncated Romanesque church of Notre-Dame-sur-l'Eau.

As early as the summer of 1943, Churchill and Roosevelt decided that Normandy would be the bridgehead for the liberation of France under the joint command of Generals Montgomery and Eisenhower. After months of intensive air attacks to destroy the occupying army's communication lines, and a day's delay because of bad weather, a fleet of more than 4,000 landing craft set sail from England during the night of 5 June 1944 for the beaches of the Calvados and Cotentin coast, landing at dawn on the 6th, D-Day.

Airborne troops were simultaneously dropped behind the coastal defences at both ends of the invasion front. On the beaches, losses were heavy but the defenders lacked air support and a vital toehold was soon won.

RETRACING HISTORY
Eight signposted circuits, covering more than 1,000km (620 miles) across the *départements* of Calvados, Manche and Orne, lead you from one history-packed place to another, tracing each step in the Battle of Normandy: Overlord, the assault; D-Day, the onslaught; Objective, a port; the Confrontation; Cobra, the breakout; the Counter-attack; the Encirclement and the Outcome. A special pass is available offering access to the numerous museums along the circuits at considerably reduced rates.

Joint landings With Caen as their objective, British, French and Commonwealth forces landed in the east, on beaches code-named Sword (**Colleville-Plage**, **Lion-sur-Mer** and **St-Aubin**), Juno (**Bernières** and **Courseulles**) and Gold (**Ver-sur-Mer** and **Asnelles**). On D-Day itself the invading force took Arromanches and began to install an enormous artificial or 'mulberry' harbour, towed across the Channel. Two and a half million soldiers and 4 million tonnes of equipment landed at Arromanches in the next three months.

Farther west, American forces landed at Omaha Beach (**St-Laurent**, **Colleville** and **Vierville-sur-Mer**) and Utah Beach on the Cotentin coast. Fierce resistance by the occupying force resulted in very heavy American losses, especially around **St-Laurent** itself (Omaha Beach).

Coastal route The D514 runs the length of the Calvados section of the 'Invasion Coast', passing many memorials, small museums and eloquent graveyards. War debris still litters the dunes and beaches and visitors are advised to tread carefully.

Museums and memorials The 60th anniversary of D-Day in June 2004 once again focused the world's attention on the area. Most of the towns which played a key role in the Battle of Normandy have World War II museums, including Caen, Alençon, Ouistreham, Bayeux, Cherbourg, Pegasus Bridge, where the original bridge has now become a memorial, and Arromanches.

At **Arromanches**, remains of the mulberry harbour are still visible, and a British graveyard lies between Ryes and Bazenville. **Colleville** and **St-Laurent** have monuments by the sea and the biggest US graveyard (Omaha Beach). The nearby German cemetery has a staggering 21,500 graves. **Utah Beach** has an impressive American memorial at La Madeleine. At Quineville a Musée de la Liberté has opened.

WHERE TO STAY
Arromanches and the lively fishing port of Port-en-Bessin are the best places to stay in this area; Courseulles, best known for its oysters, and Riva Bella are beach resorts with a number of hotels.

CLAUDE MONET
Claude Monet was born in Paris in 1840 but grew up at Le Havre, where Boudin persuaded him to paint landscapes. After studying in Paris and soldiering in Algeria, Monet settled in Paris in the 1860s, escaping to London during the Franco-Prussian war. His Le Havre painting *Impression, Sunrise* (exhibited in 1874) prompted a critic to coin the term Impressionism. Monet moved to Giverny in 1883 and died there in 1926. His dedication to his art was total. When his wife was dying, he painted her. 'Just an eye, but God what an eye!' said Cézanne.

▶ Ecouis *73D2*

This small village north of Les Andelys is grouped around the 14th-century collegiate church of Notre-Dame, an unusual, broad, brick-vaulted building with many beautiful sculptures and carved wood panels.

▶ Evreux *73D2*

The departmental capital of the Eure has risen from the ashes many times, most recently after 1944 air raids. The cathedral spires melted, but the rest of the building survived, a surprisingly elegant mixture of styles from the 12th to 17th centuries, with richly decorated north and west façades. The old bishop's palace is now the town museum, and the former abbey church of St-Taurin has a 13th-century reliquary of Taurinus, Evreux's first bishop.

▶ Falaise *72C2*

The birthplace in 1027 of William the Conqueror, son of the 17-year-old Duke of Normandy, and Arlette, a tanner's daughter, was devastated in August 1944. But the impressive castle ruins (*Open* May–Sep daily 10–6. *Admission: moderate*) have survived, with the restorers' help. The guided tour reveals the window from which the prince watched Arlette washing clothes at a fountain below, and the room where William the Bastard was born.

▶ Gaillard, Château *73D2*

Superbly sited castle ruins command a meander of the Seine and the pretty little town of **Les Andelys**. Richard the Lionheart built the castle (*Open* Wed–Mon 10–1, 2–6. *Admission: moderate*) in less than a year (1196–97). There is a steep path up to the ruins from the river, while the road passes Grand Andelys' late Gothic and Renaissance church (Notre-Dame). The **Musée Nicholas Poussin**, rue Ste-Clothilde (*Open* Wed–Mon 2–6 and by appointment) has displays on Monet, other local artists and the château.

▶▶ Giverny *73E2*

Giverny-Claude Monet Fondation Jardins de Claude Monet, 27620 Giverny. Open Apr–Oct Tue–Sun 9.30–6. Admission: moderate

Monet spent the last 43 years of his life here, turning out countless paintings of his gardens, including the water lilies. Only reproductions of Monet's paintings are on display, but the pink and green house is an original, with spectacular gardens and lily pond. The attractive **Musée d'Art Americain▶** (*Open* Apr–Oct Tue–Sun 10–6. *Admission: moderate)* nearby, which opened in 1992, displays the works of American disciples of Monet.

Monet's pink and green house in Giverny. The rooms have been restored to the artist's original designs and retain his furniture, mementoes and collection of Japanese prints

▶ Le Havre *72C3*

Built in the 16th century for François I when the port of Harfleur became unnavigable, Le Havre was all but obliterated in 1944 and the modern port is no place to linger, except for the **Museé Malraux▶** (*Open* Mon, Wed–Fri 11–6, Sat, Sun 11–7. *Admission: inexpensive*) at the port entrance, with works by Boudin and by Dufy, a native of Le Havre, and the **Espace Oscar Niemeyer**. Avenue Foch, leading from the beach to the place de l'Hôtel de Ville, is Europe's widest avenue.

▶ Lassay, Château de *72B1*

This 15th-century military fortress, complete with barbican, drawbridge and pepperpot towers, is on the main road from Bagnoles de l'Orne to Mayenne. The château's contents include the oven which baked the first porcelain made from Alençon clay.

Château de Lassay—a near-perfect fortress

▶ Laval *72B1*

The departmental capital, once known for its linen, is a textile town. The old quarter, huddled around its cathedral and château, has picturesque walls, gateways and buildings. The naïf painter Henri (Douanier) Rousseau was born in a tower of the Bucheresse gate (his father's workshop) in 1844; the château has a naïf art museum.

▶ Lisieux *72C2*

This market town is a great place for cheese lovers on market day (Saturday). The Gothic cathedral **(St-Pierre)▶** houses the tomb of Bishop Cauchon, who executed Joan of Arc. But Lisieux's focus is the vast pilgrimage basilica of Ste-Thérèse. Millions come to ride the Petit Train (summer only) linking Thérèse's family home of Les Buissonnets with the Carmelite chapel and basilica.

▶ Lyons-la-Forêt *73D3*

This flower-filled village in the thick of splendid beech woods was chosen as Yonville in Claude Chabrol's film of *Madame Bovary*. Flaubert's original model, Ry, lies to the west near Vascoeil, where the historian Michelet's château **(Martainville)▶** has interesting works of art. Lyons-la-Forêt is a good base for exploring Normandy and the immediate forest. Its sights include the 40m (130ft) Bunodière beech (signed from the N31), the ruined Cistercian abbey of Mortemer (south of Lyons) and the château of Fleury.

SAINTE THÉRÈSE

Born in Alençon in 1873, Thérèse Martin moved to Lisieux aged four and entered the Carmel order there at 15 by special papal dispensation. Her body was as fragile as her spirit was strong and responded badly to the hardships of life in the convent, where in winter only one room was heated to 10°C (50°F). After Thérèse died of TB in 1897, her autobiography, *The Story of a Soul*, was published. Its poignant account of pain and sacrifice in the quest for spiritual perfection ('my little way') proved an enormous consolation, especially during World War I. Pilgrims came to Lisieux as early as 1899, miraculous cures were reported, and Thérèse was canonized in 1925.

In Normandy, as in many other places in France, Benedictine monks of the Cluniac persuasion provided the main impetus for a wave of church-building which followed the year 1000. Duke Richard II persuaded the Abbot of St-Benigne at Dijon to found a new monastery at Fécamp in 1003, and from then until the mid-12th century there was a frenzy of building in a distinctive style which spread to Britain, southern Italy and Sicily.

The basic elements of the architectural style, christened Romanesque (*roman* in French) in the 19th century because of its similarities with Roman (*romain*) architecture, are the barrel vault and round arch. Compared with some of the highly decorative styles which developed in the south of France, the Norman version was based on a sobriety verging on the austere.

Places to visit Caen's two abbey churches (St-Etienne and La Trinité) are fine examples on a grand scale, as are the abbeys at **Jumièges** and **St-Martin-de-Boscherville** (see page 89), and, simplest of all, **Lessay's** reconstructed abbey church (north of Coutances). The truncated abbey church of **Cérisy** (southwest of Bayeux) is all the more impressive for its isolated setting at the edge of the village. **Lucerne** and **Hambye** are ruined sandstone abbeys in tranquil settings on the Cotentin Peninsula, between Coutances and Avranches. **Bayeux** Cathedral has typically Norman decoration of geometric and foliate patterning. This is the style that was exported to England after the Norman conquest; in Britain all the Romanesque architecture is known as Norman.

Rouen (above and below)—filigree stonework

Norman Gothic From the late 12th century the Gothic style (pointed arches, flying buttresses and bigger expanses of glass), born in the Ile de France area around Paris, gradually replaced the Romanesque style in Normandy.

Coutances Cathedral, famous for its splendid octagonal lantern tower, and the later cathedral-size church of St-Ouen at **Rouen** are superb examples of Norman Gothic at its most elevating and harmonious. Many other churches, if less admirably proportioned, have richer and more decorative detail to enjoy from the exuberant Late Gothic (or Flamboyant) period, which continued to be used well into the 16th century: **St-Maclou** and the cathedral at **Rouen**, **Mont-St-Michel**, **Caudebec-en-Caux** and **Evreux** Cathedral are all worth inspecting.

An 80m (260ft) granite island rises from the muddy estuary of the Couesnon river, whose tortuous course at low tide, to the west of the rock, now places Mont-St-Michel in Normandy, rather than Brittany. It has been a site of importance since prehistoric times. There are quicksands in the notoriously treacherous estuary and water races across the 16km (10 miles) of mudflats, occasionally flooding the car park. Explore the bay on foot at your peril. Land is encroaching, but a massive redevelopment of the bay (2003–2008) aims to reverse its fate.

The rock may have been a place of worship in pre-Christian times: its early name, Mont Tombé, suggests use as a burial ground. In the eighth century the Bishop of Avranches built St. Michael's Chapel there. Legend has it that it was designed according to the instructions passed on to the Bishop by the Archangel Michael in a vision. This was followed by increasingly splendid Carolingian, Romanesque and Gothic buildings, crowning the summit of the rock. A monastery was founded in the late 10th century, and throughout the Middle Ages played a dual religious and military role. As a fortress, Mont-St-Michel resisted the English throughout the Hundred Years' War.

Place of pilgrimage The pilgrim traffic began before the foundation of the monastery. Today, just under three million visitors a year file up the steep and narrow Grande Rue to La Merveille, as the abbey is known. The buildings are a combination of the finest sacred Gothic and Romanesque architecture. The most beautiful elements are the church itself (the incomplete nave is Romanesque, while the choir is soaring Gothic), the cloister and refectory. At the top of the 157m (515ft) spire, the 19th-century figure of St. Michael has been rearmed, having lost his sword in a thunderstorm. This forms the apex of a multi-tiered citadel whose outlook alone is breathtaking.

Between the souvenir shops is a limited number of hotels and an overnight stay is recommended. This gives the chance to explore the sanctuary at its least crowded—at dawn and dusk. There are regular concerts throughout the summer and guided night visits.
Mont-St-Michel (*Abbey Open* May–Aug daily 9–7; Sep–Apr daily 9.30–6. *Admission: expensive.*)

Visitors crowd into the narrow streets of Mont-St-Michel

The Pays d'Auge village of Le Bec-Hellouin presents typically well-maintained, timbered façades

▶▶▶ Pays d'Auge *72C2*

The fertile hinterland of the Côte Fleurie, between the Rivers Risle and Dives, is Normandy at its most delightful: the heartland of cider, Calvados and cheese. There are also decorative manor houses like toy châteaux with moats, red tile roofs and patterns of timber, brick and stone. Traditional thatched roofs planted with flowers are less common than tourist brochures suggest, but they do exist. **Cambremer** (west of Lisieux) and **Livarot** are at the hub of cider and cheese routes. Local tourist offices can supply maps of the routes and farms you can visit.

The towns of the Auge did not escape war damage and cannot match the charm of their surrounding countryside. **Lisieux** is the main industrial and market town of the region (see page 81). **Pont-Audemer▶▶** is prettier: an old tanning town with timbered houses on its central island between branches of the Risle. The church of St-Ouen is a mixture of Romanesque and Renaissance, with beautiful 16th-century windows.

In the Middle Ages, the abbey of **Le Bec-Hellouin▶** (*Open* Jun–Sep Mon–Fri tours at 10.30, 3, 4, 5, Sat 10.30, 3, 4, Sun 12, 3, 4; Oct–May Mon–Sat 10.30, 3, 4, Sun noon, 3, 4. *Admission: moderate*) was an important hub of learning and supplier of eminent churchmen, including Lanfranc, William the Conqueror's right-hand man and first abbot of St-Etienne in Caen. Only one tower survives of the medieval buildings. The rest is modern restoration of 17th- and 18th-century buildings. Other village attractions are the Musée de la Musique Mécanique and an excellent hotel/restaurant.

Manor houses For a good manor house tour (combining sections of the cider and cheese routes), head south from Lisieux along the river before turning west to Livarot and

PRODDING CHEESES
When selecting a Camembert for its ultimate ripe, ready-to-eat condition, don't hesitate to remove the lid and give it a good prod. The squashier it is, the better and more pungent it will be. The optimum state is when the interior is completely yellow and it runs off the table... Those marked *au lait cru* are made with unpasteurized milk.

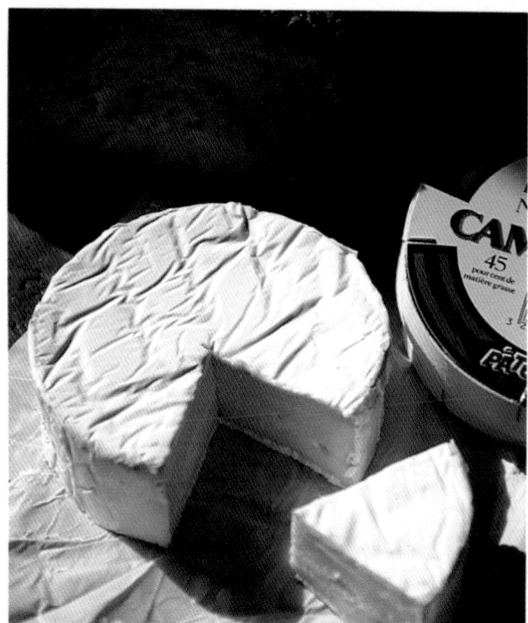

One of Normandy's great delights is its mouth-watering selection of cheeses, the Vallée d'Auge producing some of the richest milk in France

Vimoutiers (see below) and returning north to the coast at Dives, via Crèvecoeur-en-Auge and Beuvron-en-Auge. The jewel of the manor houses is **St-Germain-de-Livet▶▶** (*open* Apr–Sep Wed–Mon 10–12, 2–7; Oct–Mar 10–12, 2–5; closed Dec, Jan), south of Lisieux, a fairy-tale vision with pepperpot turrets, arcaded courtyard and pink-and-white check stonework like a gingham tablecloth.

The manor crawl continues south to **Fervaques**, its moat also fed by the Touques, **Bellou▶**, **Coupesarte▶** (a delightful moated farmhouse), and **Grandchamp**. **Crèvecoeur▶▶** assembles a moated manor house, timbered dovecote, gatehouse, chapel and farm buildings (*Open* Apr–Sep daily 11–6; Jul, Aug 11–7. *Admission: expensive*). On the way north to Cabourg, **Beuvron-en-Auge▶** is an exceptionally pretty, timbered crafts village, strong on cider; there is also a 16th-century manor house at **Cricqueville**.

Cheese country Normandy produces more than a quarter of the nation's meat and dairy produce, including the celebrated pungent cheeses of **Livarot** and **Pont-l'Evêque** and the more recently elaborated and milder **Camembert**, which is now produced throughout France in insipid imitation of the real thing. You can watch the manufacture of all three cheeses at the Musée du Fromage in Livarot (Mar–Nov). **Vimoutiers** (south of Lisieux) has an interesting Camembert museum **Musée du Camembert▶▶** (*Open* Mar Tue–Sat 2–5; Apr, Sep, Oct Mon–Sat 10–12, 2–6, Sun 2–6; May–Aug daily 10–12, 2–6. *Admission: moderate*) and a statue to Marie Harel, who launched Camembert after sheltering a priest during the Revolution in exchange for his cheese recipe. Cheese lovers will head south by the D16/246 for the hamlet of Camembert itself, where farms offer tastings.

LITTLE ANGEL & COLONEL

Perhaps the best-known Normandy cheese, Pont l'Evêque, was already renowned in the Middle Ages, known as 'angelot' (little angel). During the 19th century, Livarot, known as 'poor-man's meat', was the most popular Normandy cheese. It is still made traditionally, working the curds by hand, salting with dry salt and hand-tied with five paper 'stripes' (originally strips of willow, hence its nickname, 'colonel').

APPLE SPIN-OFFS

Cider orchards proliferate in the Auge, thanks to the dampness and clay soil. Normans prepare meat and fish in cider sauce and drink cider, corked and wired like champagne, with their food. Calvados, the best known of many local apple brandies, does not reach its best for 15 years. Normans no longer pour 'calva' down their infants' throats in the hope of producing another Conqueror (or perhaps to get some sleep), but still drink a nip with coffee, between courses (a habit known as *Le Trou Normand*), and after the meal. A distillery at Coquainvilliers (north of Lisieux) offers tastings.

Rouen's remarkably restored historic heart is full of arresting details

►►► Rouen 73D3

The capital of Normandy is a big industrial port spanning the Seine, with tall, timbered houses and great Gothic churches, all carefully restored since the war.

Central area The focal points are the cathedral and the **place du Vieux Marché**, where Joan of Arc was burned at the stake in 1431. As well as a memorial cross, there is a museum (*Open* May–Sep daily 9–7; Oct–Apr daily 10–12, 2–6.30. *Admission: inexpensive*) and a church with 16th-century stained glass (*Open* Mon–Thu, Sat 10–12.15, Fri 11–12.15. *Closed* Sun mornings and during services).

The pedestrian rue du Gros-Horloge, a main shopping axis, is spanned by a one-handed gilt 14th-century clock mounted on a sumptuously carved Renaissance arch. The nearby **Palais de Justice►►** (take rue Thouret), much restored, is the city's most splendid Renaissance palace.

One of the Gothic great churches of France, the **cathedral►►►** has a wealth of intricate carving on the outside. Inside, there are Renaissance tombs in the lady chapel. The building was damaged in the 1999 storm so some parts are closed to the public. Take the rue St-Romain to St-Maclou, a masterpiece of late Gothic (15th- to 16th-century) art on a cobbled square of timbered houses. A covered alley leads to the Aitre St-Maclou, a 16th-century court, originally a cloister used as a charnel house. Timbers are decorated with skulls.

Rue Damiette leads north to the 14th- to 15th-century **St-Ouen,** which purists consider the most harmonious and elegant of Rouen's churches (*Open* Mar–Oct Tue–Sat 10–12, 2–6, Sun 10–12, 2–5; Nov–Feb Tue, Wed, Sat 10–12, 2–6, Sun 10–12, 2–5).

Museums Another picturesque street, rue Ganterie, leads west to a cluster of the city's best museums: fine arts, ceramics and metalwork (*Le Secq des Tournelles*). To the north looms the **Musée des Beaux Arts►►►**, Square Verdrel, 76000 Rouen (*Open* Wed–Mon 10–6; Mon guided visits only. *Admission: inexpensive*), housing 4,000 paintings from Velázquez to Renoir, extensively renovated with 63 galleries. The **Museum of Antiquities►**, north of St-Ouen, has a rich collection, including tapestries and mosaics; the **Flaubert/History of Medicine Museum** is west of Vieux Marché, and the **Corneille Museum** (dedicated to Rouennais playwright Pierre Corneille, 1606–84) is near Vieux Marché.

A MAN AND HIS PARROT

Gustave Flaubert (1821–80), misanthropic and merciless chronicler of his age (*Madame Bovary, Education Sentimentale*) was the son of a surgeon at Rouen's Hôtel Dieu, where young Gustave observed disease and death at close quarters. After giving up law for literature, he based himself in a riverside villa at Croisset (right bank, a short distance downstream of Rouen), now a museum, as is Flaubert's birthplace in Rouen, which doubles up as a museum of medical history. Both have a stuffed parrot purporting to be the bird Flaubert kept on his desk while writing *Un Cœur Simple*.

▶ Sées 72C1

A peaceful, small town on the River Orne north of Alençon and the Ecouves forest, Sées scarcely seems to justify a grand 18th-century bishop's palace and **cathedral▶▶**. This is a fine twin-spired 13th- and 14th-century Gothic building with good stained glass in the crossing and a sweet 14th-century marble Virgin. A spectacular *son-et-lumière* highlights it from June to September. Over the river is a no-less-surprising 19th-century market hall, in grand classical manner. Several good hotels make Sées ideal for an overnight stop.

▶ Suisse Normande 72C2

The likeness to Switzerland of this part of France is debatable, but on its way north to Thury Harcourt (a town extensively rebuilt since 1944 with a château and park beside the river) the River Orne dives and weaves through gorges and wooded valleys, and energetic visitors can indulge a taste for a wide range of Alpine activities, from rafting to rock-climbing. At a more leisurely level, there is good fishing here, and attractive walks to rocky belvederes above the river. For campers this is a good area. The main tourist hub is **Clécy▶▶**, a good base for exploring the valley on foot, on horseback, by car or in a canoe. It also has Europe's biggest miniature railway. **Pont d'Ouilly** is a possible alternative base, a short distance downstream from the **Roche d'Oëtre▶▶**, about the most impressive of the viewpoints in Norman Switzerland. To the south, the Orne is dammed near **Putanges** to form the long **Lac de Rabodanges** (with bathing and watersports).

▶ Vire 72B2

Vire is the not-very-interesting capital of the not-very-remarkable *bocage* area, which is characterized by hedges sited on raised earth banks. These proved effective defences and made the area very difficult to advance through during the Battle of Normandy. Vire is famous for a sausage (*andouille*) of pigs' intestines, the small wrapped in the large. Scanty castle ruins command a good view of the River Vire, winding through a wooded gorge known as the Vaux de Vire. A medieval working man and songwriter of the locality gave rise to the term *Vaux de Vire* (later Vaudeville) songs. There is a museum of *bocage* crafts and traditions in the 18th-century Hôtel-Dieu (*Closed* Tue).

TAKE A WALK

The long-distance path GR36 follows the Orne from near Argentan to Caen. The section on the right bank opposite Clécy makes a good half-day's walk from the village. Take the minor road north from Clécy to join the GR36 just before the river bridge and railway crossing. The path forks right and climbs to the Pain de Sucre (sugar loaf), a good viewpoint high above a river bend, before descending south to the bridge and riverside cafés at Vey. Legs permitting, you can continue south to the Rochers des Parcs cliffs, popular with rock climbers.

The 19th-century market hall at Sées comes second only to the town's grandiose cathedral

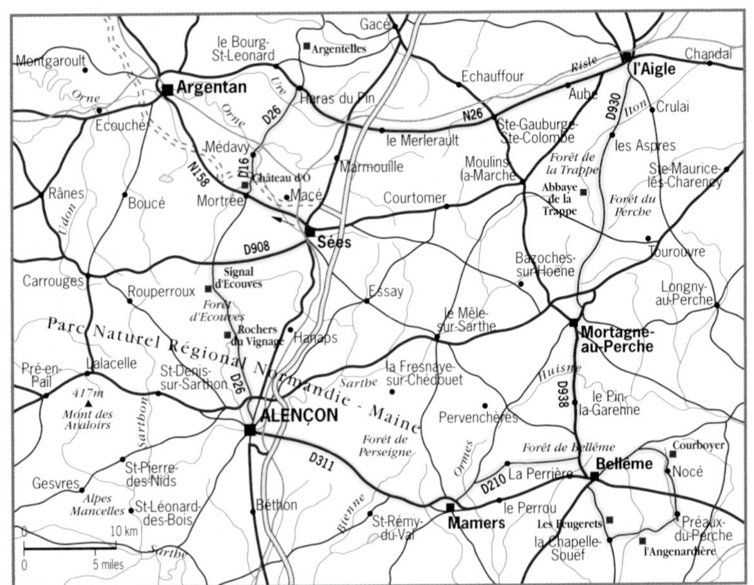

Drive

A tour of the Perche

Start from Sées.
The Perche is a region of forests, undulating hills, powerful Percheron workhorses and manor houses.

Take the N158 to Château d'O.
Built on an island in a lake, the **Château d'O's** fanciful turrets would not be out of place in the Loire.

D16/26 to Haras du Pin.
Haras du Pin is the national stud, founded in the 17th century and housed in gracious buildings and park.

N26 to l'Aigle; D930 to Abbaye de la Trappe and Mortagne-au-Perche.
La Trappe's 17th-century Abbot de Rance launched the strict Trappist rule of abstinence, silence and hard work. The abbey's setting is beautiful but the buildings are of little interest. **Mortagne-au-Perche** has an attractive Renaissance church.
D938 to Bellême; circuit to Courboyer, l'Angenardière and Les Feugerets.
Southeast of Bellême, **Courboyer**, **l'Angenardière** and **Les Feugerets** are among the finest of Perche manor houses.

Returning to Bellême, take the forest road and D210 to Mamers; the D311 to Alençon; and the D26/226/908 to Sées via the Ecouves Forest.
The biggest and most impressive of the Perche forests is part of the Normandy/Maine Regional Nature Park (information point at Carrouges), well provided with marked paths. Denizens include boar, deer, snakes and multitudinous insects, so walkers should set off prepared (for the insects, anyway).

Near the D26 and D226 crossroads, where there is a war memorial, the **Signal d'Ecouves** (417m/1,368ft) is the summit of Normandy. The GR36 path leads south from here to the Croix Madame crossroads, whence another path descends (east) to the Vignage rocks (good views), rejoining the D26 5km (3 miles) south of the war memorial.
See pages 74 and 87 for **Alençon** and **Sées**.

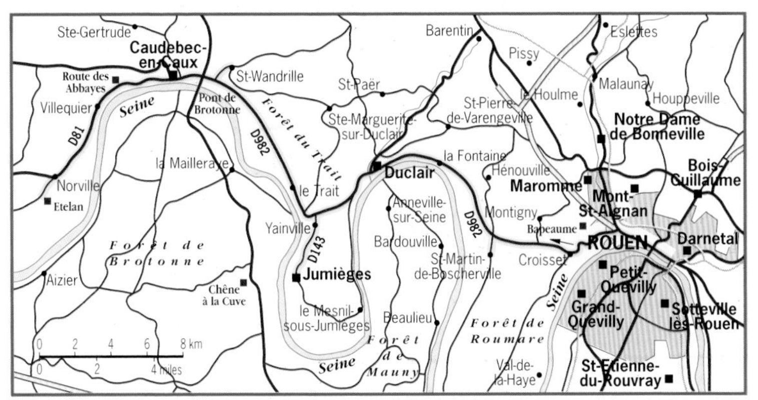

Drive

The Lower Seine Valley

Start from Rouen.
The Seine probably derives its name from its sinuous course, nowhere more evident than on either side of Rouen: from Elbeuf to Jumièges is about 20km (12 miles) as the crow flies, but 75km (47 miles) for a fish. This tour follows the main road along the right bank, passing abbeys founded as early as the seventh century. It does not follow the meandering river, but there are minor roads that do. There is no bridge across the Seine between Rouen and Caudebec-en-Caux, but there are ferries at La Bouille, Le Mesnil-sous-Jumièges, Duclair, Jumièges and Yainville. On the outskirts of **Rouen** (see page 86), Flaubert's no-longer-rustic pavilion at Croisset has memorabilia.

Take the D982 from Rouen to St-Martin-de-Boscherville.
At **St-Martin-de-Boscherville**, the 12th-century abbey church (St-Georges) has typical Norman geometric decoration on the façade and interesting capitals within, including jousting knights.

D143 to Jumièges and back.
Quietly set away from the main road, **Jumièges** is the greatest of the Seine Valley abbeys and the most ruinous, having been sacked in the 17th century and since used as a quarry. But the roofless ruins of the 11th-century church (the porch and the towers survive) and, still older, the nearby St-Pierre (10th-century) are wonderfully romantic.

Take the D982 to St-Wandrille.
After centuries of changing fortunes, during which it was used as a mill and a private home and was much damaged, altered and restored, **St-Wandrille** abbey (open to the public for daily services) is once more inhabited by monks, known for their singing and jam. The present church is a medieval barn brought from La Neuville, 50km (31 miles) away in the Eure.

Continue to Caudebec-en-Caux.
Caudebec-en-Caux has a lively Saturday market beneath the beautiful late Gothic church (Notre-Dame), which has good stained glass.

Take the D81 to Norville (Etelan).
The late Gothic **Château d'Etelan** is a magnificent sight but not normally open to the public.

❑ At Villequier, just over 4km (2.5 miles) from Caudebec, Victor Hugo's daughter and son-in-law were killed in a boating accident in 1843, victims of one of the fierce tidal currents that were a feature of the river at this point. There is a Hugo museum in the house on the waterfront, where Hugo used to live (*Closed* Tue). ❑

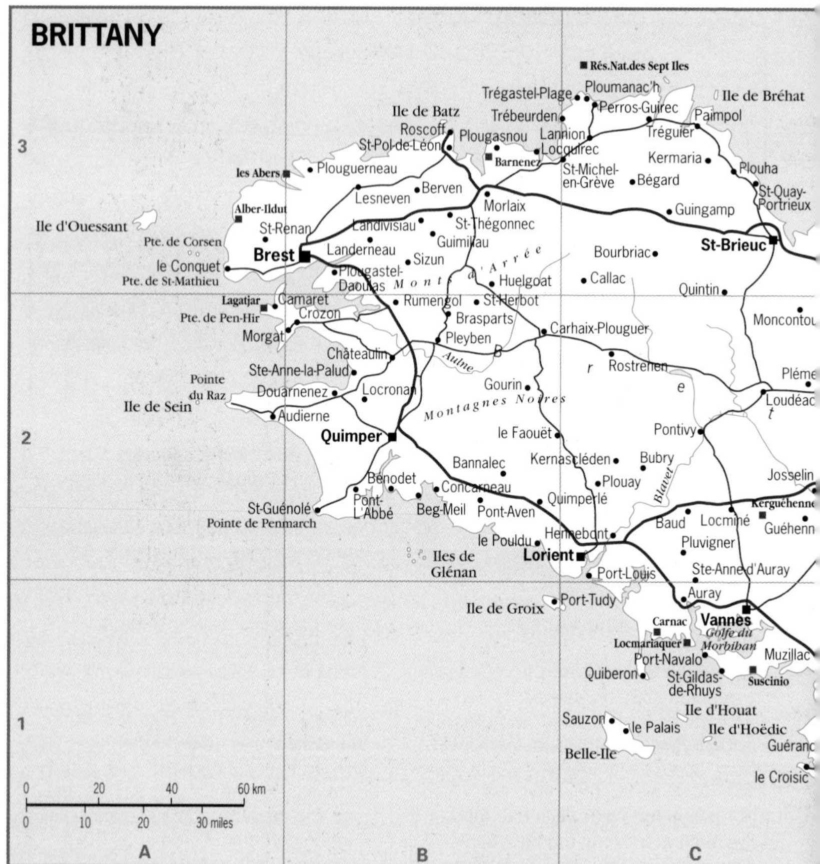

►►► REGION HIGHLIGHTS

BEFORE IT WAS NAMED 'Little Britain' by invading Franks in the early Middle Ages, Brittany was called Armorica: the land of the sea. The region's great attractions are its long coastline of golden sandy beaches, muddy estuaries with fascinating wildlife, small fishing ports, villages of low white and stone houses, and, in the extreme west, rocky capes battered by Atlantic storms. A serious oil spill in 1999 damaged an extensive area of the coast, a massive clean-up solved much of the problem, although small amounts of oil persistently drift ashore.

Inland Brittany is no longer a wasteland of heath, rocky hills and subsistence farmers, but one of the most dynamic agricultural regions of France. This is good news for the Bretons, though it does not make compelling tourism. Brittany's big towns are dull and incursions from the coast are for specific points of interest—richly decorated village churches and fortresses marking the long-disputed frontier between France and the Duchy of Brittany, independent until 1532.

A LAND APART As part of France, Brittany has been a backwater, physically remote (Brest is farther from Paris than Grenoble), poor and ignored. As a result, Brittany has kept, and recently tried hard to revive, its culture,

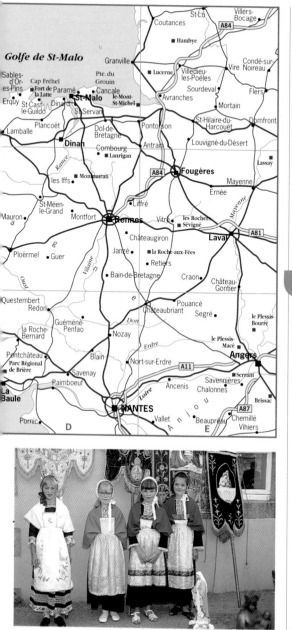

Traditional Breton dress

Attractive Breton stone dormer window

traditions and the Breton language which, although scarcely flourishing, survives in western Brittany.

This is a region of deep religious feelings, interwoven with a rich tissue of pagan myth and Arthurian legend. The combination of an intricate coastline, intriguing folklore and a good climate makes the southwest, around Concarneau and Quimper, the most picturesque corner of Brittany today.

Remarkable shutters in the village of Les Abers—a rare display of contemporary creation

LANDMARKS
Aber Ildut marks the boundary between the Channel and the Atlantic, and the nearby Pointe de Corsen is the western-most point of mainland France.

FAT FLAT OYSTERS
Bélons de Bélon is an increasingly rare entry at the top of a French menu, promising a plateful of slithery delight. *Bélons* are the most prized of flat oysters. The estuary of the Bélon river, which joins the Aven at the sea, is their traditional but not their only place of origin—hence the distinction between *Bélons de Bélon* and any old *Bélons*.

▶ Les Abers *90B3*

On the northwest coastline of Finistère, the estuaries and shallow muddy inlets are known as *abers*. It is a low-lying, bleak stretch of coast, rich in seaweed. But the small port of **Aber Wrac'h▶**, between the two main *abers*, has charm, small hotels and dunes.

▶▶ La Baule *91D1*

No longer officially part of Brittany, La Baule is the last resort before the mouth of the Loire, and the most fashionable of the long Breton coastline. Its 5km (3-mile) crescent of south-facing pine-sheltered sands boasts 2,000 hours of sunshine a year. The sprawling resort behind the beach is geared up to the young, affluent and active.

▶▶▶ Belle-Ile *90C1*

The largest of the Breton Islands is also the most lively and varied, with rocky coastal scenery, good beaches and picturesque villages, notably the little yacht marina of Sauzon and fortified **Le Palais▶**, the main port and island capital. The Citadel, rebuilt by Vauban in 1638, has been restored as a museum (*Open* Jul, Aug daily 9–7; Apr–Jun, Sep–Oct 9.30–6; Nov–Mar 9.30–12, 2–5. *Admission: moderate*). On the Côte Sauvage (fairly tame, unless you coincide with a storm), Port Goulphar has two good hotels. The biggest sandy beach is Grands Sables, south of Le Palais, but there are prettier sandy coves (Herlin, near Bangor). The ferry from Quiberon is very busy in high season. (See also page 93.)

▶ Bélon see panel.

▶ Brest *90B3*

France's great Atlantic naval base has little to offer except its beautiful setting, on a huge natural harbour: The bridge over the Elorn linking Brest and Plougastel Daoulas is a good viewpoint. The city is modern, but its history, including the building of the 17th-century port, is well evoked in the waterside château and the Tanguy Tower on the other side of the River Penfeld (Old Brest Museum). The arts museum has Pont Aven School paintings. A 'sea world', the **Océanopolis▶▶**, Port de Plaisance du Moulin Blanc (*Open* Apr–Sep daily 9–7; mid-Sep to Mar Tue–Sun 10–5. *Admission: expensive*), at the Moulin Blanc Marina, Port de Plaisance, has an impressive 2,600sq m (28,000sq ft) of exhibits and aquariums.

The many islands dotted along the Breton coastline are rich in fascinating legendary, folklorish and historical associations but, in general, fairly unrewarding to visit. The wilder the island, the more intriguing the folklore, as a rule. Belle-Ile (see page 92) is the great exception, its size according it more life and variety.

Sein▶ (access from Audierne, and Brest in summer) is an island no taller than a big wave and will be an early victim of global warming. A druids' refuge and burial ground, the island's entire active male population (130) answered de Gaulle's call by setting sail for Britain in 1940. The island's main produce is *coquilles-St-Jacques*, lobster and crayfish.

Storm-lashed **Ouessant** (access from Brest and Le Conquet) is the westernmost point of France and notorious for shipwrecks. One of its lighthouses can be climbed; another contains a museum. Here, as on some of the other islands, women work the land (little of which is workable) and make the marriage proposals.

In the more sheltered waters off the south coast, the islands closest to Belle-Ile, **Houat▶** and **Hoëdic▶** (Duck and Duckling) are also accessible from Quiberon; Duck has excellent beaches and neither has cars.

Groix (access from Lorient, and Doëlan in summer) is like a smaller Belle-Ile, with a similar mixture of rocky and sandy coast. Its main village, Port Tudy, once a tunny fishing port, sees a little tourism.

Desert isles Off Concarneau, the nine uninhabited Glénan islands are a nature reserve with a big sailing school. Despite its northern location, **Bréhat▶▶** (access from L'Arcouest, near Paimpol) has a famously mild climate and exotic vegetation. With an intricate coastline of pinkish rocks, it is a much better island for gentle walks than for bathing.

The two most spectacular capes of three-pronged Finistère (which means 'the end of the world') are **Pointe de Pen-Hir**, on the cross-shaped tongue of the Crozon Peninsula, and the more celebrated Pointe du Raz, at the tip of Cape Sizun in the extreme southwest. There is not much to choose between them: cliffs of about 70m (230ft) in both places and an overall effect whose savagery depends chiefly on the weather and crashing waves.

LEGENDARY MERMAID
Between the Pointe du Raz and the less-visited cliffs of the Pointe du Van, the little Baie des Trépassés is one of the candidate sites of the legendary city of Is, which was swallowed up by the sea as a result of King Gradlon's beautiful daughter Dahut carrying on with the devil. She has since haunted the coast in mermaid's guise, luring sailors to their deaths.

Belle-Ile's town hall lies in the port of Le Palais, dominated by a 16th-century citadel

BOG-DWELLERS
People have lived on the Brière's marshes since the 17th century. The Brièrons make clogs, punt flat-bottomed boats, spear eels, shoot game and cut peat. They harvest reeds to make their mattresses, baskets and thatch for their houses. And, in considerable numbers, they abandon the Brière for an easier life elsewhere. The regional park was created to encourage and help to keep alive the old traditions. To the west are the salt flats of Guérande, which are famous for quality sea-salt.

Investigating the heart of Concarneau

▶ Brière Regional Park *91D1*

North of St-Nazaire, the D50 runs from Montoir up through the Grande Brière—an area of peaty bogs, canals and villages on granite mounds that are islands in winter when the bogs flood. There are several of these around St-Joachim, which has places to stay and an information point for the regional park in summer. The most interesting is **Ile de Fédrun**. Punting on the reedy canals can be organized. Much of the Brière is a bird reserve.

▶ Cancale *91D3*

Cancale is a cheerful port and gourmet pilgrimage, with fine views of the bay of Mont-St-Michel. It has the most extensive oyster beds on the Channel coast, well viewed at low tide. There are two museums, one dedicated to popular crafts, the other to traditions. A museum just outside town is devoted to oysters (guided tours daily at 2pm, Feb–Oct; tel: 02 99 89 69 99 for details). Cancale's flat oysters, once appreciated by Julius Caesar, Louis XIV and Napoleon, are farmed here.

▶▶▶ Carnac *90C1*

Famous for its lines of standing stones (see page 95), Carnac is also a busy seaside resort with a splendid beach. Between Plage and Préhistoire is an ordinary town, with a museum of prehistory **Musée de Préhistoire▶▶** (Miln-le-Rouzic), 10 place de la Chapelle (centre ville), 56340 Carnac (*Open* Feb–Nov daily 10–5.30. *Admission: moderate*).

▶▶ Combourg *91D2*

This is a small lakeside town beneath a feudal fortress, the **Château de Combourg▶▶** (tel: 02 99 73 22 95. *Open* Park: Apr–Oct daily 9–12, 2–6. Château: Apr–Oct Sun–Fri 2–5.30. *Admission: moderate*). The author Chateaubriand spent a short but gloomy period of his youth here, sleeping in a tower haunted by the cat of a previous lord of Combourg. A few rooms have been made into a Chateaubriand museum, but the view is the main thing. Other outings from Dinan include the château of Montmuran and the church of Les Iffs.

▶▶ Concarneau *90B2*

One of the great fishing ports of Europe, Concarneau's walled old town (*ville close*) sits on an island within the port. The *ville close*, built by Vauban, has 17th-century walls and a fishing museum. There is a Marinarium next door, while the local marine restoration society offers sailing trips on replica 19th-century boats (tel: 02 98 65 10 00).

Megaliths (big stones) are ubiquitous in Brittany, although by no means unique to the region. There are many in the north and west, but the main concentration is on the Gulf of Morbihan in the southeast.

Carnac, on the Gulf of Morbihan, has a unique series of more than 3,000 stones in three alignments. The stones were raised over a long period, possibly beginning in 5500BC, and lasting until about 1000BC. There is an excellent museum about prehistoric civilization. (See page 94.)

Mystery system It is argued that the Morbihan megaliths form a system of astrological observation points, established over hundreds of years and focused on **Locmariaquer** (east of Carnac), where the greatest of all standing stones, weighing more than 350 tonnes, stood 20m (66ft) high. The argument leaves many experts unconvinced, and their significance remains a mystery. Several theories have been put forward for the alignments at Carnac; the most imaginative include windbreaks for Roman tents and petrified legionnaires miraculously arrested while in pursuit of an early Christian pope, Cornelius, the patron of Carnac church.

Selected sites Apart from Carnac, sites include:
Barnenez (eastern side of Morlaix estuary). Tumulus.
Gavrinis Island (access from Larmor Baden). A half-covered tumulus here has beautiful patterned carving.
Lagatjar (Crozon Peninsula, near Camaret). Alignments of 100 stones.
Locmariaquer. Doubters say the great menhir never stood, but a 17th-century sailor's description confirms that it did, before crashing and breaking into five pieces (four still in situ). There is a fine dolmen (Merchants' Table) with carvings nearby.
La Roche Aux Fées (at Retiers southeast of Rennes). A massive 42-stone monument, one of France's largest.
St-Just (north of Redon, in southwestern Brittany). Brittany's second-largest collection of standing stones.

MENHIRS AND DOLMENS
Brittany has no circles to compare with Britain's Stonehenge, but large numbers of menhirs (standing stones, from the Celtic *maen hir*, 'long stone'). These either stand on their own or in lines. Dolmens are structures with roofs, probably used as graves, and tumuli are earth-covered burial mounds with stone-walled tunnels and chambers.

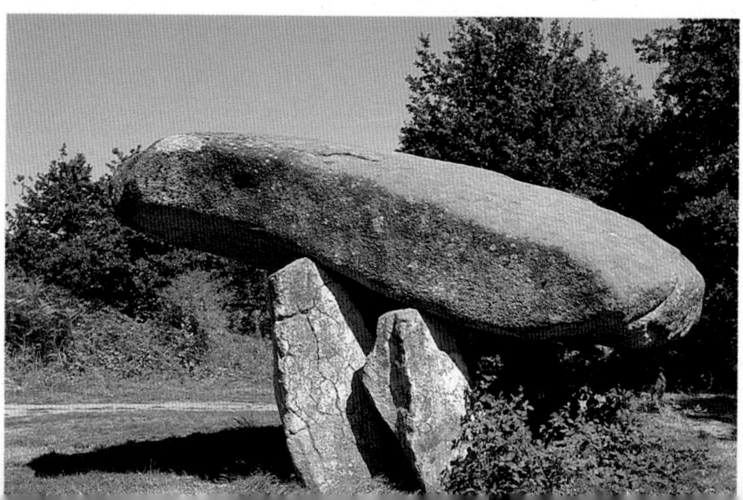

Dolmens are collective burial places with horizontal slabs over upright stones

►► Corniche de l'Armorique *90B3*

This short stretch of scenic wooded coast road runs round a W-shaped bay, from **Locquirec**—a white-washed resort with beaches on both sides of its narrow promontory—to **St-Michel-en-Grève**. The great feature of the bay is the enormous (4km/2.5-mile) beach at **Lieue de Grève►►**, punctuated by the **Grand Rocher**. This is a good viewpoint that can be reached by a short but steep path from the road. There are interesting churches at **Plougasnou** (on the coast west of Locquirec) and **Ploumilliau**, east of St-Michel. The **Pointe de Primel** is an impressive granite headland in the manner of the Breton Corniche (see below), which adds to the confusion between the two Trégastels. **Primel-Trégastel** is a more modest resort than Plage of that ilk, but has a good beach. **Lannion►**, the main town of this area, is not a bad place for a rainy day, with picturesque old houses around the central square and a fine hilltop church. South of the town, the isolated 16th-century Kerfons chapel has a calvary and beautiful rood loft.

***CRÊPES* AND *CRÊPES*...**
Ask most visitors to France where *crêpes* come from, and the most likely answer is the boulevard St-Michel in Paris, where street vendors smear them with gooey chestnut purée (or whatever), roll them into floppy cones and serve in a paper napkin. The unsweetened buckwheat *galette* is, however, a Breton export, and every village on the coast has its *crêperie*, where pancakes with a variety of fillings are served at the table, preferably with Breton cider. Wheat flour is often used instead of traditional buckwheat flour.

►► Corniche Bretonne *90C3*

Scenically, the best thing about the north coast of Brittany is the zone of strangely eroded pink granite rocks between **Trégastel-Plage►** and the fishing port and busy beach resort of **Perros-Guirec►►**. The locals, inspired by the curious eroded rock formations, have conjured some evocative names for them: Napoleon's Hat, Death's Head, the Pancake, the Torpedo, and so on. There are good views of the shoreline from the lighthouse at **Ploumanac'h**—a small fishing port between Trégastel and Perros—and from the coastal path, **Sentier des Douaniers►►**, between Ploumanac'h and Perros, a beautiful 5km (3-mile) walk. Ploumanac'h itself is divided by a municipal park—a kind of rock reserve. From Trégastel-Plage, the coast continues to **Trébeurden**, a small resort with good beaches split by a rocky promontory. From Perros-Guirec there are boat trips to the bird sanctuary archipelago of the **Sept Iles►►**. The largest of the group is the Ile aux Moines, whose lighthouse and fort can be visited.

The beaches of the Corniche de l'Armorique are sculpted by cliffs and rocks: tides leave plenty of interest in rock pools

Breton sightseeing has its limitations but the parish close (enclos paroissial) *is a fascinating local curiosity, best seen in Léon (northern Finistère). In 16th- and 17th-century Brittany, as nowhere else in France, the buildings around the village graveyard developed into an elaborate architectural complex.*

Traditionally, the parish close consists of a triumphal arch (the churchyard gate); a highly decorated church porch, where parish councils met; a separate ossuary or a charnel house, where old bones were stored to make room for the new dead; and, as the focal point, a free-standing calvary swarming with carved granite figures in modern dress, illustrating Bible stories and popular morality tales.

Origins To the obvious question—why?—the best answers are probably local rivalry between villages, the survival in Brittany of passion plays, the use of the calvaries for popular religious instruction, and the singular Breton preoccupation with death. Many church interiors have richly carved and painted wooden altarpieces, pulpits, glory beams or complete rood screens.

Close competition Rivalry played an important part in the development of the two most spectacular and complex parish closes, at **St-Thégonnec** and **Guimiliau**. Other outstanding (not all complete) parish closes are at **Lampaul-Guimiliau** (wood carvings in the church); **La Roche** (ossuary, screen); **St-Herbot** (screen and ossuary); **Sizun** (arch and ossuary); **Le Folgoët** (pilgrimage church with a magnificent 15th-century granite screen); **Brasparts** (carved Virgin in the church); **Berven** (screen); **Plougastel-Daoulas** (calvary); **Ploumilliau** (a wooden sculpture of Ankou, the Breton Father Time, with scythe) and **Kerfons** chapel (with a rood loft and calvary).

At St-Thégonnec there is a particularly elaborate example of the traditional Breton parish close

CHURCH TRAIL
Making a church route from west to east, notable closes can be seen at Pleyben (church and calvary); Notre-Dame du Crann (stained glass); St-Fiacre, near Le Faouët (an outstanding screen) and Kernascléden (15th-century frescos). Guéhenno, south of Josselin, has a parish close with a remarkable story. Its great calvary was destroyed during the Revolution, then pieced together laboriously and expertly by the villagers. In the north, near Paimpol, the chapel at Kermaria has a remarkable series of Dance of Death frescos.

Dinan's harmony arises as much from its riverside setting as from its fine granite buildings

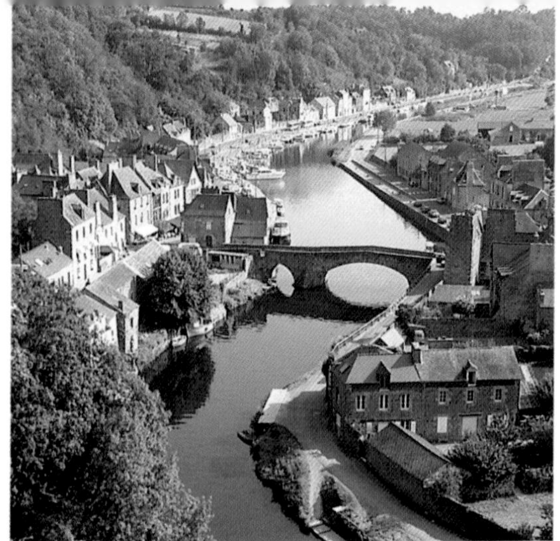

RURAL ROAMING
One of Brittany's loveliest rural areas lies inland from the Emerald Coast and can be explored starting from Dinan. Don't miss the Roman ruins at Corseul, the charming back roads radiating from Plancoët or the powerful fortress ruins of the Château de la Hunaudaye, overlooking the Arguenon river.

DEFENDED BY ONE MAN
Dinan's cherished son is Bertrand du Guesclin, who defended the town against the English by winning in single combat against a Canterbury knight in 1364. Du Guesclin's request to be buried at Dinan was complicated by the distant location of his death (caused, after a lifetime of heroics, by drinking icy spring water), in a remote region of the Massif Central. Bits of him were laid to rest in Paris, Le Puy, Le Mans and Montferrand, but the great soldier's big heart made it back to the basilica of St-Sauveur at Dinan.

►► Dinan *91D3*

Dinan is a well preserved medieval town, surrounded by 600-year-old ramparts and guarded by a fortress, high above the Rance. Its few museums are a less powerful magnet than the cobbled streets, timber-fronted houses, craft shops and weavers' workshops. There are good views from the Jardin des Anglais (Dinan had a large 19th-century British colony) and the small port.

The Rance estuary►► One of the longest and most beautiful of Breton inlets, the Rance sees huge tides of up to 13m (43ft). A short distance upstream of its mouth at St-Malo and Dinard, it is bridged by the world's first tidal power dam, which uses both ebb and flow to generate electricity. You can walk along the dam, which makes a long narrow reservoir of most of the steep-sided inlet, drive over it, and sail through it. Boat trips go up the Rance from St-Malo to Dinan (tel: 02 99 16 35 32).

► Dinard and the Emerald Coast *91D3*

Facing St-Malo, **Dinard►►** was crowned 'Queen of the Emerald Coast' by English Victorians, who 'discovered' the resort and its sheltered crescent of white sand. The town retains a certain style, with neo-Gothic villas, formal hotels, lush gardens, coastal walks and well-heeled visitors. In summer, there are musical moonlit promenades on the seafront. Just outside the town is the studio of artist Pierre Manoli, 9 rue de Suet, La Richardais (*Open* Jul, Aug daily 10.30–12, 3–7; May, Jun, Sep, Oct Sat, Sun 3–7. *Admission: inexpensive).*

Between Dinard and Cap Fréhel the coast weaves up inlets and back along rocky promontories, with the finest cliff scenery between the medieval **Fort de la Latte** and **Cap Fréhel►►►**. To the east and west lie a succession of bucket-and-spade resorts: **St-Cast-Le-Guildo** and **St-Quay-Portrieux** (both mergers) are the liveliest, both good for watersports. **Sable d'Or Les Pins►** lives up to its name with shady pines and long golden sands, and **Erquy** is a small fishing port with Breton charm, good seafood, and a beach into the bargain. The big town of the area, **St-Brieuc►**, has an unusual fortified 14th-century cathedral.

▶ Dol de Bretagne *91D3*

Dol overlooks land reclaimed from the Bay of Mont-St-Michel. **St. Samson's Cathedral▶** is a massive 13th-century granite structure. Champ-Dolent is a fine **menhir▶** (see page 95) to the south, near the Rennes road.

▶ Fougères *91E2*

An impressive fortress **Château de Fougères▶▶**, place Pierre Symon (*Open* Feb, Mar, Oct–Dec daily 10–12, 2–6; Apr to mid-Jun, mid- to end-Sep 9.30–12, 2–6; mid-Jun to mid-Sep 9–7. *Admission: moderate*), is located below the town. The ruined interior holds open-air concerts.

▶ Josselin *90C2*

This old town was named after the younger son of the baron who began building its castle, the **Château de Josselin▶▶** (*Open* Apr, May and Oct, Sat, Sun and public holidays 2–6; Jun to mid-Jul and Sep daily 2–6; mid-Jul and Aug daily 10–6. *Admission: moderate*), in the early 11th century. In striking contrast to the round towers and wall rising from the waters of the Oust, most of the building is in ornate Renaissance style. It has been much restored, houses a doll collection and has fine gardens.

▶▶ Locronan *90B2*

Between Quimper and the Crozon Peninsula, the village of Locronan has a grand ensemble of Renaissance buildings around its central square. Every second Sunday in July, Locronan has a *pardon* (pilgrimage) following the course of Saint Ronan's daily barefoot walk. The village is now a thriving arts hub.

▶ Lorient *90C2*

This is a large fishing port and naval base. Maritime museums include a World War II submarine base and oceanographic research vessel.

JOSSELIN'S RULER

The first Rohan at Josselin was the wife of Jean de Beaumanoir, who captained the winning side in 1351 when the forces of Josselin and pro-English Ploërmel agreed to a hand-to-hand fight.

LORIENT'S MARITIME PAST

Lorient prospered with the Compagnie des Indes, which built its shipyards on the Blavet estuary. Louis XVI and Napoleon transformed the port into a naval base. The German garrison held out until May 1945 and little remained standing. A festival of Celtic culture is held in August.

Dol de Bretagne's main street is flanked by timbered houses supported by 11th- and 12th-century pillars

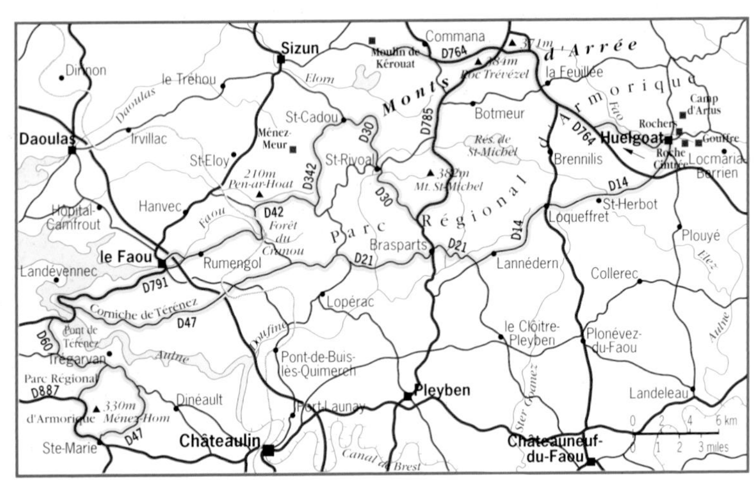

Drive

Visiting the Hill Country: Monts d'Arrée

Start at Huelgoat.
Huelgoat is a rare inland resort, beside a lake at the heart of Brittany's hill country, the **Monts d'Arrée**, now one section of the fragmented Armorique Regional Park. The 'goat' in the name, meaning forest, is no longer appropriate after centuries of deforestation and severe storm damage in October 1987 and December 1999. The main walking area is to the northeast of the village; Arthur's camp is genuinely ancient, if not Arthurian.

D764 to Roc Trévézel; D785/30 to St-Rivoal and St-Cadou.
The route skirts the reservoir and much resented nuclear power station of **St-Michel**, a surprising landmark at the heart of a regional park. Near the crossroads of D764 and 785, the **Roc Trévézel** (384m/1,260ft) is the highest point of Brittany. Millions of years ago these mountains stood as high as the Alps do now.

To the west, on the Sizun road (D764), the old hamlet of **Kérouat** has been restored as a rural ecomuseum. The Maison Cornec in nearby **St-Rivoal** shows the interior of an 18th-century peasant home. South of St-Cadou is the **Ménez-Meur** Wildlife Reserve and Regional Park information point.

D130/342/42, Forêt du Cranou, to Le Faou.
Le Faou is an attractive estuary port, with good hotels to be found on the main square.

D791 Corniche de Térénez road to Ménez-Hom (D60/47/83).
Ménez-Hom (330m/1,082ft) is the western bastion of the Monts d'Arrée, a splendidly isolated hump at the base of the cruciform Crozon peninsula. A steep road climbs to a viewing platform. At a crossroads near **Trégarvan**, north of Ménez-Hom, the old village school has been restored (Musée de l'Ecole Rurale). There are sandy beaches along the south side of the peninsula, between **Ste-Anne-la-Palud** and **Morgat**.

D47/21 to Brasparts, D14 to St-Herbot and back to Huelgoat.
Brasparts has a craft showroom and church with Renaissance porch and calvary. **St-Herbot's** Gothic church has a 16th-century ossuary, calvary and carved wooden screen. Herbot is the patron saint of horned beasts; hoping for protection for their cattle, farmers traditionally deposit locks of tail hair in the church on pardon day.

►► Morbihan, Golfe du *90C1*

Morbihan is the only one of Brittany's *départements* with a Breton name—it means 'Little Sea', after the vast mud-rimmed tidal lagoon known as the Gulf of Morbihan. The gulf forms an almost complete circle, including the **Vannes** and **Auray** estuaries and enclosing 40 inhabited islands. The entrance to the inland sea between Locmariaquer and Port-Navalo is less than 2km (1.25 miles) wide. In the first century BC the gulf was the site of a sea battle between the local Veneti tribe and the forces of Rome. Julius Caesar watched from the top of a prehistoric tumulus on the shore near Arzon.

Oyster country The best way to see the gulf is by boat, either a private yacht (tricky currents in the strait) or on a boat trip, for which Vannes is the main base. Low tide reveals huge expanses of oyster beds. The gulf (especially the area known as the Auray Peninsula) is the breeding ground for flat oysters, which grow on lime-washed tiles until they are big enough to be transported to parks all round the Breton coast.

Driving round the gulf is long and not very rewarding. Of the two main towns, Vannes is more interesting than Auray, except for one of the big *pardons* at **Ste-Anne d'Auray** and the pretty historic quarter of St-Goustan. **Locmariaquer**, the island of **Gavrinis** (from Larmor Baden) and Carnac are the highlights of Breton prehistory (see page 95). On the southern arm of the gulf, the main points of interest are the old monastery of **St-Gildas-de-Rhuys►** and the 13th- and 14th-century fortress of **Château de Suscinio ►►**, 56370 Sarzeau (*Open* Apr–Sep daily 10–7; Oct, Feb, Mar Thu–Tue 10–2, 2–6; Nov–Jan Thu–Tue 10–12, 2–5. *Admission: moderate*). **Port Navalo** provides places to stay and has summer boat trips.

The cobbled streets of Auray climb steeply from the banks of the River Loch

THE VAGARIES OF ABÉLARD

After his amorous adventure with a young pupil, Héloïse, in Paris, the philosopher Peter Abélard withdrew to the lonely job of abbot of St-Gildas-de-Rhuys in 1126. In a letter to Héloïse he expressed his hatred of Brittany and his suspicion of the Breton monks. Abélard's attempts to impose discipline in the abbey went down very badly with men he referred to as savages, who spoke a language he was unable to understand. In 1138 the resentful monks tried to poison Abélard, but he survived and escaped.

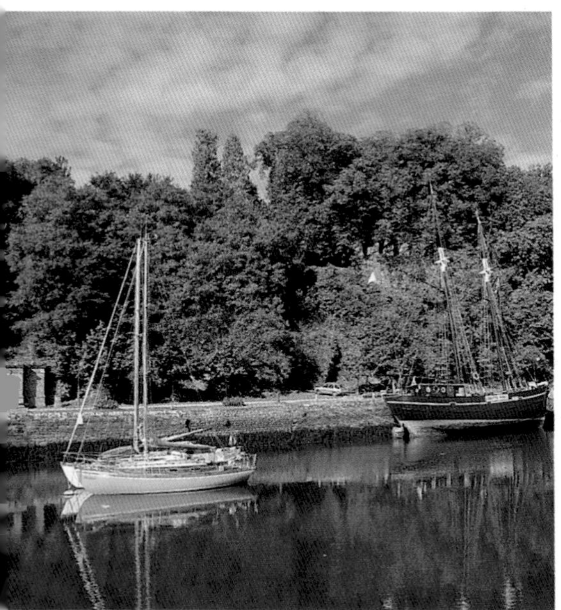

Sailing on a private yacht or an organized trip is the best way to see the sights of the Golfe du Morbihan

DARK PAST
Nantes' history has its darker moments. Gilles de Rais, the original Bluebeard, was tried and burned at the stake in the Ducal castle in 1440. Nantes later made fortunes out of the slave trade. And in 1793, it saw macabre ceremonies known as Republican Weddings, when Royalists were stripped naked, bound together in pairs and dumped in the Loire in order to make room in the city's prisons.

▶▶ Nantes 91D1

The former capital of Brittany is no longer a city of much charm. The old town is now encircled by fast ring roads, and its chief monument, the 15th- and 16th-century **Dukes' castle**, stands among tall modern blocks (*open* Wed–Mon 9–8. *Admission: moderate*). A vast restoration project was completed at the castle in February 2007. The museum, **Musée des Beaux Arts▶▶**, 10 rue Georges Clemenceau (*Open* Mon, Wed–Sat, 10–6, Sun 11–6. *Closed* public holidays. *Admission: moderate*), displays works by Perugino, Ingres and de la Tour; and the late Gothic cathedral has the beautiful Renaissance tomb of the last duke of Brittany, François II. Take time to explore the 18th-century colonial quarter that lies west of the cours des 50-Otages.

▶ Quiberon 90C1

This lively port and resort with a good beach, and famous for thalassotherapy, lies at the end of the long sandy isthmus linking the former island to the mainland. There are some good walks along the rocky west coast. Quiberon was once known for its fresh sardines, but the supply has dwindled recently. There are ferries to Belle-Ile and the other Quiberon islands (see pages 92–93).

▶▶▶ Quimper and Cornouaille 90B2

Cornouaille's sixth-century King Gradlon made Quimper his capital after the destruction of Is, and a statue of him stands between the twin spires of the Gothic cathedral. Quimper is full of well-kept charm: cobbled streets and timber-framed houses. The bishop's palace is now an excellent museum of Breton history and traditions (*Open* Jun–Sep daily 9–6; Oct–May Tue–Sat 9–12, 2–5. *Admission: inexpensive).* The town also has museums of art and Breton life, and a *faïencerie*, representing Quimper's 300-year-old tradition of making pottery. There are boat trips down the Odet Estuary.

At the mouth of the river, **Bénodet** is the largest of several family beach resorts in the camper's preferred corner of Brittany. **Beg-Meil** is the other popular focus.

The rest of the southwest corner of Brittany is disappointingly dreary. **Pont l'Abbé** is a town of needleworkers and home of the tallest of all Breton *coiffes*. **St-Guénolé▶** has a good beach, a museum and rocky coast at the back of the port and at Pointe de Penmarch.

Audierne is ideal if you prefer fishing ports. Masses flock to the **Pointe du Raz▶▶**, with its 70m (230ft) cliffs, Brittany's most spectacular rocky cape (see page 93).

PAIMPOL
In the 19th century, Paimpol was the main base of France's long-haul cod-fishing fleet, immortalized in Pierre Loti's novel *Pêcheur d'Islande*. On 20 February, most of the town's men would set sail for six months in the North Atlantic, returning in late summer. Refrigeration technology hit the industry and Paimpol is now a busy pleasure port and agricultural market place.

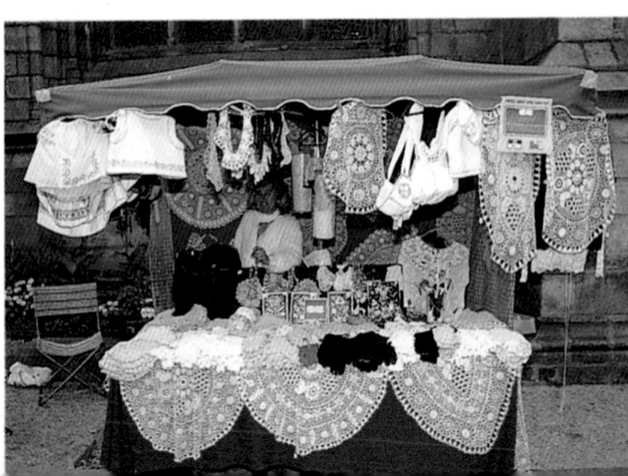

Selling lace in Quimper, also known for its hand-painted faïence, best seen at the Faïenceries H. B. Henriot (visits Mon–Fri)

The name of Pont-Aven has become inextricably linked with Paul Gauguin, the 38-year-old Paris stockbroker who gave up everything (job, wife and five children) to spend the summer there in 1886, with his fellow artist Emile Bernard.

Paul Gauguin's Breton Peasant Women *on loan from the Musée d'Orsay in Paris for a summer exhibition in Pont-Aven*

Gauguin and Bernard did not discover Pont-Aven (south-east of Quimper), which was already full of artists, mainly American. It was picturesque then as now, with walks in the Bois d'Amour by the river, and watermills outnumbering dwellings 15 to 14. There were several inns: the Julia (French academic artists), des Voyageurs (Americans, some of whom stayed all year) and the more bohemian Pension Gloannec, where Gauguin and friends holed up at 60 francs a month, including two good meals a day and cider; more often, paintings were accepted in lieu.

Model villagers Pont-Aven was a thoroughly pretty place, added to which the locals readily agreed to pose in their quaint costumes for a few sous a day. Gauguin, Bernard and disciples, including Sérusier and Maurice Denis, looked beyond these Breton charms and the naturalistic aims of Impressionism. They launched a new, more mystical art, using the local chapels for their sense of rural piety, interwoven with myth and superstition. Within walking distance of the village, the Trémalo Chapel's wooden Christ inspired Gauguin, as did Nizon's calvary (*Yellow Christ* and *Green Christ* paintings).

'When my wooden shoes ring on this granite, I hear the muffled, dull, powerful tone I seek in my painting.' — Paul Gauguin

Grand exit In 1889, Gauguin and friends moved from Pont-Aven, which they found overrun, to Le Pouldu on the coast, where Gauguin surprised walkers by his rough appearance—naked, with long hair and a spear at the ready. After this blatant rejection of his own culture and society, the artist moved to Tahiti, where he died in 1903.

PONT-AVEN PAINTINGS
Pont-Aven still has its walks, restored mills and various galleries, but go to Rennes' Musée des Beaux Arts to see original Pont-Aven paintings.

SEA CURES
The whole Léon coast is rich in seaweed: Roscoff has more than 70 varieties, which it puts to medical, chemical and agricultural use. Ordinary seaweed is an excellent natural fertilizer for artichokes, cauliflowers and onions.

►► Rennes *91D2*

The capital of Brittany was almost entirely demolished by fire in 1720 and subsequently rebuilt in a severe Classical style. Only the area between the market square (place des Lices) and the city's two waterways escaped and remains old and higgledy-piggledy. The excellent **Musée de Brittany►►** has a truly impressive collection (*open* Tue noon–9, Wed–Fri 12–7, Sat, Sun 2–7. *Admission: expensive*). The newly restored 17th-century law courts are considered to be the Parliament of Brittany (guided tours only). The rue St-Georges presents harmonious architecture; the cathedral has a fine carved wooden altar; and the hilltop Jardin du Thabor offers verdant respite.

► Roscoff *90B3*

This port and pretty seaside resort, once renowned for its pirates, is now known for the sea cure. Beautiful alabaster altar reliefs adorn the church near the port, whose Renaissance belfry bristles with cannon to warn off the English. Roscoff's 'Johnnies' (itinerant onion sellers) regularly crossed the channel in the 19th and early 20th century and the creation of a deep-water port was a key part of the strategy to revive Breton agriculture in the 1960s. Re-establishing their old Celtic links, the farmers' ferry company, Brittany Ferries, exports vegetables to England and Ireland, and welcomes ferry-loads of British tourists on the return leg. Day trips go from the old port to the sandy island of **Batz** (pronounced Baa).

► Ste-Anne-la-Palud *90B2*

West of Plonevez-Porzay is the sandy beach and hamlet of Ste-Anne-la-Palud, which hosts the most famous *pardon* (pilgrimage) in Brittany (last weekend in August).

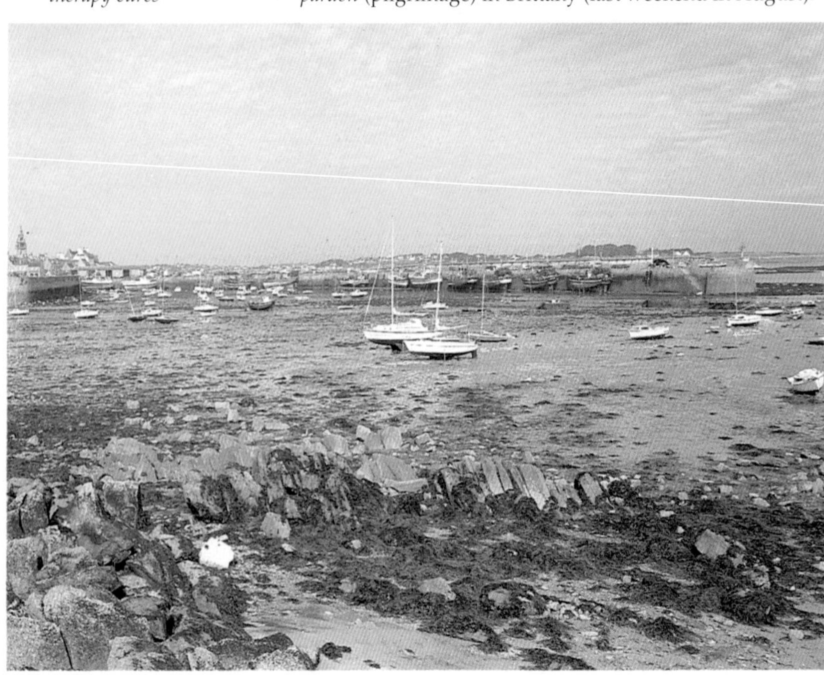

Roscoff's port at low tide reveals the seaweed used in local thalasso-therapy cures

▶▶ St-Malo *91D3*

St-Malo is a port with a long history of explorers, traders and swashbuckling corsairs (legalized pirates). The heart of their home town at the mouth of the Rance is a walled citadel (St-Malo-Intra-Muros) at the entrance to the port. Although the town had to be rebuilt after destruction in 1944, the job was faithfully done, and Intra Muros deserves a **rampart tour▶▶** and a wander. At low tide you can walk out to two islands: a Vauban fort and Grand Bé, where the 19th-century author Chateaubriand, who spent his formative years here, is buried. There are three good museums dedicated to the town's seafaring history (including the Cape Horners), the home of a local shipowner, an aquarium and, just outside the town, the home of navigator Jacques Cartier, who 'discovered' Canada. Nearby St-Juliac is one of the prettiest villages in France.

▶ St-Pol-de-Léon *90B3*

This vegetable market town near Roscoff has two beautiful **churches▶▶**, the cathedral and slightly later Kreisker chapel, famous for its slender 77m (253ft) belfry. St-Pol is one of the seven old Breton bishoprics, a tour of which every Breton should traditionally make at least once. The saint in question is the sixth-century missionary Paul Aurelian, who is said to have tamed the local dragon.

▶▶ Tréguier *90C3*

An old hillside town, well set above a deep oyster-rich inlet near busy north coast resorts, Tréguier has a celebrated pilgrimage in memory of Brittany's beloved St. Yves, a 13th-century lawyer and poor man's champion. A splendid cathedral is set on the market square. Tucked into the rocky coast to the north, little **Port Blanc** has great charm, and was appreciated by H. G. Wells and Bernard Shaw, among many other escapists.

▶▶ Vannes *90C1*

This important town in Breton history (the act of union with France was finalized here in 1532) has old walls and fortified gateways intact, commanding the Gulf of Morbihan. A canalized waterway reaches the foot of the town walls. The old central area is touristy and picturesque, with timbered and gabled houses overhanging the narrow streets around the cathedral. Around 30km (19 miles) north lies a superb 19th-century park dotted with site-specific contemporary sculptures, the **Domaine de Kerguèhennec▶▶**, 56500 Bignan (*Open* (park) all year; (information point) Tue–Sun 10–6; Jun–Sep 10–7. *Closed* mid-Dec to mid-Jan. *Admission free*).

▶▶ Vitré *91E2*

Set at the foot of a fine turreted 14th-century castle on the River Vilaine, **Château de Vitré▶▶** (*Open* Jul–Sep daily 10–6; Oct–Mar Wed–Fri 10–noon, 2–5.30, Sat–Mon 2–5.30, *closed* Tue; Apr–Jun daily 10–12, 2–5.30. *Admission: moderate)*, Vitré rivals Dinan as a medieval time warp. Lots of old interesting houses line the streets that run between the castle and the church. Literary tourists may want to visit the nearby **Château des Rochers-Sévigné▶** (*Closed* Tue out of season), home of Madame de Sévigné.

PARDONS

Pardons are a mixture of religious and pagan festival: pilgrimages undertaken to seek anything from forgiveness to a bumper harvest. These remain serious religious occasions, but also provide a chance for a costume display and, following, a bunfight. The most important are at Rumengol (15 August and Trinity Sunday), Perros-Guirec (15 August), St-Jean-du-Doigt (23/24 June), Ste-Anne-la-Palud (last weekend in August), and Tréguier (3rd Sunday in May). The biggest pilgrimage focuses are Le Folgoët (main event in early September) and Ste-Anne-d'Auray (last Sunday in June). Locronan has an extra-large *pardon* every six years.

'Vannes and his wife' look out over their home town

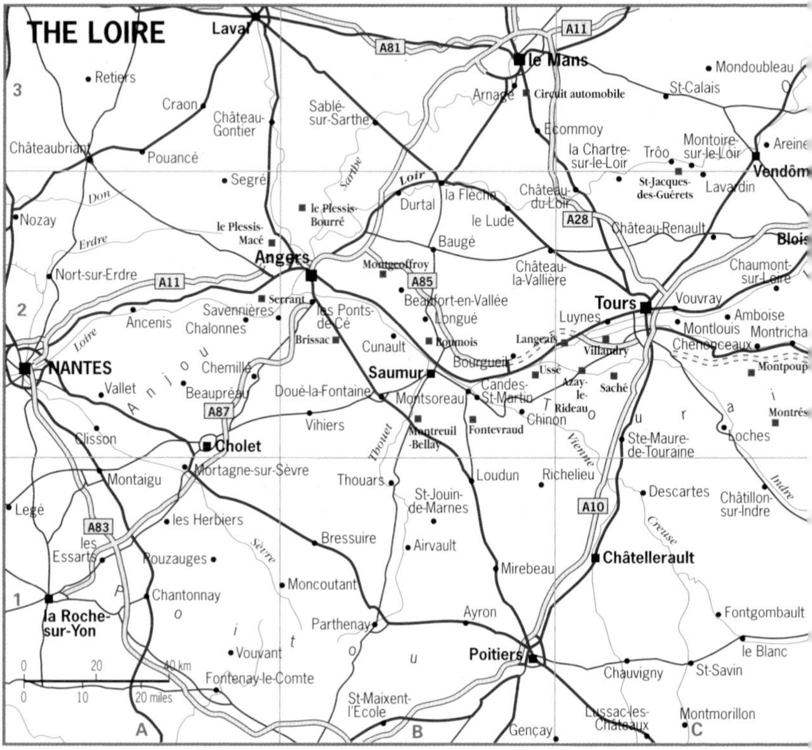

One of the most popular of the Loire Valley châteaux: Azay-le-Rideau

The Loire

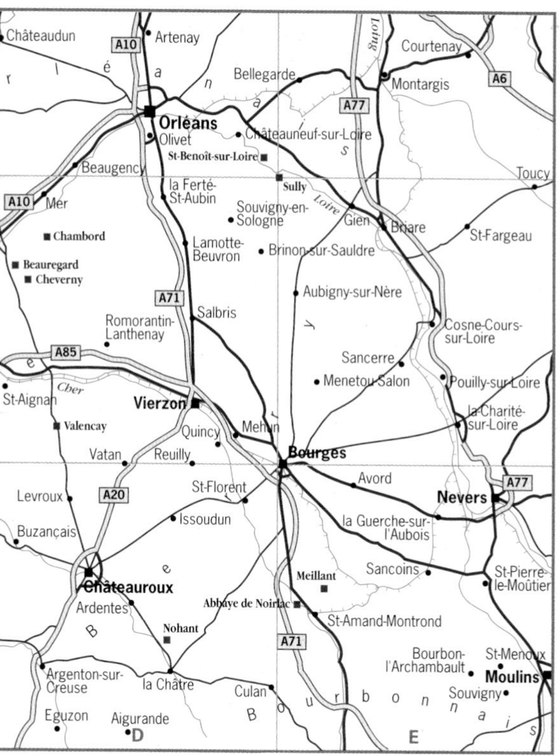

THE VAL DE LOIRE, in the form of the ancient provinces of Anjou, Touraine, Orleanais and Berry, is the historic heart of France, and is now a World Heritage Site. As capital of the Plantagenet kings' Angevin Empire, which at its zenith stretched from the north of England to the Pyrenees, it was the focus of almost three centuries of war between the French and English, which culminated in the expulsion of the English in 1453.

GRACIOUS LIVING The resulting ascendancy of French pride engendered a period of fervent building, and as a result the countryside around the Loire Valley is incomparably rich in Renaissance châteaux, built of milky-white tufa. With their turrets and towers, steep, slate roofs, galleries and pleasure gardens, they are a perennially popular part of the tourist itinerary. It may come as a disappointment to realize, during a lengthy guided tour (in French), that for many châteaux the main interest is in their historical associations. It pays to make a careful selection and to include one or two of the more intimate, inhabited châteaux.

THE RIVER The wide, shallow Loire flows sluggishly between mud banks and silt islets, past looming nuclear power stations and busy towns and highways. Its prettier tributaries are punctuated with white and stone villages and fringed by forests, orchards and fertile cultivations, justifying the area's claim to be the garden of France.

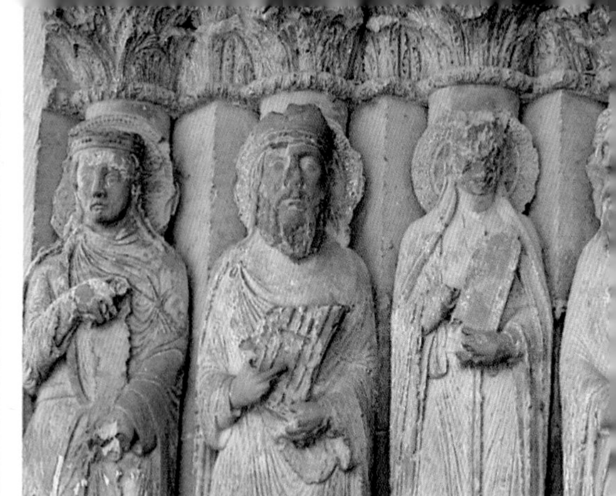

Detail from the entrance of Angers' St-Maurice cathedral. Inside are 12th-century stained-glass windows

►►► REGION HIGHLIGHTS

LEONARDO'S RETIREMENT

In 1516, François I, determined to lure to Amboise as many distinguished Italian artists as he could, persuaded Leonardo da Vinci to enjoy a quiet retirement as *premier peintre et ingenieur et architecte du roi.* He thrilled the court with dramatic *son-et-lumières,* firework displays and pageants, using mechanical special effects; he also drew up plans for a new Venetian-style town. In the gardens of his former home, le Clos Lucé, there are life-size models constructed (in 2003) according to his designs, including his famous flying machine.

►► Amboise *106C2*

This small and attractive town was one of the earliest Loire settlements. It became the site of one of the greatest royal châteaux after Charles VIII (who was born here in 1470) embarked on building a new style of palace. He was inspired by the exuberant Renaissance buildings he had seen on an otherwise unsuccessful campaign in Italy. Only fragments of the château at Amboise remain today, but a guided tour is well worth taking in order to visit the superb Flamboyant chapel of St-Hubert, containing the tomb of Leonardo da Vinci. The extraordinary Tour des Minimes, with a spiral ramp, is said to have been able to accommodate horses and carts. It is also worth visiting the **Pagode de Chanteloup►**, an oriental folly.

►► Angers *106B2*

A large town on the banks of the Maine, Angers lies in the area known as Black Anjou on account of the local rock, which in contrast to the white tufa of Touraine, farther east, lends a forbidding tone to the buildings. The black shale fortress walls of the **Château d'Angers►►**, promenade du Bout du Monde, 49100 Angers (*Open* May–Aug daily 9.30–6.30; Sep–Apr 10–5.30. *Closed* public holidays. *Admission: expensive*) are relieved by white stripes; 17 drum towers remain to evoke its military past, when Angers was an outpost of the French kings on the border of hostile Brittany. Angers is well endowed with buildings of interest. Around the early-Gothic cathedral are many old houses (see page 109), including the 16th-century Maison d'Adam and the Renaissance Hôtel Pincé, a fine museum. Across the river lies the Doutre district, cradle of contemporary tapestry, full of architectural curiosities to explore.

►►► Azay-le-Rideau *106C2*

Open: Apr–Jun, Sep, Oct daily 9.30–6; Jul, Aug 9.30–7; Nov–Mar 10–12.30, 2–5.30. Closed: public holidays. Admission: expensive. See page 113.

► Beaugency *107D3*

Another important Loire bridgehead, delivered from the English by Joan of Arc in 1429, Beaugency is now a compact small town with a cluster of sights by the river, and picturesque cobbled streets.

Tapestry weaving in Europe is believed to have started in the 12th century, although the techniques were probably used in classical Greece and Rome. From the 14th to the 17th centuries the art reached its peak. The main workshops were in Paris, Arras, Bruges, Tournai and Brussels; later, royal workshops were established at the Gobelins factory in Paris, and at Aubusson.

The most famous tapestry to have survived from the early period is the incomplete but superb series of 70 works illustrating the Apocalypse of St. John the Divine, commissioned by the Duc d'Anjou in 1375, and made in Paris by Nicolas Bataille from cartoons by Hennequin de Bruges. These huge works (100m/330ft long and 5m/16ft high), intended for Angers Cathedral, provide a graphic illustration of St. John's writings, depicting rivers of blood and whores of Babylon against a more gentle background of *mille-fleurs*, with humorous touches such as rabbits popping in and out of holes in the border.

COVERS AND RUGS
Tapestries were used not only for wall hangings in churches and houses of the rich, but as covers for beds, chairs, tables and cushions, and as horse blankets and rugs.

Survival over the centuries The preservation of these tapestries is nothing short of miraculous. In 1843, the Bishop of Angers set about buying all the fragments he could find and having them carefully restored. Now they hang in the **Château d'Angers** (see page 108). You can appreciate them on different levels: by following the story, Bible in hand, admiring the technical details, or simply looking at the faces, whose emotions are as vivid as ever, even after 600 years.

Detail from an Angers tapestry

Tapestries for today On the opposite side of the river, the **Ancien Hôpital de St-Jean**, home of the **Musée Jean Lurçat/Musée de la Tapisserie Contemporain**, 4 boulevard Arago, 49100 Angers (*Open* mid-Jun to mid-Sep daily 10–7; mid-Sep to mid-Jun 10–noon, 2–6. *Admission: inexpensive*), is the setting for a remarkable series of contemporary tapestries created in Aubusson by the painter and designer Jean Lurçat. Inspired by the Apocalypse, Lurçat created intense and vivid symbolic works entitled *Le Chant du Monde* ('The Song of the World'). Against a black background, he depicted his fears of the future of the world; the first four panels (including *The Man of Hiroshima* and *The Great Charnel House*) are the more pessimistic ones. Originally there were to have been 17 panels; only 10 were created, over a period of nine years, before Lurçat's death in 1966.

► Beauregard, Château de *107D2*

Like Chambord, Beauregard was one of François I's hunting lodges. Unlike Chambord, this château is still inhabited, and although on the popular châteaux trail, it is relatively unfrequented, and well worth visiting. There is a portrait gallery of 327 famous people, echoed in the new Jardin des Portraits, a Delft tile floor, and some fine timbered and coffered ceilings.

►► Blois *106C2*

The busy town of Blois could be considered the tourist capital of the Loire Valley. Picturesque and lively, it is a good base for visitors without a car, with a selection of sightseeing coach tours on offer from the tourist office, and bicycles to rent opposite the château (in summer) or from Velo-Cycles Leblond (all year, tel: 02 54 74 30 13). Taking pride of place on a cliff top north of the river is the great royal **Château de Blois►►►** (*Open* Jan–Mar, Nov–Dec daily 9–12.30, 2–5.30; Apr–Jun, Sep–Oct 9–6; Jul, Aug, 9–7. *Closed* public holidays. *Admission: expensive*) (see pages 112–113), whose architectural variety—with parts ranging from the 13th to 17th centuries—reflects its history as the preferred royal residence until Louis XIV moved the court to Versailles.

Architectural detail at the royal château of Blois

JACQUES COEUR

Jacques Coeur's remarkable talents for commerce and his consequent royal patronage led, in 1451, to his imprisonment instigated by a band of jealous courtiers. After a dramatic escape, he offered his services to the Pope but died soon after.

►► Bourges *107E2*

This large industrial town is notable for one of France's great Gothic **cathedrals►►►** (mainly 12th- and 13th-century), famous for its Romanesque side doors. Bourges also possesses a perfect example of a Gothic mansion, the **Palais Jacques Coeur►►**, rue Jacques Coeur (*Open* daily. Guided visits only. Phone ahead for times of tours: 02 48 24 79 42. *Admission expensive*). On summer evenings follow the blue lanterns, which take you on an illuminated tour of the city and monuments.

►► Brissac, Château de *106B2*

Brissac is yet another example of a château which combines medieval foundations and towers (which resisted all attempts at destruction) with a later building: In this case the more recent addition is an elegant 17th-century central wing, richly decorated.

► Candes-Saint-Martin *106B2*

At the confluence of the Loire and the Vienne stands the quiet farming village of Candes, where the fortified church of **St-Martin►►** (12th- and 13th-century) has much of interest, including a richly sculpted façade and soaring Angevin vaulting. The steep path behind the church offers attractive river views.

►►► Chambord *107D2*

41250 Chambord (Open Apr–Sep daily 9–6.15; Oct–Mar 9–5.15. Closed: public holidays. Admission: expensive)

At the western edge of the Sologne lies the huge forest estate and hunting reserve of Chambord. There are public avenues and paths, and game observation posts (dawn and dusk are the best times). At the heart lies the 440-room Château de Chambord, transformed by François I from a simple hunting lodge (see pages 112–113).

►► Chaumont-sur-Loire *106C2*

This small riverside town is overlooked by a hillside park whose tall cedar trees almost hide one of the finest early Renaissance châteaux in France, home for many years to the scheming Catherine de Médicis and her rival, Diane de Poitiers. The interior illustrates the rather spartan lifestyle enjoyed by its noble inhabitants. There are fine stables in the grounds, also home to a landscape gardening school.

►► Chenonceaux *106C2*

The village of Chenonceaux is well provided with hotels and other tourist facilities, and an overnight stay is worth considering to beat the morning crowds at the **Château de Chenonceau**, 37150 Chenonceau (*Open* Mid-Mar to mid-Sep daily 9–7; mid- to end-Sep 9–6.30; 1–15 Oct, 1–15 Mar 9–6; 16–31 Oct 9–5.30; 1–15 Nov, Feb 9–5; 16 Nov–31 Jan 9–4.30. *Admission: expensive*; see page 113).

CHAUVIGNY

On the east bank of the Vienne, east of Poitiers, the small town of Chauvigny has a fine hilltop fortress. On the same hill, the church of St-Pierre has remarkable grotesque capitals; and to the south of the town, the little church of St-Pierre-les-Eglises has interesting frescoes.

Chauvigny Market has little to do with the ruins of five enormous châteaux up above

BLOOMS

Chaumont's flourishing horticultural school, a recently created national institution, gives rise to a blooming festival every summer (mid-June to mid-October). International landscape gardeners indulge their talents by creating a thematically inspired garden.

The great age of châteaux-building in the Loire Valley followed the campaigns of Joan of Arc and the subsequent expulsion of the English from France in 1453. With peace, a new feeling of national pride and optimism was engendered, which resulted in an ambitious royal building programme. The failure of successive military forays to Italy by Charles VIII, Louis XII and François I between 1494 and 1525 was mitigated by their exposure to the Renaissance movement in that country. Italian architects, artists, artisans and gardeners were brought to the French court, and schools were established first at Amboise, then at Tours, Blois and Fontainebleau.

In the Loire Valley's ancient hunting grounds of kings and courtiers, the new climate of peace changed the need for fortification, and emphasis was placed instead on comfort and elegance. Massive walls, machicolations, battlements, moats and drawbridges were gradually to give way to ornamental details: Open loggias, finely sculpted exterior staircases, mullioned and dormer windows, columns and pilasters were all part of the new style.

Chenonceau, spanning the River Cher (right) and a detail from Blois (below)

Inspired designs In the transitional period of the early 16th century, Renaissance features were grafted onto Gothic ones; later influences were the Mannerist decorative architectural arts of Rome, providing inspiration for the school of Fontainebleau. This period was followed (in the 17th century) by a more dignified Classical approach for exteriors, combined with brilliantly profuse rococo decoration. No motif was too elaborate: scrolls, nymphs, shells, luxuriant foliage and wreaths were applied in stucco, wood or papier mâché to walls, ceilings and furniture.

Four of the most beautiful and most popular Loire châteaux from the Renaissance period are **Azay-le-Rideau**, **Blois**, **Chambord** and **Chenonceau**.

Azay-le-Rideau This graceful, small white château, its image reflected in a moat formed by the River Indre, retains its medieval appearance, but combines this with the new ornamental style. It boasts a beautifully decorated staircase with straight flights, a departure from the conventional spiral. The interior has been arranged as a Renaissance museum (itinerant *son-et-lumière*, nightly in Jul, Aug; Fri, Sat and Sun in May, Jun, Sep).

Blois The royal château of Blois is interesting for its variety of styles. From the 13th century onwards, a succession of buildings was erected around a central courtyard. The most impressive is the elegant François I wing (adorned by a magnificant spiral staircase tower), which was partly demolished by François Mansart in order to build the Gaston d'Orléans wing, in sharply contrasting Classical style.

A guided tour of the interior features heavily restored rooms and much historical detail, including a description of the bloody murder of the Duc de Guise in 1588. More rewarding, perhaps, is a *son-et-lumière* performance in the courtyard, or a visit to the recently revamped Musée des Beaux Arts.

Chambord Designed by an Italian architect, this monumental château was built as a superior hunting lodge by François I. Its size defies most camera lenses, and lends an air of fantasy to the building, which may seem to have more in common with Disney than the Renaissance. The most memorable exterior feature is the extraordinary sculpted roofscape, consisting of numerous chimneys, bell turrets, dormer windows, spires and capitals; it served as a viewing terrace from which to observe the start and finish of hunts, as well as tournaments and pageants, and was also a place for court assignations and intrigues.

Inside, the most outstanding feature is the famous double spiral staircase, by which people can ascend and descend simultaneously without meeting each other, thought by some to have been designed by Leonardo da Vinci. The château is sparsely furnished and evokes little of the life of former times, but you can visit without a guided tour.

The exterior aspect of Chambord is best enjoyed before or after popular tourist visiting hours; at dawn or dusk, it assumes an almost magical quality.

Chenonceau A supremely elegant château whose arched gallery spans the River Cher. The building work was supervised by Katherine Bohier, the wife of Thomas Bohier, royal tax collector and embezzler. Following confiscation by François I, the château came under the influence of Diane de Poitiers and then, more significantly in architectural terms, Catherine de Médicis, who added a gallery to the bridge.

The interior is well furnished and is visited without a guided tour (explanatory notes are available). There are fine formal gardens and a park; other attractions include temporary art exhibitions and sampling Chenonceau's wines in the 16th-century cellars. (Note that the village of Chenonceaux is spelt with an 'x', unlike its château.)

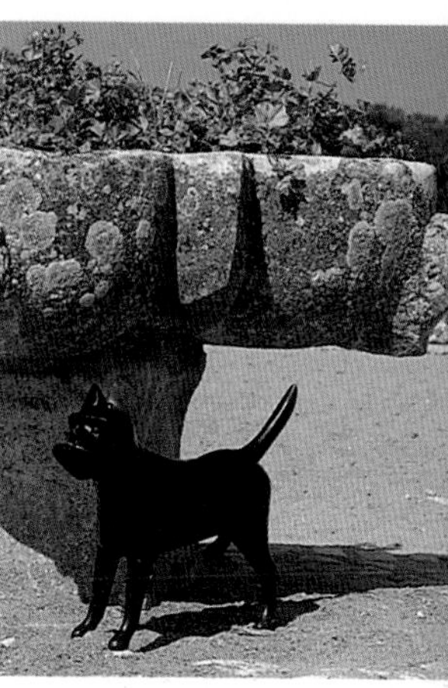

Chenonceau's gardens attract some odd visitors

A WOMAN'S WORK
Created for the financier Gilles Berthelot in the early 16th century, Azay-le-Rideau is one of several chateaux in the Loire Valley, Chenonceau included, where the building work was directed by a woman—in this case, Berthelot's wife.

CHINON EXTRAS
Nuclear power fans or foes can visit France's first nuclear power station at Avoine, 12km (7.5 miles) north of Chinon. It is no longer in use. Less stressful perhaps is a one-hour trip on the 1900s steam train from Chinon to Richelieu (services every weekend Jul, Aug). Rabelaisian-inspired foodies may like to visit La Dévinière (at Seuilly, 6km/4 miles west of Chinon), the birthplace and museum of the creator of Gargantua—the writer François Rabelais. Every August there is a medieval market where the vendors dress in period costume.

An onion-seller in Chinon

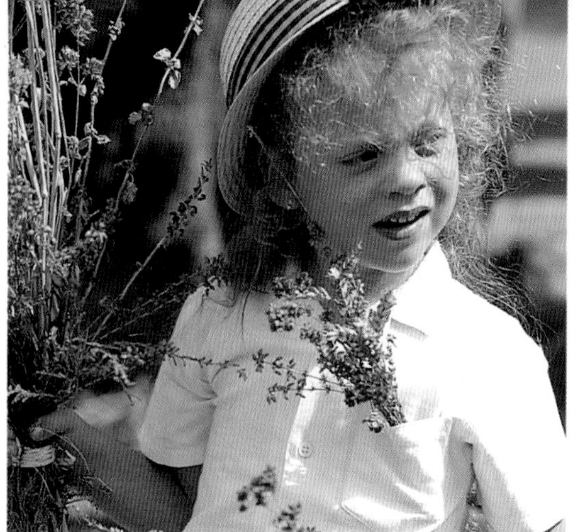

►► Cheverny, Château de *107D2*

This is a rigorously symmetrical classical château, supremely harmonious, whose interior has been largely unaltered since its completion. Sumptuously decorated and furnished in Louis XIII style, it is one of the few Loire châteaux to evoke the feel of a home; it is still privately owned and inhabited. Expect to wait a long time for the guided tour in high season. Cheverny is famous for its liveried hunt; in the grounds of the château, the kennels and trophy room can be visited.

►► Chinon *106B2*

A busy and interesting small town and tourist hub on the leafy Vienne, Chinon is dominated by the ample ruins of its medieval castle, a royal residence best known as the place where, in 1429, Joan of Arc first persuaded the Dauphin Charles to let her take command of an army in order to drive the English out of France.

Chinon is an attractive base for a short stay (there are several hotels and restaurants, as well as a riverside campsite). The picturesque cobbled streets of the old town are lined with half-timbered houses; the principal focus of activity is the Grand Carroi crossroads.

►► Cunault *106B2*

On the south bank of the Loire northwest of Saumur lies the beautiful Romanesque church of Cunault, part of a former Benedictine monastery. Tall and slender, its pure white tufa stone broken only by fragments of fresco, Cunault is renowned above all for its wealth of remarkable sculpted capitals, best admired through binoculars.

► Doué-la-Fontaine *106B2*

Troglodyte structures of one sort or another abound here, but of particular interest are the quarry from which monolithic sarcophagi were hewn in Merovingian times, and the remarkable anonymous late 16th-century bawdy sculptures in the caves at **Dénezé-sous-Doué** (sadly unprotected). A labyrinth of caves, waterfalls and tropical vegetation in another disused quarry provides refuge for more than 500 animals (mainly threatened species) at the imaginatively run **Zoo de Doué►**.

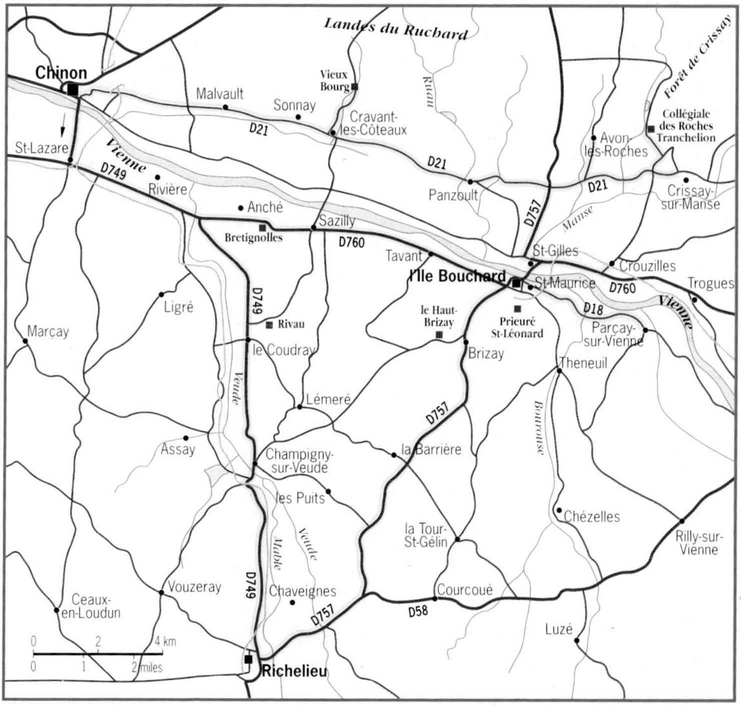

Discovering the River Vienne

Start at Chinon.
The Vienne is an intimate and secretive river, bordered by gardens, orchards, willows and poplars.

D749 to Champigny-sur-Veude and Richelieu.
The chapel of Sainte-Chapelle at **Champigny-sur-Veude** is part of a former château demolished by Cardinal Richelieu in a fit of jealousy. Saved only by the intervention of Pope Urban VIII, it is a wonderful example of the marriage of Renaissance with Gothic. In the town of **Richelieu**, to the south, the Cardinal's own château was demolished in the Revolution. Fine parks remain; of more interest, however, are the results of 17th-century classical town planning.

D757 to l'Ile-Bouchard. Take the D760 to Crouzilles, the D18 to Parçay-sur-Vienne, or the D757/D21 to Avon-les-Roches, Les Roches-Tranchelion and Crissay-sur-Manse.
The area southeast of Chinon, along the Vienne Valley, is rich in early churches. At **l'Ile Bouchard**, fine capitals remain in the ruins of St-Léonard priory. Various detours offer the opportunity to visit the Romanesque churches of **Crouzilles**, **Parçay-sur-Vienne** and **Avon-les-Roches**, the Gothic/Renaissance collegiate church of **Les Roches-Tranchelion**, or the Carolingian church of **Vieux-Bourg-de-Cravant**.

Return to Chinon direct on D21 via Cravant-les-Côteaux, or go back to l'Ile-Bouchard and take the D760 via Tavant, Sazilly and Anché; rejoin the D749 to Chinon.
The tiny Romanesque church of **Tavant** has lively frescoes that are full of realism (for access apply to the Mairie).

NOBLE REFUGE
Fontevraud Abbey was established in the early 11th century, catering for both monks and nuns, as well as fallen women and lepers. Each unit had its own church, cloister and living quarters. Headed by an abbess, the Order became popular with noblewomen, and acquired great wealth under the patronage of the rich and the royal. It was also the chosen resting place for the Plantagenet Henry II, his queen, Eleanor of Aquitaine, and their son Richard the Lionheart, whose effigies lie in the abbey church.

►► Fontevraud *106B2*

Abbaye Royale de Fontevraud, 49590 Fontevraud (Open: Jun–Sep daily 9–6; Apr, May, Oct 10–5.30; Nov–Mar 10–5. Closed: public holidays. Admission: expensive)
Relatively little remains of the great 11th-century abbey of Fontevraud (even the few buildings that survived the Revolution had to serve for more than 150 years as a national prison). Apart from the soaring abbey church, the most interesting part is the kitchen, a rare example of secular Romanesque architecture, flanked by apsidal chapels. The gardens are also impressive.

► Gien *107E2*

A bridgehead town and useful stop on the rather dull stretch of Loire east of Orléans, Gien is known mainly for its faïence. The factory west of the central area contains a museum and offers tours. Gien's red-brick **castle►** contains a museum of hunting; next to it, the modern church of Ste-Jeanne-d'Arc fits in well with its surroundings.

►► Langeais, Château de *106C2*

One of the most interesting late medieval royal châteaux to have come down to us largely unaltered, Langeais illustrates the transition from Gothic (fortress exterior, drawbridge and barbican) to Renaissance (interior). Unusually, it has a wonderful collection of contemporary furnishings, tapestries and works of art, which evokes the lifestyle of the time of Charles VIII and Anne of Brittany. The château lies in the busy heart of an otherwise unexciting small town (*Open* daily. *Admission* moderate).

►► Loches *106C2*

Above the modern town of Loches lies the heavily fortified medieval city, whose fierce keep and dungeons, purportedly the deepest in the Loire, served for many centuries as a state prison. The château is perhaps best known as the home of Agnès Sorel, extravagant mistress of Charles VII; a guided tour reveals among other things the tiny prayer cell of Anne of Brittany. It's worth wandering around the ramparts and through the old quarter leading up to the medieval city.

Powder horns in the Museum of Hunting at Gien

▶▶ Le Loir *106B2*

The confusingly named tributary of the Loire, Le Loir, meanders slowly through peaceful agricultural countryside. Although within easy striking distance of its more famous sister, Le Loir is off the main tourist track, with the exception of the **Château du Lude▶▶**. Its towns and villages preserve an everyday charm, in the past appreciated by Ronsard and today by fishermen. *Dégustations* of the local wines, Jasnières and Coteaux de Vendômois, are readily available.

Church country Le Loir is of particular interest to lovers of early churches (like the stretch of the Vienne described on page 115). Along its banks is a succession of small Romanesque buildings, most of which were on a medieval pilgrimage route leading to Santiago de Compostela in Spain. Orders of Benedictines, Cistercians and Knights Templar housed and fed the pilgrims, and in **Montoire** and **Trôo** hospices and hospitals offered comfort to the sick.

The Loir churches are of special interest for their bright frescoes; some are remarkably well preserved. A good area for a church crawl is on the stretch of river between **Vendôme** and **La Chartre-sur-le-Loir**. Particular buildings to seek out include the church in the little village of **Areines▶**, the site of a Roman settlement, on the eastern side of Vendôme (take the D917 east, followed by the first road on the left); St-Genest in **Lavardin▶▶**, which has especially fine mural paintings dating from the 12th to the 16th centuries; and **St-Jacques-des-Guérets▶**, on the south bank of the Loir just outside the village of Trôo, which also has a superb series of paintings.

Town sights The towns along this stretch of Le Loir offer plenty of interest, too. **Vendôme▶▶** not only has a fine Gothic abbey church (La Trinité), with a rich Flamboyant west front, but is also a picturesque place built on several islands, with waterside gardens. The attractive market square of **St-Martin** has a beautiful Renaissance bell-tower. **Montoire** possesses some of the best frescoes of all the Loir churches, in the tiny chapel of St-Gilles; it is also remembered as the site of a meeting in 1940 between Marshal Pétain and Hitler.

TODAY'S CAVE-DWELLERS

The Loire Valley's soft tufa stone has long provided shelter, in conditions of constant temperature and humidity, for wine-storage and mushroom cultivation. Along Le Loir the banks are riddled with tufa caves which are used for troglodyte dwellings. Now no longer only simple peasant abodes, troglodyte caves are sought-after second homes, with central heating to supplement the log fire (the chimney sticks out of the ground above), and conservatories tacked on to the front. Some have been turned into restaurants and a good place to visit is the troglodyte museum at Rochemenier.

THE UNEXPLODABLES

River transport was once vital in the Loire region, carrying passengers, wine and other produce in flat-bottomed barges. In 1832, a steamboat service started between Orléans and Nantes, vastly reducing journey time but also leading to deafeningly exploding boilers. New 'unexplodable' steam-boats were introduced, but the development of railways in the 1850s led to their gradual disappearance.

The Loire Valley is often where France's varying weather changes: clouds stop and the southern sun starts here

In the village of Luynes

LOIRE WINES
The Loire Valley produces every style of wine. The best appellations for dry whites are: Muscadet de Sèvre-et-Maine; Pouilly-Fumé and Sancerre, and the cheaper Reuilly, Quincy and Menetou-Salon; Savennières, and the individual vineyard appellations of Coulée de Serrant and La Roche aux Moines. For reds: Saumur-Champigny; Bourgueil and St-Nicolas-de-Bourgueil; Chinon. For sparkling whites: Saumur; Vouvray and Montlouis. For sweet whites: the superb Quarts de Chaume and Bonnezeaux, and the larger area of Côteaux du Layon; Vouvray and Montlouis.

24 HOURS
The first race at Le Mans, in 1923, was won by a Chenard & Walcker which cruised at an average speed of 92kph (57mph). The prize for the fastest lap went to a Bentley, which clocked 107kph (66mph).

▶ Luynes *106C2*

Just off the north bank of the Loire, west of Tours, the village of Luynes is overlooked by yet another of the valley's sentinels—the Château de Luynes (*Open* Apr–Sep daily). The current building (mainly 13th-century) replaced an earlier fortress, which in turn was built on the site of a Roman castrum. The **aqueduct** which served this, and the town of Tours, can still be seen to the northeast of the village.

▶▶ Le Mans *106B3*

Known for its world-famous 24-hour automobile race every June, the industrial city of Le Mans, on the River Sarthe, serves as a crossroads town between Normandy and the Loire Valley. This ancient city still preserves its Gallo-Roman ramparts, and the beautiful Romanesque/Gothic **cathedral of St-Julien▶▶▶** is rich in interest, with vivid stained glass, Renaissance tombs, and a 12th-century south doorway which could rival that of Chartres. Within the ramparts there are antique and craft shops, more churches and several fine houses, some of which can be visited: The Maison de la Reine-Bérengère houses a local history and ethnography museum, while the **Tessé mansion▶** has a rich collection of paintings.

On a different track Racing enthusiasts will not want to miss the 13.5km (8.5-mile) circuit, off the D139 to the south of the city, and the **Musée de l'Automobile▶▶**, Circuit des 24 Heures du Mans, BP 23454, Le Mans (*Open* Oct, Nov, Mar–May daily 10–6; Jun–Sep 10–7. *Closed* Dec–Feb. *Admission: moderate*), which houses an excellent collection of elegant vintage cars. Le Mans also has a gigantic Renault factory.

▶▶ Meillant, Château de *107E1*

South of Bourges, the Château de Meillant is the finest in the Berry. Similar to many of the Loire châteaux in its combination of fortress and palace, Flamboyant Gothic and decorative Renaissance, the still-inhabited Meillant rivals the better-known châteaux nearby for the interest of its interior, beautifully decorated and furnished.

▶ Montgeoffroy, Château de *106B2*

About 20km (12 miles) east of Angers, this elegant and harmonious 18th-century château has remained in one family since it was built, and the Louis XVI furniture, wood panels and wall hangings are all original. The tour of the house includes some beautiful rooms, as well as kitchen garden, saddle room and the stables, with a collection of carriages (*Open* Easter to mid-November, daily).

▶ Montreuil-Bellay *106B2*

Southwest of Saumur, the large hulk of the 15th-century Château de Montreuil-Bellay dominates the small village above the very leafy little Thouet River; the château comprises several parts, including a pyramid-shaped kitchen reminiscent of that at Fontevraud (see page 116), complete with cooking utensils. The former chapel is now the village church.

▶ Montrichard *106C2*

This attractive little market town on the banks of the Cher has a beach, half-timbered houses by the river, and one of the many fierce keeps to be built in the 11th century by Foulques Nerra, Count of Anjou. On the outskirts of town are stretches of former tufa quarries, now housing wine or mushroom cellars, or troglodytes.

OUT OF MONTRICHARD
The elegant Château de Montpoupon stands 12km (7.5 miles) to the southwest. An early Renaissance building with a striking gatehouse, it overlooks a wooded valley. An amusing hunting museum is housed in the outbuildings (*Open* Oct–Dec, Feb, Mar Sat, Sun and holidays 10–12, 2–4; Apr–Sep daily 10–12, 2–4. *Admission: expensive*).

The Château de Montreuil-Bellay, where the intrepid Duchess of Longueville once rode up the main staircase on horseback

▶▶ Nohant, Château de *107D1*

Nohant (Open: Oct–Mar daily 10–12.30, 2–5; Apr–Jun, Sep 9.30–12.45, 2–6.30; May–Jun 9.30–12, 2–6.30; Jul, Aug 9.30–7. Admission: expensive)

Near La Châtre, this was George Sand's home and is now a museum. The nearby countryside features in her novels.

▶▶ Noirlac, Abbaye de *107E1*

18200 Bruère-Allichamps (Open: Feb–Sep daily 9.45–12.30, 2–5; Oct–Dec Wed–Mon 9.45–12, 2–5. Closed Jan. Admission: moderate)

In the Berry, south of Bourges, this former 12th- to 14th-century abbey is typical of the austere style of Cistercian buildings. Some of the monks' living quarters are furnished, giving an idea of 12th-century monastic life.

GEORGE SAND
Born in Paris in 1804, Aurore Dupin (alias George Sand) soon moved to Nohant. Here she lapped up the mysteries of this typical Berry countryside and transferred them to her novels. After her marriage to an uninspiring baron, she would make nocturnal escapes from the château, disguised as a peasant, to join the more rambunctious nightlife of La Châtre. She died at Nohant in 1876.

The cloisters of the Abbaye de Noirlac (see page 119)

LOIRE GASTRONOMY
Food delicacies of the Loire include river fish, particularly pike (*brochet*), carp (*carpe*), shad (*alose*) and salmon (*saumon*), served with a sorrel sauce (*à l'oseille*) or a sauce of butter, vinegar and shallots (*beurre blanc*); early vegetables, particularly asparagus, and mushrooms; game, particularly in the Sologne; cold, potted pork (*rillettes* and *rillons*), and pork with prunes, a Tours dish; fresh cream cheeses (*crèmets*), eaten with sugar and cream; goats' cheeses, especially from Poitou; caramelized upside-down apple tart (*tarte Tatin*).

▶ Orléans *107D3*

Indelibly associated with Joan of Arc, who delivered it from the English in 1429 after a siege of eight months, the industrial city of Orléans has long been the site of decisive battles. From the early days when Orléans stopped the hordes of Attila, through the Wars of Religion and the Revolution, and finally during World War II, Orléans suffered much destruction. Now it is the regional capital and a lively university town, although it cannot be said to brim with charm. References to The Maid abound (road and house names, statues and a museum devoted to her); other sights include a much altered cathedral with fine carved panels, and an arts museum, **Musée des Beaux Arts▶▶**, Place Sainte-Croix (*Open* Tue–Sat 9.30–12.15, 1.30–5.45, Sun 2–6.30. *Admission: moderate*).

▶▶ Plessis Bourré, Château du *106B2*

4960 Euvillé (Open: Feb–Mar, Oct–Nov Thu–Tue 2–6; Apr–Jun, Sep Fri–Tue 10–2, 2–6, Thu 2–6; Jul, Aug daily 10–6. Closed: Dec & Jan. Admission: expensive)

This magnificent moated fortress, north of Angers, is not only one of the finest houses in Anjou, but also one of the best examples of secular architecture of the late 15th century. Built by Jean Bourré (also responsible for Langeais) during the period that marked the transition from heavy feudal fortress to elegant abode, Le Plessis is Bourré's sumptuously decorated dwelling.

▶ Plessis Macé, Château du *106A2*

On a hill 13km (8 miles) northwest of Angers, Plessis Macé retains much from the days when it was strategically important. The original 11th-century fortress was partly destroyed during the Hundred Years' War, but the 15th-century additions are of more interest, particularly the splendid Flamboyant Gothic courtyard balcony, which served as a ladies' viewing area during tournaments.

▶▶ Poitiers *106B1*

An industrial and university city, much damaged during World War II, Poitiers is best known for its Romanesque churches, and its high-tech theme park, **Futuroscope▶▶**, BP 3030 86130 Jaunay-Clan, Poitiers, (tel: 05 49 49 11 12; www.futuroscope.fr *Open* daily from 10–dusk. *Closed* part of Jan–Feb. *Admission: expensive*). On the great pilgrimage route to Santiago de Compostela, the province of Poitou saw the emergence of a distinct school of Romanesque architecture; today, the finest example is the church of **Notre-Dame-la-Grande▶▶**, on Poitiers' market square. Another exceptional building is the fourth-century baptistery, which is unattractively situated but well worth seeking out for its medieval frescos. The **Musée Sainte-Croix▶** displays archaeological and medieval artefacts.

▶ St-Aignan *107D2*

A small town on the Cher, St-Aignan has narrow streets of half-timbered houses climbing up wooded slopes below a Renaissance château (access only to the terrace). The Romanesque church has beautiful capitals and frescos in the crypt.

▶▶ St-Benoît-sur-Loire, Abbaye de *107D3*

The site of St-Benoît was a sacred druid place of worship before the monastery of St-Pierre-de-Fleury was founded in the seventh century. Renamed St-Benoît after receiving the relics of the saint, the abbey became an important place of pilgrimage and enjoyed increasing prosperity. The beautiful basilica which you see today was built between the 11th and 13th centuries, and is one of the finest examples of Romanesque art and architecture in the country—tall and light, with harmonious proportions and wonderfully sculpted capitals. The abbey has now been revived as a monastic community, and daily services with Gregorian chants are held.

▶▶ St-Savin *106C1*

The abbey church at St-Savin-sur-Gartempe is another beautiful Romanesque church, notable for its extraordinarily vivid life-size mural paintings. (Binoculars are well worth renting to appreciate the detail.)

FUTUROSCOPE
The so-called 'European Park of the Image' is a vast complex of futuristic constructions offering some extraordinary technological attractions aimed at all ages. Cinema experiences include moving seats, images in relief, hemispherical screens viewed through special glasses or 360-degree screens. Interactive water-games and countless other high-tech attractions complete the range.

The village of St-Benoît-sur-Loire does not always reflect its impassioned spiritual past

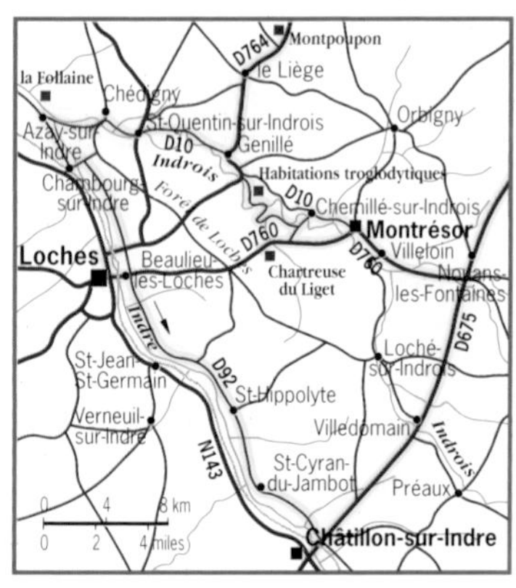

Drive

Tributaries of the Loire

Start at Loches. East to Beaulieu-les-Loches, then D92 along the Indre to Châtillon-sur-Indre. D675 to Nouans-les-Fontaines.
The Indre and Indrois are quiet and beautiful tributaries of the Loire, meandering through chalky escarpments, lined with willows, alders and poplars. Despite being less well endowed with grand châteaux than other parts of the region, the area is very rewarding for an unhurried tour on minor riverside roads through sleepy villages, past small churches, ruined abbeys and mills, and troglodyte caves.
Châtillon-sur-Indre, on the northern fringe of the Brenne marshlands, is an important market town for agricultural produce and equipment, with views from the fortress-topped old town (and a beautiful Romanesque church). The 13th-century church in **Nouans-les-Fontaines** also merits a short detour to see the large and very fine altarpiece by Jean Fouquet.

D760 to Montrésor, then the D10 to Chemillé-sur-Indrois, and a short detour to Chartreuse du Liget.
For those suffering from withdrawal symptoms, the medieval fortifications and interior manor of the **Château de Montrésor** will come as a timely architectural injection; it's beautifully furnished by the Polish family who set about restoring it in the mid-19th century. Montrésor is also notable for an elegant Renaissance doorway on the church. **Chemillé-sur-Indrois** has a small leisure complex on a lake. At the edge of the Forest of Loches lie the remains of the Carthusian monastery of **Le Liget**.

Follow the Indrois Valley west on minor roads to Genillé, and the D10 to St-Quentin-sur-Indrois and Azay-sur-Indre.
Azay-sur-Indre, **St-Quentin-sur-Indrois**, **Genillé**, **Chemillé-sur-Indrois** and **Villeloin** are all attractive villages with old houses, abbeys or small castles.

Follow the Indre southeast on the D17 back to Loches. Visitors leaving the area to head northeast via the Cher could additionally take in the Château de Montpoupon, on the D764 from Loches to Montrichard.

❑ Like several other monasteries, Le Liget was founded by Henry II in expiation for the murder of Thomas Becket; ask for the keys to visit the frescoed Chapelle St-Jean, and take a glance at La Corroierie, a former annexe of the monastery, on the Montrésor road. ❑

▶ Saumur 106B2

Saumur's main fame (apart from the pepperpot-towered castle which dominates the town and surrounding countryside) derives from the tufa which gives this area its name of 'White Anjou'. The many caves and cellars carved out of the soft white chalk in and around Saumur shelter thousands of bottles of sparkling wine and around 70 per cent of the country's cultivated mushrooms. This may be reason enough for visiting the town (guided tours and tastings are offered at many of the wine houses), but an additional attraction is offered by Saumur's Cadre Noir, the corps of instructors at its famous **Cavalry School**, with its annual display in July (Apr–Sep: trial runs can be watched). No less than three museums are devoted to various aspects of the horse and horsemanship (one in the château, which also houses a **museum of decorative arts▶▶**; *closed* during 2007).

The **Chateau-Musée de Saumur▶▶**, 49400 Saumur (*Open* Apr–Sep Wed–Mon 10–1, 2–5.30; Oct–Mar groups and by appointment. *Admission: inexpensive*) has been much altered since the days when it was depicted so beautifully in the book of miniatures, *Les Très Riches Heures du Duc de Berry*, and has served as a prison and barracks. There are good views from the watchtower.

▶ Serrant, Château de 106A2

Guided tours are given of this large Renaissance-style château near Angers. They reveal opulent décor and furniture; in the chapel, designed by Hardouin-Mansart, is the baroque tomb of the Marquis de Vaubrun by Coysevox.

▶ Sologne 107D2

This area is an infertile plain of marshland and forest, bounded by the large loop of the Loire between Blois and Gien. The D922 between **La Ferté-St-Aubin** and **Romorantin** is signed as a tourist route, passing typical Sologne countryside and lakes bright with water lilies. Attractive village features include low brick and timber houses and galleried churches: fine examples can be found at **Souvigny-en-Sologne▶▶** and **Brinon-sur-Sauldre**. An interesting museum housed in a converted mill in Romorantin offers the opportunity to learn about Solognote life. The **Etang du Puis** is a large lake with watersports facilities.

HUNTIN', SHOOTIN' AND FISHIN'

The Sologne's main activities have long been huntin', shootin' and fishin'. Local prosperity depended on royal popularity; when the court returned to Paris in the 17th century, there followed a period of neglect and stagnation. After reafforestation, the Sologne began to thrive again. Thousands of pheasants are now reared to provide recreation for weekend gun-slingers, and the lakes and rivers are rich in pike, carp and perch.

Looking at the Loire across Saumur: the bridge saw a heroic stand by cavalry cadets in 1940 against the German advance

The quintessential fairy-tale Château d'Ussé was built in the 15th century around a medieval fortress

SULLY
Henri IV's right-hand minister and shaper of the fortunes of France, Maximilien de Béthune, was given the title of Duke of Sully after he purchased the château in 1602. Always a confirmed workaholic, later in life Sully would rise at 3am to pen his memoirs and even installed a printing press in one of the towers. He also greatly embellished the fortress.

BALZAC'S TOURAINE
Born in Tours, the great novelist Honoré de Balzac (1799–1850) referred constantly to his beloved Touraine, encapsulating the charms of the countryside in *Le Lys dans la Vallée*. This novel, among many others, was written in the Château de Saché (near Azay-le-Rideau), in which he frequently sought refuge from the bustle of Parisian life. Balzac's rooms in the château have been arranged as a museum and contain manuscripts and proofs covered in such an abundance of notes that many a publisher must have been driven to despair.

► Sully, Château de *107E3*
This feudal fortress is notable for one of the finest medieval timber roofs in existence, which was fashioned out of chestnut by ships' carpenters (*Open* Feb–Dec).

►► Tours *106C2*
The thriving industrial and university city of Tours is encircled by tower-block outskirts, but the city has managed to preserve (with much recent restoration) its historic heart, and the wide boulevards have excellent shops. For visitors without a car, Tours makes a good base from which to take coach tours of the châteaux; and the lively old town is well provided with restaurants and bars. Sights include **Musée des Beaux Arts►►**, 18 place Francois-Sicard (*Open* Wed–Mon 9–12.45, 2–6. *Admission: moderate*), other museums devoted to medieval art, craft guilds, waxworks and wine, as well as a Gothic **cathedral** with beautiful stained glass.

► Ussé, Château d' *106B2*
This is the wonderful fairy-tale château of everyone's dreams, used by the writer Perrault as the model for his setting of *Sleeping Beauty*. Ussé's woodland backdrop is appropriately romantic. Topped by turrets and tall chimneys, unfortunately the outside is more captivating than its interior, with the exception of the Renaissance chapel (*Open* Feb to mid-Nov).

► Valençay, Château de *107D2*
This vast domed château, in a well-stocked park, is a very fine example of the classical Renaissance style (*open* Apr–Aug daily; Sep–Mar by appointment. *Admission: expensive*). Most famously associated with the 19th-century politician Talleyrand, the château is furnished in mainly Louis XV, Louis XVI and Empire styles. In the summer it has a sound and light show.

►► Villandry, Château de *106C2*
37510 Villandry (Open: daily, times vary. Admission: (gardens) moderate; (château and gardens) expensive).

A much altered château that retains only the keep from its original fortress building, though it has recently been restored, Villandry is notable for the re-creation of its 16th-century gardens, a fine example of the formal style known as *à la française*. Arranged on three terraces, it combines symbolic designs and decorative effects with practical use (vegetables, herbs and fruit). The planting, clipping and pruning statistics are mind-stretching.

When Charles VIII returned from northern Italy filled with a desire to copy the ornamental architecture of the Italian Renaissance, he brought with him not only the best architects, artists and craftsmen, but also a very talented garden designer, Pacello da Mercogliano. French gardens before the 16th century were mainly of practical use (orchards and areas for vegetables and medicinal herbs), with only a rare concession to ornament. The châteaux gardens at Amboise and Blois were to break new ground.

Setting a trend Larger and more vibrant than traditional gardens (those at Blois covered an area five or six times that of the palace), and with a greater variety of flowers, Amboise and Blois were to be the first of a series of royal pleasure gardens, which became increasingly decorative and fanciful as the century progressed.

Style change The other, more subtle change concerned the composition of the garden, which became symmetrical, conceived as part of the overall design of a building. The classical garden, *à la française*, was developed with genius by the great royal gardener **Le Nôtre**; at its best it was supremely ordered, and, under Louis XIV, inescapably grand. Le Nôtre was one of the first gardeners in France to recognize the importance of trees in a landscape composition; he also used water, in the shape of tranquil ornamental ponds (unlike the Italian style of fountains or informal streams and lakes), to great effect. Three gardens sum up Le Nôtre's legacy: those at the **Tuileries**, **Vaux-le-Vicomte** and **Versailles**.

The gardens at Versailles ...

Le Style Anglais The French garden could be said to be the very opposite of the English garden (called 'romantic'), whose natural rambling style, punctuated by architectural ornaments such as fake temples, pagodas and Gothic ruins, became increasingly popular in France. The style reached its peak in the 19th-century parks created by Napoleon III as a result of his long exile in London—most famously the **Bois de Boulogne** and the **Bois de Vincennes**.

... and at the Château de Villandry

New directions On a more modest level, in town or village, the French garden of today betrays its ancestry: Formal and symmetrical patterns of bold and contrasting hues, red with blue, orange with white, are popular and widely employed; their discipline is far removed from the apparent disorder and subtle tones of the English cottage garden. In the last few years, however, a renaissance in landscape-gardening has begun to take place, producing innovatory approaches such as the **Parc André Citroën** in Paris and countless replantings.

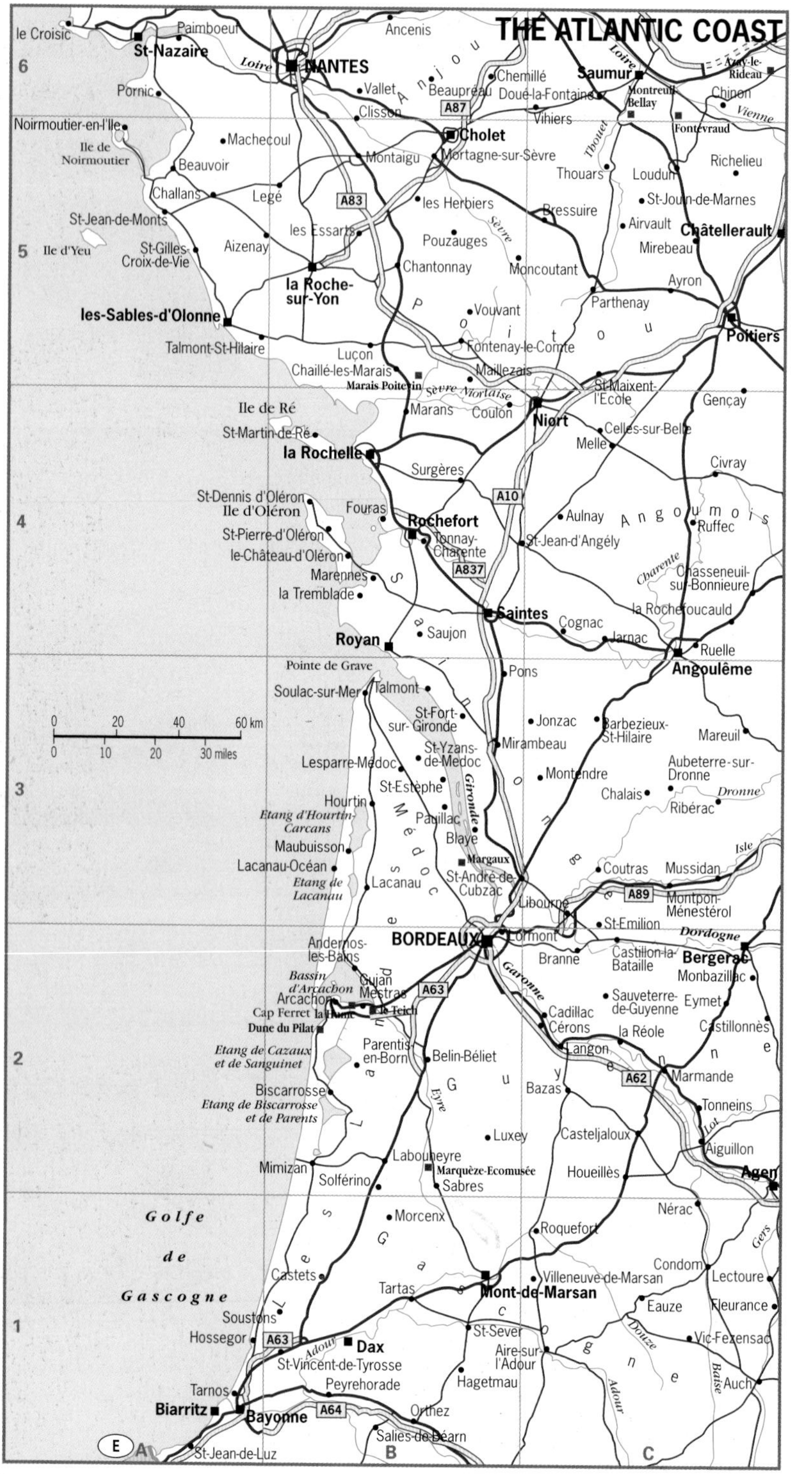

THE ATLANTIC COAST

le Croisic
St-Nazaire
Paimboeuf
Ancenis
Loire
NANTES
Pornic
Vallet
Anjou
Beaupréau
Chemillé
Doué-la-Fontaine
Saumur
Montreuil-Bellay
Azay-le-Rideau
Chinon
Vienne
Clisson
A87
Vihiers
Fontevraud
Noirmoutier-en-l'Ile
Ile de Noirmoutier
Machecoul
Cholet
Thouet
Montaigu
Mortagne-sur-Sèvre
Thouars
Loudun
Richelieu
Beauvoir
Challans
Legé
A83
les Herbiers
Bressuire
St-Jouin-de-Marnes
St-Jean-de-Monts
Sèvre
Airvault
Châtellerault
Ile d'Yeu
St-Gilles-Croix-de-Vie
Aizenay
les Essarts
Pouzauges
Mirebeau
Moncoutant
Chantonnay
Ayron
la Roche-sur-Yon
Parthenay
les-Sables-d'Olonne
Vouvant
Poitou
Poitiers
Talmont-St-Hilaire
Luçon
Fontenay-le-Comte
Chaillé-les-Marais
Maillezais
Marais Poitevin
Sèvre Niortaise
St-Maixent-l'Ecole
Gençay
Ile de Ré
Marans
Coulon
Niort
St-Martin-de-Ré
Celles-sur-Belle
Melle
la Rochelle
Surgères
Civray
St-Dennis d'Oléron
Ile d'Oléron
Fouras
A10
Rochefort
Aulnay
Angoumois
Ruffec
St-Pierre-d'Oléron
Tonnay-Charente
St-Jean-d'Angély
le-Château-d'Oléron
A837
Charente
Chasseneuil-sur-Bonnieure
Marennes
la Tremblade
Saintonge
Saintes
la Rochefoucauld
Cognac
Royan
Saujon
Jarnac
Ruelle
Angoulême
Pointe de Grave
Pons
Soulac-sur-Mer
Talmont
St-Fort-sur-Gironde
Jonzac
Barbezieux-St-Hilaire
Mareuil
St-Yzans-de-Médoc
Mirambeau
Lesparre-Médoc
Aubeterre-sur-Dronne
St-Estèphe
Montendre
Chalais
Dronne
Hourtin
Gironde
Ribérac
Etang d'Hourtin-Carcans
Médoc
Pauillac
Maubuisson
Blaye
Isle
Margaux
Coutras
Mussidan
Lacanau-Océan
St-André-de-Cubzac
Etang de Lacanau
Lacanau
Libourne
A89
Montpon-Ménestérol
St-Emilion
Andernos-les-Bains
BORDEAUX
Lormont
Dordogne
Branne
Castillon-la-Bataille
Bergerac
Bassin d'Arcachon
Gujan Mestras
Monbazillac
Arcachon
A63
Sauveterre-de-Guyenne
Eymet
Cap Ferret
la Hume
le Teich
Garonne
Cadillac
Dune du Pilat
Cérons
la Réole
Castillonnès
Etang de Cazaux et de Sanguinet
Parentis-en-Born
Belin-Béliet
Langon
Guyenne
Marmande
Biscarrosse
Bazas
A62
Etang de Biscarrosse et de Parents
Eyre
Tonneins
Lot
Luxey
Casteljaloux
Aiguillon
Mimizan
Labouheyre
Marquèze-Ecomusée
Houeillès
Agen
Solférino
Sabres
Nérac
Golfe de Gascogne
Morcenx
Roquefort
Les Landes
Gers
Condom
Castets
Mont-de-Marsan
Villeneuve-de-Marsan
Lectoure
Tartas
Eauze
Fleurance
Soustons
Gascogne
Douze
St-Sever
Hossegor
A63
Dax
Adour
Vic-Fezensac
St-Vincent-de-Tyrosse
Aire-sur-l'Adour
Baïse
Tarnos
Peyrehorade
Hagetmau
Auch
Biarritz
Bayonne
A64
Orthez
E
St-Jean-de-Luz
Salies-de-Béarn

0 20 40 60 km
0 10 20 30 miles

6
5
4
3
2
1
A
B
C

The Atlantic Coast

WHEN THE FRENCH mass-migrate for two months to the beach every summer, all roads leading to the Mediterranean are jammed, while on the Atlantic coast an infinity of pines, dunes and sandy beaches await. From Bordeaux to the Pyrenees, the map reveals only a scattering of resorts.

FAMILY FORMULA Do not expect pretty ports or coastal villages of the unspoiled 'hidden gem' variety. Aquitaine provides huge horizons and wide open spaces, ideal for family holidays to a formula—a simple apartment or a campsite, sun and sand, lots to do but comparatively little to see. Lakes near the sea offer safe bathing and water-sports. Surfers head for the ocean rollers in Biarritz.

THE NORTHERN STRETCH The **Vendée** and **Charente** coasts are more varied, with bays, fishing ports, islands and a rural economy of oysters, mussels, vineyards and salt pans. But here, too, the land is flat, and resorts are best for families requiring little more than a beach for the kids and French food and wine in the supermarket for mum and dad, who will return home with fond memories of *mouclade* (mussels in white wine) and a souvenir bottle of Pineau des Charentes, the local cognac-based aperitif. Of the towns, only the old port of **La Rochelle** has much style and *joie de vivre*.

ENGLISH LINKS Northern and southern coasts are separated by the Gironde, a deep incision where most of the rivers in southern France reach the sea. **Bordeaux** was the capital of English territory in France after Louis VII rashly lost Eleanor of Aquitaine to the future king of England, Henry Plantagenet, in 1152. The English were not chased out until 1453, by which time bibulous Albion had acquired a taste for 'claret', as the English still call red bordeaux. The region has not severed its British links of trade, blood and vineyard ownership.

WINE COUNTRY In the land of the most aristocratic of wines, connoisseurs can gaze with awe at the immaculate vineyards of **Latour**, **Lafite** and **Yquem**, whose precious grapes are picked one by one. Tasting is another matter: Many of the châteaux are less than welcoming to visitors. The wine villages are dull, with the notable exception of **St-Emilion**.

▶▶▶ REGION HIGHLIGHTS

TRAPPED AROMAS
One of the more bizarre, not to say dubious, traditions of Landais gastronomy is eating ortolan buntings. Having been caught in nets, the birds are nourished and gradually poisoned by a diet of milk mixed with a daily increasing quantity of armagnac. They are roasted in their own fat, served on paper and consumed by diners with napkins over their heads to ensure that no fume of the delicate bouquet escapes.

Monolithic church of St-Jean, Aubeterre

▶ Arcachon and Côte d'Argent *126C4*

The Aquitaine coast consists of two sandy beaches: 100km (62 miles) from **Soulac** to **Cap Ferret**, 125km (78 miles) from **Arcachon** to the outskirts of **Bayonne**. With dunes blocking the way to the sea, rivers feed a string of inland lakes. The River Eyre alone has broken through. Its estuary is the wide but tight-lipped bay of **Arcachon▶▶▶**, famous for oysters and popular with yachtsmen, migrant birds and Bordelais sun-seekers. Between Arcachon and the smelly oyster capital **Gujan Mestras** is a crafts village and farm animals (La Hume). **Le Teich** bird reserve has marked walks and, sometimes, storks in residence.

▶▶ Aubeterre *126B2*

Midway between Angoulême and Bordeaux, carved out of the white cliff from which it gets its name, lies the attractive town of Aubeterre. Theories abound concerning the exact origins of many of its more famous buildings—the breathtaking **monolithic church of St-Jean▶▶▶** and the so-called Couvent des Cordeliers—as well as the site's powers to cure madness! The river Dronne is a good spot for swimming and canoeing.

▶ Aulnay *126C3*

The beautiful Romanesque pilgrimage church of St-Pierre is set among cypresses on the edge of a small village between Poitiers and Saintes. It has outstanding stone carving on the west and south façades and the capitals inside the church (note the Indian elephants and Delilah cutting Samson's hair).

▶▶ Biarritz *126A1*

Biarritz was a small whaling port until Empress Eugenie brought Napoleon III for a six-week stay in 1854 and thereby launched the Atlantic coast's only rival to the Riviera. Her villa, later the Hôtel du Palais, has been sumptuously restored along with the casino, and the excellent **Musée de la Mer** (*Open* Jun–Sep daily; Oct–May Tue–Sun) and **Musée du Chocolat** are worth a visit. Biarritz has long had a rather shabby image but this is changing, partly due to its surfers visiting its superb beaches.

▶▶▶ Bordeaux *126B2*

A sea port 100km (62 miles) from the Atlantic, Bordeaux is France's most elegant provincial city, a creation of the Enlightenment dedicated to the civilized business of exporting fine wine. Like Paris, only a century earlier, it was rationalized with the creation of wide boulevards, public gardens and a colonnaded **Grand Theatre▶▶**. Eighteenth-century palaces line the Garonne and the place de la Bourse is a splendid gateway to the intriguing streets of **old Bordeaux▶▶**. The place du Parlement is its focus. Other sights include a vast cathedral and impressive **Musée d'Aquitaine▶▶**, covering the region's archaeology, history and culture (*Open* Tue–Sun 11–6. *Admission: free*). The rue St-Catherine and the cours Clemenceau are best for shopping. The tourist office and Maison du Vin (with tastings) are on the cours 30-Juillet near the theatre. Urbanization projects along the riverfront are underway.

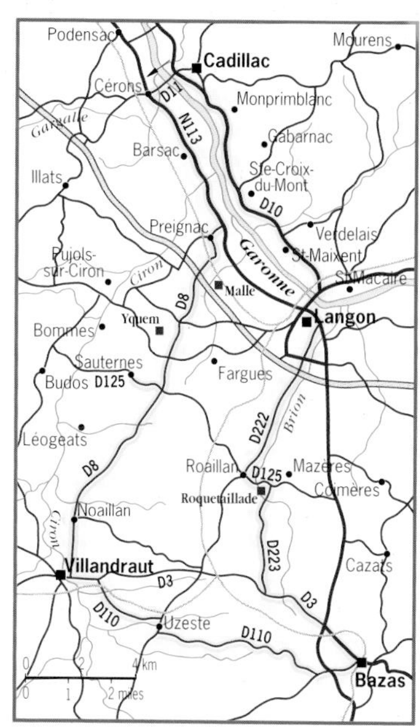

The crest of the Château d'Yquem, closed to visitors but visible from the road north of Sauternes

Drive

Entre-Deux-Mers and Sauternes

Start at Cadillac. D11 to Cérons; N113 to Barsac, Preignac.
Cadillac, an old walled village, is at the edge of the vineyards of **Entre-Deux-Mers**, about 40km (25 miles) south of the medieval town of **St-Emilion**. Cross the Garonne into pudding wine country. Near Preignac the beautiful **Château de Malle** is the best Bordeaux château to visit.

D8/125 to Sauternes.
Barsac and **Sauternes** have Maisons du Vin with tastings and wine for sale. The prestigious **Château d'Yquem** is closed to visitors, but worth admiring from the road (D116E north of Sauternes).

D8 to Villandraut; D3/110 to Uzeste; Bazas; D3/223 to Roquetaillade; D125/D222 to Langon.
Bertrand de Got, the 14th-century Pope Clement V, built a fortress at Villandraut and lies buried in the church at Uzeste. His nephew built the **Château de Roquetaillade**. The entrance ticket also covers a rural museum. Bazas has an interesting church on an arcaded square. François Mauriac's home, Malagar, at St-Maixent, is a haven of peace.

D10 to Ste-Croix-du-Mont and Cadillac.
Ste-Croix-du-Mont makes a sweet white wine modest only by Sauternes' standards. It can be tasted in caves below the church.

Wine country: Sauternes

The hinterland of the Aquitaine coast, between Bordeaux and the Basque country, is a vast triangle of pine forest, covering 6,450sq km (2,490sq miles). It was planted in the 19th century to stabilize shifting dunes and to drain a marshy heath populated only by bees, mosquitoes, sheep and shepherds who went about on stilts.

WHO LIVES HERE?
Illustrious inhabitants of Les Landes have included turn-of-the-20th-century writer François Mauriac, who described its wealthy pine forests in his many novels. Some 25,000 years earlier, the Dame de Brassempouy left her ivory image there to be unearthed in 1894 as the first female icon of prehistory (a cast of it is exhibited at St-Germain-en-Laye; the original is not on view: see page 63). More recently, former President Mitterrand and his faithful labrador enjoyed its seclusion in his forest home.

New life Logging and resin tapping, followed by coastal tourism and a modest oil industry (on and around the Lac de Parentis) transformed the life of the region.

The Landes towns are on the fringe of the forest. **Mont de Marsan** is a good place to watch a *course landaise* (a race) starring nimble *écarteurs* (literally 'dodgers') who, among other tricks, leap over charging cows. Also worth visiting is the Musée Despiau-Wlérick, with its collection of sculpture from the first half of the 20th century.

In the woods The forest itself is disconcerting, empty of spirit: no views, no flowers, little wildlife, few villages, just the smell and sight of pine trees and the piercing whine of cicadas. In small clearings there are low timber and brick farmhouses, each surrounded by a maize field, a vegetable patch and a few farm animals.

Ecomuseum The best reason to venture inland from a Côte d'Argent campsite is the Landes Ecomuseum at **Marquèze**, reached by train from Sabres. This is a fascinating all-round presentation of the pastoral life and ecology of the area in the pre-pine age, including a traditional farm. It is part of the regional park, through which runs the River Leyre, now opened up for canoeing.

At the traditional Landes village of Levignacq there is a charming 14th-century church with frescoes decorating the interior. **Luxey's** ecomuseum has an old resin distillery and by-products.

Recreating Landes life in the ecomuseum at Marquèze

Old-time travel to the Marquèze Museum in the Landes region

▶ Marais Poitevin *126B5*

This wide area of reclaimed marshland is punctuated by 'island' villages (**Marans, Chaillé**). Punts are the traditional means of transport for fishermen and can be rented with or without pilot at **Coulon. Maillezais**, with splendid abbey ruins, also has boats to rent.

▶ Pornic *126A6*

A fishing port on a rocky creek, Pornic has charm, unlike the notorious owner of its château, Gilles de Rais (Bluebeard), who gave up a military career for satanism and infanticide. There are summer ferries to **Noirmoutier**.

▶ Rochefort *126B4*

Rochefort is often overlooked by tourists who prefer to visit larger La Rochelle nearby. The historic rivalry between these two ports dates back to Rochefort's foundation in the 17th century, by Colbert, as France's largest shipyard. Be sure not to miss the reconstructed 18th-century frigate, and the **Corderie Royale**, the **Musée de la Marine▶**, 1 place le Gallissonière, Rochefort (*Open* Apr–Sep daily 10–6.30; Oct to mid-Dec, mid-Jan to Mar Tue–Sun 10–12, 2–6. *Closed* mid-Dec to mid-Jan. *Admission: moderate*) and the idiosyncratic home of author Pierre Loti.

▶▶ La Rochelle *126B4*

La Rochelle is a prosperous user-friendly city: It was the first city in France to place free bicycles at the disposal of visitors. In the old port, twin towers still guard the narrow port entrance. The nearby **Tour de la Lanterne▶** gives good views. The old central area has kept its houses (rue des Merciers, rue de l'Escale), mostly 16th- and 17th-century. The **Musée de Nouveau Monde▶▶**, 10 rue Fleuriau (*Open* Wed–Sat, Mon 10.30–12.30, 1.30–6, Sun 3–6. *Admission: moderate*) relates La Rochelle's trading history; the **l'Aquarium▶▶▶**, Port des Minimes, 17000 La Rochelle (*Open* Apr–Jun, Sep daily 9–8; Jul, Aug 9–11; Oct–Mar 10–8. *Admission: expensive*) is excellent. Plentiful local beaches include **Châtelaillon▶**.

▶▶ Saintes *126B4*

An ancient town on one of the main pilgrimage routes (and the autoroute) to Spain, red-brick Saintes is a good base for visiting the Romanesque churches along here. St-Eutrope itself is but a fragment of a former great pilgrimage church, with the fourth-century martyred bishop's tomb in its beautiful crypt. Roman vestiges remain.

APERITIF AND DIGESTIF

Unique blends of twice-distilled eau-de-vie made from white grapes grown in the confusingly named Grande and Petite Champagne areas around Cognac make up one of the world's most prestigious *digestifs*. If your nose doesn't lead you to one of the distilleries in the old part of Cognac, your eyes will spot the black stains caused by alcohol evaporation from the distilleries' oak barrels, fondly known as the 'angels' share'. For a fascinating *dégustation*-cum-history tour, head for the Château des Valois. Throughout the Charente you will find the *aperitif* known as *pineau*, made from grape juice and cognac.

HIT THE ISLANDS

Hugely popular summer holiday resorts, the offshore islands of Ré, Noirmoutier and Oléron are all accessible by toll bridge from the mainland. **Ré▶▶▶** is the most interesting, with vineyards, farms, white-washed villages and the fortified port of St-Martin. Noirmoutier mostly consists of salt-pans, but the old village has pine woods and a good beach at hand; Oléron has vast oyster parks off the old port of Château d'Oléron. From Aix (ferries from Fouras and Boyardville on Oléron) Napoleon left France in 1815; his house displays Imperial memorabilia. Yeu (ferries from Fromentine and La Fosse, on Noirmoutier) is an island of granite cliffs, lobster pots and tuna fishing. Marshal Pétain was imprisoned there from 1945 until his death in 1951.

The Bordeaux vineyard area is the most productive fine wine district in the world. The five main districts are Médoc (red), Sauternes (sweet white) and Graves (white) on the left banks of the Garonne; and St-Emilion and Pomerol (red) on the right bank of the Dordogne. Less prestigious wines (with exceptions) are produced between the rivers (Entre-Deux-Mers) and on the eastern side of the Gironde (including Côtes de Blaye and Côtes de Bourg).

HIT THE BOTTLE
Signs marked *dégustation, visite des chais* or *vente directe* mean wine-sampling and potential purchasing. 1988, 1989 and 1990 were excellent Bordeaux vintages; 1991, 1992, 1993, 1994 less so. 1995 just missed being the year of the century due to rain but was still a good year, as was 2005.

Bordeaux vineyards: a treat for the eye as well as for the palate

Divisions and ranks Each region is divided into many *appellations* (**Médoc, Haut-Médoc** and **St-Emilion** being the most famous for red wine). Within the *appellations* village names may be added, Pauilliac and St-Julien for example in AC Haut-Médoc. The finest Médoc châteaux were ranked into five categories of *crus classés* in 1855 (from *premier* to *cinquième*); there have been only minor changes and additions since.

This system of classification varies slightly from region to region, and is not an infallible guide to quality; many wines in the lower *crus classés* are often as good. The *crus bourgeois* are good value and, of the *appellations*, **St-Estèphe** and **Haut-Médoc** are good value and worth seeking out.

Along the D2 from **Bordeaux** to **St-Vivien-de-Médoc** are some of the most prestigious wine châteaux in the world: **Margaux**, **Latour** (south of Pauillac), **Mouton-Rothschild** and **Lafite** (north of Pauillac). Not all are open to the public.

Interesting châteaux in the Médoc are:

Château Batailley near Pauillac: 18th-century château; by appointment (tel: 05 56 59 01 13).

Château d'Issan near Margaux: 17th-century moated château; by appointment (tel: 05 57 88 35 91).

Château Loudenne near St-Yzans: wine museum; by appointment (tel: 05 56 73 17 80).

Château Margaux: by appointment; closed August and harvest time (tel: 05 57 88 83 83).

Château Mouton-Rothschild near Pauillac: wine museum; by appointment (tel: 05 56 73 21 29).

There are Maisons du Vin (information offices) at **Margaux**, **Moulis**, **St-Estèphe**, **Bordeaux** and **Pauillac.** Visit www.bordeaux.com for the official wine site.

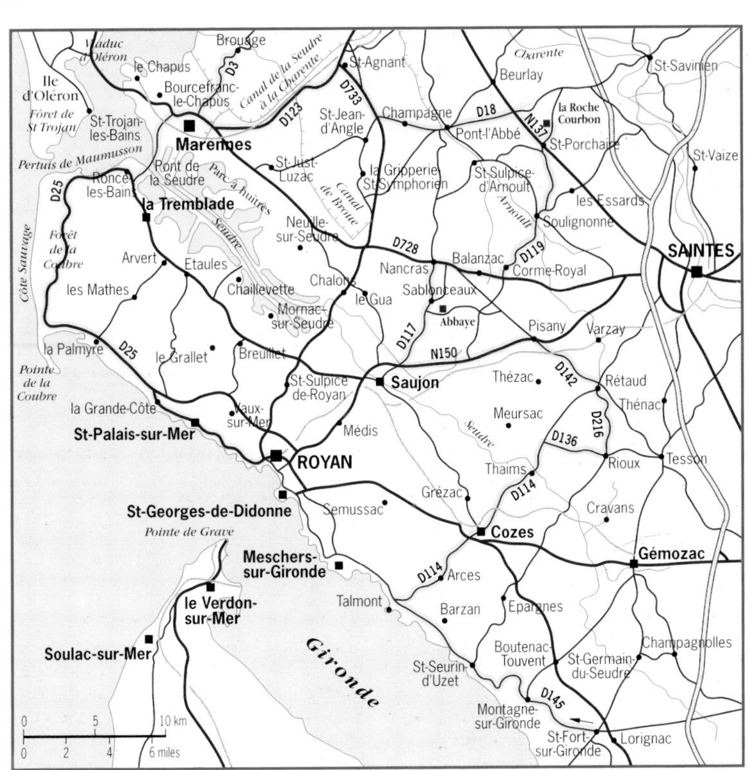

Drive

Churches, beaches and the Gironde Estuary

Start at St-Fort-sur-Gironde.
St-Fort is 50km (31 miles) north of Blaye, Louis XIV's key defensive position on the Gironde. In the vineyards north of Blaye there are roadside invitations to taste and buy *pineau* (a grape juice and cognac aperitif). **St-Fort** and nearby **Talmont** have interesting churches.

D114/136 to Rioux; D216 to Rétaud; D142/N150/D117 to Sablonceaux; D117/728 to Corme-Royal; D119 to St-Porchaire; D122 to La Roche Courbon and back.
Rioux and **Rétaud** are the highlights of the inland church tour, also featuring Sablonceaux Abbey and Corme-Royal. **La Roche Courbon** is a richly decorated moated château set in lovely gardens.

N137/D18/D7/D123 to Marennes; D3 to Brouage and back; D25 to Ronce-les-Bains and Royan.
Brouage was a 17th-century salt port and mighty royal fortress, but the sea has retreated and left a sleepy village. Tablets commemorate Champlain, the locally born founder of Québec, and the affair of Louis XIV and Marie Mancini, who came to Brouage after the king chose a Spanish princess instead. At the mouth of the Seudre, **Bourcefranc-le-Chapus** and **Marennes** are the best places for local oysters. There are beaches and campsites along the wooded Grande Côte and Côte Sauvage in the direction of Royan, but bathing is often hazardous. **Royan** is a big resort that has been developed in bleakest post-war functional style, redeemed only by its shallow beach and its proximity to the excellent La Palmyre zoo.

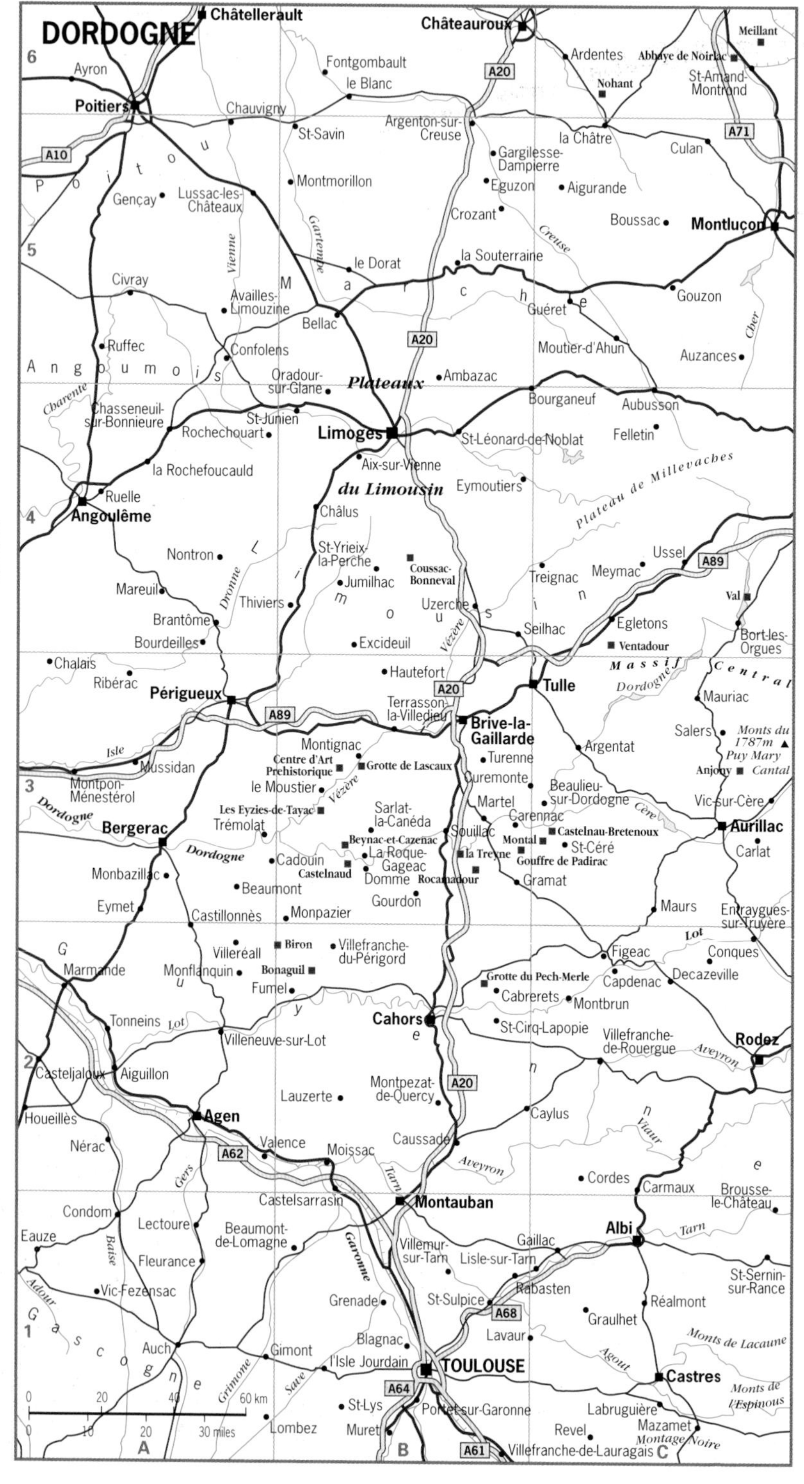

DORDOGNE
Châtellerault
Châteauroux
Meillant
Ardentes
Abbaye de Noirlac
Nohant
St-Amand-Montrond
Fontgombault
le Blanc
A20
Ayron
Poitiers
Chauvigny
St-Savin
Argenton-sur-Creuse
la Châtre
A71
Culan
A10
Gargilesse-Dampierre
Eguzon
Aigurande
Poitou
Gençay
Lussac-les-Châteaux
Montmorillon
Crozant
Boussac
Montluçon
Vienne
Gartempe
Creuse
le Dorat
la Souterraine
Civray
Availles-Limouzine
Marche
Guéret
Gouzon
Bellac
Ruffec
Confolens
Moutier-d'Ahun
Auzances
Cher
Angoumois
Oradour-sur-Glane
Plateaux
Ambazac
Charente
Chasseneuil-sur-Bonnieure
St-Junien
Bourganeuf
Aubusson
Rochechouart
Limoges
St-Léonard-de-Noblat
Felletin
la Rochefoucauld
Aix-sur-Vienne
Eymoutiers
Plateau de Millevaches
du Limousin
Ruelle
Angoulême
Châlus
Nontron
St-Yrieix-la-Perche
Coussac-Bonneval
Ussel
Treignac
Meymac
A89
Mareuil
Jumilhac
Dronne
Limousin
Val
Thiviers
Uzerche
Brantôme
Egletons
Bort-les-Orgues
Bourdeilles
Excideuil
Vézère
Seilhac
Ventadour
Chalais
Hautefort
Massif Central
Ribérac
Périgueux
Tulle
Dordogne
Mauriac
Terrasson-la-Villedieu
Brive-la-Gaillarde
Salers
Monts du Cantal
1787m
Puy Mary
Montignac
Isle
Centre d'Art Préhistorique
Grotte de Lascaux
Turenne
Argentat
Anjony
Mussidan
Curemonte
Montpon-Ménestérol
le Moustier
Beaulieu-sur-Dordogne
Martel
Cère
Vic-sur-Cère
Les Eyzies-de-Tayac
Sarlat-la-Canéda
Carennac
Bergerac
Trémolat
Souillac
Castelnau-Bretenoux
Aurillac
Beynac-et-Cazenac
Montal
St-Céré
Carlat
La Roque-Gageac
la Treyne
Gouffre de Padirac
Cadouin
Castelnaud
Domme
Rocamadour
Monbazillac
Gramat
Beaumont
Eymet
Gourdon
Maurs
Entraygues-sur-Truyère
Castillonnès
Monpazier
Lot
Biron
Villefranche-du-Périgord
Villeréall
Figeac
Conques
Marmande
Monflanquin
Bonaguil
Grotte du Pech-Merle
Capdenac
Decazeville
Fumel
Cabrerets
Montbrun
Guyenne
Tonneins
Cahors
St-Cirq-Lapopie
Villefranche-de-Rouergue
Rodez
Villeneuve-sur-Lot
Aveyron
Casteljaloux
Aiguillon
Montpezat-de-Quercy
Lauzerte
Caylus
Houeillès
Agen
Viaur
Nérac
Valence
Caussade
Moissac
A62
Gers
Tarn
Cordes
Carmaux
Brousse-le-Château
Castelsarrasin
Montauban
Condom
Lectoure
Beaumont-de-Lomagne
Albi
Eauze
Garonne
Villemur-sur-Tarn
Gaillac
Baïse
Fleurance
Lisle-sur-Tarn
St-Sernin-sur-Rance
Vic-Fezensac
Rabastens
Adour
Grenade
St-Sulpice
Réalmont
A68
Graulhet
Gascogne
Blagnac
Lavaur
Monts de Lacaune
Auch
Gimont
Agout
l'Isle Jourdain
TOULOUSE
Castres
Grimone
Save
A64
Monts de l'Espinouse
St-Lys
Portet-sur-Garonne
Labruguière
Mazamet
Lombez
Muret
Revel
Montagne Noire
A61
Villefranche-de-Lauragais
0 20 40 60 km
0 10 20 30 miles
A
B
C
1
2
3
4
5
6

Bergerac, on the banks of the Dordogne River

THE DORDOGNE is a river flowing from the Massif Central to join the Gironde at Bordeaux, and an administrative *département* that includes a section of this river and an area to the north fondly known to the French as Périgord—home of the truffle, the walnut and the bloated liver of force-fed geese. It is also the region of Europe that has yielded most to students of prehistory; the area is uniquely rich in cave paintings.

To its many visitors, the Dordogne embraces a much larger and more diffuse area of southwest France, stretching from the undulating farmland of Limousin to the bleak limestone *causses* of Quercy and the orchards of the Lot Valley. It signifies French country life at its most delightful: old villages of golden stone with rust-hued roofs, fortress ruins on wooded river banks, markets groaning under the weight of fresh local produce, and small-scale cultivation. The typical Dordogne farmer has a handful of animals, an area of maize to feed them, fruit trees and walnuts and a small vineyard. Less idyllic, but highly significant to France's economy, are the hydroelectric power installations along the rivers.

So irresistible is the Dordogne's charm that many visitors have made it a second home, in some cases forming 95 per cent of the population. Foreign money has pushed prices up and the hunt for a cheap French ruin has moved on, but some of the prettiest villages now contain large colonies of expatriates, particularly British and Dutch. The most popular section of the Dordogne Valley, between **Sarlat** and **Trémolat**, may now seem too neatly restored, with too many foreign voices.

PROTECT AND SURVIVE In the Middle Ages the land between the Lot and Dordogne valleys was a border zone between French territory and English-controlled Aquitaine. As well as isolated fortresses commanding the river valleys, the rival factions built fortified towns (*bastides*). Some of these survive, little changed.

▶▶▶ **REGION HIGHLIGHTS**

TOULOUSE-LAUTREC
Count Henri Marie Raymond de Toulouse-Lautrec was born in Albi in 1864. At the age of 14, he fell and suffered the first of two leg injuries which contributed to his deformity. Later Lautrec studied in Paris, where he immersed himself in the low life depicted in his paintings, drawings and posters. His childhood home, Château du Bosc (48km/30 miles northeast of Albi, at Naucelle), has daily tours.

ARMAGNAC
The Romans brought vines to Gascony, the Arabs brought the alambic and the Celts imported casks; thus began Armagnac, the world's oldest *eau-de-vie*. Produced in only three areas of Gascony, it is matured for up to 30 years before blending according to 'recipes' secretly guarded by local distillers.

For 500 years Aubusson has been synonymous with exquisite tapestry, and remains so today. It still produces carpets and wall-hangings; the tapestry museum shows weaving methods

▶ Agen *134A2*

Succulent *pruneaux d'Agen*, stuffed with marzipan or marinated in cognac, are in a league of their own. This market town has a cluster of narrow streets in its old quarter, a 12th-century **cathedral▶▶** and an aqueduct. The **Musée Municipale des Beaux Arts**, place du Dr Esquirol (*Open* Wed–Mon 10–6; 10–5 in winter. *Closed* public holidays. *Admission: inexpensive*), occupies four Renaissance town houses. It has an impressive collection of 19th-century art and a Greek marble Venus unearthed by a local farmer in 1876. See also the bastide of **Puymirol▶▶**.

▶▶ Albi *134C1*

This big, brick-red town beside the Tarn is dominated by its warlike Gothic cathedral. Built with funds seized from heretics or alleged *pénitents*, it formed a fortress in a time of inquisition, torture and simmering popular resistance. Instead of stained glass to illuminate the faithful, **Ste-Cecile▶▶▶** has narrow apertures like arrow slits. Only the delicate 15th-century doorway lightens the effect. Inside, gruesome Last Judgement scenes adorn the west wall. The bishop's palace (Palais de la Berbie) has the **Musée Toulouse Lautrec ▶▶▶**, Palais de la Berbie, place Ste-Cecile, 81000 Albi (*Open* Nov–Feb Wed–Mon 10–12, 2–5; Mar, Oct Wed–Mon 10–12, 2–5.30; Apr, May Sep daily 10–12, 2–6; Jul, Aug daily 9–6. *Admission: moderate*). Formal gardens overlook a river spanned by an 11th-century bridge.

▶ Argentat *134C3*

The sleepy old village of **Argentat** straddles the Dordogne just before it flows into a series of reservoirs among wooded gorges. Upstream is the Argentat dam and a hydroelectric power station. The left (south) bank is by far the prettier side, where a terrace of yellow-fronted, *lauze*-tiled houses with chestnut balconies hangs over the water. Nearby are the ruins of the Tours de Merle.

▶ Aubusson *134C4*

The tapestry town of Aubusson nestles in the **Creuse Valley▶▶** and galleries and workshops can be visited all over. The **Musée Départemental de la Tapisserie** (*Open* Sep–Jun Wed–Mon 9.30–12, 2–6; Jul, Aug Wed–Mon 10–6, Tue 2–6. *Admission: moderate*) illustrates 500 years of weaving, including ultramodern abstracts, and the **Maison du Tapissier** contains 17th- to 19th-century tapestries and a reconstructed workshop. During the summer the Hôtel de Ville holds regular exhibitions.

During the Middle Ages, the English fought for centuries to gain control of this part of France. Countless reminders of this turbulent period can be seen on hilltops and strategic vantage points throughout the region, in castles, fortified churches and bastide towns (see panel, page 139).

War and peace Some grand châteaux date from, or were rebuilt during, later, less warlike centuries, and more closely resemble the pleasure palaces of the Loire. But the typical castle architecture of the Dordogne is unmistakably military. Grim fortresses glare at each other from either side of the river—English on one bank, French on the other—almost close enough to hurl insults. Much of the damage they have suffered dates not from the Hundred Years' War but from the wars between Catholics and Protestants during the 16th century. Some castles have been restored, and are used as private residences, hotels or wineries. Others are open to the public; many of these can be visited only on lengthy guided tours (in French).

Above: Bonaguil castle; below: Medieval siege warfare is explained in Castelnaud's military museum

Beynac-et-Cazenac One of the Dordogne's most spectacular and memorable fortresses towers above a huddled village on a sheer cliff commanding a beautiful stretch of the Dordogne. The keep dates from the 13th century; the main building from the 14th.

Biron A massive and intimidating château perched on a volcanic crag, Biron has a huge view of surrounding countryside. The buildings date from the 12th century, gradually mellowing in more gracious times.

Bonaguil One of the best surviving examples of late 15th- and early 16th-century military architecture. The cruel Berenger de Roquefeuil insisted on making his castle impregnable, even though he outlived the age when this was necessary.

Castelnaud Beynac's opposite number on the English (south) bank has almost equally splendid views. It houses an impressive museum devoted to the military history of the Middle Ages, and includes weapons and reproductions of fearsome bombardment machines in its collection.

Coussac-Bonneval This 14th-century castle has machicolated pepperpot towers and contains fine furnishings, tapestries and woodwork associated with Achmet-Pasha, the eccentric mercenary who was born here (*Open* Jun–Sep, afternoons only).

Montbrun Dating from the 13th century, this lovely moated castle was reconstructed in the 15th century. It was besieged unsuccessfully by Richard the Lionheart. (The castle is private.)

PUFFERS
Tobacco first appeared in France in 1560. Powdered into snuff, it was recommended by the Portuguese ambassador as a cure for Catherine de Médicis' migraines. Louis XIII first taxed, then outlawed the habit, but the nation was hooked. And so it remains. In spring and summer the dark leaves fill plots around the valleys of Bergerac and the Lot-et-Garonne. Later they are dried before being dispatched to the newly privatized *Régie Nationale des Tabacs* for processing into that Gallic aroma.

▶ Beaulieu-sur-Dordogne *134C3*

This waterfront market town has as appealing a setting as its name suggests, and among its older streets are several well-preserved mansions. Its great glory, however, is the Benedictine **church of St-Pierre▶▶**, best known for its elaborate south portal, carved in 1125. Damaged in parts, this vigorous sculpture is still one of the region's best examples of Romanesque art. A *Last Judgement* takes up the tympanum. The old monastery buildings can be seen from place des Pères; the Chapelle des Pénitents from the riverside.

▶ Bergerac *134A3*

Though now encased in suburbs of little interest, Bergerac's older quarter repays exploration. It is one of the Dordogne's largest towns, a former capital of Périgord, and is an important commercial and agricultural gateway to the Médoc plains. Bergerac's own wines are no mean rivals to the products of nearby towns downstream, the most celebrated being the sweet dessert wine of Monbazillac, to the south.

Trading activities Bergerac always had strong Protestant connections from its Huguenot community and its geographical and trade associations with Britain and the Low Countries, and it was much battered in the religious conflict that swept through France. Although Bergerac lost political status to Périgueux, the town made a canny entrepreneurial living through the centuries from river-borne trade. Modern preoccupations are as diverse as tobacco (a principal local cash-crop) and nitro-cellulose, used in paint and plastics. Rostand's hero Cyrano (he of the unfortunate nose) has only tenuous links with the town, but has been enthusiastically adopted as a citizen worthy of a statue.

What to see Bergerac's main sights and most picturesque buildings lie among the narrow streets north of the historic port area. The **Cloître des Récollets** is a lovely half-timbered convent where the Regional Wine

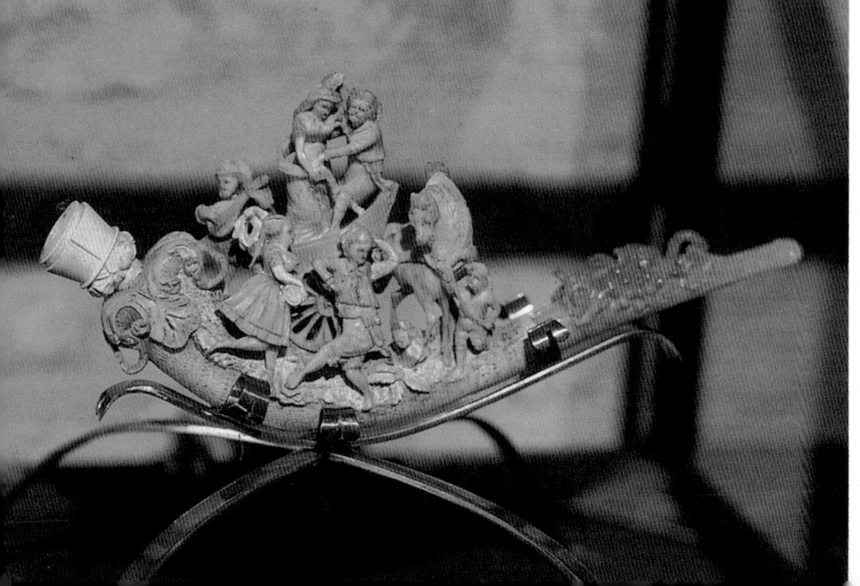

A cigar-holder becomes a work of art at Bergerac's Musée du Tabac

Council meets annually to deliberate the merits of the *vendange*. The museum contains an interesting section on the river and port. The turreted 15th-century Maison Peyrarède houses the intriguing **Musée de Tabac▶**, place du Feu (*Open* Tue–Fri 10–12, 2–6, Sat 10–12, 2–5, Sun 2.30–6.30. *Closed* Sat, Sun mid-Nov to mid-Mar). The Gothic church of Notre-Dame contains several valuable paintings and tapestries.

▶ **Brantôme** see page 147

▶ Cadouin *134A3*

This large village on the edge of the Besside Forest was once an important place of pilgrimage. Its Cistercian abbey **Cloitre et Musée du Suaire▶▶** (*Open* (church) daily 8.30–7; (museum) Jul, Aug 10–12.30, 1.30–7; Sep–Jun daily 10–noon, 2–5. *Admission: moderate*), founded in 1115, stood on the route to the Spanish shrine of Santiago de Compostela. During the Middle Ages, kings and princes halted here to pay homage to its Holy Shroud, later discredited as an 11th-century Egyptian textile. Inside, the church is dark, but the cloisters are beautifully carved. Bikers should head for the Musée du Vélocipède.

▶▶ Cahors *134B2*

Encircled by a natural moat, a *cingle* of the Lot, Cahors was a worthy prize to the English, who besieged it during the Hundred Years' War. They gazed at it without attacking, and the impregnable town was eventually ceded by treaty in 1360, to the great disgust of its inhabitants. The old town still bristles with ramparts, battlements, barbicans, fortified towers and no fewer than 280 ornate doorways (12th to 19th century). Much more interesting, though, is the unique 14th-century **Valentré Bridge▶▶▶** (the only one of three still standing), its curious proportions emphasized by three pointed towers from which unfriendly missiles could be directed at intruders.

Local produce Within this pleasant market town, many shops display tempting local produce, particularly supplies of the robust local 'black wine'. The narrow streets leading from the main square to the river ramparts make a fascinating area for unscheduled wandering. Worth seeing are the **Maison de Roaldès** (Henry IV's Mansion) and the **Cathedral of St-Etienne▶**, with Byzantine domes in Périgord style, a fine carved north doorway and interior frescos.

▶ Carennac *134B3*

Carennac is one of the Dordogne's most charming and peaceful villages, where medieval and Renaissance houses overlook an island in the river, and orchards of greengages flourish. François de Salignac (Fénélon) wrote his masterpiece *Télémaque* here while he was Prior in the 18th century. Not to be missed is the splendid Romanesque doorway of St-Pierre, where *Christ in Majesty* occupies the tympanum, encircled in a strange oval halo known as a *mandorla*.

▶ **Collonges-la-Rouge** see page 151

BASTIDES

Southeast of Bergerac, the border country of the Hundred Years' War is studded with *bastide* towns. Their purpose was military: As well as massive fortress garrisons, both the English and the French created a permanent civilian guard. Built on a grid pattern, often with an arcaded market square and fortified church tower as a refuge during times of siege, the *bastide* towns had streets too narrow for a mounted knight to wield weapons effectively. Best of the *bastide* towns are Monpazier, Monflanquin, Villeréal, Villefranche-du-Périgord, Beaumont and Eymet. Sometimes over-restored, several of these towns now verge on the chic.

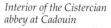

Interior of the Cistercian abbey at Cadouin

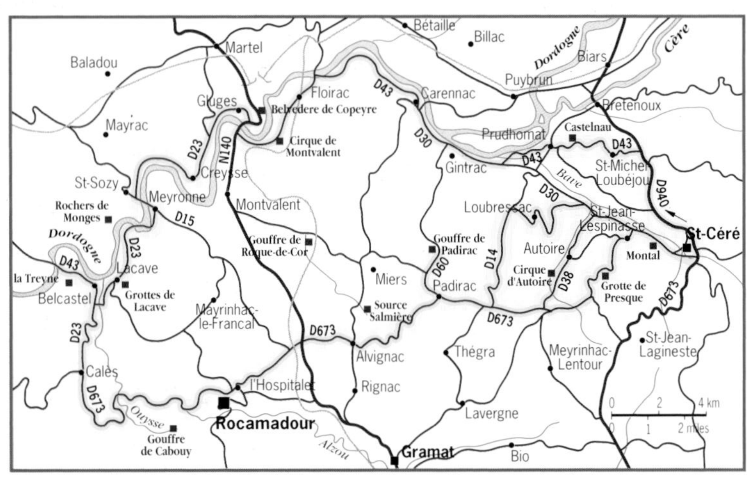

Drive

River valley and open land

Start at St-Céré.
St-Laurent castle in St-Céré was the home of Jean Lurçat, the great tapestry designer of the 1930s. His work is displayed in the Casino.

D940 and D43 to Castelnau.
One of Quercy's most formidable castles is **Castelnau**. This vast 12th- and 13th-century fortified castle was saved from ruin by an opera singer whose sumptuous furniture and lapidary collection can be seen.

D43 and D30 to Carennac; D43 to Cirque de Montvalent and N140 to Gluges; D43 and D23 to Creysse and D114, D15 to Meyronne.
The River Dordogne curves through lush meadows dotted with villages. Most strikingly set is **Gluges**, at the foot of sheer cliffs; **Creysse** and **Meyronne** have castle remains.

D23 south to Grottes de Lacave.
At **Lacave**, a lift and underground railway lead to limestone caverns.

D23 to Belcastel; D43 to la Treyne.
The terrace of **Belcastel**'s mighty château offers a splendid panorama of a wooded river-bend. A short way west is the **Château de la Treyne**, part 14th-century. It is now a hotel.

D23, D673, D90 to Gouffre de Padirac.
The **Gouffre de Padirac** (*Open* Apr–Jun, Sep daily 9–12, 2–6; Jul 9–6; Aug 8.30–6.30; Oct, Nov 10–12, 2–5. *Closed* Dec–Mar. *Admission: expensive*) is a giant sinkhole imbued with satanic associations and in season spoiled by crowds. A lift descends the fern-lined walls; a boat tours the caves.

Divert from D673 on to D14 and D118 to Loubressac or D38 to Autoire; then join D30 and D673.
Loubressac is a hilltop bastide, with a vast view from its 15th-century château. A long-distance footpath, the GR652 (480), leads through Loubressac to **Autoire**, where farmhouses have been snapped up as second homes. Nearby is a beauty spot, the **Cirque d'Autoire**.

D673 to Montal and St-Céré.
The romantic Renaissance château of **Montal** was built by Jeanne de Balsac d'Entraygues as she waited for her son Robert to return from the wars in Italy. He never did, and *Plus d'Espoir* ('Hope No More') is carved beneath one of the château windows. Inside, the Renaissance staircase is encrusted with sea monsters and shells, testifying to the dedication of Maurice Fenaille, a philanthropic historian who restored the château and later gave it to the state.

►► Creuse, Vallée de la *134C5*

The River Creuse rises on the Millevaches Plateau, on the granite foothills of the Massif Central. Dozens of small streams eventually form this picturesque waterway, beloved by George Sand, who set several of her novels here. From its infant course past the tapestry towns of **Aubusson** and **Felletin**, the river flows through a landscape of gorges, reservoir lakes and farmland. Landmarks include the great fortress of **Crozant**, the lovely village of **Gargilesse►►** and the giant dam at **Eguzon**, behind which stretches the serpentine **Chambon Lake**. At **Fontgombault►** there is an abbey founded by the hermit Gombault, which has a tall choir and decorated capitals. The Benedictine order has returned (it was suppressed in 1714) and goats' cheese is sold in the outbuildings.

► Culan *134C5*

A massive fortress (*Open* Jul, Aug daily 10–8) clings to the overgrown rocks overlooking the Arnon Gorges. Among many illustrious visitors, the castle numbers Joan of Arc, sheltering here after Orléans, and Louis XI, and it contains a collection of furniture and tapestries, as well as a 'neo-medieval' garden.

►► Domme *134B3*

Few fail to be impressed by Domme's picturesque location on a rocky cliff high above the Dordogne. A *bastide* town, its hilly setting proved too difficult for the classic grid-patterned rectangle, and getting around Domme, particularly in high season, is best accomplished on foot. In the main square is a covered market hall; below it is an entrance to some small stalactite caves, once used as a refuge for the townsfolk. Animal bones found in the caves are on display at the **museum►** in the château, and a regional museum exhibits traditional crafts and objets d'art. From the Belvedere de la Barre there are stupendous views of the river looping through fields far below. Most striking of the surviving gateways is the Porte des Tours, whose burly round towers once imprisoned many hapless Knights Templar, falsely accused of heresy and perversion by Philip the Fair.

►► Hautefort, Château de *134B3*

24390 Hautefort (Open Apr, May daily 10–12.30, 2–6.30; Jun–Sep 9.30–7; Feb, Mar, Oct, Nov Sat, Sun 2–6. Admission: expensive)

The formidable silhouette of Hautefort Château, overlord of the Ans country from the 14th century, is a striking feature of the Périgord Blanc. Hautefort has been rebuilt several times, most recently after a disastrous fire in 1968, and is now restored to its largely 17th-century grandeur. The moat is dry and the drawbridge is fixed.

Domme's magnificent setting high above the Dordogne defeated the traditional geometric bastide plan

Basket-weaving in Domme

CUREMONTE

You really do feel in a time warp when walking the two main streets of this extraordinary village, dominated by three castles in varying states of repair. Don't be put off by 'ye olde' shop fronts down the far end (intentionally left in situ from the last film set); the old ladies knotting bunches of garlic on their doorsteps, in the shadow of the castle, are for real, and the garlic is for sale!

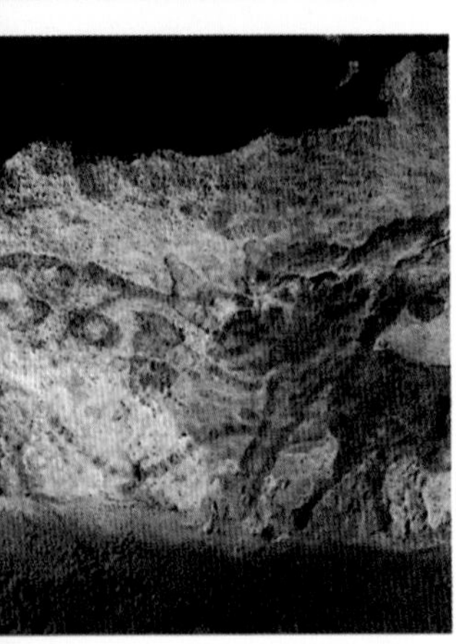

The limestone caverns of the Massif Central are famous for their beautiful formations; those in the Dordogne are better known for prehistoric animal paintings. The Périgord region has been inhabited by man since palaeolithic times: The earliest skeletal traces of Neanderthal type were found at Le Moustier near Les Eyzies-de-Tayac in 1909. Many other remains (tools, tombs, bones, weapons, ornaments) have been unearthed, but by far the most exciting discovery occurred in 1940, when some boys out rabbiting with a dog stumbled by chance upon the cave of Lascaux, one of Europe's most important and most beautiful prehistoric finds.

The Museum of Prehistory, set into the rock face at Les Eyzies-de-Tayac

The paintings at Lascaux and other caves in the Dordogne are probably between 12,000 and 20,000 years old, and were executed by Cro-Magnon man, a taller, vastly more sophisticated creature than the earliest flint wielders. The most interesting prehistoric sites in the Dordogne lie between **Les Eyzies** and **Montignac** in the Vézère Valley, and near Cabrerets on the Lot, but there are numerous lesser caves all over the region with animal drawings or stalagmites and stalactites. The best museums and exhibitions of prehistory are at **Les Eyzies**, **Périgueux**, **Sarlat** and **Le Thot.** Some sites become very crowded; advance booking is advisable.

Damaging breath Lascaux itself was thronged with curious visitors from the end of World War II, and alarmed officials soon realized that just two decades of warm, carbon dioxide-exhaling tourists had done more damage to the paintings than 17,000 years of lying undisturbed. A film of greenish micro-organisms was creeping steadily across the walls. Quickly, the original cave was closed to all but a handful of privileged researchers. Meanwhile a replica cave, perfect down to every last contour, with all the dyes synthesized from the same ingredients, was created nearby, **Lascaux II**. To visit this cave you must reserve tickets in advance at the tourist office in **Montignac**, year-round, or at the site, Nov–Mar (tel: 05 53 51 95 03. *Open* Feb, Mar, Oct–Dec Tue–Sun 10–12.30, 2–5.30; Apr–Jun, Sep daily 9.30—6.30; Jul, Aug daily 9–8. *Closed* Jan. Very popular, with limited capacity. A ticket bought in the morning will usually ensure a visit the same day. *Admission: expensive*). It is awe-inspiring to emerge from the air-lock system amid a herd of galloping bison, deer and horses in brilliant shades of red, ochre and black.

At **Le Thot**, 7km (4 miles) southwest, a prehistory exhibition (tel: 05 53 51 95 03) houses displays of cave art, audio-visual shows, and in the surrounding park wild animals roam among life-size animated mammoths.

Les Eyzies-de-Tayac revels in its soubriquet 'Cradle of Prehistory' because of the prehistoric riches discovered in the immediate surroundings. The **Musée National de Préhistoire▶▶**, 24620 Les Eyzies-de-Tayac (*Open* Jul, Aug daily 9.30–6.30; Sep–Jun Wed–Mon 9.30–12.30, 2.30–5.30. *Admission: moderate*), housed in a 13th-century fortress halfway up a rock face, is worth a visit. Just outside the town is the **Grotte de Font-de-Gaume▶▶▶**, where the highly sophisticated animal drawings are originals, not copies. Numbers of visitors are restricted, so book early in the morning (tel: 05 53 06 86 00. *Open* mid-May to mid-Sep Sun–Fri 9.30–5.30; mid-Sep to mid-May Sun–Fri 9.30–12.30).

Smaller caves with animal drawings include the **Grotte des Combarelles▶** and the **Abri du Cap Blanc**, to the east. The **Roque-St-Christophe▶▶** is a series of rock galleries in a cliff where traces of troglodytes have been found. **La Madeleine** is an excavated Magdalenian village with cave dwellings. In the caves at **Rouffignac (les grottes)▶▶** (*Open* Apr–Jun, Sep–Nov daily 10–11.30, 2–5; Jul, Aug 9–11.30, 2–6. *Closed* Dec–Mar. *Admission: moderate*) visitors take an electric train through 4km (2.5 miles) of galleries decorated with hundreds of animal engravings.

On a lighter note, the Disney-like **Préhistoparc** presents an everyday story of cave people. Farther south, above the River Célé, a tributary of the River Lot, are the **Grottes de Pech-Merle▶▶**, at Cabrerets

PREHISTO-INDUSTRY
'Prehistoric tourism' is big business in the Périgord: More than 300,000 tourists visit Lascaux II alone every year. Many sites are at saturation point, others forbid access altogether and several other facsimilies are under discussion. But the flow continues and visiting out of season is recommended to try to avoid the crowds.

Pictures from another age: painting of a horse at Lascaux II—not an original but a faithful replica

(tel: 05 65 31 27 05. *Open* Apr–Oct 9.30–12, 1–5.30; maximum 700 visitors so make a reservation. *Admission: expensive*). Here there is a huge series of caverns containing limestone formations, as well as some exquisite animal paintings, silhouetted handprints and a frieze of bison and mammoths. Among these curiosities are the mudprints of prehistoric feet dating back some 15,000 years. The chambers are next to a heavily didactic museum.

The porcelain industry in Limoges took off with the discovery of high-quality kaolin (china clay) at St-Yrieux in 1768; today Limoges produces about half of France's porcelain, mostly tableware

LIMOGES ENAMEL
The process of firing enamel dates back to the sixth century, but it developed to a much more sophisticated art in Limoges during the 12th century with the invention of the *champlevé* technique: successive coats of enamel are spread on engraved copper, each fired at decreasing temperatures, resulting in a deep, jewel-like glow. Painted enamels are still produced at Limoges.

►►► **Lascaux** see page 142

►► **Les Eyzies** see page 143

► Limoges — *134B4*

The ancient crafts of enamel firing and porcelain-making still figure largely in Limoges' economy, but the old town has now spread along both banks of the Vienne. The most interesting part is the **Quartier de la Boucherie►►**, a web of narrow alleys lined with half-timbered houses. Don't miss the Cathedral of St-Etienne in ambitious Gothic style. Two excellent museums chart the history of Limoges's major industries: the **Musée National Adrien-Dubouché►►**, place Winston Churchill (*Open* Sep–Jun Wed–Mon 10–12.30, 2–5.40; Jul, Aug Wed–Mon 10–5.40. *Admission: moderate*), is devoted to the history of ceramics; the Musée Municipal contains a splendid collection of Limousin enamels.

►► Martel — *134B3*

This quiet truffle town on Quercy limestone is rich in history and fascinating to explore. The town is named after Charlemagne's grandfather, Charles Martel, who defeated the Saracens in the eighth century and built a church here. Streets full of ancient mansions stretch past the sturdy fortified church of St-Maur, the Mirepoises Cloisters and the Maison Fabri.

►► Moissac — *134B2*

The modern town of Moissac is unprepossessing, but the reason to visit it is the ancient abbey church of **St-Pierre►►** on the right bank of the Tarn. It has suffered many vicissitudes since its Benedictine foundation in the seventh century, but still has a remarkable Romanesque south doorway depicting St. John's Vision of the Apocalypse. The ornately carved capitals in the cloisters are among the best in France.

► Monbazillac, Château de — *134A3*

From the lovely hilltop château with its massive pepper-pot towers, well-combed vineyards stretch as far as you can see. The luscious white wine for which Monbazillac is famous is said by some to be sweeter and richer than Sauternes. The château dates from about 1550. Today it is looked after by a wine co-operative and houses a tasting area, restaurant and shop.

► Montauban — *134B1*

Modern suburbs do little for this pink brick bastide on the rich plains of the Garonne and Tarn, but its historical and artistic associations are impressive. A Protestant stronghold, Montauban resisted Louis XIII's besieging troops for more than three months in 1621. The picturesque quarter surrounds the 17th-century arcaded place Nationale, where rose-hued houses are linked by angled porticoes. The best thing in town is the **Musée Ingres►►**, Palais Episcopal (*Open* Jul, Aug daily 10–6; Sep–Jun Tue–Sat 10–12, 2–6, Sun 2–6. *Admission: moderate*), in the bishop's palace near the river, where the 19th-century artist's work is displayed; and the best event is the annual jazz festival in July.

History and peacefulness in the village of Martel

▶ Montpezat de Quercy *134B2*

Besides its agreeable old houses and arcades, this little Quercy town is worth a visit to see the Collegiate Church of St-Martin. Its main treasures are the lavishly worked tapestries in the sanctuary, which depict scenes from the life of St. Martin, and the tombs of the local great family, the des Prés, several of whom became famous clerics.

▶ Moutier d'Ahun *134C5*

A church is again the main focus of interest here: the part-Romanesque, part-Gothic building dates originally from the 12th century, but later suffered at the hands of pillaging Protestants. Between 1673 and 1681, its finest feature was incorporated: a magnificent display of oak woodcarving. See also the 14th-century bridge over the River Creuse.

▶ Oradour-sur-Glane *134B4*

Most French towns quickly repaired wartime damage, but what happened in Oradour was too dreadful to forget. So it has been left exactly as it was, an effective monument to the horrors of war. On 10 June 1944, a group of SS troops swept through the town on a mission of vengeance. They were still smarting from their humiliation after D-Day and angered by the deaths of two outriders at the hands of Resistance snipers in a nearby village. They rounded up all the citizens of Oradour, putting women and children in the church, men in the surrounding outbuildings, and systematically massacred them. Many died in machine-gun fire, others burned to death when the church was set on fire. The total death toll was 642, of whom over 200 were children. Today the old village of Oradour is just the same as when the Nazis left: bullet marks on walls, charred shutters, old—now vintage—cars parked in garages, trailing telegraph wires. The ruins and the cemetery can be visited. Nearby, new Oradour and its modern church have risen phoenix-like from the ashes.

NUTS
Walnuts are best sampled when at their autumnal freshest. Originally brought by the Romans, walnut trees are now found throughout the region. Europe's largest walnut forest is at Doissat, outside the lovely medieval village of Belvès.

FAITHFUL CLIMBERS
The faithful who visit Rocamadour climb the long stairway halfway up the side of the cliff to an assembly of seven chapels, where the miraculous shrine of St. Amadour is believed to lie beneath the altar of a smoke-blackened Virgin. The annual pilgrimage get-together is 8 September.

▶▶ **Padirac** see page 140

▶▶ Périgueux *134A3*

The capital of Périgord is a large, lively agricultural and commercial hub, where truffles, *foie gras*, walnut sweets, honey, wine and liqueurs are stacked temptingly high in the windows of chic *épiceries* in the old quarter. A regular open-air market (Wed and Sat) adds to this cornucopia. The pedestrianized narrow streets around the cathedral and the houses by the river offer fascinating architectural detail at every turn and much effort has been put into restoration. The Romans who patronized the Vésone spring have left plenty of evidence, notably Vesunna's Tower, a stumpy cylindrical structure of yellowish stone. Other finds from the Gallo-Roman period can be seen in Périgueux's excellent **Musée du Périgord** (*Open* Apr–Sep Mon, Wed–Fri 10.30–5.30, Sat, Sun 1–6; Oct–Mar Mon, Wed–Fri 10–5, Sat, Sun 1–6. *Admission: moderate. Closed* Tue). The St-Front Cathedral's white domes and spiky turrets evoke some Islamic Levantine scene rather than a Catholic stronghold, but it was badly restored in the 19th century by Paul Abadie, the controversial architect of Sacré-Cœur in Paris. The original cathedral, the massive **St-Etienne-de-la-Cité,** is now hemmed in by traffic.

▶▶ Rocamadour *134B3*

Rocamadour's setting is irresistibly dramatic, particularly early or late in the day, when the light is indirect. The town clings to a sheer limestone spur rising from a dry canyon. An excellent view can be had from the belvedere at **L'Hospitalet**, across the valley. Close up, the fortified village loses some of its magic in an undignified scuffle for parking places and a jangling of souvenir cash-tills. The town hall has fine modern tapestries by Jean Lurçat. On the skyline is a château fortress, partly 14th-century. There are falconry displays at the Rocher des Aigles.

CRUMBLING
In 1956, several people were killed in rockfalls at La Roque-Gageac as the cliffs collapsed. Today the village is safely shored up.

▶▶ La Roque-Gageac *134B3*

The crumbling cliffs of golden limestone into which La Roque-Gageac is built make it one of the most remarkable settings on the Dordogne. Traditional flat-bottomed *gabares* (boats) ferry tourists past numerous châteaux. The **Château de la Malartie** is a 19th-century folly, the **Manoir de Tarde** genuinely 16th century.

▶▶ St-Cirq-Lapopie *134B2*

Huddled on its wooded limestone cliffs more than 80m (260ft) above the Lot, this gold-stone village is popular with tourists. Formerly a wood-turners' colony, many of its houses are now owned by artists inspired by surrealist André Breton. The 15th-century church juts out of the rock face to survey a dizzying sweep of Lot and Cère valley.

Lush countryside surrounds Périgueux at the heart of Dordogne département

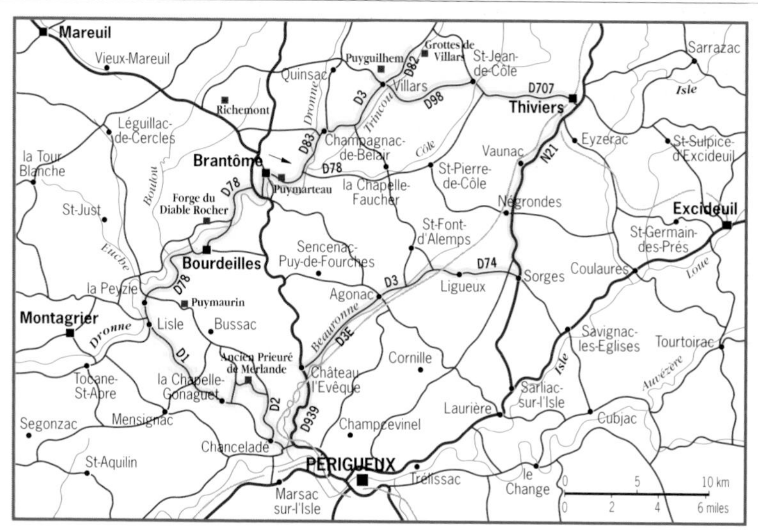

Drive

Exploring Périgord Vert

Start at Brantôme.
Brantôme lies in the heart of Périgord Vert. Its riverside setting and good food make it a popular. An imposing Benedictine abbey and 11th-century clock-tower (good view from top) hide ancient troglodyte dwellings and an extraordinary Last Judgement carving in the cliffs behind.

D78, D83, D82, D3 to Puyguilhem and D82 to Grottes de Villars.
Northeast lies the 16th-century château of **Puyguilhem**, restored after World War II (guided tours. *Closed* Mon except July, Aug). Also northeast are the **Grottes de Villars** (*Open* Apr–Jun, Sep daily 10–12, 2–7; Jul, Aug 10–7.30; Oct 2–6.30. *Admission: expensive*), limestone caves decorated with animal engravings believed to be 30,000–40,000 years old.

D98 from Puyguilhem to St-Jean-de-Côle and D707 to Thiviers.
St-Jean-de-Côle has a typically Périgordian assembly of brown and gold stone houses. The 11th-century priory church and Château Marthonie are its most notable buildings. **Thiviers** has a good foie gras and truffle market (Sat); and there are bizarre carvings in its 12th-century church.

N21 to Sorges; then D74 and D3 to Agonac, D3E to Château l'Evêque and D939 and D2 to Chancelade.
Sorges has a truffle museum in the local Syndicat d'Initiatif; in winter you can join a truffle trail through nearby oak woods. Northwest of Périgueux lie the monastic ruins of **Chancelade**, where the abbey church and chapel of St-Jean remain of a once-great 12th-century community (Jul–Aug, afternoons).

D2 and side road to Prieuré de Merlande; join D1 to Lisle, then D78 to Bourdeilles and Brantôme.
At **Merlande**, an isolated chapel in a woodland clearing is all that remains of an associated priory, remarkable for its Romanesque carving. Heading back to the swift-flowing Dronne, you will encounter the town of **Bourdeilles**, dominated by a high medieval and Renaissance castle. Hastily patched up to receive a proposed (but unfulfilled) visit by Catherine de Médicis, it has excellent views over the rocky green river. The drive back to Brantôme passes beneath spectacular overhanging rocks. This stretch of the Dronne is ideal for canoeing.

EDIBLE BLACK DIAMONDS
Périgord's buried treasure, truffles, look like lumps of coal, and their aroma is questionable. Yet these unappetizing fungi are the subject of an abstruse Périgordian science, tales of aphrodisic powers and gourmets' dreams, with a per kilo price to match: typically around 600 euros. Truffles come in about 30 different species, weigh about 100g (3.5oz), and flourish on the roots of sickly oak trees. Their appearance any time between November and March sends farmers and poachers with trained pigs or dogs to nose them out. Truffles figure regularly on Périgordian menus.

► St-Junien 134B4

Glove-making has been the local industry here since the 11th century and today its factories supply many of the finely crafted leather goods for Hermès, Dior, Cacherel, Kenzo, etc. St-Junien's church is a fine Romanesque building in Limousin style. North of town lies the Vallée de la Glane, home to a pastoral view that inspired the painter Corot. The **Château de Rochechouart►**, containing 16th-century murals and a contemporary art museum (*Open* Mar–Sep Wed–Mon 10–12.30, 1.30–6; Oct to mid-Dec 10–12.30, 2–5) is 10km (6 miles) southwest.

►►► Sarlat 134B3

This beautifully restored gold-stone town is now one of the most popular places in the central Dordogne, and suffers accordingly from crowds. Sarlat stages many cultural events and holds an annual theatrical festival. Its buildings are of minor interest, but they form a harmonious grouping, despite the busy road known as the Traverse which now bisects the old town. The cathedral's belfry is 12th century; the rest was rebuilt in the 16th and 17th centuries. The strange conical-towered building is the Lanterne des Morts, a funerary memorial. On the main square is a Renaissance house where the poet Boétie was born. Other noteworthy mansions include the Gothic Hôtel Plamon, the Renaissance Hôtel de Maleville and the entire rue des Consuls.

► Souillac 134B3

A bustling commercial hub, Souillac is also a popular resort and officially one of the prettiest village in France. Its old quarter is quite limited, but the prize is the domed church of **Ste-Marie** and its fine doorway, now visible inside the nave. The carvings depict episodes from the life of Theophilus, who retracted a pact with the devil. The 12th-century church of St-Martin is now used for exhibitions.

St-Léonard-de-Noblat

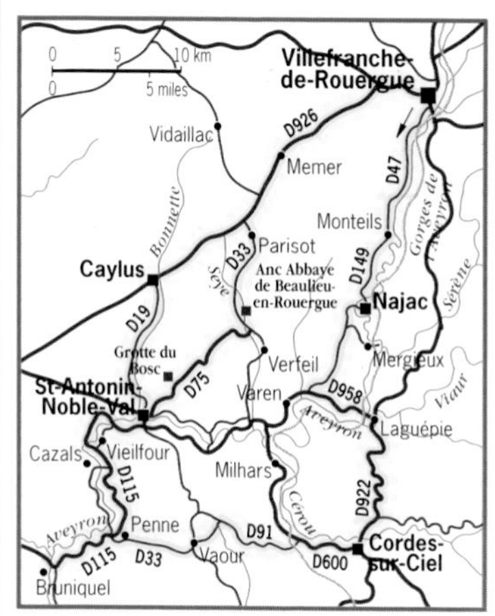

Drive

Along the Aveyron Valley

Many different route variations are possible around the Aveyron Valley. This long, meandering river follows a picturesque course to meet the River Tarn through a southerly spur of Quercy.

Start at Villefranche-de-Rouergue; then D47 and D149 to Najac. From Villefranche-de-Rouergue, a 13th-century bastide town with a fine central square, follow the river south to Najac.

Of all the many medieval fortresses in France, **Najac** is a classic example. Set high on a cone-shaped bluff, its defensive walls are extended by a dizzy cliff plunge to one of the Aveyron's looping bends. To reach it, you walk along the one village street of ancient houses to the castle keep set on its promontory.

D564, D594 and D106; then D958 to Laguépie. D922 to Cordes.

Farther south, leaving the river temporarily, the beautiful hilltop bastide of **Cordes** has been well preserved and is now a popular artists' colony, resuming a tradition of craftsmanship dating back to the 14th century.

Head west along the D91 and take D33 to Penne.

At one of the valley's most beautiful sections, **Penne** reveals yet another ruined and rugged fortress on a hill. This village was batted to and fro like a shuttlecock during the Hundred Years' War, and suffered during the Albigensian Crusade. Now its peaceful streets are lined with escutcheoned, half-timbered houses, leading up to the castle ruins.

D115 to Bruniquel

The cruel Visigothic princess Brunhilda is said to have founded the castle at **Bruniquel**; she was eventually tied to the tail of a wild horse and trampled to death. The castle still retains very early sections; the Knight's Hall and guardroom chimneypiece are worth seeing (*Open* Apr–Oct).

Return on D115 to St-Antonin-Noble-Val.

This ancient town is set opposite a sheer rock wall, the **Rochers d'Anglars**. Its tiered merchants' houses have roofs covered in round *lauze* tiles, and its former town hall (actually a belfry), one of the oldest in France, houses a prehistory collection. Notice the 14th-century calvary on the market square.

Leaving the Aveyron to follow its tributary the Bonnette, head north on the D19 to Caylus.

Caylus has a huge covered market and fortified church, with a striking modern crucifix by Ossip Zadkine.

An alternative route via the D75 and D33 leads to Beaulieu-en-Rouergue.

This route passes the **Grotte du Bosc,** a smallish cave in a dry underground riverbed displaying limestone formations. At **Beaulieu**, the abbey church dates back to the mid-13th century and has a seven-sided apse. The dormitory now houses a modern art gallery.

Return to Villefranche-de-Rouergue via the D33 and D926.

DOWN THE GULLET
All over the Dordogne, cheerful, healthy-looking geese roam the fields, munching whatever they choose. These are the lucky ones—they haven't yet encountered the *gavage* process, in which maize is poured down their gullets through funnels to enlarge their livers. If you enjoy *foie gras* (goose liver) visit a pâté farm to see what happens. Force-fed geese stay inside dark sheds, for they can hardly waddle, and endure five or six weeks' involuntary gluttony.

►► Toulouse *134B1*

During the Middle Ages, Toulouse was an important hub of learning and culture, and the present university is second in size only to the Sorbonne. The city has much high-tech industry (including the assembly plant for Airbus) and European Space Park, **La Cité de l'Espace**, Avenue Jean-Gonord Toulouse (tel: 05 62 71 48 71. *Open* Jul, Aug daily 9.30–7; Sep–Dec, Feb–Jun Tue–Fri 9.30–5, Sat, Sun 9.30–6. *Closed* Jan. *Admission: expensive*). Toulouse has horrific traffic problems, but its distinctive pink buildings include many attractive Renaissance mansions. Recommended shopping streets include the rue Croix Baragnon, the rue des Arts and around the place Wilson.

The **Basilique de St-Sernin►►►**, place St Sernin, 31000 Toulouse (*Open* Jul–Sep daily 8.30–5.45; Oct–Jun daily 8.30–11.45, 2–5.45. *Admission: free*), is the biggest Romanesque church in France, dedicated to a saint martyred by bulls in AD250. The **Eglise des Jacobins** is a stern Gothic hall church with an unexpectedly flamboyant interior. Equally unusual is the lopsided cathedral, **St-Etienne**, and its pretty square. The **Musée des Augustins►►**, 21 rue de Metz, 31000 Toulouse (*Open* Thu–Mon 10–6; Wed 10–9. *Admission: inexpensive*), housed in the 14th- to 15th-century convent, contains remarkable collections including medieval sculpture rescued from demolished churches, and the **Musée St-Raymond►►** has a collection of Roman art. The fine Renaissance **Hôtel d'Assézat►** is home to the Bemberg Foundation, renowned for its paintings, including 30 works by Bonnard. The **Espace d'Art Moderne et Contemporain**, housed in the former abattoir in the revitalized St-Cyprien district, is further proof of the city's determinedly cultivated image.

An 11th-century relief at the basilica of St-Sernin

►► Uzerche *134B4*

The 'Pearl of Limousin' stands on a rocky spur above the waters of the Vézère, and is moated on three sides. Densely packed buildings sprouting belfries and turrets are linked by steps and interspersed with 14th-century fortifications. The 12th-century church of St-Pierre has capitals carved with animals and foliage, and a splendidly ornate crypt.

► Ventadour *134C4*

These romantic castle ruins above the rocky Luzège gorge can be reached by foot from Moustier-Ventadour. Home of the Viscounts of Ventadour before they grew weary of feudal plumbing and decamped to Ussel, this was also where the troubadour Bernard de Ventadour developed his talents. Of humble birth (some say he was the son of the Viscount by a kitchen-maid), Bernard's courtly love songs were inspired by his illicit passion for the Viscountess.

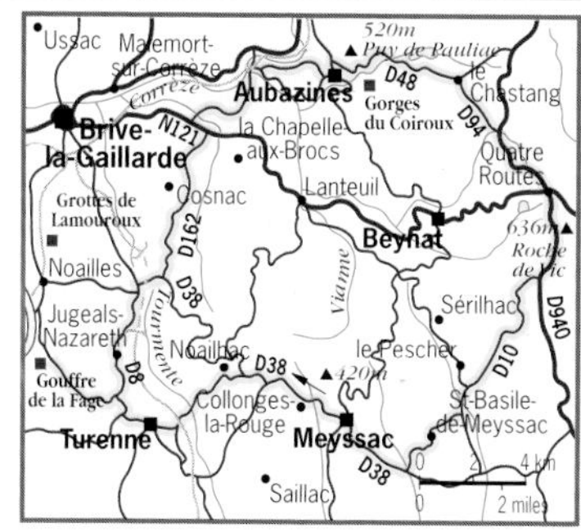

Drive

Between the Dordogne and the Corrèze

Start at Collonges-la-Rouge.
The buildings of **Collonges-la-Rouge►►►**, fashioned from brilliant magenta sandstone, vie with each other for attention. The corbelled Maison de la Sirène bears a mermaid; whimsical turrets adorn the Hôtel de la Ramade de Friac and Hôtel de Beuges; the Castel de Vassignac sports mullions, watch-towers, and loopholes for firing missiles.

D38 and D150 west to Turenne.

Turenne is built of more typical pale limestone, but its vainglorious hilltop castle, reduced by the Revolution to two ruined towers, is striking. Turenne's bankrupt overlords were forced to sell their birthright to Louis XV in 1738, but during the Middle Ages the viscounts of Turenne held sway over 1,200 villages, minted their own currency and collected their own taxes. Today the village is full of 15th- and 16th-century houses. Northwest lies the **Gouffre de la Fage**, a series of limestone caverns.

Take the D8, D38 (east), D162 (crossing the N121) and D48 to Aubazines.
The Cistercian abbey church of St- Stephen is **Aubazines**' main feature of interest, originally dating from the 12th century. The church has amusing 18th-century choir-stalls, and St. Stephen's splendid Gothic carved tomb. The restored abbey still houses a religious community but can be visited by guided tour.

D48 to Gorges du Coiroux and Puy de Pauliac.
The summit can be climbed on foot for a panoramic view.

D48, D94 and D940 to Roche de Vic, and D10 and D38 to Collonges-la-Rouge.
The Roche de Vic is a hilltop vantage point crowned by a chapel.

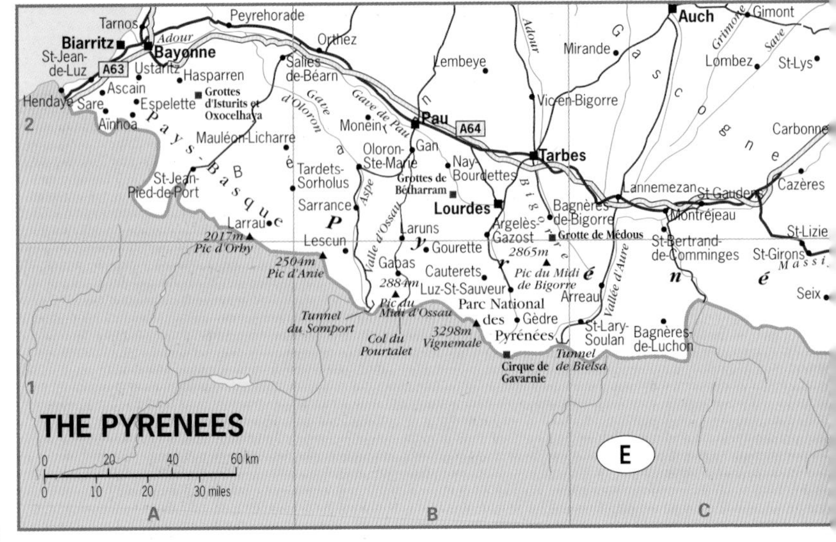

▶▶▶ REGION HIGHLIGHTS

CLIMBING ABRUPTLY FROM the plains of Gascony, the Pyrenees—rich in history, even richer in natural beauty—are a formidable natural barrier between France and the Iberian Peninsula. There are two mountain chains, stretching for more than 400km (250 miles) between the Bay of Biscay and the Mediterranean, and overlapping where the Garonne rises in the Valle d'Aran, a corner of Spain on the northern side of the watershed. Elsewhere, natural and national frontiers mostly coincide.

This is France's second-highest mountain range after the Alps. The highest point, Pic d'Aneto (in Spain), is 3,404m (11,168ft). Their width is about 100km (62 miles), and the passes over the mountains are steep, particularly on the northern side, where there are deep, narrow valleys, forested and with cascades falling down their sides. There is a marked contrast between the forests and pastures of the damp and cool Atlantic Pyrenees, and the vineyards and orchards of the sun-drenched Mediterranean flank, one of the driest corners of France.

The region's many thermal and mineral springs made it fashionable in the 19th century, with the result that many of its main resorts are slightly run-down old spas, and the development of winter sports facilities still has some way to go—the mountains are relatively uncluttered by ugly modern resorts and cable-car pylons. For many visitors, the unfashionable nature of the Pyrenees is their great appeal. Prices are low, lodgings unpretentious, the welcome warm and unaffected. The flowers are spectacular, the wildlife abundant (only the Camargue is better for bird-watching), a few species surviving only in the Pyrenees. A Grande Randonnée trail (the GR10) follows the range from coast to coast and takes hikers into a spectacular wilderness. If the resorts are disappointing, the Pyrenees are a backpacker's paradise.

There is plenty for sightseers: pilgrimage places past and present, including Lourdes, probably the most

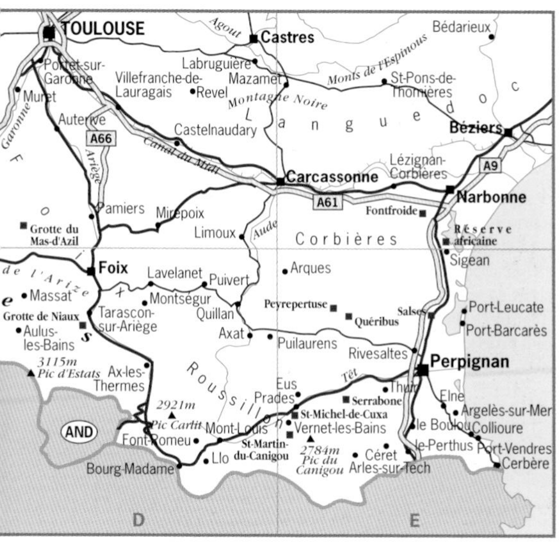

popular invalids' pilgrimage in Christendom; the showpiece fortified city of Carcassonne and dizzy citadels where medieval heretics sheltered from persecution; and a wealth of inventive art in the Romanesque churches of Catalonia. The Basque country offers a beautiful coastline, picturesque old villages and an ancient and cherished language.

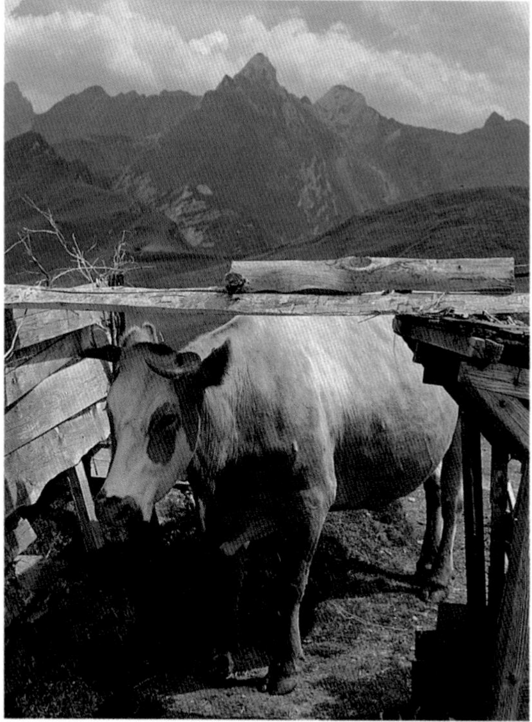

Houses in Bayonne incorporate mountain chalet styles

► Andorra 153D1

Straddling the spine of the Pyrenees, Andorra is a small co-principality nominally subject to the French president and the Spanish bishop of Urgel. It is actually proudly independent—and making a good living from tourism, much of it generated by Andorra's tax-free status. Almost all Andorra lies on the Spanish side of the Port d'Envalira (2,407m/7,897ft), the highest main road pass in the Pyrenees. The Spanish language prevails except at Pas de la Case (2,091m/6,860ft), a rather ugly modern ski resort on the French border. Villages along the main road down the Valira Valley have been ruined by messy modern development, and the capital, Andorra La Vella, is a traffic-jammed supermarket city. However, Andorra does have some of the best skiing in the Pyrenees, in five separate areas.

MOUNTAIN CHORUS

A troupe of Chanteurs Montagnards (mountain singers) toured Europe in the 19th century, enchanting Second Empire society audiences with their recitals of Pyrenean songs, glorifying the delights of the Bigorre. The chorus still exists at Bagnères de Bigorre.

► Arles-sur-Tech 153E1

This market town makes a more attractive base than nearby Amélie les Bains. Its old **abbey church▶** has interesting Romanesque carving on the façade, a Gothic cloister and a baroque altarpiece which illustrates the story of the town's patrons, a pair of third-century Kurdish martyrs. The Fou cascades down a narrow gorge (access only on foot) to join the Tech, 2km (1 mile) above Arles-sur-Tech.

► Aure, Vallée d' 152C1

The Neste d'Aure (*neste*, like *gave*, is a local Pyrenean word for river) flows from the slopes of the 3,000m (9,840ft) Massif de Néouvielle to join the Garonne at Montréjeau. The middle section of the valley is pleasantly rural, and the old town of Arreau makes a good base or overnight halt. The main alternative is **St-Lary-Soulan,** a fashionable and stylish resort by Pyrenean standards, with a cable car to good ski slopes. Above St-Lary, the road narrows and climbs into wilder country. From Fabian, it is a slow 14km (9-mile) drive up to a cluster of high lakes beneath the snowy walls of the **Néouvielle▶▶**, some of the most impressive Pyrenean scenery. Marked GR hiking trails lead over the massif to Barèges.

▶▶ Bayonne *152A2*

The capital of the French Basque country is famous for its ham, chocolate and bayonets. On the left bank, the twin spires of its 13th-century Gothic **cathedral** dominate an attractive precinct of old streets. The arcaded rue du Port-Neuf has mouthwatering *confiseries* and old-fashioned tea shops; the place de la Liberté is the focus of café society. The right-bank half of the old town has the **Musée Bonnat▶** 5 rue Jacques-Laffitte (*Open* May–Oct Wed–Mon 10–6.30; Nov–Apr Wed–Mon 10–12, 2–6. *Admission: expensive*), with a rich art collection. **Musée Basque quai des Corsaires** (*Open* May–Oct Tue–Sun 10.30–6.30; Nov–Apr 10–12.30, 2–6. *Admission: moderate*) covers the history and traditions of the Basque.

▶ Bétharram, Grottes de *152B2*

65270 St-Pe-de-Bigorre (Open: 25 Mar–25 Oct daily 9–12, 1.30–5.30; 3 Jan–25 Mar Mon–Fri 2.30–4. Closed Dec. Admission: expensive)

This 5km (3-mile) complex of grandiose underground chambers, rich in stalactites and stalagmites, is reached by minibus and toured by boat and train. Bétharram would be a powerful attraction in any region; so close to Lourdes (14km/9 miles east), it is often dauntingly crowded.

▶▶ La Bigorre *152B1*

The Bigorre is the heartland of the high Pyrenees and its main tourist area. The route from Arreau to Luz-St-Sauveur crosses the pastoral **Col d'Aspin▶** and wilder **Col du Tourmalet▶** (2,114m/6,936ft), notorious as the most punishing climb in the Tour de France. From the pass, a re-made road (open only in summer) and funicular provide alternative access to the observatory station on the **Pic du Midi du Bigorre▶▶▶** (2,865m/9,400ft; see panel). **La Mongie** is a rather unsightly ski resort linked by chairlift to Barèges, a small resort with sulphur springs and summer campers. **Bagnères de Bigorre** is an older and larger spa—there are impressive stalagmites and stalactites in the nearby **Grotte de Médous**. Cauterets and Luz-St-Sauveur are the other main resorts (see separate entries).

▶ Le Canigou *153E1*

Lonely eastern bastion of the Pyrenees, 50km (31 miles) from the Mediterranean, the Canigou (2,784m/9,132ft) is the holy mountain of the Catalans, who come annually from France and Spain to light fires on the summit on midsummer's night. From Vernet-les-Bains, jeep trips are organized up the rough forest road to the Chalet-Hôtel des Cortalets (2,175m/7,136ft), two hours' walk (a slog, but not difficult) from the summit. There is a longer and slightly less difficult road from Prades via Villerach. The classic Canigou experience is to stay overnight at Cortalets and walk to the top in time to see dawn break over the sea.

BIGORRE'S HIGHPOINT

The highest museum of astronomy in Europe opened to the public in 2000. Some 200,000 tourists per year now share the Pic du Midi du Bigorre and its observatory with scientists. Take a cable car from Taulet to the observatory for extraordinary views, and a spectacular lift to the top floor of the observatory. The Futuroscope-like cinema show, Pentascope, free to all in the A64 Toulouse-Pau-Bayonne motorway halt (the Aire du Pic du Midi), and the special effects and film projections on the rocks and snow along the funicular route from the Gare de l'Ayre to Barèges, are all part of this vast project, Pic 2000.

Since the Basques came down from the high passes to ambush Charlemagne's rearguard and kill Roland at Roncevaux in 778, they have been no friends of the French. Yet the beret and the rope-soled espadrille are just two Basque contributions to the national way of life. Of obscure origin, the Basques speak an apparently impenetrable tongue, once thought to have been the pre-Babel language. The Devil is said to have mastered only three words of it after seven years of study.

Most of the Basque country lies on the Spanish side of the Pyrenees and only one in ten of the half-million speakers of the Basque language are French. Although the Basques are conscious of their cultural and ethnic solidarity—'Zazpiak Bat' ('the seven are one') is a popular slogan—Spanish and French Basques have evolved differently. In Spain, the mineral-rich region was quick to industrialize and Basques have been prominent in the economic and political life of the nation. In France, the Basque country, consisting of the three provinces of Labourd, Basse Navarre and Soule, was a remote backwater of farmers and fishermen until tourism reached the coast in the 19th century.

Traditionally, they are a humble and reserved people not associated with the acts of separatist violence committed by some of their Spanish cousins. Even in France, however, demonstrations in the middle of towns, usually about political prisoners, are not uncommon. To those unfamiliar with the politics, it is hard not to view these processions with banners and chanting as another example of Basque folklore, like the costumed displays of traditional Basque dancing and music.

Celebrating the Basque festival in Bayonne in August dressed in unseasonal shaggy sheepskins

The national game 'Basque pelota' is not one game but many variations of the old *jeu de paume*, featuring a hard ball hit against a wall (*fronton*) which is a conspicuous feature of every village in the southwest. The fastest version of the game (*cesta punta*) takes place in an indoor court (*trinquet*); players wear long, curved scoop-like gauntlets (*chistera*) to catch the ball and return it in a single swing of the arm. When played well, this is one of the most exciting and graceful of ball games. At a simpler level (as played by children against the village *fronton*), bare hands or a wooden bat (*pala*) are used. Most of the major championships and important matches are held at Biarritz. St-Jean-de-Luz is another good place for pelota watching.

Labourd Well watered to a fault, the Labourd is the prettiest of the three Basque regions, with a beautiful coastline of cliffs and sandy coves fronting a bumpy landscape of green hills and immaculately kept, red and white timbered villages. Sare, Ainhoa and Ascain are outstandingly pretty, with typical Basque churches, of which the main characteristics are sex-segregated seating arrangements and small circular gravestones bearing the Basque swastika emblem. On the coast, **Biarritz** (see page 128) is the grand resort and surfing capital of Europe. The old fishing port of **St-Jean-de-Luz** has a perfectly sheltered sandy beach (a rare commodity on the Atlantic coast), lots of good fish restaurants, elegant shops and lashings of Basque charm in the vibrant streets of its pedestrianized central zone. The house where Louis XIV spent the month (May/June 1660) before his marriage to the Spanish Infanta Maria Teresa stands by the waterfront. His fiancée stayed in the beautiful house next door. Their marriage took place in the spectacularly ornate church of St-Jean Baptiste. After the ceremony, the door used by the royal couple was blocked. The border town of **Hendaye** is dreary by comparison, but has a vast beach.

Bayonne (see page 155), the capital of Labourd, is the acknowledged capital of the French Basque country. It has a core of streets in typically vivid Basque style, and is worth a visit for sightseeing. In early August it hosts the largest Basque festival, with much dancing of fandangos and other dances to tunes played on the *txistu* (three-holed flute) and *ttun-ttun* (tambourine).

Inland From the Col de St-Ignace, between Ascain and Sare, a railway (Apr–Nov) ascends the Rhune (900m/2,953ft), which is a superb viewpoint commanding the coast.

BASQUE CUISINE
Typical ingredients in Basque cuisine are tomatoes, peppers, garlic and onions: mixed with eggs these make *piperade*, a Basque omelette. Chicken, kidneys and grilled tuna are often served *à la Basquaise*, with a sauce of red peppers, garlic and onions. Traditional *gâteau* Basque has lemon and black cherries from Itxassou (south of Cambo les Bains). The best Basque wine is Irroléguy, from the area around St-Etienne-de-Baïgorry.

The red and white houses of Ainhoa, one of the most characteristic villages of the Labourd, founded in the 12th century

Espelette has a pimento fair (last weekend Oct) and is a market place for *pottoks*, diminutive semi-wild horses which inhabit the local hillsides (fair: last Tue–Wed in Jan).

Soule (see page 166) cannot rival the coastal region for the prettiness of the villages, but has magnificent countryside of forests and sheep pastures still managed, as they have been for centuries, by committees of communal representatives.

Carcassonne's magnificent fortifications

SOLAR OVEN
Built in 1969, the Odeillo solar oven at Font-Romeu consists of 9,500 mirrors forming a concave surface area of 1,800sq m (19,375sq ft), concentrating the sun's rays into an 80cm (30in) oven where the temperature can reach 3,500°C (6,330°F). Since 1986 it has not been used for power generation, but there are other highly technical scientific uses to which the mirrors are put, as explained in the permanent exhibition on site.

►►► Carcassonne *153E2*

Set apart from a thriving modern town beside the Aude stand the towers and walls of a mint-condition medieval fortified city, one of the great sights of Europe. The fortifications were of little use in 1209, when Carcassonne lasted less than a month before opening its gates to the crusading army of Simon de Montfort. Tourism rules in the narrow streets and the chateau **Cité Medieval et Chateau Comtal-Carcassonne** (*Open* city all year; château Apr, May, Oct daily 9.30–6; Jun–Sep 9.30–7.30; Nov–Mar 9.30–5. *Admission: city free; château expensive*), but nothing spoils the time warp in the beautiful grassy area between the city's twin curtain walls. The massive towers buttressing the inner wall show clearly visible Gallo-Roman masonry. The outer wall was built after the 1209 siege. Inside the city, the basilica of **St-Nazaire►** has both a Romanesque nave and a Gothic choir.

► Cauterets *152B1*

A 19th-century spa proud of its boiled sweets (*berlingots*), Cauterets is a good all-round resort, full of animation in midsummer and a good base for excursions into the Parc National des Pyrenées. The park information point has a good exhibition of Pyrenean ecology. A cable car hoists skiers to the Cirque du Lys, known for the most reliable snow in the Pyrenees. For walkers, the classic excursion is by road past waterfalls to **Pont d'Espagne►►**, from where trails lead up to the highest peak in the French Pyrenees, the Vignemale (3,298m/10,820ft).

► Cerdagne *153D1*

Cerdagne/Cerdanya is the beautiful upper Segre Valley, divided between France and Spain according to the terms of the 1659 Pyrenean treaty. It is a famously sunny region and its main resort, **Font-Romeu**, boasts a solar oven (see panel). Much used for high-level athletics training, it is also a pilgrimage site, with an 18th-century hermitage on the site of a spring where a miraculous statue of the Virgin was uncovered by a bull. There are other interesting churches at **Llo►**, a picturesque old village, and Hix, near the border at Bourg Madame.

The Albigensian crusade, launched by Pope Innocent III in 1209 to eradicate the Cathar heresy which flourished in southwestern France, is one of the more compelling stories of internecine butchery and bravery in the annals of medieval history. Apart from wiping 400 villages off the map, it brought about royal control of Languedoc and the destruction of the Raymond dynasty of the Visigoths, a multicultural civilization of great refinement, which had flourished at the court of Toulouse.

Kill them all! Promised remission for all sins past and future and the annulment of all debts in exchange for 40 days' service, an army of land-grabbing northern French crusaders went south. Even contemporaries were shocked when Béziers was singled out for exemplary massacre on 22 July 1209; Cathars and Catholics were slaughtered indiscriminately. Towns soon opened their gates to the crusaders but the Cathar *parfaits* and *parfaites* (the mystical corps of Cathar priests) retreated to remote fortresses in the foothills of the eastern Pyrenees.

The Cathar strongholds The two most exciting of these ridge-top eyries to visit are Peyrepertuse and Quéribus. **Quéribus** is set 500m (1,640ft) above the main valley, with superb views of the Canigou and other high peaks to the south. Its siege in 1255, which succeeded only through treachery, was the last episode of the intermittent crusading effort. **Peyrepertuse** is a larger complex of ruins, crowning a ridge. **Montségur château** (*Open* daily Feb 10.30–4; Mar 10–5; Apr 9.30–6; May–Aug 9–7.30; Sep, Oct 9.30–6; Nov 10–5.30; Dec 10.30–4.30. *Admission: moderate;* same ticket for museum and château) is equally impressive, but you are less likely to have it to yourself. There is a steep path to the ruins from the pass on its western flank and a museum in the village. **Puivert** and **Puilaurens** are other good examples beside the Foix-Perpignan road near Quillan.

SIEGE OF MONTSÉGUR

The Cathars' headquarters on the rock of Montségur, southeast of Foix, was besieged by 10,000 Catholics throughout the autumn and winter of 1243–44. A truce was eventually concluded but all 207 Cathars declined to abjure their faith or escape, and walked calmly into the flames of a huge bonfire on the morning of 16 March 1244.

A stronghold formed by Nature and by man: Peyrepertuse

▶ Céret 153E1

Céret attracted leading Cubist artists at the turn of the 20th century and has an excellent modern art museum, the **Musée d'Art Moderne▶▶**, 8 boulevard Marechal Joffre, 66400 Ceret (*Open* Jun to mid-Sep daily 10–7; mid-Sep to May Tue–Sun 10–6. *Admission: expensive*). A canopy of plane trees adds to the pleasures of a stroll through the old part of town.

St-Bertrand-de-Comminges (above)

The Devil's Bridge at Céret (right)

▶▶ Le Comminges 152C2

The heart of the Comminges region is the upper valley of the Garonne. In 72BC Pompey founded a city, Lugdunum Convenarum, on an isolated hill at the entrance to the mountain valley. The old walled village of St-Bertrand-de-Comminges now stands on the site, dominated by its **Cathédrale▶▶** (*Open* Feb, Mar, Nov, Dec Tue–Sun 10–5; Apr–Jun, Sep, Oct daily 10–6; Jul, Aug daily 10–7. *Closed* Jan. *Admission: moderate),* which used to be an important stop on the pilgrimage road to Spain. All that survives of the original 12th-century building is the façade and three sides of the cloister, with beautiful capitals and an open gallery giving a fine mountain view. The choir has outstanding 16th-century carved wooden choir stalls and screen. At the foot of the hill there are some excavations of the Roman city and the delightful 11th-century basilica of **St-Just▶**, largely built of recycled Roman masonry. Roman inscriptions and columns are easily identified.

▶ Le Couserans 152C1

Between the Pays de Foix and the Comminges, the Couserans is an out-of-the-way region of quiet valleys without major sights or spectacular mountain scenery. The traditional local ways of life have survived better than in most places, but depopulation is as great an enemy as overdevelopment. The Bethmale Valley, well known for its local dress (including extravagantly upturned wooden footwear, see the Begouen Collection, St-Lizier), is now quiet holiday-home country. **Aulus-les-Bains**, a spa once known for its bear tamers, is now well past its prime but set among beautiful mountains near the Spanish border ridge and a good base for hikes to mountain lakes and waterfalls (the 110m/360ft Cascade d'Arse, notably). **Seix** is popular for canoeing.

EXTRA-CURRICULAR

Céret's sights include a monument to toreadors, and in July bull-running hits the streets. The traditional regional dance, *la sardane*, peaks on the last Sunday in August with strict choreography to the sounds of an 11-piece band, *la cobla*, of tambourines and strident flageolets.

ST-LIZIER

At the northern edge of the Couserans lies the small town of St-Lizier, with its third-century Gallo-Roman ramparts still intact. Immediately to the south lie the church of St-Lizier, famous for its Romanesque cloister and its remarkable ninth-century apse frescoes, and the 18th-century pharmacy in the Hôtel-Dieu next door, still used as a stopover for pilgrims *en route* for Santiago de Compostela.

Drive

Pays de Foix

This tour combines the best Pyrenean cave with beautiful hill driving.

Start at Foix.
Foix is less enchanting than is suggested by a distant view of its **Château**, 45 cours Gabriel-Fauré (*Open* Sep–Jun daily 9.45–12, 2–6; Jul, Aug daily 9.45–6.30. *Admission: moderate*), but the town has good restaurants.

Take the N20 to Tarascon-sur-Ariège. Excursions possible to Grotte de Niaux (D8) and Grotte de Lombrives (N20).
The **Grottes de Niaux** (*tel: 05 61 05 88 37 to book*; *extremely limited numbers daily. Admission: expensive*) are some of the finest prehistoric painted caves in Europe. You can also visit the replica in Tarascon-sur-Ariège's **Parc Pyrenéen de l'Art Préhistorique**, Tarascon-sur-Ariège (*Open* daily Sep–Jun 10–6; Jul, Aug 10–7. *Admission: expensive*). On the other side of the mountain, **Lombrives** (two-hour guided tour) is a network of prehistoric caves used as a refuge and burial place.

Take D618 to Massat and Biert, then D18/D17 via Col de la Crouzette, Sommet de Portel and Col des Marrous back to Foix.

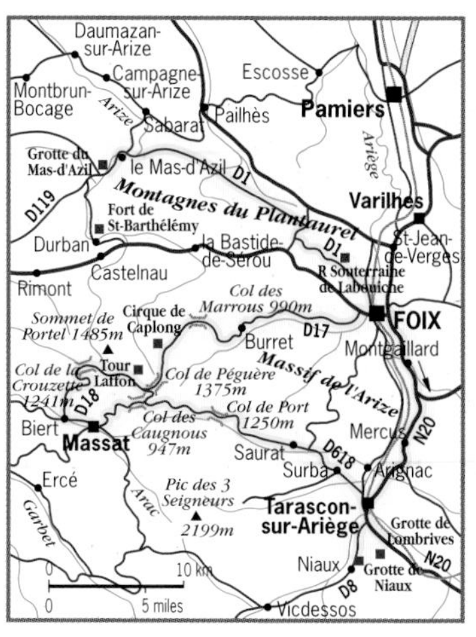

The rest of the tour is a long scenic drive, which can be abbreviated by taking the narrow road that climbs steeply from the Col des Caugnous (6km/4 miles east of Massat) to the Col de Péguère near the Tour Laffont, a fine viewpoint a few minutes' walk from the road. The view from the Sommet de Portel (1,485m/4,872ft) is better still.

From Foix excursions can be made to Rivière Souterraine de Labouiche and Grotte du Mas d'Azil by D1 (30km/19 miles each way).
Visiting the underground Labouiche River involves a 1.5km (1-mile) boat trip, with stalagmites, stalactites and a waterfall to admire. South of the village of le Mas d'Azil, the D119 runs through a superb 420m (460yd) tunnel carved by the River Arize. Side caves (guided tour) were inhabited by prehistoric man, and finds are well displayed on site.

The red-roofed town of Foix

►► Cirque de Gavarnie *152B1*

The most celebrated mountain beauty spot in the Pyrenees is the huge circus of cliffs, waterfalls and snowy peaks to the south of Luz-St-Sauveur. The classic way to see the cirque is by donkey (or on foot) along the 5km (3-mile) path from the car parks at the village of Gavarnie (where there are lodgings) to the foot of the cliffs.

► Isturits and Oxocelhaya (Grottes) *152A2*

These two caves in the Basque country are within easy reach of the coast for a rainy-day outing. The higher chamber (Isturits) has yielded important evidence of occupation by prehistoric man; Oxocelhaya is more beautiful, with well-lit stalactites and stalagmites (*Open* mid-Mar to mid-Nov, guided tours only).

BRECHE DE ROLAND
A tough three-hour walk from the Col de Gavarnie/Boucharo leads to the Brèche de Roland, a cleft in the rock wall where, according to the *Chanson de Roland*, Charlemagne's expiring lieutenant smashed his sword on the rock to prevent it falling into infidel hands.

► Lourdes *152B2*

Lourdes is an astonishing manifestation of contemporary faith. Rows of stretcher cases inch closer to the holy taps, the candles and the screen of votive crutches at the entrance to the miraculous riverside grotto where a young country girl, Bernadette Subirous, saw the Virgin Mary on 11 February 1858 and on 17 subsequent occasions. Shop after shop peddles plastic Virgins, bottles of holy water and exorbitantly priced candles to light at the shrine. The cavernous underground basilica has room for 20,000 pilgrims.

Lourdes was once an important strategic stronghold. An impressive fortress overlooks the Gave de Pau and houses a good regional museum.

LOURDES BUSINESS
The infrastructure for the world's leading pilgrimage is enormous: more than 270 hotels (only Paris has more) and scores of sanatoria, all dependent on voluntary helpers.

► Luchon (Bagnères-de-Luchon) *152C1*

The Romans' preferred spa in the Pyrenees still has a certain chic, with tree-lined avenues, a casino and thermal baths set in a handsome park. At a junction of high mountain valleys, Luchon makes an excellent base for excursions. From the woods and waterfalls of the Val de Lys it is a splendid hairpin drive up to the mini-resort and lofty belvedere of Superbagnères (1,800m/5,905ft). The former Hospice de France refuge (10km/6 miles southeast) and the Col de Pierrefitte (above **Bourg d'Oeil►**, 22km/14 miles northwest) are better starting points for walks.

► Luz-St-Sauveur *152B1*

This picturesque old village and modest resort between Lourdes and Gavarnie is an attractive alternative to the larger resorts in the area. Once the capital of a self-governing republic, it has an unusual fortified **church►**. There is a national park information station next door.

LUCHON'S DISTEMPERS
'Beastly dens...sufficient to cause as many distempers as they cure.' — Arthur Young, on Luchon, 1787.

► Montségur see page 159

►►► Niaux, Grotte de *153D1*

See **Pays de Foix Drive**, page 161

► Oloron-Ste-Marie and Vallée d'Aspe *152B2*

Oloron-Ste-Marie is a busy market and chocolate-making town at the confluence of the Aspe and Ossau *gaves*, on the old pilgrimage route to Spain. Its showpiece is the 12th-century marble doorway of Sainte-Marie, richly carved with Biblical figures.

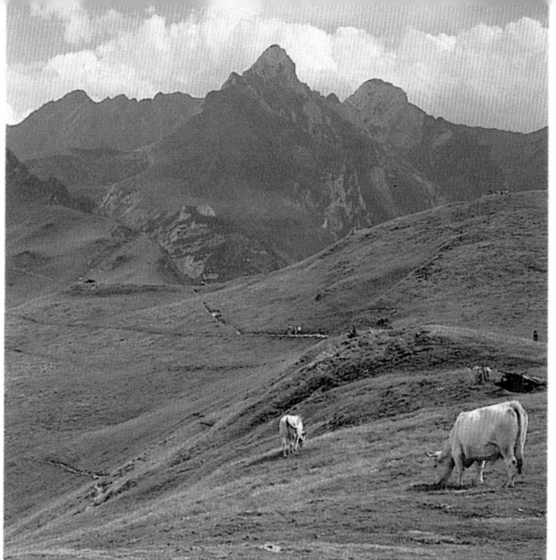

Accessible from June to early November, the D918 linking the valleys of the Gave d'Ossau and the Gave d'Arrens offers a scenic drive over the Col d'Aubisque

Running north from the Col du Somport (1,632m/5,354ft) is the beautiful **Aspe Valley▶▶▶**. Its relative peacefulness and its dwindling population of bears are threatened by a new road tunnel. The Pyrenees national park office at Etsaut gives hiking information. Above the valley, the rough stone village of **Lescun** is a good hiking base with simple lodgings, beneath superb peaks including the Pic d'Anie (2,504m/8,215ft).

▶ Ossau, Vallée d' *152B2*

One ridge to the east of the Aspe, the Ossau Valley runs north to Pau from the Spanish border at the Col du Pourtalet (1,794m/5,886ft); the two valleys combine to make a circuit via Jaca in Spain. The upper Ossau Valley is beautiful wild country, with a few bears lurking around Laruns, and rather more isards (Pyrenean chamois) on the slopes of the Pic du Midi d'Ossau (2,885m/9,465ft), focal point of the famous view from Pau. From Gabas, a narrow road climbs steeply to the artificial Lac de Bious (1,420m/4,659ft); from here it is a two-hour walk to a cluster of natural **lakes▶▶** among splendid scenery at the foot of the Pic du Midi. Hiking trails link to form a full circuit of the mountain.

On the other side of Gabas, a cable car and mountain railway lead to the **Lac d'Artouste▶** via the panoramic Pic de la Sagette (2,031m/6,663ft). There is a hiking trail back to Gabas from the lake. From Laruns, it is a beautiful drive east over the Col d'Aubisque (1,709m/5,607ft).

▶▶ Pau *152B2*

The one-time capital of Béarn has two claims to fame: Henri IV (*'le Béarnais'*), best loved of all French monarchs, was born there in 1553; and the boulevard des Pyrénées gives a famous view of the mountain range, best when the distant peaks are snowy.

At the western end of the boulevard des Pyrénées, the much-restored château is a mixture of medieval, Renaissance and Second Empire. The interior has a collection of 17th- and 18th-century tapestries and many Henri-related items, including his cradle, a turtle shell.

BRINGING UP HENRI

Henri IV's mother, Jeanne d'Albret, queen of Navarre, sang Béarnais songs when she was giving birth in order not to produce a cry-baby; her father rubbed the newborn's lips with garlic and Jurançon wine, to make him grow into a big strong man. Both the strategies worked. The French crown fell to him when the Valois line expired with Henri III in 1589. Although the new king was a Protestant (his mother had abandoned the Roman faith), finding the gates of Paris closed to him, he renounced his Protestantism with the famously pragmatic words: 'Paris is well worth a mass'.

NOT SO PAU-FACED

Pau enjoyed a vogue in 19th-century Britain as a place to winter, or as a permanent residence. It has not entirely lost its sedate atmosphere. The fashion started when the Duke of Wellington's soldiers, on their way home from war in Spain and a successful encounter with Marshal Soult at Orthez in 1814, were fêted as liberators at Pau. Many settled there, advertised the alleged curative powers of Pau's mild climate, and introduced racing, golf and fox-hunting. Hunts still meet on winter Saturdays.

The High Pyrenees cover more than half the 400km (250-mile) length of the range, from the Pic d'Anie (2,504m/8,215ft) above Lescun in the Aspe Valley to the Pic Carlit (2,921m/9,583ft), east of Andorra. Apart from the Somport and Pourtalet passes in the west and the Garonne Gap (the Spanish Valle d'Aran) where the two Pyrenean chains overlap to the south of Luchon, there are no easy frontier passes in this wilderness area of spectacular peaks and rocky cirques mirrored in mountain lakes. The area has a rich and fascinating ecology, with the best examples of high-mountain flora and fauna in Europe.

A narrow strip (110km/68 miles by 15km/9 miles at its widest) of the frontier mountains in the west, from Lescun to the Néouvielle Massif above St-Lary, is part of the Parc National des Pyrénées.

Climbers' challenges The highest Pyrenees are in Spain (due south of Luchon, the Maladeta Massif culminates at the 3,404m/11,168ft Pic d'Aneto), but the northern side has the most famous and beautiful peaks, including the Vignemale (3,298m/10,820ft), highest point of the frontier, the terraced cliffs and waterfalls of the **Cirque de Gavarnie** (see page 162), and the mighty **Pic du Midi d'Ossau** (2,885m/9,465ft), an isolated bastion that is the climber's preferred playground in the range. The Pic du Midi was first climbed in 1787 (the year after the first ascent of Mont Blanc) by a shepherd from the Aspe Valley.

South of **Cauterets**, the remotest of the Pyrenean spas, the uninterrupted 800m (2,625ft) wall of the north face of the **Vignemale** is a formidable challenge for mountaineers. The Vignemale has the biggest glacier in the Pyrenees and was the adopted home of one of the more eccentric characters in the history of mountaineering, Count Henry Russell (1834–1909), who dynamited seven caves (including one only just below the summit) to inhabit and use for dinner parties. Russell climbed the Vignemale more than 30 times and had guides bury him to the neck in scree on the summit for closer communion with the mountain he described as his own. This was no exaggeration: Barèges gave it to him on a 99-year lease. Luchon Museum has a section devoted to Russell and there is a statue of him at Gavarnie.

The High Pyrenees have some of the best wild flowers in Europe

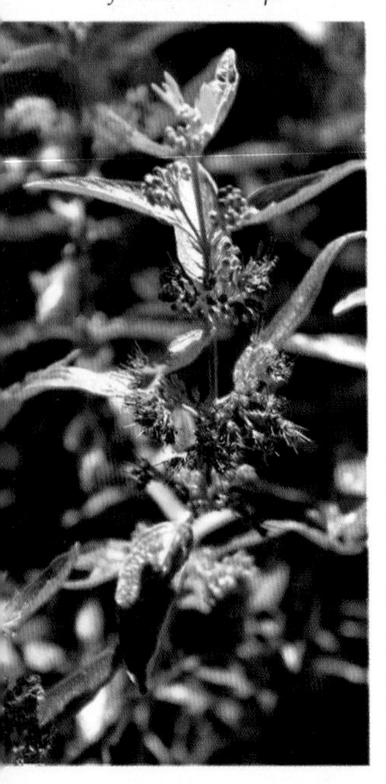

Pyrenean wildlife Bears, the most celebrated specimens of Pyrenean wildlife, do not inhabit the high mountains but instead choose to live on the fringe of human habitation at medium altitude (invariably below the tree-line). Other inhabitants of the mountains include marmots, isards (Pyrenean chamois) and *desmans*, nocturnal voles with webbed feet and a long trunk that are found only in the streams in the Pyrenees and the Caucasus.

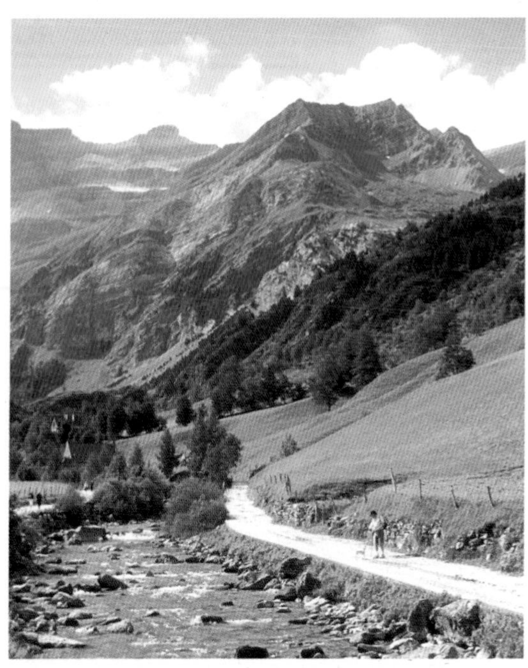

Stunning Pyrenean mountain scenery in the Parc National des Pyrénées. Guided hikes can be arranged through park offices in the main valleys

Undisputed king of the Pyrenees, however, is the lammergeier or bearded vulture, the largest of European vultures (more than 1m/3ft long with a wingspan of up to 3m/10ft) and a unique link in the food chain—its preferred food is bone marrow, which it obtains by dropping bones on to rock from a great height. Lammergeiers nest on mountain ledges in the wildest locations and shun the company of other vultures at a carcass. When it is seen on the wing it is a magnificent sight, clearly distinguishable from other vultures by its size and narrow pointed wings and tail.

The hiker's Pyrenees An 8km (5 miles) rough road leads from **Gavarnie** to the **Barrage d'Ossoue** reservoir, along a valley where you might glimpse isards, marmots and (if you're lucky) bearded vultures. From the lake it is about three hours' walk to the foot of the Vignemale's Ossoue glacier and one of Russell's caves.

The **GR10** hiking trail crosses from Atlantic to Mediterranean on the northern side of the chain, passing through the national park via numerous refuges. No rock climbing is involved, but in many places the isolation and high altitude of the path brings it into the realm of mountaineering. A Pyrenean **Haute Route** (the HRP, for experienced climbers only) takes a higher line along the crest of the frontier mountains, crossing into Spain in several places.

There are national park information stations at Tarbes, Cauterets, Luz-St-Sauveur, St-Lary-Soulan and Etsaut. Or you can obtain information from Féderation Française de Randonnée Pedestre, 64 rue du Dessous des Berges, 75013 Paris; tel 01 44 89 93 93; www.ffrandonnee.fr.

PYRENEAN TRAIL
Pont d'Espagne, south of Cauterets, is the point of departure for some of the most celebrated, not-too-arduous walks in the Pyrenees. You can take a chair-lift to the beautiful Lac de Gaube (otherwise an hour on foot). From the lake, the GR10 continues up the valley to Les Oulettes refuge (2,151m/7,057ft) with increasingly impressive views of the north wall of the Vignemale. From there it climbs steeply to a high col (another two hours) on the mountain's eastern shoulder and down to the Barrage d'Ossoue.
Another path from Pont d'Espagne follows the beautiful Marcadeau Valley to the refuge Wallon (1,866m/6,122ft, two hours from Pont d'Espagne). The trail, much used by wayfarers and smugglers down the centuries, continues over the mountains to Panticosa in Spain via the Port du Marcadeau (2,541m/8,337ft).

BASQUE AMBUSH
From St-Jean-Pied-de-Port, the modern road to Roncevaux follows the Valcarlos road, where Charlemagne's rearguard, under Roland, Count of Blaye, with the valiant support of Olivier le Preux and Bishop Turpin, was ambushed and annihilated by rock-throwing Basques in 778. Legend, in the form of the great epic poem the *Chanson de Roland*, transformed Basques into Saracens and translated the action to the Ports de Cize route to the east, now open only to hikers (GR65).

►► St-Jean-Pied-de-Port *152A2*

An old Basque town with great charm and a long tradition of hospitality for passing wayfarers, St-Jean was where medieval pilgrimage routes converged before crossing the mountains to Roncevaux in Spain. Pilgrims walked down the cobbled Rue de la Citadelle from the Porte St-Jacques to Porte d'Espagne. Old pink sandstone houses and a fortified church (Notre Dame du Pont), built into the fabric of the ramparts, overlook the right bank of the River Nive. The great military engineer Vauban added a citadel and a new system of fortifications on the left bank in the 17th century.

► St-Martin-du-Canigou *153D1*

Abbaye St-Martin-du-Canigou, 66820 Casteil (Open Jun–Sep daily; Oct–May Wed–Mon; tour times vary but usually on the hour 10–4. Accessible on foot or by jeep—30-min walk. Admission: moderate)
This much-restored abbey is sited on the western side of the Canigou above Vernet-les-Bains (see opposite).

► Prieuré de Serrabona *153E1*

(and Jardin Méditérranéen) 66130 Boule d'Amont (Open daily 10–6. Closed public holidays. Admission: inexpensive)
The 11th- to 12th-century abbey church (see opposite) here sits in a wild setting among scented scrub-covered hills to the south of the Prades–Perpignan road.

St-Jean-Pied-de-Port huddles beneath the peak of Roncevaux

► Haute Soule *152A2*

Soule is the easternmost province of the Basque country and, in terms of charm, the least interesting. **Mauléon-Licharre**, the capital, manufactures typical Basque products—espadrilles and pelota bats. The churchyard at Gotein (3km/2 miles south) is characteristically Basque, with triple-crowned belfry wall and adjacent *fronton* (pelota court). Patient drivers can traverse the beautiful beech forests and wild pastures of the Haute Soule, still managed by the traditional collective syndicates of Soule communes, either driving 42km (26 miles) from St-Jean-Pied-de-Port to Larrau (via the Col Bagargiak 1,327m/4,354ft), or 36km (22 miles) from St-Jean to Tardets-Sorholus via Ahusquy, a more pastoral route.

In wild country south of Tardets, the D113 leads past the entrance to the **Gorges de Kakouetta►**, a narrow canyon accessible only to walkers (proper hiking boots are needed). At **Ste-Engrâce's** Romanesque pilgrimage church, the Queen of Sheba rides an elephant on one of the pillar capitals.

ON THE ROAD
The edible scallop takes its French name, *coquille St-Jacques*, from the emblem of the medieval pilgrimage to Compostela, Spanish burial place of the Crusaders' patron saint, Sant Iago (St. James or St. Jacques), on the scallop-rich coast of northwest Spain. Wearing the pilgrim's uniform (cap with cockle badge, stick and gourd) pilgrims crossed France on set routes from Paris, Arles, Le Puy, Vézelay and Tours. Pilgrimages continued throughout the Hundred Years' War but the vogue waned by the 16th century. So-called pilgrims were mistrusted as spongers, and the term *coquelin* (now *coquin* in colloquial French) took on a pejorative meaning.

Medieval Catalonia was a prosperous and cosmopolitan region, with trade links all over the Mediterranean. Its architecture from the Romanesque period, before the lumpish northern Crusaders descended on the southwest to snuff out tolerance and invention, seems to reflect its open society. There is a remarkable and fruitful fusion of influences, from as far afield as southern Spain (so-called Mozarabic style) and Lombardy in northern Italy, home of many specialist masons.

Serrabone This is the most exciting church in the region, thanks to the contrast between the dour exterior of the 11th- to 12th-century priory church, which stands alone in a scrubby sub-mountainous wilderness, and the wealth of delicate carving on roseate marble inside.

Abbaye de St-Michel de Cuxa 66500 Codalet (*Open May–Sep 9.30–6; Oct–Apr 9.30–5. Closed Sun (mornings) and religious holidays. Admission: moderate*). The 10th- to 11th-century buildings of the powerful abbey are red tiled, and there is a handsome four-floor crenellated tower. Half the cloister, found incorporated in surrounding buildings, was exported to New York to form The Cloisters Museum; the remainder has been reconstructed, with its delightful capitals.

Corneilla de Conflent Ste-Marie has a carved doorway and windows and 12th-century (wooden) and 14th-century (marble) Virgins inside (key next door).

Above: The abbey of St-Martin-du-Canigou; below: detail at abbey church of Ste-Foy in Conques

St-Martin-du-Canigou This spectacularly sited rocktop monastery, more than 1,000m (3,280ft) above Vernet, has superimposed 10th- and 11th-century churches and a cloister of impressive simplicity. Best reached on foot (40 minutes) from Casteil above Vernet-les-Bains. Guided tours.

Eus A small Romanesque chapel (St-Vincent) sits at the bottom of an old village on a slope, with a good view of the Canigou. North of Prades by D35.

St-Martin-de-Fenollar This small chapel, with 12th-century frescoes, is signed from the N9, 6km (4 miles) north of Le Perthus. (*Open* daily; winter afternoons only.)

St-Génis-des-Fontaines Carvings of Christ and apostles over the doorway (AD1020) of this church and cloisters on the D618 between Le Boulou and Argelès.

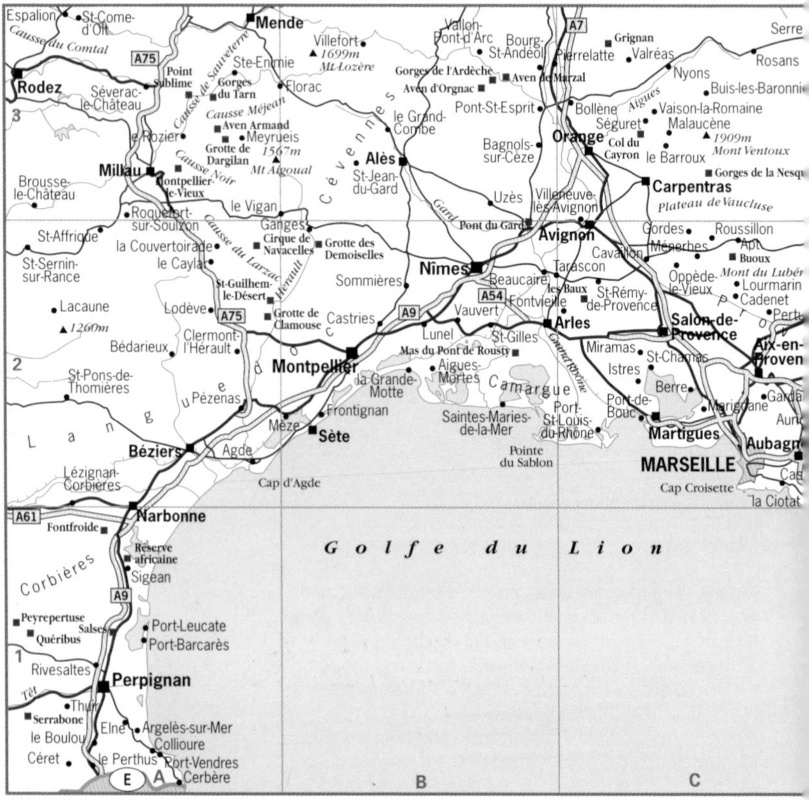

The palm-tree lined promenade des Anglais in Nice

The Provence Coast

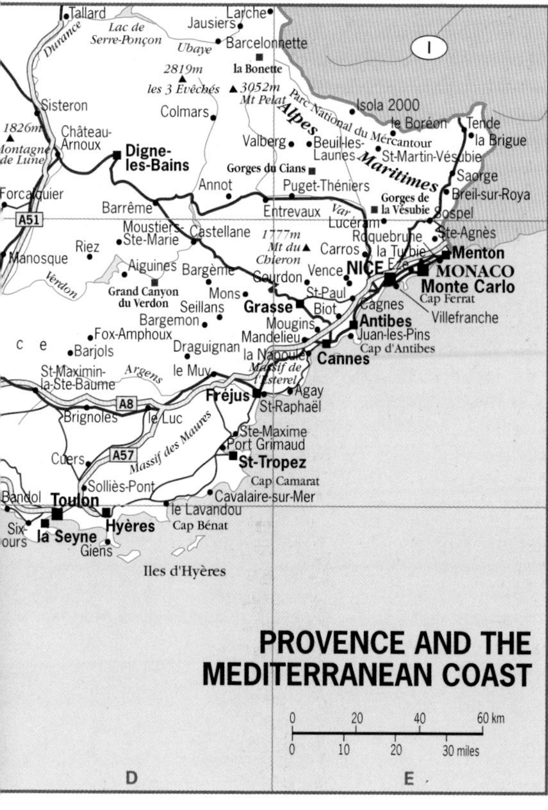

THE FRENCH CALL it le Midi, where the sun is high in the sky and hot. The winter sun is warm enough for lemons at Menton, and launched the south of France as a winter playground. Now tourists prefer the white heat of the summer. It is a harsh climate, prone to the howling Mistral (north wind) that fans devastating fires every summer. Only the Riviera is sheltered from its forces.

It is an area of enormous diversity of life, landscape and history. The Mediterranean coast has the spectacular mountains and fashionable urban resorts (with urban traffic problems) of the Riviera; and the long tracts of featureless sands of the Languedoc coast.

The French make for the sea *en masse* in July and August. The marshlands of the Camargue and the high mountain country of the Maritime Alps have their own wilderness appeal. Between the two lies the hill country of rural Provence, an ideal retreat: bright hues and lavender-scented air, and scores of old villages, which are ideal for sitting in the shade of a plane tree sipping *pastis* and watching a game of boules. The sightseeing glories of the south are Roman—great amphitheatres and triumphal arches to rival the best in Italy. There are medieval treasures, too—the Papal city of Avignon—and a wealth of artistic associations: scenery made famous by Van Gogh and Cézanne, and great modern art museums. Artists follow money and the sun. In the south, there is plenty of both.

The shifting marshy area, half land and half sea, of the Rhône delta is desolate but uniquely appealing. It is a wilderness full of potent, exotic images—wild horses, costumed cowboys (les gardians)*, rosy migrant flamingos and flamenco festivals.*

OTHER POINTS OF INTEREST
Mas du Pont de Rousty: an open-air museum, Musée Camarguais, beside the main Saintes-Maries to Arles road. A 3km (2-mile) walk through specimen Camargue-scapes (*Closed* Tue, in winter). Pont de Gau: a big bird sanctuary and information station near Les Saintes-Maries. St-Gilles: a small pilgrimage town on the northern edge of the Camargue, with an old church; the façade is decorated with beautiful but damaged 12th-century sculptures.

Here land and sea have an unstable relationship. A fragile ecosystem exists, where wildlife and society are threatened by irrigation, agriculture and, of course, tourism. The Camargue is an ornithologist's pilgrimage, with more than 100 migrating species, including flamingos. The best chance of seeing them is in the spring at **Etang de Fangassier** in the southeast. There is a good information point at **la Capelière**, on the eastern side of the main lagoon (Vaccarès), with guided tours on request (*Closed* Tue). Several traditional Camargue ranches (*manades*) are open to visitors and run riding excursions. Méjanes, on the Etang de Vaccarès, has a highly commercialized example.

Towns and ports The main resort is **Les Saintes-Maries**, where the Holy Maries (Salomé and Jacobea) landed on the beach with a black servant girl Sarah, the patroness of gypsies. On 24 and 25 May gypsies flock from all over Europe for the pilgrimage, which is followed by a Camargue festival of dancing, costume displays, bullfights and rodeos. Les Saintes-Maries is a rather seedy resort, but worth visiting for its church, a windowless fortress full of ex-votos. There is a good sandy beach and boat excursions on the Petit Rhône.

At the western edge of the Camargue lies **Aigues-Mortes**, purpose-built by Louis IX in the 13th century as a fortified port. The grid of old streets is encircled by ramparts, which you can climb and tour, for views over the Camargue and empty marshes.

Two other modern resorts nearby are **Port Camargue** and **Le Grau du Roi**.

Souvenir of Saintes-Maries, depicting a gardian *(traditional cowboy of the region) astride a native Camargue horse, which is descended from prehistoric horses. The coats of these horses turn white aged 4 to 7 years*

►► Aix-en-Provence 168C2

Chic and cultured, Aix is one of Europe's loveliest small cities, still seemingly inhabited by the spirit of Provence's last great ruler, *le bon roi* René d'Anjou (1409–80). Once a spa, it is still a fountain-rich city of classical town houses. Parking is very difficult. Café life and traffic jams focus on Aix's main boulevard, the **cours Mirabeau►►**, shaded by a magnificent canopy of plane trees, flanked by some of the best façades and most populated café-terraces.

Old town To the north lies the old town, a maze of narrow cobbled streets, with a lot of restoration of old buildings. This is the most interesting part to explore, with an excellent daily market on Place Richelme. **St-Sauveur Cathedral►** (*Open* daily 9–12, 2–5) has elements from all periods, Merovingian to Renaissance, with a Romanesque cloister. The great treasures are the triptych of *The Burning Bush*, painted by Nicolas Froment for King René, and the carved prophets and sibyls on the main doors. Both are kept shut, but a key holder is usually on hand. Near the cathedral, on the rue Saporta, the former archbishop's palace has an excellent collection of 17th- and 18th-century **Beauvais tapestries►** (*Closed* Tue). The **Atelier de Cézanne►**, 9 avenue Paul-Cézanne, is the artist's former studio (*Open* daily Apr–Jun, Sep 10–12, 2.30–6; Jul, Aug 10–6; Oct–Mar 10–12, 2–5. *Admission: moderate*).

On the south side of the cours Mirabeau in the quieter Mazarin quarter, the **Musée Granet►►**, place St-Jean-de-Malte (*Open* Mon, Wed–Sun 10–noon, 2–6. *Admission: inexpensive*), has an outstanding collection of works by Ingres, Rubens, Bernini and Giovanni Bologna. A room is devoted to Cézanne, who was born at Aix in 1839 and died there in 1906. The nearby 17th-century Fontaine des Quatres Dauphins (rue Cardinale) is one of the most delightful of Aix's many fountains. (See also page 174.)

► Antibes 169E2

A lively old port at the heart of a big modern town, full of narrow back streets, pretty squares and a good market. Overlooking massive 17th-century fortifications, the Château Grimaldi now houses the **Musée Picasso►►**, place Mariejol (*Open* Jun–Sep Tue–Sun 10–6; Oct–May Tue–Sun 10–12, 2–6. *Admission: moderate*). (See page 174.) The former cathedral dates from the 12th to 17th centuries, and has a good Renaissance altarpiece (the local Brea school) in the south transept.

The flower market in Aix-en-Provence is held on Tuesday, Thursday and Saturday mornings on the place de l'Hôtel de Ville

Aix's fountains witness a lively international music and opera festival every July

►►► REGION HIGHLIGHTS

PROVENCE'S NOBEL PRIZE
In 1854, Frédéric Mistral and six fellow poets writing in the Provençal language of the medieval troubadours formed a group, *les Félibres*, dedicated to reviving the language. Mistral wrote two epic love poems, *Mireio* and the *Song of the Rhône*, produced a Provençal dictionary and founded the Provençal museum (Muséon Arlaten) in Arles in 1896. In 1904 he won the Nobel Prize for literature and used the money to refurbish the Hôtel Laval-Castellane, the Muséon's present home.

END OF A DREAM
Van Gogh dreamed of establishing an artists' colony in Arles, with Gauguin as its 'abbot'. The two shared Van Gogh's 'yellow house', decorated with sunflower paintings, but after a quarrel and the cut ear incident, Gauguin left. Van Gogh entered an asylum in 1889. His house, later a café, was bombed in 1944.

►►► Arles *168B2*

Spiritually, if not officially, Arles is the capital of Provence. It is one of the great tourist hubs of the south with spectacular Roman and medieval buildings, a beautiful old town, good museums, cultural events, costume festivals and bullfights. The heart of town is the leafy place du Forum, which has a statue of the poet Mistral, café tables under the plane trees and live music in the evenings. To the south, the boulevard des Lices monopolizes promenaders. A global entrance ticket covers all the town's museums and monuments (available in situ).

Amphitheatre and theatre see page 188

St-Trophime►► The 12th-century reliefs of the *Last Judgement* on the façade are a masterpiece of Romanesque carving. St-Trophime also has one of France's most beautiful cloisters.

Museums The most unusual is the dusty old **Muséon Arlaten (Arles Museum)►►**, 29 rue de la République (*Open* Jun–Aug daily 9–1, 2–6.30; Apr, May, Sep daily 9.30–12.30, 2–6; Oct–Mar Tue–Sun 9.30–12.30, 2–5. *Admission: moderate*), the grandfather of folklore museums and still one of the best. In 1995, a strikingly designed museum, **Musée de l'Arles Antique►►**, avenue de la Première Division Francaise Libre (*Open* Nov–Feb daily 10–5; Mar–Oct daily 9–7. *Admission: moderate*), opened near the Roman circus, west of the middle of town.

Les Alyscamps One of the most famous burial grounds in medieval Christendom is now rather a let-down. Most of the tombs lining the shaded avenue have gone (some to the archaeological museum).

Espace Van Gogh This is an initiative to transform the old Hôtel Dieu into a commercial and cultural space, painted in Van Gogh's preferred primary hues, with flower beds to match. Van Gogh lives again, too, at the **Pont de Langlois**, an old wooden bridge painted by him, unobtrusively signed near the Sémence de Provence factory on the Salon road, and at the Fondation Van Gogh, opposite the arena, with an excellent collection of work by modern masters inspired by Van Gogh.

►►► Avignon *168C2*

A historical heavyweight city beside the Rhône, its old heart still enclosed by 4km (2.5 miles) of medieval walls, Avignon is an essential stop on the Provençal sightseeing trail. It is often windswept and can seem a rather joyless place, but comes alive during the annual drama and dance festival (2nd week July for three weeks), when the **place de l'Horloge►** cafés work round the clock. Avignon owes its fame to the 12th-century bridge, Pont St-Bénézet, of the popular song *Sur le pont d'Avignon*, long reduced to four spans jutting out into mid-stream, and the 14th-century 'Babylonian Captivity', as the scandalous papal residence at Avignon was known.

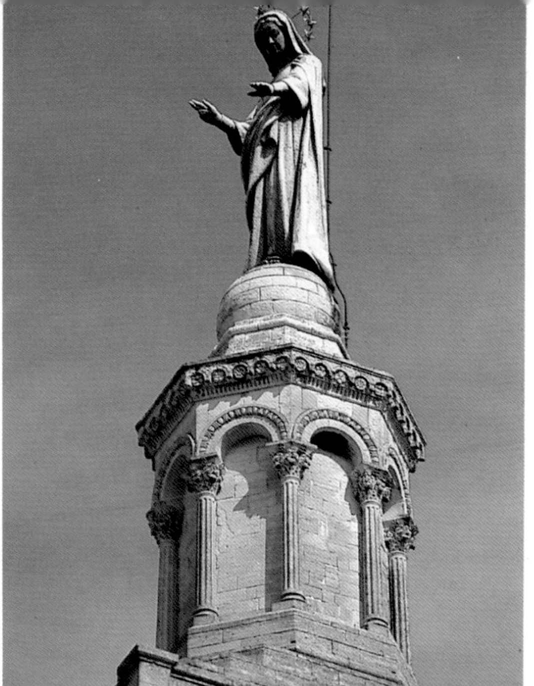

PAPAL PRESENCE
In the 14th century, Avignon was a Provençal city surrounded by papal land. Fed up with the insecurity of life in Rome, Pope Clement V brought the papal court to Avignon in 1309. Six French popes succeeded him, buying Avignon from the Countess of Provence in 1348 and building the magnificent Papal Palace. In 1377, Gregory IX took the curia back to Rome but in 1378 a group of cardinals returned to Avignon with a French rival to the Italian pope. Thus began the Great Schism, lasting until 1417.

A fresco by Simone Martini (now restored and in the Papal Palace) once adorned Avignon's cathedral, itself a fine example of Provençal Romanesque architecture

The popes gave Avignon its walls and the magnificent **Palais des Papes▶▶▶**, place du Palais (*Open* Jul–Sep daily 9–8 (until 9 during festival); Oct, mid-Mar to Jun 9–7; Nov to mid-Mar 9.30–5.45. *Admission: expensive*). The palace has a rock-solid façade, which defied all attempts to dismantle it after the Revolution. Its interior, though, was turned into a barracks. The rooms are unfurnished except for beautiful 14th-century frescoes, many inspired by *mille fleurs* tapestries. The monumental central courtyard is used during the festival for major theatrical productions.

Town and gown Outside the rule of French law, the city was a haven for outlaws and assorted disreputables so the 'town and gown' contrast of low life and the curia's ostentatious opulence was real enough.

There are good views from the Rocher des Doms Gardens, and two excellent museums: the **Musée de Petit Palais▶**, place du Palais (*Open* Jun–Sep Wed–Mon 10–1, 2–6; Oct–May Wed–Mon 9.30–1, 2–5.30. *Admission: moderate*), an old papal guesthouse with an outstanding collection of Gothic and Renaissance art; and the **Musée Calvet▶▶**, 65 rue Joseph Vernet (*Open* Wed–Mon 10–1, 2–6. *Admission: moderate*), in a fine 18th-century town house, with good art, furniture and wrought ironwork.

Villeneuve-lès-Avignon Sited on the opposite bank, this suburb was popular with cardinals. French kings built impressive fortifications to remind the popes of French power. The 14th-century Villeneuve's Carthusian monastery, **Chartreuse du Val de Bénédiction▶▶**, allée des Muriers (*Open* Apr–Sep daily 9–6.30; Oct–Mar daily 9.30–5.30. *Admission: expensive*), is now a cultural space.

FOCAL POINTS
Away from monumental central Avignon, the most picturesque part of the town is the old gypsy quarter, where the cobbled rue des Teinturiers was the home of the 19th-century calico cloth dyers. The focus of café life is the place de l'Horloge. The main north/south axis of the walled town, the rue de la République, has the best shopping.

Near the end of the 19th century, artists made their way to southern France, attracted by the special quality of the region's light and hues. Avant-garde artists followed Van Gogh and Cézanne, coming south to paint, and society artists followed society to Nice and Monte Carlo when the Riviera hit the social jackpot in the last quarter of the 19th century.

Above: Nice is an art-loving place: its contemporary art museum is the latest addition

Below: Matisse designed Vence's Rosary Chapel in gratitude to the nuns who looked after him between 1943 and 1948, when he withdrew there, overworked and exhausted

In the first category, Signac discovered the old fishing port of St-Tropez in 1892; artists who followed him there included Bonnard and Matisse. In 1905, Matisse and André Dérain worked together at Collioure. 'The light here is very strong,' wrote Dérain, 'the shadows very luminous. I am learning to rid myself of the whole business of the division of tones.'

This approach earned Dérain, Matisse, Dufy and others working on the coast the name *fauves*—the wild beasts of paint. One of many to fall under the influence of Cézanne was Georges Braque, whose landscapes at L'Estaque, in the first decade of the 20th century, first elicited the term 'cubist'. Matisse and Dufy settled in Nice and recorded all the brilliance and *joie de vivre* of the Riviera. Picasso settled in the south of France in 1946, revived the flagging ceramic industry at Vallauris, and lived there, at Cannes, at Vauvenargues and finally at Mougins, until his death in 1973. Max Ernst was another painter seduced by Provence's charms at Seillans. As well as providing inspiration for many great modern artists, the south is a rich store of their works in private and public collections. Only one painting by Van Gogh can be seen in Provence, *Les Wagons du Chemin de Fer*, in the Fondation Angladon-Dubrujeaud in Avignon. The Musée Granet in Aix has several small Cézannes.

Aix-en-Provence Cézanne's studio is open to the public, but it is a sadly inadequate memorial. To admire the Mont Ste-Victoire, Cézanne's much painted subject, take the Le Tholonet road east from Aix and circle the mountain, taking in views of one of Picasso's abodes, the château at Vauvenargues on the way (not open to the public).

Antibes One floor of the Grimaldi château is filled with paintings, drawings, sculptures and ceramics by Picasso, most of it the inspired output of a single year (1947).

Biot An interest in ceramics brought Fernand Léger to Biot shortly before he died in 1955. The museum of his work is one of the best modern museums in the south.

Cagnes Renoir painted on despite arthritis so severe he was unable to wield the brush unaided. His home and studios at Les Collettes are open to visitors. The Château also displays collections of work by artists who worked and lived locally, including Dufy and Vasarely.

Pot plants decorate the forecourt of the Musée Matisse in Nice's Cimiez district

Fréjus The Chapelle de Cocteau (4km/2.5 miles from Fréjus on the N7. *Open* May–Oct Tue–Sun 9.30–12.30, 2–6; Nov–Apr Tue–Sun 9.30–12.30, 2–5) has an unfinished interior by Jean Cocteau.

Menton Jean Cocteau designed a museum (*Closed* Tue) to himself in the old port fortifications, and also decorated the Salle des Mariages in the town hall (Mon–Fri).

Nice In the Cimiez district is the **Musée Matisse**, 164 avenue des Arènes (*Open* Wed–Mon 10–6. *Admission: moderate*) and the **Musée Chagall**, near the bottom of the avenue de Cimiez, designed for Chagall's biblical work (*Closed* Tue). In the middle of town there is the **Musée International d'Art Naïf Anatole-Jakovsky**, avenue de Fabron, and the **Musée d'Art Moderne**, promenade des Arts (*Open* Tue–Sun 10–6. *Admission: moderate*), near the theatre and acropolis conference/exhibition space.

St-Paul-de-Vence There are dozens of mediocre art galleries within the walls and, outside, the architecturally intriguing Maeght Foundation **St-Paul-de-Vence, Fondation Marguerite et Aimé Maeght ▶▶▶**, Montée des Trious (*Open* Oct–Jun daily 10–12.30, 2.30–6; Jul–Sep 10–7. *Admission: expensive*), with exemplary summer exhibitions and a permanent collection.

St-Tropez Musée de l'Annonciade, quai Saint-Raphael, 83990 St-Tropez (*Open* Jun–Sep Wed–Mon 10–1, 3–10; Oct, Dec–May Wed–Mon 10–12, 2–6. *Closed* public holidays and November. *Admission: moderate)* has a small private collection of Post-Impressionist paintings, including works by Bonnard and Matisse.

Vence Chapelle du Rosaire, 468 avenue Henri Matisse (*Open* Mon, Wed, Sat 2–5.30; Tue, Thu 10–11.30, 2–5.30. *Closed* Mass 10am Sun, Fri and Nov. *Admission: inexpensive*), was designed and decorated by Matisse (1947–51).

Villefranche The 14th-century Chapelle St-Pierre (*Closed* Mon) was decorated by Cocteau in 1957.

'The future of the new art lies in the South. The painter of the future will be a colourist such as never existed.'
— Van Gogh, 1888.

'Sunlight cannot be reproduced, but must be represented by something else—by colour.'
— Paul Cézanne, native of Aix, 1876.

TROUBADOURS
Troubadours were court poets in Occitan-speaking southern France during the 12th century. Some were noblemen, including William IX of Aquitaine, who wrote freely about his prowess in the lists of love. Most troubadours were more discreet, scarcely mentioning the object of devotion. As the French kings extended their control over the southwest, the poets retreated to Provence, where the fashion died out at the end of the 13th century.

▶▶ Bandol 169D1

Bandol is a lively weekend resort between Toulon and Marseille, with marina, sandy beaches and the best of Provençal red wines. It is a few minutes by boat to the small island of Bendor, a purpose-built craft village with sailing and diving schools, and an alcohol museum (*Open* Apr–Aug) exhibiting 8,000 bottles.

▶▶▶ Les Baux—Citadel 168C2

Musée d'Histoire des Baux and Citadel▶▶ (*Open* Mar–May, Sep, Oct daily 9–6.30; Jun–Aug 9–8; Nov, Feb 9–6; Dec, Jan 9–5. *Admission: expensive*) 'The Petra of France' (Augustus Hare) is a ruined citadel in a savagely romantic setting on a spur of the jagged Alpilles chain, almost invisible from below. Richelieu demolished the fortress and Les Baux was all but deserted by the 19th century. It now teems with people visiting its museums, as well as the château, shops and restaurants. To appreciate the ghostly beauty of the place, visit at sundown or out of season.

▶▶▶ Béziers 168A2

A wine town at the foot of the Minervois hills, Béziers stands for rugby, Spanish bullfights and the most savage atrocity of the Albigensian crusade: on 22 July 1209 Simon de Montfort's crusaders massacred 30,000 inhabitants, not bothering to distinguish Catholic from Cathar. 'Kill them all,' said the Abbot of Citeaux, 'God will recognize his own'. The main points of interest are the former cathedral and the two museums nearby: the Musée du Vieux Bitérrois et du Vin (local history, archaeology and wine) and the **Musée des Beaux Arts▶** (paintings).

▶▶▶ Biot 169E2

This picturesque and usually overcrowded old village in the scented hinterland of the Riviera is long famous for its ceramic industry and more recently for its glass and the **Musée National Fernand Léger▶▶**, Chemin de Val de Pome (*Open* Jul–Sep Wed–Mon 10.30–6; Apr–Jun Wed–Mon 10–12.30, 2–6; Oct–Mar Wed–Mon 10–12.30, 2–5.30. *Admission: moderate*; see page 174). You can visit the main glassworks (Verrerie) and watch the blowing process. There are potteries and galleries in the heart of the village, which has kept its 16th-century gates and arcaded square.

A relaxing game of boules at Bandol; a year-long pastime helped by Bandol's 320 days of sun

Provence is hill country, and on almost every hilltop there perches a village: a rhapsody of crumbling honeyed walls, pink tiled roofs and steep cobbled alleys too narrow for cars. A shady little square with a café and a fountain at the heart of the village, long views over vineyards, lavender fields, olive groves or the sea make each a paradise on earth.

The most spectacularly sited villages overlook the sea high above the Riviera—**Eze**, **Gorbio**, **Ste-Agnès**, **La Turbie** and **Roquebrune**, with its 10th-century castle. Even old **Monaco** counts as a perched village, naturally pretty but about the most tawdry of them all. Other beauty spots near the coast, all often overcrowded, are **Biot** (famous for its pottery and glass), **Tourrette-sur-Loup** (a weaving village), **Gourdon** (a souvenir village) and **St-Paul-de-Vence**, the most famous of all the artists' villages. For all its fame, St-Paul remains a place of style and irresistible charm, with a plane-shaded *boules* pitch outside the Café de la Place at the gates of the old walled village. Opposite the café, the prestigious Colombe d'Or hotel is full of masterpieces of modern art, accepted in lieu of payment by the proprietor, M Roux. Deeper into the mountainous hinterland of Nice, **Peillon** and **Luceram** are worth visiting for their church paintings. Strung across a precipice high above the Roya Gorge, **Saorge**'s setting is the most startling of all. It is easier to reach by car than looks likely from below, and fascinating to explore on foot.

Farther west, the landscape of the interior is less wild, the hill villages more welcoming. **Bargème**, **Mons**, **Bargemon**, **Seillans** and **Fox Amphoux** all have great charm. In the fashionable Lubéron/Vaucluse area, **Gordes** and the orange ochre village of **Roussillon** are the touristy beauty spots. Quieter villages include **Oppède le Vieux**, where the imposing Renaissance houses are now being rescued; and **Ménerbes**, recently invaded by Britons. **Le Barroux**, **Crestet** and **Séguret** are beautifully restored villages on the flanks of the jagged Dentelles de Montmirail.

HILL VILLAGES
Hill villages evolved to defend the area from attack in the lawless centuries that followed Roman peace. Since the 18th century many of the hill villages have gradually been abandoned by their inhabitants. Most have been revived by tourism and new residents seeking a peaceful alternative to the coast. The most picturesque have now evolved from artists' colonies to popular beauty spots.

Eze, one of the most dramatic of the Provence hill villages

Baroness Béatrice Ephrussi-de-Rothschild's collection is housed in the Villa Ile-de-France, Cap Ferrat, set among 7ha (17 acres) of gardens

CASSIS CALANQUES
The coastal landscape between Marseille and Cassis is unexpectedly wild and beautiful: cliffs and inlets (*calanques*) of bleached rock, clear water and pocket-handkerchief beaches, accessible only on foot (an arduous marked GR path follows the coast) or by boat. Sormiou and Sugiton *calanques* can be reached on foot from Marseille (start near the university). Prehistoric depictions of animals, similar to those at Lascaux in Dordogne, were discovered recently in a cave at Sormiou. The three eastern *calanques* are served by boat trips from Cassis: Port-Miou (accessible by car); Port-Pin; and En-Vau, the prettiest of all.

▶▶ Cannes *169E2*

Cannes is the glamorous focus of the Riviera, with expensive yachts and spectacular beaches along the palm-lined promenade, La Croisette (see page 182).

▶ Cap Ferrat *169E2*

A beautiful walk circuits this rocky cape. Set in the Villa Ile-de-France, in superb gardens, the **Villa Ephrussi-de-Rothschild▶▶**, Cap-Ferrat (*Open* mid-Feb to mid-Nov daily 10–6; mid-Nov to mid-Feb Mon–Fri 2–6, Sat, Sun 10–6; first week in Jan 10–6. *Admission: expensive)*, houses Baroness Beatrice's art collection. The resort and marina of **St-Jean-Cap-Ferrat** reflects the cape's muted opulence.

▶ Carpentras *168C3*

Carpentras is a busy medieval market town, famous for its truffles and sweets (*berlingots*). Sights include a 15th- and 16th-century cathedral, a small Roman triumphal arch and the beautiful Hôtel Dieu.

▶ Cassis *168C2*

This charming fishing port beneath the 400m (1,300ft) cliffs of Cap Canaille has waterfront cafés, fish restaurants and small hotels—a Mediterranean idyll. Boats travel to the rocky inlets, good for scuba diving and rock climbing.

▶▶ Esterel, Massif de l' *169E2*

The 32km (20-mile) coast road between La Napoule and St-Raphael offers the most spectacular scenery in the south. Flame-red porphyry mountains drop to the rocky shores and rough and narrow forest roads lead into the mountains. A track branching south 3km (2 miles) west of the **Auberge des Adrets** takes you within walking range of the highest peak, the **Mont Vinaigre** (618m/2,028ft). The **Pic de l'Ours▶▶**, near the coast (496m/1,627ft), is equally dramatic. There are few bathing spots, but there is red sand at Agay, a small resort on a sheltered horseshoe bay.

▶ Fréjus *169D2*

Fréjus was the first big Gallo-Roman port, with a ruined aqueduct and **amphitheatre▶** (see page 188). Outstanding cathedral buildings form the heart of town: **Fréjus cathedral close, museum and cloisters▶▶** (*Open* Apr–Sep daily 9–6; Oct–Mar Tue–Sun 9–noon, 2–5. Baptistery guided tour only), an archaeological museum (*Open* Apr–Sep daily 9–6; Oct–Mar Tue–Sun 9–12, 2–5) and the Gothic cathedral itself.

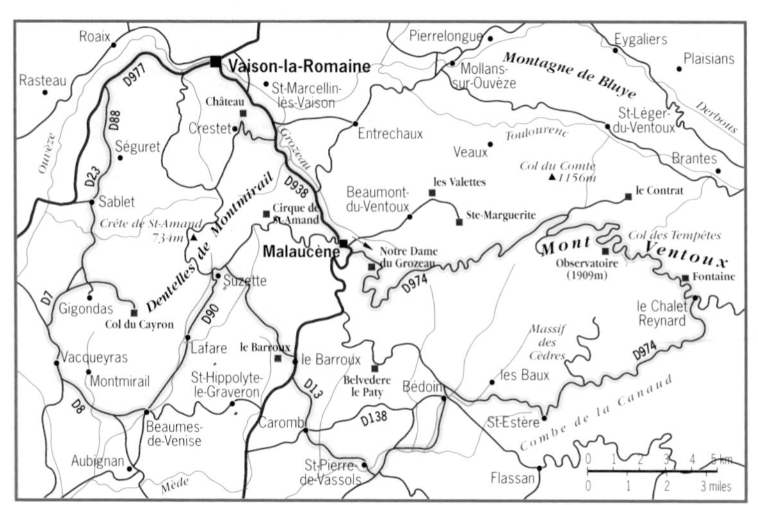

Drive

The Dentelles de Montmirail and Mont Ventoux

Start at Malaucène.
Malaucène is a lively market town at the foot of **Mont Ventoux**, France's highest mountain outside the Alps and Pyrenees. Its bare scree slopes make the Ventoux look snow-capped all year; in winter it is, and there is skiing on both flanks.

D974 via Mont Ventoux.
The road loops round the summit (crowned by ugly towers and a café), giving enormous views. On the eastern side is a memorial where cyclist Tommy Simpson died during the 1967 Tour de France.

From Mont Ventoux continue to Bédoin.
The road down to Bédoin through thick woodland was long used for time trials and still has the skid marks to prove it. **Bédoin** is an attractive village with a naturist holiday zone nearby.

D138 as far as Caromb and the D13 up to Le Barroux.
Caromb and **Le Barroux**, the latter dominated by an ill-proportioned Renaissance château, both have excellent small hotels.

Continue north to Suzette.
The slopes above Le Barroux lead to the dramatic jagged crest of the **Dentelles de Montmirail**. There are good views of the crags from **Suzette**.

D90 to Beaumes-de-Venise.
The tour now takes in some Rhône wine villages: **Beaumes-de-Venise**, **Vacqueyras** and **Gigondas**. The Dentelles de Montmirail are signed from Gigondas. The road surface soon turns rough, climbing through vineyards to a pass at the foot of the central spine of the Dentelles, the Col du Cayron. From here it is a steep 15-minute walk up an obvious path to a breach in the rocks, giving spectacular views. There are many possibilities for extending the walk: paths along the eastern flank of the rocky crest, or through the vineyards from the Col du Cayron, a long hike to Séguret (see below).

D7 and D23 to Séguret; then the D88 and 977 to Vaison, taking the D938 back to Malaucène.
The circuit continues to **Vaison-la-Romaine** via the restored village of **Séguret**. On the other side of the hill, **Crestet** has a medieval castle, an arcaded square and fountain, and a fine view.

▶ Fontfroide 168A1

This Cistercian abbey, set among the Corbières vineyards near Narbonne, was abandoned at the Revolution and was privately owned for most of the 20th century. The buildings, a mixture of Romanesque and Ancien Régime styles, have been well restored and complemented by delightful gardens.

▶ Fontvieille 168C2

Fontvieille is known for a pretty windmill on a wooded hillside to the south—the Moulin of Alphonse Daudet's *Lettres de Mon Moulin*, although the author neither owned nor wrote from it. The mill has been restored and houses a museum of Daudet memorabilia.

▶ Giens Peninsula 169D1

Two 5km (3-mile) spits of sand enclose working salt pans and link the village of Giens to the motherland near Hyères. There are pine woods and some modest resort development (Hyères Plage) along the eastern sand bar. The biggish town of Hyères, once a health resort of some cachet, no longer attracts many tourists, although the old upper town around the place St-Paul has some charm and fine public gardens.

OFFSHORE HYERES
Easily reached by boat from Hyères and Giens, the lovely islands of Porquerolles, Port Cros and Levant offer forest walks, good beaches and no cars. The largest, Porquerolles, has a small village resort. Mountainous and luxuriant, Port Cros and surrounding waters are a national park. Its only hotel is booked months in advance. The Ile du Levant has naturists in the west, and a small resort (Héliopolis). The eastern half is a naval base.

▶ Grasse 169E2

The world capital of the perfume industry is an old town in a sheltered, south-facing setting. Queen Victoria wintered here, but modern Grasse has no trace of Riviera chic. The old town has a tumbledown charm, though, with a narrow arcaded market place, the place aux Aires. Stalls surrounding the fountain are filled with local fruit, flowers and herbs.

The massive 12th-century **cathedral▶** has three works by Rubens, as well as a rare religious piece by Grasse's most famous son, Jean Honoré Fragonard (1732–1806). Fragonard left Grasse at the age of six and returned only briefly in 1790, bringing with him a series of paintings, The *Pursuit of Love*, rejected as too frivolous by their intended owner. Copies of the originals are on display in the villa where he stayed, with one good self-portrait and a number of works by his son Alexander.

Several scent producers (including Fragonard) offer free factory tours. The **International Perfume Museum** is worth visiting for its carefully researched herb garden and historical collection of perfume accessories.

▶▶ Lubéron 168C2

The 65km (40-mile) mountain ridge between the rivers Durance and Coulon is divided into Petit and Grand Lubéron by the only road over the ridge, between Bonnieux and Lourmarin. The Lubéron is wild country, protected by regional park status but developing nevertheless. Now ultra-fashionable, the quiet villages on the wooded north slope have become the latest corner of Provence to experience the questionable benefit of a second-home renaissance, spurred on by the phenomenal success of Peter Mayle's books. Ménerbes, Bonnieux and the Marquis de Sade's Lacoste are examples of reviving villages. Oppède-le-Vieux, a place of romantic ruins, is in the process of rescue from abandonment.

THE NOSE KNOWS
Grasse took to perfumery when scented gloves came into fashion in the 16th century. It takes 500kg (1,100lb) of roses to produce 1L (34fl oz) of essential oil; many local plants are still used and a few are unique to the Var. A specialist sniffer *(le nez)* chooses the fragrances.

Drive

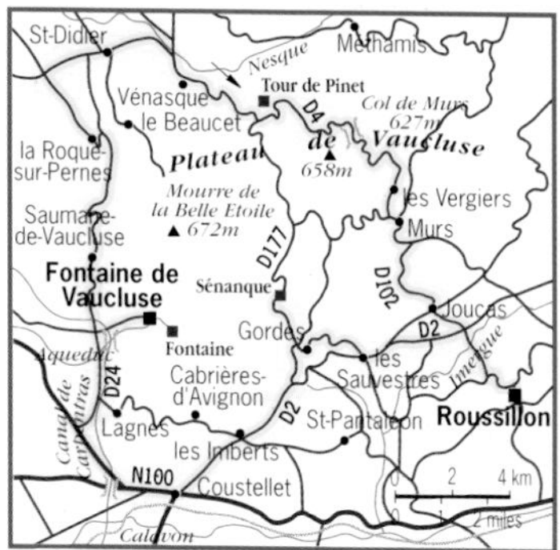

The Vaucluse Plateau

Start at Vénasque; take the D4 to Murs.
Vénasque is a fortified village on a ledge of the Vaucluse Plateau. It was a bishopric in the early Middle Ages and gave its name to the papal territory, Comtat Venaissin. Beside the church is an intriguing ancient chapel. The road climbs through oak woods to the **Col de Murs** before descending into the fashionable second-home territory of the Vaucluse/Lubéron.

D102 to Roussillon.
The orange/red village of Roussillon is a tourist trap, but not to be avoided for that. The vivid tones of the buildings and the sculptural ochre quarries of the surrounding hills are astonishing.

❑ When the noble Tricline Carbonnelle fell for the young poet Guillaume de Cabestan, her jealous husband killed him and had his heart served for supper. When the severed head was produced for pudding, Tricline realized what she had eaten and jumped out of the window. The earth of Roussillon was stained red for evermore. ❑

Back along the D102 and then the D2 to Gordes; D177 to Sénanque and back.
Gordes is another busy beauty spot, carefully restored and expensive, at the heart of *borie* country (see below). An imposing Renaissance château and turreted church command the plain and the steeply terraced village. A narrow road winds to the Cistercian abbey of Sénanque, set among fields of lavender.

D2/N100/D24 to Fontaine de Vaucluse.
Fontaine de Vaucluse was made famous by its romantic associations in Petrarch's love poetry. The site and nearby village are now thoroughly commercialized.

Walk

The Fort de Buoux

The ruins of the medieval fortifications are on the site of a much older citadel, south of the hamlet of Buoux (turn off the D113 at a *colonie de vacances*); later used as a Protestant refuge, it was dismantled in the 17th century. Walking possibilities include a two-hour tour. For a longer haul, follow marked paths across the Lubéron to Lourmarin or Vaugines; or along the crest of the Grand Lubéron to the Mourre Nègre (1,125m/3,690ft), and down to Auribeau (north side) or Cabrières (south).

❑ Dome-shaped dry-stone dwellings are found as far afield as southern Italy, the Balearics and Ireland. Dating back in origin to the Ligurian inhabitation of the region 4,000 years ago, the Vaucluse/Lubéron area has thousands of these *bories*, some inhabited until the 19th century. Gordes is the *borie* capital, with a restored museum village of the dwellings. ❑

Menton's dowdy, Monte's brass
Nice is rowdy, Cannes is class

The French Riviera has changed profoundly in the past few decades, primarily in becoming a summer instead of a winter playground. But the words of the old song still say plenty about the differences of style between the resorts which form an almost unbroken urban sprawl along the mountainous coastline between Cannes and the Italian border. This is the Riviera proper, although the term Côte d'Azur is often used to include the less densely developed coast between Cannes and Marseille.

ISLAND ESCAPE
If the Riviera buzz is getting too much, make an easy escape by using the regular boat service from Cannes to the tranquil Iles de Lérins, 15–30 minutes across the waves. The closest, Ste-Marguerite, offers walks through pine and eucalyptus woods, swimming off rocks and a marine museum. Smaller but equally seductive, St-Honorat has an ancient fortified monastery, part of which can be toured, and a new one still functioning—a popular place for retreats.

Larger-than-life musicians at the Nice Mardi-Gras

Cannes The Riviera at its most showy: the promenade of La Croisette, lined with palm trees and palatial hotels, is a perfect catwalk. Unlike many Riviera resorts, Cannes has a good sandy beach, divided into expensive private concessions, many of them attached to hotels and with classy lunch restaurants.

There is a public beach at the west end of the Croisette, near the gleaming conference facility separating the prom from the expensive yacht-filled port. It is also naturally picturesque, overlooked by the trees and medieval towers of **Le Suquet**, a small hill where some traces of an old village survive. The Croisette, the rue d'Antibes and side streets between them have the best shops. Boat trips go from the port to the Lérins Islands, Ste-Marguerite and St-Honorat, both with dense woods. Ste-Marguerite has some old prison buildings.

Juan-les-Pins Popular with Americans in the '20s (Frank Gould, Scott Fitzgerald, Hemingway, Harpo Marx, Mary Pickford and many others), Juan-les-Pins is less smart now, a young place with fast food and discos. A monument at nearby **Golf Juan** commemorates Napoleon's landing after his escape from Elba in 1815.

Antibes see page 171

Nice The capital of the Alpes Maritimes and the Riviera is, if not rowdy, a big city. The promenade des Anglais (endlessly due to undergo extensive restructuring for pedestrian benefit) is a roaring dual carriageway but has kept many of the domes and façades of its belle époque buildings (notably the Hotel Negresco).

An Italian city (Nizza) until 1860, and the home town of Garibaldi, Nice has kept more than a hint of Italian style in the gardens and arcaded neoclassical buildings around the place Masséna and the port, and especially in the narrow backstreets behind the quai des Etats Unis and the broad plaza of cours Saleya. This is Nice's open market and the best place for cafés and restaurants. This old

quarter is separated from the port by the so-called château—a hill with gardens and views.

Many of Nice's Victorian visitors (including the Queen) stayed at Cimiez, a hill suburb and site of the Roman settlement, with good museums and ruins (see pages 175 and 188). The other museums are in the striking modern complex north of the place Garibaldi. Nice goes mad for its two-week pre-Lent carnival, which ends with fireworks and a battle of flowers.

Cap Ferrat see page 178

Villefranche The most sheltered bay on the Riviera has an unspoilt fortified village above the fishing port (see also page 175).

Monaco/Monte Carlo Every inch of the Grimaldi family's tiny principality is occupied, and Monaco continues to grow upwards (skyscrapers) and outwards, on new man-made promontories. The old clifftop village of Monaco is now a toy-town pink-and-yellow tourist village with white-suited policemen, waxwork and doll museums, the Grimaldi's Marzipan Palace (a Napoleon museum and some of the interior are open to visitors), a gruesome 19th-century cathedral with good Renaissance paintings and the **Musée Océanographique**, avenue Saint-Martin (*Open* Apr–Sep daily 9.30–7; Jul, Aug daily 9.30–7.30; Oct–Mar daily 10–6. *Admission: expensive*). Traffic is strictly controlled: Signs to Monaco lead into underground car parks, with lifts up to street level.

Monte Carlo is the heartland of Monaco: plush shops, luxury hotels and the exuberant casino and Hôtel de Paris. A 3km (2-mile) circuit is used for the Grand Prix in May.

Menton Mild winters and lemons brought fame to Menton (it has a lemon festival in February). A baroque belfry and high, pastel-painted houses overlook the beach. Summer concerts are held on the small piazza outside the church of St-Michel. See also page 175.

Despite its casino, Menton's atmosphere is the slowest of the Riviera

THE CORNICHES

Three corniche roads hug the mountainous coastline from Nice to Menton. The lower corniche (N98) runs through all the resorts: a 33km (20.5-mile) journey of many hours in summer. The middle corniche (N7) is much quicker and passes the perched village of Eze; the upper or Grande Corniche (D2564) goes through La Turbie and over the Col d'Eze. Both upper and middle corniches bypass Monaco. Above this there is now a fourth corniche, the A8 motorway. With its fast drivers, sharp bends, tunnels and multiple exits, the motorway demands full concentration. Princess Grace of Monaco (the former actress Grace Kelly) was one of the corniches' many victims.

THAT SOUP
Quintessential product of the Mediterranean, *bouillabaisse* (fish soup) originally developed in Marseille as a fishermen's stalwart. Hundreds of pale imitations are offered along the Côte d'Azur, but there is a strict etiquette to its concoction (types and combinations of fish) and to its service: The fish must be dissected by the waiter at table.

▶ Marseille 168C2

The Mediterranean's biggest port and France's second city is an acquired taste—notorious for corruption and gangsterism, and a sure break from the tourist trail. The Greeks founded the city in the sixth century BC, but it is the modern life of the city that intrigues and repels in equal measure. The city is a melting pot of Arab, African and Latin cultures, with France's biggest community of Algerians. Racial tension simmers—National Front leader Jean Marie le Pen has his roots here.

The once celebrated **Canebière▶** is the main shopping street. There is an Arab market, a spectacular morning fish market at the **old port▶** (a good area for restaurants) and cheap souks near the Porte d'Aix.

Marseille's most famous monument is a former prison—the rocky island of **Château d'If▶** (boat trips from the old port). There are many excellent museums: archaeology and ethnography in the superbly restored 17th-century hospice, **La Vieille Charité▶▶**; fine arts; local history in the beautiful Renaissance **Maison Diamantée**; fashion; and natural history.

The best of the smaller museums are the faïence museum at **Château Pastré** and **Grobet-Labadié▶**, a 19th-century collector's house and contents preserved intact. The whole city is overlooked by its symbol, the spectacular basilica and statue of **Notre-Dame-de-la-Garde▶**, reached by a steep walk (or a tourist train) from the old port. Another of Marseille's attractions is the garden setting of the Parc and Palais du Pharo and **Parc Borély▶▶**.

Local produce from the Massif des Maures also includes strong-tasting chestnut-tree honey

▶ Maures, Massif des 169D2

This wild hinterland of hill country between Fréjus and Hyères is named after its dark mantle of pines, chestnuts and cork oaks. The interior is little visited, as the roads over the hills are narrow and very slow (except the D25 from Ste-Maxime to Draguignan), though scenic. The D558 Grimaud/La Garde crossing is more rewarding.

Le Lavandou/Bormes▶ is the main resort agglomeration, with a big marina. La Croix Valmer and Cavalaire are smaller resorts. There are boat trips to the Hyères Islands (see page 180) from Cavalaire and Le Lavandou.

▶ Montpellier *168B2*

A dynamic city of high-tech industry, bold new architecture and buzzing student life, Montpellier has cast off its traditional mantle of donnish stuffiness. One of the few big southern cities without a Roman history, its medieval growth was fostered by developing trade with the eastern Mediterranean.

The 17th- and 18th-century **promenade du Peyrou▶▶** is an impressive ensemble of triumphal arch, statue of Louis XIV and water tower at the head of the aqueduct that used to quench the city's thirst. The view from the terrace is splendid. People congregate around the **place de la Comédie▶**, Esplanade Gardens and on the place Jean Jaurès in the fashionable **old town▶▶**, where elegant mansions and museums line narrow winding streets.

Antigone is modern neoclassical residential area. The **Musée Fabre▶▶**, 2 rue Montpelliéret (*Open* Tue–Fri 9.30–5.30, Sat, Sun 9.30–5. *Admission: moderate*), has a fine collection of Old Master and 19th-century paintings. One of the benefactors was Alfred Bruyas, a rich patron of Courbet, Delacroix and others. There is a dance festival at the end of June and a wine fair in October.

▶ Narbonne/Languedoc–Roussillon Coast *168A2*

This coastline, sandy from the Petit Rhône to the Pyrenees, has thin strips separating sea from enclosed lagoons. The resort style is modern: the pyramid apartment blocks of **La Grande Motte** are an aggressive 1960s monument, while newer resorts have adopted a less obtrusive style. **Port Camargue** is an interesting marina-based design. The biggest development of all is **Cap d'Agde**, with a 41-court tennis club and a naturist area (Port Nature). Between Montpellier and Béziers is the fishing port of **Sète▶**, built in the 17th century.

Southern resorts Farther south, **Port Leucate** and **Port Barcarès** are big new resorts with marinas, on a sand bar between sea and salt lake. For 30km (19 miles) before the Spanish border, after the concentration of campsites at **Argelès sur Mer**, stretches the scenic **Côte Vermeille▶▶**. **Collioure▶▶** was, at one time, popular with Matisse.

Other areas of interest:

Agde Founded by Greeks when it was a sea port, Agde has a fortified black lava church.

Elne The cathedral has a beautiful medieval cloister.

Narbonne▶ This wine town once hit the news because of race riots. The twin towers of an unusual, unfinished Gothic cathedral dominate the town and surrounding vineyards. Excavations in the central square have unearthed part of the Roman road from Italy to Spain, the Via Domitia; there is an archaeological museum nearby.

Salses The well-preserved 15th-century fortress here was altered by Vauban.

Sigean Safari Park African wildlife (*Admission: expensive*).

MONTPELLIER MEDICINE
Pre-Renaissance Europe did not read Greek, and medical knowledge filtered in from the east via the spice trade, of which Montpellier was a hub from the 12th century. The university specialized in medicine and attracted Petrarch and Rabelais among its students.

HERBS
Herbs grow throughout the south of France; in Provence they are an important industry, and every market sells them in quantity. Buis-les-Baronnies, renowned for its *tilleul* fair in early July, has a good weekly *marché provençal* on Wednesdays.

BULL-TEASING
All summer the Roman amphitheatres at Nîmes and Arles and the modern arena at Béziers are the setting for the *corrida*, the traditional gory Spanish bullfight. The Camargue specializes in a more informal and slightly less cruel encounter, the Provençal *course à la cocarde*. In makeshift arenas bullfighters (*razeteurs*) try to snatch a rosette (*cocarde*) from the horns of Camargue bulls, which survive to fight again. The *razeteur* escapes by vaulting over the ringside hoardings.

Between the mouth of the Var and the Italian border, the Alps drop abruptly into the Mediterranean with no transition between mountains and coast. This cramps life by the sea and offers plenty of escape routes from the heat and crowds into the cooler, cleaner air of the mountains.

Old perched villages of the immediate hinterland (**Eze**, **Peillon**, **Peille**, **Gorbio**, **Lucéram**, **Coaraze**) are the obvious short-haul targets. Longer journeys involve heading up any of the four main river valleys which have their sources at altitude near the Italian border: the **Tinée**, **Var** and **Vésubie** (which end up as one, the Var); and the **Roya**, which crosses into Italy about halfway down to the sea. Connoisseurs of river gorge drives will want to see the **Vésubie** Gorges (between Plan du Var and St-Jean-la-Rivière) and the **Cians** gorge between Pont de Cian and Beuil (tight driving). The source of the Tinée is near the **Col de la Bonette**, at the northern limit of the Maritime Alps; the **Bonette** road, Europe's highest, is a rugged and beautiful route north, for visitors who are not in a hurry.

The **Roya** Valley is of more varied interest; either follow the river up from Ventimiglia (Italy) or drive up from Menton to Sospel and over the Col de Brouis, joining the Roya near **Breil**, a small town with simple lodgings. North of Breil, the Roya cuts impressive gorges, especially below the balcony village of **Saorge**, well worth a detour to explore on foot. **La Brigue** is the best base in the upper valley, with an interesting church and remarkable 15th-century frescoes in the nearby chapel. On the other side of the valley are **Lac des Mesches** and **Casterino**, reached from St-Dalmas-de-Tende, the start of hikes to the Vallée des Merveilles around Mont Bégo (2,872m/9,420ft). The valley is accessible only from July to early October.

The **Mercantour** is mainland France's youngest national park, covering a long stretch of high mountain country along the Italian border. Gateways to the park (with information points) include the summer and winter resort of **Valberg** and **St-Martin-de-Vésubie**.

Le Boréon (near St-Martin) is a good starting point for a hike.

VALLEY MARVELS
The ancient artistic marvels of the Vallée des Merveilles date from the Bronze Age (1800–1500BC). They were traced into the schist surface using silex or quartz tools and mostly represent human or bovine figures, pointing to the Ligurian people's cult for the all-powerful Mt. Bégo and for bulls. To visit the 100,000-odd rock drawings you must be accompanied by a guide. There are several visits a day starting from the main refuges and from the Lacs Jumeaux (Jul–Aug; apply to tourist office in Tende tel: 04 93 04 73 71). Less hardy walkers might find an overnight stay at the mountain refuge of Merveilles helpful.

High mountain country in the Mercantour National Park

Swimmers in the Gardon River, near Pont du Gard, escape the stifling mid-summer heat

▶▶ Nice 169E2

See pages 175, 182–183 and 188.

▶▶ Nîmes 168B2

The birthplace of denim (serge de Nîmes) is best known for extreme heat, its Roman amphitheatre **Les Arènes▶▶▶**, boulevard des Arènes (*Open* daily, Apr–Sep 9–7; Oct–Mar 10–5. *Admission: moderate*), and temple (see page 188) and a state-of-the-art contemporary art museum **Musée d'Art Contemporain Carré d'Art**, place de la Maison Carrée (*Open* Tue–Sun 10–6. *Admission: moderate*), designed by Norman Foster.

▶ Orange 168C3

Orange has a fine Roman arch, which, with its still finer Roman **Théâtre Antique▶▶▶** (*Open* daily, Apr–Sep 9–7; Oct–Mar 9–6. *Admission: expensive*; includes admission to the museum opposite), is a compelling reason to visit (see page 189). Orange is an important market town for the Rhône Valley's fruit and wine.

EXPORT ORANGES
In the 16th century, the principality of Orange passed to the House of Nassau. The first prince of this House was William the Silent, who led the rebellion of the Netherlands against Spain, becoming the province's Stadtholder in 1580. A century later, William of Orange mounted the English throne as the husband of Mary.

▶ Perpignan 168A1

The capital of French Catalonia, red-brick Perpignan was the medieval HQ of the kingdom of Majorca—an offshoot of the ruling house of Aragon. Their low-rise fortress covers a large area at the heart of the city. The streets around the cathedral (Gothic) and medieval town gate (Castillet) are more entertaining. Catalan is spoken here, and there is Hispanic music in the streets on summer evenings. The most beautiful building in the town, the Gothic Loge de Mer (a trading house), is now a burger restaurant. Outside Perpignan is Tautavel, an important prehistoric site and museum.

▶▶ Pézenas 168A2

Now a small town of fewer than 10,000 inhabitants, Pézénas once enjoyed a glorious reputation as the Versailles of the south. The old town around the place Gambetta has kept many beautiful 17th-century houses and a medieval **Jewish ghetto▶**. Outstanding among them are **Hôtel Lacoste▶** and the **Hôtel d'Alfonce▶**, where Molière's troupe performed in 1655. Abundant crafts shops and workshops add vitality and interest.

▶▶▶ Pont du Gard 168B2

This Roman aqueduct spanning the River Gardon near Nîmes is one of the greatest pieces of Roman architecture in France (see page 189).

The Romans enjoyed the south of France. They colonized it early, romanized it intensively and adorned it with temples, theatres, amphitheatres, monumental arches, aqueducts and bridges. No other region outside Italy is so rich in Roman remains, many of which are still in use today.

ROMAN INVASION
Colonization began in 125BC when consul Sextius responded to an appeal from the Greek port of *Massilis* (Marseille) and destroyed a native power base on the Entremont plateau. A new *Provincia* (Provence) was established in 118BC. Marseille lost its privileges in 49BC. Its commercial role was taken over by Arles, Fréjus and Narbonne, which became the capital of the renamed Provincia Narbonensis in 27BC.

Aix-en-Provence The first Roman town in Gaul, founded as *Aquae Sextiae* by consul Sextius, has little left to show for itself, apart from the Musée Granet's items from the pre-Roman settlement at Entremont.

Arles Once the capital of Gaul and Constantine's preferred base, Arles has a spectacularly well-preserved amphitheatre (Arènes), as well as the Théâtre Antique, seating 12,000 and still in use for bullfights and real drama. The amphitheatre (first century AD) held more than 20,000 spectators, nearly half the town's present population. The structure was converted into a medieval fortress and later a town within a town, which was dismantled in the 19th century. The Musée de l'Arles Antique groups Roman artefacts with early Christian exhibits.

Fréjus This Roman port with surviving fragments of theatre, aqueduct and Gaul's oldest amphitheatre now hosts bullfights and concerts. The 11th-century cathedral houses an archaeology museum.

Nice-Cimiez The hill town of *Cemenelum* was the capital of the Roman province of Maritime Alps. Between the monastery and the once grand hotels of Victorian Cimiez is an area of excavations, including a small amphitheatre, the **Musée Archéologique▶▶**, 160 avenue des Arènes (*Open* Wed–Mon 10–6. *Admission: moderate*), and a large area of baths, used every July for Nice's great jazz festival.

Nîmes The amphitheatre (dating from the first century AD) and temple known as the Maison Carrée (first century BC) are the best preserved buildings of their kind in the Roman world. After a 1,500-year hiatus, the full three-level amphitheatre again echoes with the roars of fighting bulls and an excited

The first-century amphitheatre at Nîmes

public. The Maison Carrée has done service as a town hall, private home, stable and a church.

Orange As at Nîmes, two outstanding Roman buildings attract tourists to an otherwise uncaptivating town. Founded in 46BC, Arausio was three times as populous as modern Orange. The Roman theatre (first century BC) is the only one with its backstage wall standing. A statue of Augustus is above the stage, still used for summer concerts. The triumphal arch (first century BC) is a roundabout on the N7 at the northern gateway to town. In the interests of traffic flow, do not attempt to admire it from behind the wheel.

Pont du Gard This three-tiered section of the Uzès to Nîmes aqueduct, spanning the River Gardon, is made of massive stones without mortar, still standing after 2,000 years. You can no longer drive across the bridge but must approach from either side of the river. Nor can you walk along the top. New landscaping is designed to enhance access to the bridge's beautiful woodland setting, with information points and two museums.

St-Rémy-Glanum and Les Antiques Among trees to the south of St-Rémy, utterly uncluttered by fencing or graffiti, stand two beautiful Roman monuments (late first century BC). The triumphal arch has lost its top but not all its decoration of fruit and captives. Beside it stands a well-preserved and elegant memorial to two grandsons of Augustus. Not far away, on the other side of the road, lie the extensive excavations of **Glanum,** a pre-Roman town, probably a spa, which was later romanized, then abandoned in the fourth century.

La Turbie Only partial remains survive of the 50m (170ft) Trophée des Alpes, built in 6BC to celebrate Augustus' successful Alpine campaigns. There is a good museum on site with a magrette, photos of a similar trophy in Romania, and old engravings of the Trophée as a medieval fortress. There are tremendous views of the coast from the surrounding park.

Vaison-la-Romaine A Roman bridge spans the River Ouvèze and separates medieval Vaison from the modern town and the excavations of the Roman Vasio. Ruins include a shopping street, a villa, public lavatories, a theatre and a museum, all in an attractive setting of rosebeds.

DEVELOPMENT
The many Alpine tribes resisted Rome longer than the rest of Gaul and were not conquered until the campaign of Augustus (24–12BC). This success allowed the completion of the Via Aurelia from Rome to Arles and was commemorated with the 50m (170ft) Alpine Trophy. Nîmes flourished throughout the first two centuries AD, while Arles emerged as the focus of the new Christian religion.

The Roman theatre in Orange comes to life every July during a prestigious opera festival

VAN GOGH'S FOOTPRINTS
Various places where Van Gogh planted his easel in and around St-Rémy and the asylum of St-Paul have been furnished with explanatory notices and reproductions of the relevant paintings. The tourist office of St-Rémy can provide maps and organizes tours of the *Lieux Peints* several times a week. More energetic hikers can tackle the marked path (GR6) from Les Antiques to the ruined town of Les Baux along the crest of the Alpilles. Due to forest fires, access to areas of Les Alpilles is forbidden between mid-June and mid-September.

St-Tropez still retains a sense of identity, despite its 'glam' status

▶ Port Grimaud *169D2*

The Venice of the Riviera is an ingenious modern resort at the head of the Gulf of St-Tropez, designed for a yacht-owning (or renting) clientele. Its streets are waterways spanned by footbridges linking clumps of holiday homes, each with its own mooring outside the front door. The architecture is inspired by the local style and, with shady squares on many of the hotel clusters, Port Grimaud achieves the simulation of ordinary village life, except that there are no ordinary villagers.

▶ St-Raphaël *169D2*

A big family resort at the foot of the Esterel, popular in Roman times and revived a century ago, modern St-Raphaël has no great cachet, but the Riviera ingredients are there—beaches, marina, palm trees, traffic jams and golf courses.

▶ St-Rémy *168C2*

This cheerful little plane-shaded town at the foot of the mini-mountainous range of Alpilles, has **Glanum▶** and Les Antiques (see page 189) on its doorstep. The main square is a good place for a drink in the shade, except on Wednesdays when the market takes over. On the edge of town is the former monastery of **St-Paul-de-Mausole▶**, the asylum where Van Gogh lived for a year from 1889. The restored Romanesque church and cloister are usually open to visitors, but there is nothing else to see: even the bust of Van Gogh by Zadkine has been stolen.

▶▶ St-Tropez *169D2*

Among an arty élite, the old fishing port of St-Tropez and its surrounding coast and mountains have been no secret since the turn of the 20th century, when the painter Paul Signac settled there. But it was Brigitte Bardot in the 1950s who made 'St Trop' a cliché for liberated youth. This it remains, although the original habitués are ageing and liberated youth arrives in herds from nearby campsites. The port has exorbitant hotels, low-rise and studiously informal; stars hiding in high-walled villas; fat yachts in the port; lots of denim and leather and loud rock music. Out of season and early in the morning, the close-knit old port remains its old self, as portrayed on scores of canvases in the excellent museum (see page 175). In the evening the place des Lices at the back of the old town becomes a vast *boules* arena. The port has no beach to speak of, but the Ramatuelle peninsula has long tracts of sand, which are part of St-Tropez mythology (Tahiti, **Pampelonne▶**, **l'Escarlet▶**). The old hill villages set back from the coast (**Ramatuelle▶▶**, **Gassin▶** and Grimaud) now have more chic and less hubbub than St-Tropez itself.

▶ Ste-Maxime *169D2*

Facing St-Tropez across a wide bay, Ste-Maxime was originally a Phoenician colony. It is a much quieter and more sheltered resort, with a fishing port, marina and a sandy beach. The bay provides safe sailing and good windsurfing.

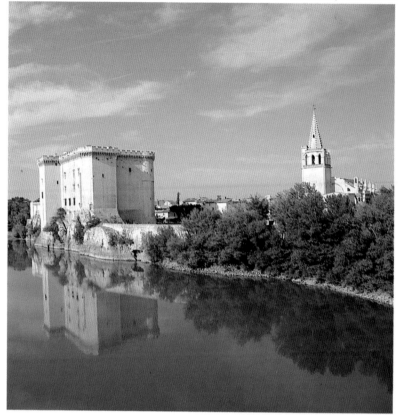

The well-preserved Château de Tarascon, sitting on the bank of the River Rhône

▶ Sisteron *169D3*

Sisteron is one of the natural gateways of northern Provence, a fortress town with an impressive **citadel▶**, described by Henri IV as the most powerful in the realm. Its position was unfortunately strategic enough to attract heavy bombing in 1944. The citadel has been restored and is used for the summer festival. There is a 12th-century former cathedral and picturesque streets.

▶ Tarascon/Beaucaire *168B2*

Their imposing medieval fortresses confronting each other across the Rhône, Beaucaire and Tarascon vividly commemorate the medieval frontier between French Languedoc and Imperial Provence. The **Château de Tarascon▶▶**, boulevard du roi René (*Open* Apr–Sep daily 9–7; Oct–Mar, 10.30–5. *Admission: expensive)*, is one of the best preserved of its kind, and is open to visitors. The next-door **church▶** has a Romanesque door, paintings by Provence-based artists and the tomb of St. Martha in the crypt. St. Martha tamed the legendary monster La Tarasque, celebrated by a vibrant June festival. Tarascon also has a popular museum, the so-called house of the fictional Tartarin de Tarascon, anti-hero of Daudet's comic novels. The **Musée Souleïado▶** displays examples of sunny Provençal fabrics, still made today by the Souleïado company.

TAMING THE BEAST
St. Martha found Tarascon terrorized by a monster with a lion's head, six twisted bear claws and an unhealthy appetite for women and children. She tamed the beast and led it back to the Rhône. King René organized a celebration in 1474, parading a model through the streets, knocking down anyone in its way. A less destructive version still takes place in June.

▶ Toulon 169D1

France's main Mediterranean naval port features more prominently in history books than on holiday itineraries. The young Captain Bonaparte covered himself in glory during the eight-month siege of English-occupied Toulon in 1793, and in November 1942, 60 French ships were scuttled in the port when the Nazis moved into Vichy France. Ironically, in 1995 the city council became National Front. The dingy backstreets of the old town of Toulon may have *louche* appeal and certainly have cheap restaurants, and you can count on finding a hotel room when the rest of the south of France is taken. The area is now undergoing a huge renovation project.

Otherwise, Toulon's main attractions are the renovated Naval Museum at the eastern end of the arsenal complex and Mont Faron, the rocky mountain ridge dominating the city and reached either by cable car or a narrow hairpin road. As well as a splendid view, there is a museum devoted to the Allied landings in 1944. The 19th-century fort is still occupied by the military.

RACING DUKES

The dukes of Uzès have been the official first dukes of France since the 17th century. King Louis XIII announced that all peers should get their titles confirmed by chancery and that future precedence would reflect the speed at which this was achieved. In the ensuing race the carriages of Uzès and Luynes converged at speed in the narrow rue St-Thomas du Louvre. The Luynes team was overturned and Uzès was the first duke home.

▶ Uzès 168B3

This dignified old town, robbed of its fortifications by Richelieu because of its Protestant leanings, stands on a high plateau of rocky garrigue, the southeastern ledge of the Massif Central. At the heart of the town, near the arcaded main square, is the **Duché d'Uzès▶▶**, place de Duché (*Open* Jul to mid-Sep daily 10–12, 2–6.30; mid-Sep to Jun 10–12, 2–6. *Admission: expensive*), still inhabited, with a medieval tower and a fine Renaissance façade. The round 12th-century **tower▶▶** (Tour Fenestrelle) is all that remains of the Romanesque cathedral. In 1662, Jean Racine was sent to Uzès to forget dreams of a literary career and prepare for holy orders. Racine liked the town, but could not understand the people, who spoke southern dialect, not rhyming Alexandrine couplets. He returned to Paris, and the rest is tragedy.

▶ **Vence** see opposite

▶▶▶ Grand Canyon de Verdon 169D2

Between Castellane and Moustiers is the most spectacular gorge in Europe, with limestone cliffs plunging 700m (2,300ft) to the narrow river bed. The best way to see it from a car is to follow the Route des Crêtes, a circuit which leads from La Palud on the north bank. The road passes the **Châlet la Maline**, one terminus of the tough day's walk (14km/9 miles) along the bottom of the canyon, via numerous tunnels (torch/flashlight essential), to a car park near the Point Sublime. For a taste of the gorge scenery, park at this end of the path and walk down to the water.

The main tourist destination is **Moustiers-Ste-Marie▶**, an interesting old village straddling a mountain ravine and waterfall. Long famous for its ceramics and lavender, Moustiers is well worth a stroll, if you can park. The church has an unstable look—bulging walls and unaligned Gothic choir and Romanesque nave. Below Moustiers, the Verdon is dammed to form a vast reservoir. There are a few villages and campsites beside the lake: only **Ste-Croix-du-Verdon** has any charm.

TONS OF LAVENDER

Corduroy fields of lavender are popular aspects of Upper Provence, for a brief midsummer period between flowering and harvest: July is best. Lavender grows naturally above 600m (1,970ft) and thrives on the climate and chalky soil. A hybrid plant (*le lavandin*, not *la lavande*) has been developed to grow at lower altitude. Provence produces 100 tonnes of lavender essence and 1,000 tonnes of lavandin essence each year.

Drive

Vaison-la-Romaine, Nyons and the Baronnies

Start at Vaison-la-Romaine.
Vaison-la-Romaine is a good base for excursions. The Ouvèze separates medieval Vaison, beneath a hill fortress, from the modern and Roman towns.

D938/D538 to Nyons.
Nyons has an olive museum and oil mills open to visitors: most interesting during the winter pulping season. A jumble of vaulted lanes (Quartier des Forts) climbs from the place Bufaven to a tiny pilgrimage chapel.

D94 to Curnier; D64 to Buis-les-Baronnies.

A beautiful drive over the **Col d'Ey** to **Buis-les-Baronnies** passes a riverside lavender distillery at

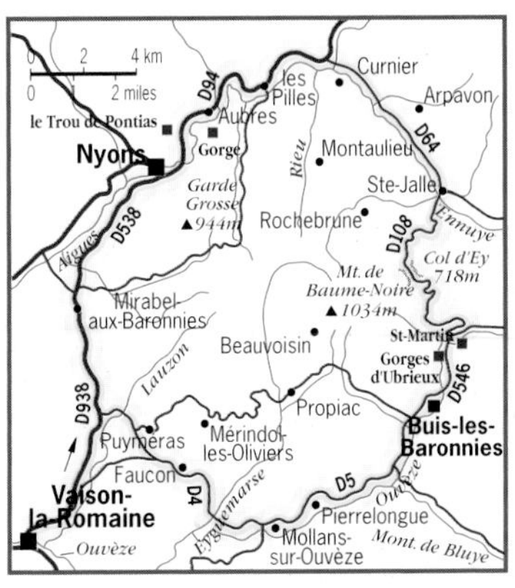

Ste-Jalle. Buis-les-Baronnies is the main trade hub for the popular lime blossom (*tilleul*) infusion.

D5 back to Vaison.

Drive

Vence, Col de Vence, Gourdon

Start at Vence.
Vence is a busy hill town with three medieval gateways and a square (place du Peyra) on the site of the Roman forum. The former cathedral has Roman inscriptions in the façade. Matisse's **Rosary Chapel** (see pages 174–175) is near the St-Jeannet road.

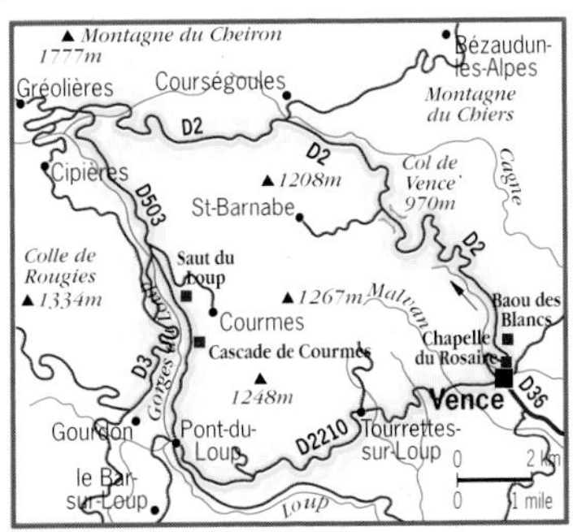

Follow D2 northwest to Col de Vence.
There are fine views from the 970m (3,180ft) **Col de Vence**.

D2 to Courségoules and Gréolières.
Beneath the impressive walls of the Montagne du Cheiron, **Gréolières** and **Courségoules** have good Renaissance paintings in their churches. Enthusiasts of mountain motoring can continue to the ski resort of **Gréolières les Neiges** or round the **Massif Cheiron**.

D3 to Gourdon and Gorges du Loup.
Gourdon is a former Saracen stronghold in a superb setting dominating the Loup Valley and surveying the coast. The Loup has impressive views, but few safe stopping places except at a café that charges for a sight of a waterfall, the Saut du Loup.

D2210 via Tourrettes-sur-Loup.
Tourrettes-sur-Loup is a pretty, old hill village, a hub of the violet industry and now a thriving arts and crafts village.

Return on D2210 to Vence.

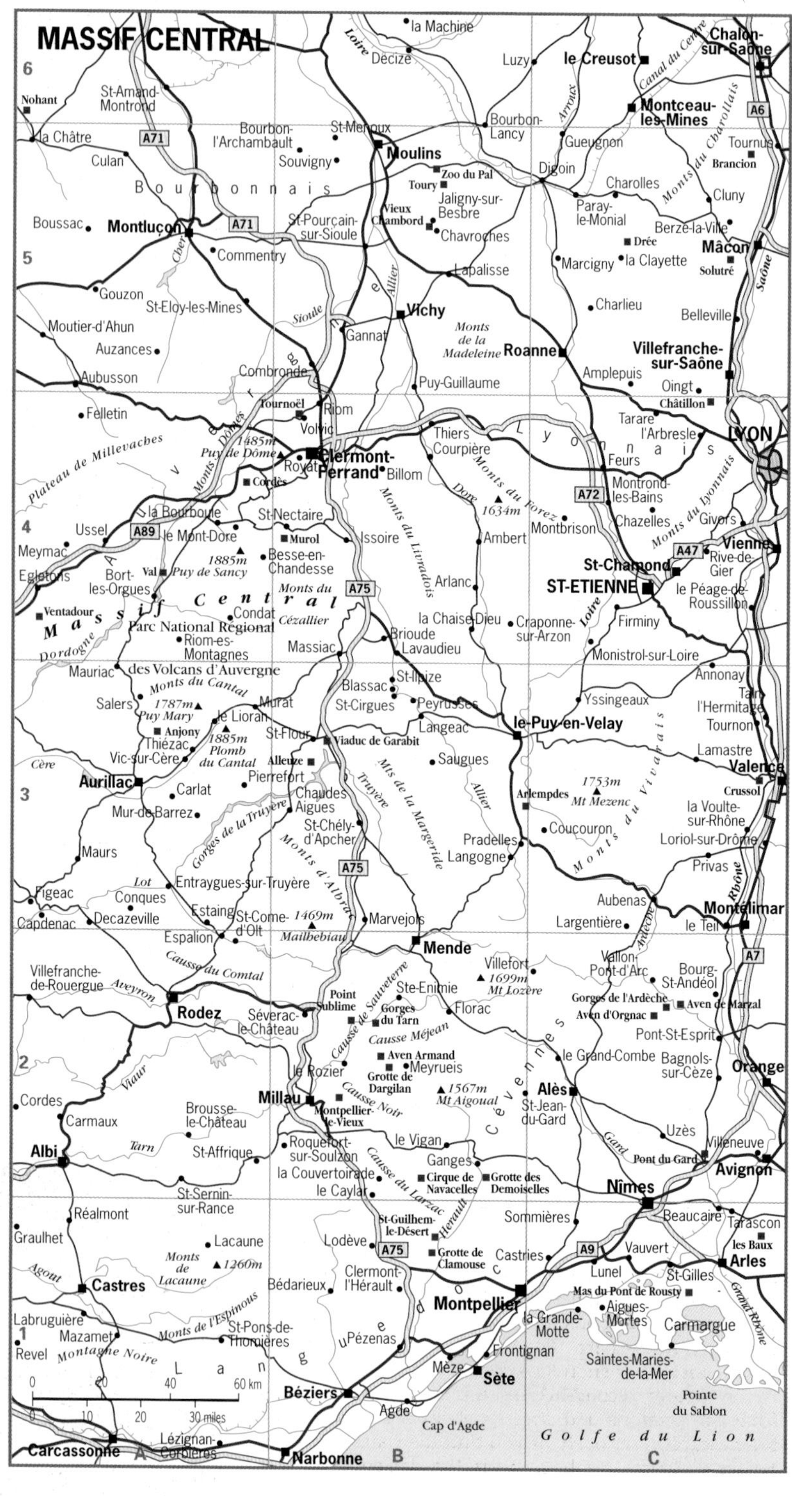
MASSIF CENTRAL
la Machine
Loire
Decize
Luzy
le Creusot
Canal du Centre
Chalon-sur-Saône
Nohant
St-Amand-Montrond
Arroux
Montceau-les-Mines
A6
la Châtre
A71
Bourbon-l'Archambault
St-Menoux
Bourbon-Lancy
Gueugnon
Monts du Charollais
Tournus
Culan
Souvigny
Moulins
Zoo du Pal
Digoin
Brancion
Toury
Charolles
Bourbonnais
Jaligny-sur-Besbre
Paray-le-Monial
Cluny
Boussac
Montluçon
A71
St-Pourçain-sur-Sioule
Vieux Chambord
Chavroches
Berzé-la-Ville
Dreé
Mâcon
Cher
Commentry
Allier
Lapalisse
Marcigny
la Clayette
Solutré
Saône
Gouzon
St-Eloy-les-Mines
Sioule
Vichy
Charlieu
Belleville
Moutier-d'Ahun
Gannat
Monts de la Madeleine
Roanne
Villefranche-sur-Saône
Auzances
Combronde
Amplepuis
Aubusson
Puy-Guillaume
Oingt
Tournoël
Riom
Châtillon
Felletin
Volvic
Thiers
Tarare
Lyonnais
LYON
1485m Puy de Dôme
Courpière
l'Arbresle
Plateau de Millevaches
Monts Dômes
Clermont-Ferrand
Royat
Billom
Monts du Forez
Feurs
Cordès
Dore
1634m
A72
Montrond-les-Bains
Monts du Livradois
Monts du Lyonnais
la Bourboule
St-Nectaire
Chazelles
Givors
Ussel
A89
le Mont-Dore
Murol
Issoire
Ambert
Montbrison
Meymac
1885m Puy de Sancy
Besse-en-Chandesse
St-Chamond
A47
Vienne
Rive-de-Gier
Egletons
Val
Bort-les-Orgues
Monts du Cézallier
A75
Arlanc
ST-ETIENNE
le Péage-de-Roussillon
Ventadour
Massif Central
Condat
Parc National Régional des Volcans d'Auvergne
la Chaise-Dieu
Craponne-sur-Arzon
Loire
Firminy
Dordogne
Riom-es-Montagnes
Massiac
Brioude
Lavaudieu
Monistrol-sur-Loire
Mauriac
Annonay
Monts du Cantal
Blassac
St-Ilpize
Salers
1787m Puy Mary
Murat
St-Cirgues
Peyrusse
Yssingeaux
Tain-l'Hermitage
Anjony
le Lioran
1885m Plomb du Cantal
Langeac
le-Puy-en-Velay
Tournon
Thiézac
St-Flour
Viaduc de Garabit
Lamastre
Cère
Vic-sur-Cère
Alleuze
Saugues
Valence
Aurillac
Pierrefort
Mts de la Margeride
Truyère
Allier
Arlempdes
1753m Mt Mezenc
Crussol
Carlat
Chaudes-Aigues
Monts du Vivarais
la Voulte-sur-Rhône
Mur-de-Barrez
Gorges de la Truyère
St-Chély-d'Apcher
Coucouron
Loriol-sur-Drôme
Maurs
Monts d'Aubrac
Pradelles
Langogne
A75
Privas
Lot
Entraygues-sur-Truyère
Rhône
Figeac
Conques
Aubenas
Montélimar
Capdenac
Decazeville
Estaing
St-Come-d'Olt
1469m Mailhebiau
Marvejols
Largentière
le Teil
Espalion
Mende
Ardèche
A7
Causse du Comtal
Villefort
1699m Mt Lozère
Vallon-Pont-d'Arc
Bourg-St-Andéol
Villefranche-de-Rouergue
Aveyron
Ste-Enimie
Gorges de l'Ardèche
Aven de Marzal
Rodez
Sévérac-le-Château
Point Sublime
Gorges du Tarn
Causse de Sauveterre
Florac
Aven d'Orgnac
Causse Méjean
Pont-St-Esprit
Aven Armand
Cévennes
le Grand-Combe
Bagnols-sur-Cèze
Viaur
le Rozier
Meyrueis
Orange
Grotte de Dargilan
1567m Mt Aigoual
Alès
Cordes
Millau
Causse Noir
St-Jean-du-Gard
Carmaux
Brousse-le-Château
Montpellier-le-Vieux
Gard
Uzès
Tarn
Roquefort-sur-Soulzon
le Vigan
Villeneuve
Albi
St-Affrique
Causse du Larzac
Ganges
Pont du Gard
Avignon
la Couvertoirade
Cirque de Navacelles
Grotte des Demoiselles
Nîmes
St-Sernin-sur-Rance
le Caylar
Hérault
Réalmont
St-Guilhem-le-Désert
Sommières
Beaucaire
Tarascon
Graulhet
Lacaune
Lodève
A75
Grotte de Clamouse
Castries
A9
Vauvert
les Baux
Agout
Monts de Lacaune
1260m
Clermont-l'Hérault
Lunel
Arles
Castres
Bédarieux
Montpellier
St-Gilles
Mas du Pont de Rousty
Languedoc
Monts de l'Espinouse
Aigues-Mortes
Labruguière
Grand Rhône
St-Pons-de-Thomières
la Grande-Motte
Camargue
Mazamet
Pézenas
Revel
Montagne Noire
Frontignan
Saintes-Maries-de-la-Mer
Mèze
Sète
0 20 40 60 km
0 10 20 30 miles
Béziers
Pointe du Sablon
Agde
Cap d'Agde
Golfe du Lion
Lézignan-Corbières
Carcassonne
Narbonne
A
B
C
1
2
3
4
5
6

Massif Central

THE MASSIF CENTRAL is no single mountain range, but an enormous highland region between the Loire and the Mediterranean, covering about one sixth of France. More southern than central, it is certainly massive. Diversity comes as no surprise.

HIGH GROUND The highest peaks are in the northern region, Auvergne, a land of rich pastures and a mountain diet of ham, hard cheese (Cantal) and dark bread: food built to last through a long winter of isolation. Its villages are drab and, as a holiday area, so is its image. The main resorts are spas and, by Alpine or Pyrenean standards, the mountains are unimpressive unless you like volcanoes, with no glaciers, no snow-capped peaks in summer, few rock faces to excite climbers, and no great lakes. Just big hills, ugly hydroelectric reservoirs, and dreary old spas—albeit full of fading grandeur.

QUIET SIMPLICITY On the other hand, Auvergne tourism is quiet, prices are low, and the value in simple hotels is often outstanding. There is a little skiing (more than a little for cross-country skiers) but in general the slopes and rough old mountain villages have escaped the ravages of ski development. Summits are accessible to walkers and are quite high enough to be rewarding. With good fishing and canoeing, Auvergne is a fine area for an active outdoor holiday, with some sightseeing thrown in—hilltop castle ruins, beautiful old churches and a range of extinct volcanoes, small but perfectly formed.

WILD COUNTRY Farther south, the Causses and Cévennes form less high but wilder and not as well-trodden country. For fishing rivers and green valleys, substitute white water and rocky gorges; for cow pastures, windswept limestone plateaux with no spring water, only dewponds and sheep; and for creamy St-Nectaire, razor-sharp Roquefort. This is wilderness France, an area of enormous appeal to a growing minority of visitors, second-homers and permanent refugees from the comforts and stresses of town life, who take their escapism seriously. If you find the charms of rural France a bit tame, try the southern Massif Central.

▶▶▶ REGION HIGHLIGHTS

Canoeists set off from the river beaches by the Pont d'Arc in the Gorges de l'Ardèche

►► Aigoual, Massif de l' *194B2*

Aigoual means wet. Thanks to the convergence of Atlantic and Mediterranean air currents, the southern bastion of the Massif Central (1,567m/5,141ft) is the wettest place in France. The slopes have been reforested to try to reduce flood damage. There are roads to the summit from north and south, big views from the top and an arboretum (**Hort de Dieu**) just below it, signed from the road. **Meyrueis►** is a popular tourist base with a Cévennes National Park information point (Chateau de Roguedols, tel: 04 66 45 62 81). It's well placed for excursions to **Aven Armand** and **Dargilan** grottoes and drives along the **Jonte** and **Tarn** gorges or south to **Dourbie gorge►►**.

► Allier, Gorges de l' *194B3*

West of Le Puy-en-Velay, the Allier runs north through dark gorges of granite and volcanic rock, best seen from the train, between tunnels. It is an area for riding, fishing, canoeing (information from the tourist offices at **Brioude►** and **Langeac**). There are interesting churches (*Open* Jul–Aug) with frescoes near the river north of Langeac—**Peyrusses**, **St-Cirgues**, **Blassac**. **St-Ilpize** is a picturesque old village with ruined **fortress►**.

► Anjony, Château d' *194A3*

A well-preserved 15th-century fortress overlooks the village of Tournemire (north of Aurillac) and its bright volcanic-stone church, proud possessor of a thorn from Christ's crown. The **Château d'Anjony**, 15310 Tournemire (*Open* daily 8 Feb–15 Nov 2–6.30; Jul, Aug Mon–Sat 11–noon, 2–6.30, Sun 2–6.30. Guided tours. *Closed* late Nov, Dec, Jan. *Admission: expensive)*, contains interesting Renaissance murals.

►► Ardèche, Gorges de l' *194C2*

The D290 from Vallon Pont d'Arc to Pont St-Esprit is the great Ardèche road, a succession of roadside belvederes high above the river. Objects in view include a natural archway (the **Pont d'Arc**) spanning the river and, usually, a dense traffic of canoeists doing the Ardèche properly. In summer, the pace of the river is comfortable; operators at **Vallon** rent out two-man canoes and organize return buses from **Sauze**, near **St-Martin d'Ardèche**, 32km (20 miles) and about six hours' paddling and drifting downstream, via many good sunbathing and picnic places. To the south of Vallon is the magnificent **Aven d'Orgnac►►** pothole (guided tours, long staircases). **Aven de Marzal►** is a shorter detour from the Ardèche road, and is almost as spectacular.

RAIN

The Massif de l'Aigoual has an annual rainfall of more than 2m (80in). More than 52cm (20in) of rain fell in 24 hours in February 1964. The 100-year-old Meteo-France departmental observatory has superb views (*Open* to the public May–Sep daily 10–7. *Admission free*).

Drive

The Cévennes and Mont Lozère

Start at Florac.
This long circuit through some of France's wildest country is easily abbreviated by using the D998 Florac/Pont-de-Montvert road along the upper valley of the Tarn. **Florac**, **Mende** or **St-Jean-du-Gard** will do as overnight stops. Mende is the largest, a quiet cathedral town by the Lot. Florac is the HQ of the Cévennes National Park and the start of the classic drive down the Tarn gorges.

Take the D907 and Corniche des Cévennes road to St-Jean-du-Gard.
The western leg between **Mende** and **St-Jean-du-Gard** includes the Corniche des Cévennes road, which runs through *camisard* (18th-century outlawed Protestants) country. The **Musée des Vallées Cévenoles,** 95 Grand Rue, 30270 St-Jean-du-Gard (*Open* Nov–Mar Wed, Thu 9–12, 2–6, Sun 2–6; Apr–Oct daily 10–12.30, 2–7; Jul, Aug 10–7. *Admission: moderate*), shows the traditional lifestyles of the region.

Follow D983, 984 and 29 (crossing the N106), and the D35 to the Col de la Croix de Berthel, and Le-Pont-de-Montvert; then the D20 to the Col de Finiels and Le Bleymard.

The eastern leg from St-Jean to **Le Bleymard** is 90km (56 miles) of narrow mountain roads and the granite mass of **Mont Lozère**. From the **Col de Finiels** and from the **Châlet du Mont Lozère** (4km/2.5 miles north) there are paths to the summit (1,699m/5,574ft).

Take the D901 and N88 to Mende and Balsièges, then the N106 via the Col de Montmirat to Florac.

Walk

Footpath across the Massif

One of the old transhumance trails is now the GR7 path, which crosses the massif from **Le Bleymard** to the **Col de la Croix de Berthel**, via the **Col de Finiels**. The best section is between **L'Hôpital** and **L'Aubaret** (about two hours). Both can be reached by car from **Le Pont-de-Montvert**. Along the GR7, farm buildings and isolated bell-towers have been restored as part of the Lozère Ecomuseum.

❑ Protestants were outlawed in 1685 and took to the hills (*désert*). They became known as *camisards*, after their white shirts. There is a *camisard* museum at **Le Mas Soubeyran-Musée du Désert**, St-Jean-du-Gard (*Open* Mar–Jun, Sep–Nov daily 9.30–12, 2–6; Jul, Aug 9.30–7). *Admission: moderate*), 11km/7 miles east of St-Jean-du-Gard by D50. ❑

CANTAL CHEESE
Auvergne's number-one cheese, Cantal, was already being made 2,000 years ago. Some 450L (100gal) of cow's milk are required to make a dense 45kg (100lb) cheese, which forms a huge 41cm (16in) diameter cylinder. The best Cantal is said to be made at Salers, and for a really sharp taste always choose the riper variety (*vieux Cantal*, aged in cellars) as opposed to the young cheese or halfway-there variety (*entre deux*).

▶ Besbre, Vallée de la *194B5*

The fertile country southeast of Moulins has a rich concentration of small châteaux. The busy main-road town of **Lapalisse▶** has the most magnificent of them, rebuilt and decorated by a marshal who brought home a taste for Italian Renaissance art from the Italian war (*Open* Apr–Nov daily 9–12, 2–6. Guided tours. *Admission: moderate*). Downstream are other châteaux: **Chavroches**, **Vieux Chambord**, **Jaligny** and **Toury**, a delicious pinkish château in miniature. There is an amusement park/zoo at **Le Pal**, and a Trappist monastery at Sept-Fons.

▶ Besse en Chandesse *194A4*

With the ski slopes of Super-Besse 7km (4 miles) away, the picturesque old town of Besse is a year-round mountain resort, popular in summer as a base for hiking, fishing and cycling (cycles can be rented locally), and is worth visiting also for its old houses, town gates and church (a mixture of Romanesque and late Gothic), all built of black lava. The deep, round **Lac Pavin▶** (southwest of Besse) is one of the prettiest of Auvergne's volcanic crater lakes. The summit of **Puy de Montchal** (1,411m/4,629ft) is half an hour's walk from the lake.

▶ Bort-les-Orgues *194A4*

This small town on the upper Dordogne sits beneath a remarkable cliff of massive pillars of volcanic rock, the **Orgues▶** (organ pipes). Walk to the foot of the cliff from the road, then drive on up to the plateau above for good views of the valley and the long reservoir above Bort's hydroelectric dam, the first of five on the Dordogne. When full, it makes an island of the picturesque turreted 15th-century **Chateau du Val▶**, Bort les Orgues, 5270 Lanobre (*Open* 15 Sep–15 Jun Wed–Mon 10–12, 2–5.30; 15 Jun–15 Sep daily 10–12, 2–6.30. Concerts on Wed during summer, exhibitions and illuminations 15 Jun–15 Sep. *Admission: moderate)*. There is a small beach nearby, with boat trips.

▶ Bourboule, La *194A4*

La Bourboule is a big spa spanning the young Dordogne downstream from Le Mont-Dore. There are gardens and hill walks down from the **Charlannes Plateau▶**, reached by gondola lift. French parents often send their asthmatic children here to benefit from the waters.

► Cère, Vallée de la *194A3*

The most beautiful part of the Cère is its upper valley in the Cantal Mountains, from its source at **Le Lioran** to **Aurillac**. The village of **Vic-sur-Cère** is an excellent base for driving tours or hiking, notably along the peaks from the **Plomb du Cantal** (1,855m/6,086ft), reached by cable car from **Super-Lioran**, to the **Col de Curebourse** (997m/3,271ft) above Vic. On the other side of the valley, the **Puy de la Poche** (1,503m/4,931ft) and **Puy Griou** (1,694m/5,558ft) are rewarding targets, the latter hard-going near the top.

*Conques' name derives from the shell-like shape (*concha *in Latin) of its wild, hilly site*

► La Chaise-Dieu *194B4*

High up in logging country north of Le Puy-en-Velay, La Chaise-Dieu is a base for outdoor sports. It has a superb 14th-century abbey church **La Chaise-Dieu►►** (*Open* May–Oct 9–12, 2–7; Nov–Apr 10–12, 2–5. *Closed* Sun mornings; Mon in Dec–Feb. *Admission: moderate*). It is worth paying to see the tomb of Pope Clement VI, beautiful tapestries, the fresco and Gothic cloister. There is a music festival at the end of August.

GRIMALDI POWER
For a century and a half before the Revolution, the Vallée de la Cère was controlled by the Grimaldis of Monaco, who are still viscounts of Carlat (a château, no longer standing, east of Aurillac). They stayed, as do many tourists today, at Vic-sur-Cère.

► Clermont-Ferrand *194B4*

An industrial city, Clermont-Ferrand's dark streets are dominated by the black lava cathedral, a soaring Gothic building. Nearby **Notre Dame du Port►** is one of the region's most important Romanesque churches. To the west, situated in a fine 16th-century house, the **Musée du Ranquet,** rue des Gras**,** boasts a calculator made by the scientist Blaise Pascal, born locally in 1623. Many elegant houses on and around the rue des Cordeliers have been restored; the **Musée d'Art Roger Quilliot,** place Louis Deteix, displays their salvaged contents (*Open* Tue–Sun 10–6. *Admission: moderate*). The archaeological Musée Bargoin and Musée du Tapis et des Arts Textiles (textiles and carpets) share premises in rue Ballainvilliers.

RUBBER INDUSTRY
Clermont-Ferrand is the home of the French rubber industry, started by the Barbier (later Michelin) family in the early 19th century.

►► Conques *194A3*

Tucked away in a remote fold of hill country to the south of the Lot, Conques is a delightful village with a great pilgrimage church. Thanks to the relics of an early Christian martyr, St. Foy, the monastery won a mention in the pilgrim's guide of the day and in the late 11th century went on to build the **Abbaye de St-Foy►►►** (*Open* Treasury: Jul, Aug daily 9–6; Sep–Jun 9–12, 2–6; 11am Sun. *Admission: expensive*). There is a fine Last Judgement carving over the main doorway.

▶ Lioran, Le 194A3

With nearby **Super-Lioran**, this is the Cantal's main ski resort, in a forest setting near the Col de Cère (1,294m/4,245ft): a watershed between the beautiful upper valleys of Cère and Alagnon, which feed the Dordogne and Loire respectively. Both upper and lower resorts are open in summer, as is the cable car from Super-Lioran to the **Plomb du Cantal▶** (1,885m/6,184ft). On the other side of the pass, there is no mechanical help for the ascent of conical **Puy Griou** (1,694m/5,558ft). Its last stage is more arduous than most Auvergnat climbs (see page 199).

MOUNTAIN HIKE

Take the cable car from the source of the Dordogne to a point not far below the summit of the Puy de Sancy, at 1,885m (6,184ft) the high point of the Massif Central. From here you can hike along the hills to the Capucin (1,465m/4,806ft) and take a cable car down to Le Mont-Dore. For the very fit, a full circuit of the amphitheatre, starting and finishing at Le Mont-Dore, is possible in a day. Take the Capucin lift and proceed via the Puy de Sancy, descending to Le Mont-Dore at a 30m (98ft) waterfall (Grande Cascade).

▶▶ Lot, Vallée du 194A3

The Lot is one of France's best-loved rivers, less touristy than the Dordogne, more welcoming than the wilder Tarn. A number of unspoiled small towns with medieval bridges reflected in the water complement the scenic drive along the middle reach of the river: **St-Côme-d'Olt**, **Espalion**, **Estaing▶** and **Entraygues▶**, where the Lot is fed by the Truyère, all have great charm. A minor road continues along the right bank to the turn-off for **Conques** (see page 199). The landscape is at its loveliest along the **gorges▶▶** between Estaing and Entraygues, with steep wooded slopes above the river, swollen by the hydroelectric Golinhac Dam below Estaing.

The lower section of the River Lot twists past villages with Romanesque churches, châteaux and vineyards that produce Cahors wine

▶ Le Mont-Dore 194A4

Le Mont-Dore is at the foot of an amphitheatre of mountains. In winter, it is one of the Massif's main ski resorts. The odorous baths, housed in a 19th-century temple-like building, are worth visiting (*Open* mid-May to mid-Oct), and car tours combine mountains, lakes (with bathing and watersports at **Lac Chambon**), churches (**St-Nectaire**, **Orcival**), châteaux (**Cordés**, north of Orcival, and **Murol**) and cheeses. Besse, Murol and Orcival are alternative bases for exploring the area. A cable car (*funiculaire/téléphérique*) to the summit of **Puy de Sancy** gives total panoramas (*Open* Dec–May, Sep daily 9–5; Jun 9–12.30, 1.30–5; Jul, Aug 9–6. *Closed* Oct–Nov).

MUROL

Murol is a small resort village beneath the ruins of a medieval fortress, which was strengthened and embellished during the Renaissance but used as a quarry after the Revolution. Enough remains for an interesting visit.

Unlike most landscapes of volcanic origin in Europe north of Naples, the area to the west of Clermont-Ferrand looks the part. The Monts Dômes, more than 100 abrupt conical peaks, form a chain on a north–south axis. Rising from the fertile surrounding landscape, some of the old volcanoes (puys) are grassy, others wooded.

The Auvergne volcanoes show almost every style of seismic activity; most have craters, in some cases as neatly decapitated as boiled eggs. Vulcanologists warn that it is much too early to write them off as extinct. As indicated by the many hot springs (**Royat**, **Le Mont-Dore**, **Vichy, Volvic,** etc), underground Auvergne is far from tranquil. The spring water at **Chaudes Aigues** (south of St-Flour) is the hottest in Europe.

The Puy de Dôme The highest of the chain has a road winding to the summit, a superb viewpoint. Immediately to the north, the **Puy de Pariou** and **Petit Puy de Dôme** both have twin craters. They stand inside the boundaries of a military firing range and access (on foot from the Puy de Dôme, or by car and footpath from the Clermont–Pontgibaud road) is at restricted times.

To the south of the Monts Dômes are surviving fragments of older and much larger mountains, the **Monts Dore** and the **Monts du Cantal**. **Puy Griou**, near the Plomb du Cantal, is one of the chimneys at the middle of the original crater. On its northern flank beneath the Puy Violent, the village of Salers occupies one of many lava plateaux, known as *planèzes*.

All these volcanic massifs are included in a regional natural park, the **Parc Régional des Volcans d'Auvergne**, Centre d'Information et de Découverte Montlosier, 63970 Aydat (Centre & Museum) (*Open* daily, school holidays, 1.30–5; Jul, Aug daily 10–12.30, 2.30–6. *Admission: inexpensive*).

The main information points are located at **Aurillac**, **Montlosier**, **Volvic**, **Egliseneuve d'Entraigues** and **Riom ès Montagnes**. The area around **Le Puy-en-Velay** falls outside the boundaries of the park, but is also volcanic in origin (see page 202).

ANCIENT VIEW
Motorists wanting to combine a scenic drive and a short panoramic walk should head for the Pas de Peyrol, east of Salers by D680. From the car park it is less than half an hour's walk to the Puy Mary (1,787m/5,863ft) at the end of a crest of peaks commanding a magnificent view of the Cantal Mountains and valleys, like the ruins of a vast natural fortress, 20 million years old.

The high tops of Cantal can be very bleak, but meadows on the lower slopes are famous for their wild flowers and for butterflies (above: Scarce Copper)

Le Puy-en-Velay's medieval chapel of St-Michel-d'Aiguilhe reaches dizzy heights, perched precariously 85m (280ft) up on an outcrop of volcanic rock

LACE-MAKERS
From Louis XIV's time until the 20th century, much of the female population of the Vélay region made lace. Now that machines do the work more cheaply, country village squares are no longer filled with women deftly manipulating their *fuseaux*. But Le Puy-en-Velay still has a lace-making *conservatoire* (rue du Guesclin), with a small display of old lace and craftswomen to demonstrate and explain techniques. Training for 'professional aptitude' takes three years of eight hours a day. Lace-making courses for the public are also given in the gallery-cum-boutique at 38–40 rue Raphael.

▶▶ Le Puy-en-Velay *194B3*

Le Puy-en-Velay fills an old crater punctuated by outcrops of volcanic rock, on the spikiest of which sits **St-Michel-d'Aiguilhe▶**. The lava-cobbled rue des Tables climbs the main hill, passing costumed lace-makers, to **Cathédrale Notre-Dame-du-Puy▶▶** (*Open* daily Mar–Sep 8.30–7.30; Oct–Feb 8.30–6.30. *Admission free.* Shorter hours and admission fees for the Cloisters and Museum). The cathedral (see page 203) is now a UNESCO World Heritage Site. This was the official start of the medieval pilgramage route to Santiago de Compostela. North of Le Puy-en-Velay, look left for the ruined **Château de Polignac▶**.

▶ Riom *194B4*

The old lava-built heart of Riom, ringed by boulevards, is of interest for its Renaissance **palaces▶**, the 14th-century statue of *Virgin, Child and Goldfinch* in Notre Dame du Marthuret (rue du Commerce) and a regional museum. There are superb fortress ruins at **Château de Tournoel ▶▶**, 63530 Volvic (*Open* Apr–Jun Wed–Mon 2–6; Jul, Aug daily 10–12.30, 2–7; *closed* Oct–Mar. *Admission: moderate).*

▶ Rodez *194B4*

The town has recently benefited from a modest revival in its fortunes, and the pedestrian central area and ramparts have been restored. The great red **cathedral▶** is a mixture of late Gothic and Renaissance ornament.

▶ Royat *194B4*

A Roman spa overlooking Clermont-Ferrand, Royat was the height of Second Empire fashion. Now it is a comfortable suburb with unexceptional hotels, extensive sports facilities and a Romanesque church. A toll-road leads up to the summit of the **Puy de Dôme▶▶▶** (see page 201).

▶ St-Guilhem-le-Désert *194B1*

After a long career in the armed service of Charlemagne, William of Orange retired to found an abbey at the foot of the Causses. He brought a fragment of the Cross, which put St-Guilhem on the medieval pilgrimage map.

In a region of dour villages it may come as a surprise to find that the local version of the Romanesque style is bright and full of invention. The builders of these churches, one feels, had fun exploiting the range of local granite, sandstone and lava to create mosaics of geometric and speckled patterns decorating the walls of churches large and small.

Clermont and surrounding area

Clermont-Ferrand: Notre-Dame du Port. The most perfect example of the local style: vivid stonework, beautiful capitals, a reproduction black Virgin in the crypt.

Chauriat (east of Clermont-Ferrand): look out for decorative stonework and good capitals.

Marsat (near Riom): features include a severe black Virgin in a golden cloak, and a wheel around which 3km (2 miles) of wax (the distance from Riom) is threaded.

Mozac (on the edge of Riom): the church is no beauty, but the capitals (including Jonah and a group of acrobats) and reliquary are outstanding.

Monts Dore

Orcival: a harmonious pilgrimage church, with a 12th-century Virgin, set in a pretty village. Note the good capitals in the choir.

St-Nectaire Trésorerie (*Open* Apr–Oct daily 9–7; Nov–Mar 9–6. *Admission free*), a handsome 12th-century church prominently set above a small spa, has outstanding capitals and treasure.

South of Clermont

Brioude: the biggest and most majestic of all, Brioude has decorative stonework even on the floor. Entertaining rustic themes can be made out in the carved capitals. Look for the 14th-century 'Leprous' wooden Christ.

Issoire: this grand central church was not enhanced by its 19th-century decorators; but it does boast a beautiful east end and fine capitals.

Lavaudieu (southeast of Brioude): a 12th-century former abbey church (entrance charge) with a cloister, frescoes and octagonal belfry.

Le Puy-en-Velay: set on a steep slope and constructed on several levels, the cathedral has a patterned west end and an unusual vault of oblong domes. There are good frescoes and a superb cloister (see page 202). The earlier 10th- and 11th-century chapel of St-Michel d'Aiguilhe, erected on a spire of rock, has intricate scalloped decoration surrounding the door, apparently inspired by Moorish art.

VIEWING

The striking similarities with the spirit of oriental art probably reflect crusading contacts. Enjoyment of a Romanesque church is never complete without a good look at the back: a fan of chapels in a rhythmic interplay of curves. Inside the church, every capital tells a lively story.

Clermont-Ferrand's cathedral

TAKING THE WATERS
The waters of Vichy were known to the Romans but the resort's boom time was the 19th century, when it acquired most of its exotic architecture. Marshal Pétain lived at the Pavillon Sévigné, formerly the residence of the celebrated 17th-century correspondent Madame de Sévigné, who came for her rheumatism, found the water foul-tasting and described the cure routine as purgatory.

Stained-glass windows at Vichy's church join the town's Second Empire and belle époque architecture

▶ Salers 194A3

Salers is a well-preserved old village of turreted houses, ramparts and gateways on the western flank of the Cantal Mountains and at the heart of cheese country. With several good hotels, it is a good base for exploring the Cantal Mountains and Monts Dore. The **church▶** has a painted sculptural group of the Entombment.

▶ Souvigny 195B5

Once an important Cluniac abbey, pilgrimage and burial place for the Bourbon dukes, Souvigny is now a peaceful place, with only the great **abbey church▶▶** to remind visitors of its past glory. There is interesting sculpture inside the church (two splendid ducal tombs) and in one of the two museums housed in the adjoining abbey buildings (*Open* Wed–Mon 9–noon, 2–6; Jul, Aug 9–noon, 2–7. *Admission: moderate*). St-Ménoux (6km/4 miles north) also has a beautiful 12th- to 13th-century church.

▶▶▶ Tarn, Gorges du see pages 206–207 194B2

▶ Thiers 194B4

Still dedicated to its traditional manufacture of cutlery, Thiers is remarkably old-fashioned in appearance. The old timbered houses lining the steep narrow streets still house traditional workshops (visits: rue Durolle and rue de la Coutellerie). There is a **cutlery museum** (*Open* Sep–Jul Tue–Sun 10–12, 2–6; Jul, Aug daily 10–12.30, 2–6, 2–6.30). The Vallée des Rouets (3km/2 miles east of Thiers), where the knife sharpeners worked, can also be visited (*Open* Jun–Sep Tue–Sun noon–6; Jul, Aug noon–6.30).

▶ Truyère Gorges 194A3

Once a tributary of the Allier, the Truyère now abruptly changes course near the old town of **St-Flour▶**, beneath a long railway bridge (Viaduc de Garabit) built, before his more famous tower, by Eiffel. Here it swells into the largest of a series of narrow reservoirs on its way to join the Lot at Entraygues. No road follows the valley, but the road from **Pierrefort** to the **Barrage de Sarrans** runs through some of the best scenery. The best thing about St-Flour, the highest cathedral town in Europe (887m/2,910ft), is its setting on a volcanic outcrop, well viewed from the Clermont-Mende road (N9). About 14km (9 miles) south, the ruins of the **Château d'Alleuze** overlook a finger of the top lake. At **Pont de Tréboul**, a submerged 14th-century bridge resurfaces when water is low. **Entraygues▶** has a 13th-century bridge and château overlooking the confluence of the rivers Lot and Truyère.

▶ Vichy 194B5

The great spa has lost its share of the fizzy water market and most of its cachet as a resort, partly by association with the 1940–44 period of German occupation, which is often referred to simply as Vichy, and partly because staying at a spa is now a cheap holiday for those with a sympathetic doctor. In season, *curistes* still wait for a drink at the taps in the Parc des Sources, amble in gardens on the banks of the Allier and avail themselves of Vichy's many seasonal entertainments and sports facilities.

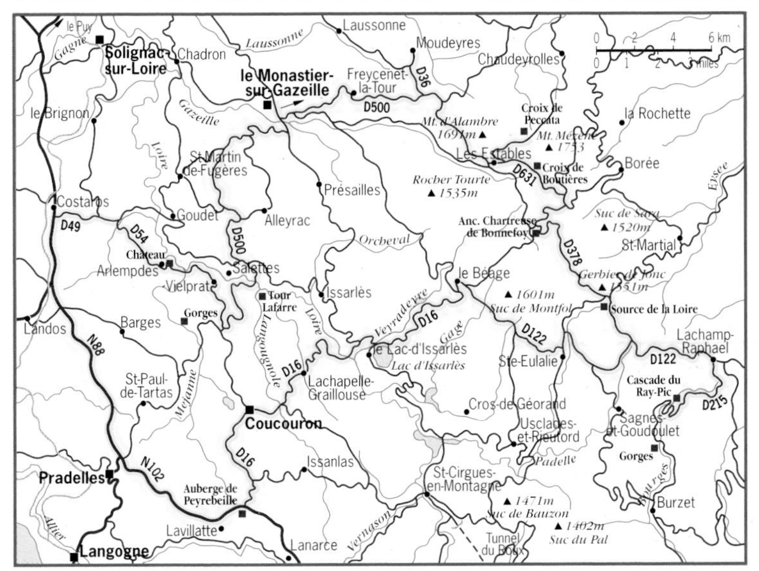

Drive

Mont Mézenc and the source of the Loire

The appeal of this tour is the scenery of Mont Mézenc (1,753m/5,751ft) and the Gerbier de Jonc, a cone of volcanic rock marking the source of the Loire.

Start at Le Monastier. D500/36 to Moudeyres, Les Estables.
Moudeyres has an excellent hotel; Les Estables has good cross-country skiing.

D274 to Croix de Peccata; D631/400/378 to Gerbier de Jonc (D122-215 to Ray Pic and back—see Walk, below).
The Ray Pic waterfall is 15 minutes' walk from the road by an easy path.

D122 to Le Béage, D16 to Lac d'Issarlès, Coucouron, and Auberge de Peyrebeille.
The volcanic crater Lac d'Issarlès has a beach and restaurants. Coucouron is a cheese-making village with a Wednesday market. The lonely highland inn, Auberge de Peyrebeille, has a grisly history. Pierre and Marie Martin, who ran the inn in the early 19th century, killed at least 53 guests in 26 years, pocketing their money and burning the bodies. Exposed in 1833, they were guillotined in front of the inn.

N102/88 north to Costaros, D49/54 to Arlempdes.
Arlempdes has a simple hotel beneath a medieval fortress high above the Loire.

Return to Le Monastier.

Walk

Mont Mézenc and the Gerbier de Jonc

Marked paths lead to the summit of Mont Mézenc from the road at Croix de Péccata (half an hour) and Croix de Boutières (slightly longer). The Gerbier de Jonc is a steeper but shorter walk from the roadside, unmarked but obvious.

Alternatively, a round trip of the Mont Mézenc from Les Estables takes about three hours.

Most of the large area between the upper Lot Valley and the Mediterranean coast of Languedoc consists of a high limestone plateau, or causse, *divided into four by rivers which have cut gorges like great wounds into the land. There are other* causses *in France, but these are the serious ones: high, wide, wild, windswept and empty.*

LARZAC RESISTANCE
The Larzac is the best known of the Grands Causses, thanks to the outcry provoked by a government plan in the 1970s to expand its military camp at the expense of a few sheep farms. The farmers took their sheep to demonstrate in Paris; angry youth found the military a soft target, and Sauvons Le Larzac fitted nicely on a T-shirt. Suddenly everyone cared about one of the more desolate parts of the country. Worry about Roquefort output may also have influenced opinion. On his election President Mitterrand lost no time abandoning the project.

High and wild country: the Causse Méjean

From north to south, the four Causses are: **Sauveterre**, between the Lot and the Tarn; **Méjean**, the highest and wildest, between the Tarn and the Jonte; the **Causse Noir**, between the Jonte and the Dourbie; and the **Larzac**, the largest, to the south of the Dourbie. The river gorges can be admired on foot, by boat (in a few places) and by car. Speleomanes can explore potholes equipped with lifts and staircases and artfully lit to show off delicate translucent curtains of rock and underground lakes.

Chaotic rocks Above ground, chaotic collections of rocks make natural imitations of ruined cities and give a small village like **Le Caylar** the look of a fortified town. **Montpellier-le-Vieux**, on the Causse Noir south of Le Rozier, is an overgrown maze of dolomitic rocks among which it would be easy to get lost without the plan available on site. Elsewhere, retreating rivers have left bends like natural amphitheatres, or *cirques*: **Navacelles** is the finest example, near the small town of Ganges. Throughout, civilization takes a back seat. Sheep are the most numerous inhabitants and their cheese, the pungent Roquefort, is the main output. Small dry-stone shelters for man and beast dot the landscape like lonely mausoleums.

Access Inhospitable as they are, the Causses are not inaccessible. A toll-free section of the A75 motorway travels across the Massif Central from St-Flour to Montpellier; a good, if winding, road follows the **Tarn Gorges**; and the old pilgrimage route across the Causse du Larzac is now a fast main road (N9 from Millau to Montpellier), passing a series of villages with evocative names like **La Cavalerie** and **L'Hospitalet**, built by the Templars and Hospitallers, the area's medieval landlords. **Ste-Eulalie** was the original Templar base, but **La Couvertoirade** (north of Le Caylar, off the main road) is the least modernized, with much of its old ramparts, towers and gates intact. South of Le Caylar the road descends from the Causse in a few hairpins at the **Pas de l'Escalette**, where earlier wayfarers had to use a staircase in the 300m (985ft) cliff.

Celebrated gorge The most famous river gorge, and the easiest gorge road, is the Tarn between **Ste-Enimie** and **Le Rozier**. There are cliffs of up to 500m (1,640ft) on either side, vividly patterned when sunlit; caves in the rock walls, brilliantly clear water and occasional fertile openings in the narrow gorge, with small villages, orchards and riverside châteaux. From **La Malène** there are organized boat trips through a section of the gorge known as **Les Détroits** (the Straits) with beautiful caves, to **Baumes Hautes**. Canoeists can tackle the same section, but should not continue downstream, where a rocky chaos (the Pas du Souci) is a dangerous obstacle. **Le Rozier** is a good base for energetic hikers: there are spectacular cliff paths above the Tarn and Jonte, with exposed sections where ladders have been installed. From **Les Vignes** (below the Pas du Souci) a hairpin road scales the right bank wall and leads to the **Point Sublime**, one of the few easily accessible places where the gorge can be viewed from above.

Other options The other sections of gorge scenery, much less crowded but with slower driving, are the Jonte between **Meyrueis** and **Le Rozier**; and the Dourbie, where two sections of tight gorges are interrupted by a more open valley around the village of **St-Jean-de-Bruel**, a cheerful resort among orchards.

Potholes The Causses' potholes are the grandest in France, although lacking the extra dimension of prehistoric art. The most spectacular are **Aven Armand**, north of the Jonte near Meyrueis, with its 'Virgin Forest' of stalagmites; and the **Grotte des Demoiselles** near Ganges.

Other places to visit

Grotte de Dargilan (near Meyrueis), **Grotte de Clamouse** (near St-Guilhem-le-Désert): stalagmites and stalactites, almost as good as Aven Armand and less crowded.

Hyelzas (4km/2.5 miles west of Aven Armand): restored traditional Causse farm.

La Jasse (beside the N9, between Millau and La Cavalerie): Larzac Ecomuseum, a splendid all-round presentation of the history and ecology of the Causse du Larzac (summer only).

Roquefort-sur-Soulzon: where the cheese comes from; caves open to visitors all year.

Sauveterre (north of Ste-Enimie): small village with typical old Causse houses.

BLUE-VEINED AROMAS

When it comes to blue-veined cheese made from the untreated milk of Lacaune ewes, there is Roquefort and Roquefort. These days most of it is made mechanically in southern France and Corsica. But a small amount is produced in the traditional manner at Roquefort-sur-Soulzon, south of Millau, using a natural mould from huge decomposed loaves of two-month-old bread. The cheeses are stored for many months in cold, damp natural caves beneath the village before being wrapped in tin foil and stamped with their red sheep insignia. The caves are open to visitors.

The Cirque de Navacelles, where the course of ancient rivers can still be seen in the land

REGION HIGHLIGHTS

Annecy, Lac d' *page 210*
Aravis *page 211*
Chamonix *page 214*
Lyon *page 217*
Pérouges *page 221*
Queyras *page 212–213*
La Vanoise *page 222*
Vénéon Valley *page 220*
Vercors *page 222*

FROM LAKE GENEVA to the Mediterranean, the Alpine chain is dominated by the pinnacles and glaciers at the shoulders of Mont Blanc (4,807m/15,771ft), a pilgrimage for mountaineers from all over the world. The Alps have their place in the history books, but are primarily a region for sport and leisure in a context of natural beauty. In two uninhabited national parks (**Vanoise** and **Ecrins**) eagle, ibex and gentian enjoy protection and hikers have to make do with simple refuges. The Queyras and Vercors Regional Parks have been set up to foster traditional crafts and ecosensitive tourism.

FRENCH ACQUISITIONS The southern province of Dauphiné was sold to France in 1349 and traditionally ruled by the heir to the throne, or *dauphin*. Grenoble became its capital and remains the metropolis of the French Alps, a dynamic industrial and university city. **Savoie** was a transalpine independent duchy with capitals on either side of the chain at **Chambéry** and **Turin**. In 1860 Chambéry's half voted to join France.

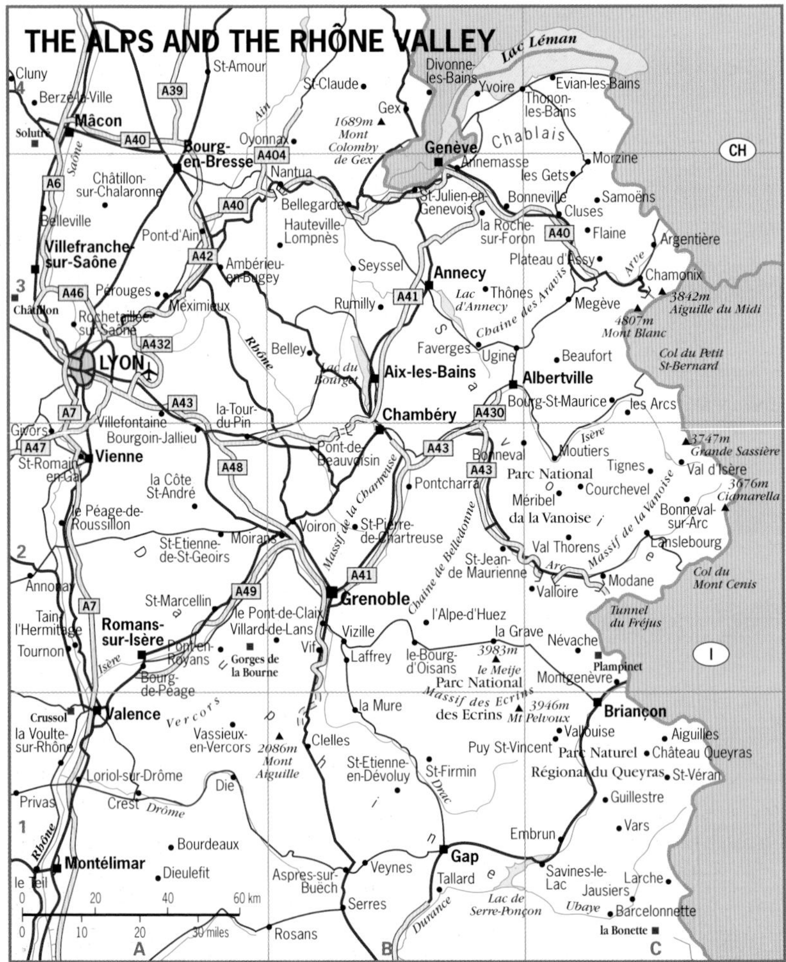

The Alps & Rhône Valley

Savoie More accessible than Dauphiné, Savoie is greener in summer and whiter in winter, and more developed for tourism. There are old spas and lakeside resorts with casinos and windsurfing schools; pre-war resorts grafted on to old chalet villages among woods and pastures; and high modern resorts planned for convenient skiing, cheap self-catering and never mind the aesthetics.

Facelifts The current effort is to improve the looks of the new resorts and broaden their summer appeal. Climbing and hiking, golf, horse-riding, mountain biking, tennis, paragliding, rafting and summer skiing are widely available. For the young and hyperactive, the high resorts are great. For cowbells and pretty chalets, look elsewhere.

Cable cars and high roads bring the glories of the Alpine landscape within the reach of even the least energetic visitor. Fine weather (never predictable in the mountains) is vital to a good holiday, and the high resorts and road passes open for a short summer season.

The Rhône Valley is a great thoroughfare, much traversed and little visited. Its capital, **Lyon**, is a city of merchants, bankers and gourmets, with a Renaissance heart, now a World Heritage site. While others pass through on the way south, gastro-tourists target the Rhône Valley to feast at the tables of Blanc, Bocuse, Chapel and other high priests of gourmet food.

Annecy's 12th-century Palais de l'Isle

CAPTIVATING CHATEAU
Annecy's château, glowering from its hilltop site, represents four centuries of architectural history (12th–16th) and now, to reflect this varied past, groups wide-ranging museum displays. Ultra-contemporary revamped exhibition halls explore Alpine ecology (aquariums) and anthropology, as well as regional archaeology, painting, religious sculpture and contemporary art. Illustrious past owners of the château include the Counts of Geneva, the Dukes of Savoie and the military (1742–1947).

►►► Annecy, Lac d' *208B3*

An old town at the head of a beautiful mountain lake, flanked by elegant villas and smart hotels, Annecy is the French showpiece of lakes-and-mountains beauty. The only complaint may be its popularity: Annecy itself, the most dynamic and prosperous town in Savoie, has industrial and residential suburbs spreading far beyond the old central area, and the banks and waters of the lake are approaching saturation with villas and boats. Once very polluted, the waters are now clean enough for the local delicacies, *lavaret* (lake trout) and *omble chevalier* (char).

The heart of town is a delightful canal zone where the Thiou flows from the lake, overlooked by the towers of a vast 16th-century fortress. Promenading around is the main attraction (especially on market days, Tue, Fri and Sun mornings), but there are a few specific sights: Renaissance frescoes in the church of **St-Maurice**, and the **Château-Musée Annecy**►►, 74000 Annecy (*Open* Jun–Sep daily 10–6; Oct–May Wed–Mon 10–12, 2–6. *Admission: moderate)*. The Palais de l'Isle, a picturesque old prison in mid-stream, is open for visits. There are extensive gardens beside the lake, with boat trips from beside the Hôtel de Ville. The best place for bathing and watersports is at the eastern end of the long avenue of planes (**avenue d'Albigny**) near the splendidly restored Imperial Palace Hotel.

On the west bank, it is a fine drive up the wooded Semnoz Mountain to the **Crêt du Chatillon**► (1,699m/5,574ft) and back to the lake at **Sevrier** via the **Col de Leschaux**, giving good views of the lake and the more interesting mountains climbing steeply from the eastern shore: the cliffs of **Mount Veyrier**, jagged **Dents de Lanfon** and towering crags of **La Tournette** (2,351m/7,713ft). The best alternative way to enjoy the scenery is a boat ride from Annecy to **Talloires**►, the most fashionable resort on the lake, with prestigious hotels and restaurants in an idyllic leafy setting, sheltered by the 150m (500ft) **Roc de Chère** cliffs, a nature reserve of primarily botanical interest. Facing Talloires across the narrowest part of the lake, the picturesque **Château de Duingt** is not open to visitors.

Nearly 14km (9 miles) long but rarely more than 1km (0.5 miles) wide, Lac d'Annecy's natural beauty has long been a magnet for writers and artists

►► Aravis, Massif des *208C3*

The Aravis is Haute Savoie at its most charming: high mountains, rich pastures, woods, old chalets with flowers on the balcony, creamy *reblochon* cheese. The **Cimetière des Glières** and **museum** (*Open* Jul, Aug Mon–Sat 10–12, 3–7; Sep–Jun Mon, Wed, Sat 9–12, 1.30–5.30, Tue, Thu, Fri 9–12. *Admission: inexpensive*) commemorate the exploits of Resistance forces based on the Glières plateau (to the north) in 1944 in **Thônes►**. This attractive small market town, has a Savoyard onion-domed church, good cheese shops and a small local museum (*Open* Mon–Sat). **La Clusaz**, reached along the D909, is one of Haute Savoie's oldest and biggest ski resorts, with chalet-style hotels, lots of sport and good walks from the Beauregard cable car and the Col des Aravis (1,498m/4,915ft), which commands a famous **view►►** of Mont Blanc. From here, the return to Annecy, via **Manigod** (D16) and **Col de la Forclaz** (D12, N508, D42), is slower driving through particularly beautiful pastoral scenery with good views over the lake.

► Assy, Plateau d' *208C3*

This institutional resort high above Le Fayet has a superb view of Mont Blanc. The former TB clinics are not a cheerful sight, but the modern church of **Notre Dame de Toute Grace►►** is well worth the long hairpin climb: its decorators included Lurçat (tapestry behind the altar), Léger (exterior mosaic), Rouault (windows), Chagall and Matisse. If you are bound for Chamonix, take the minor road via **Servoz** and the **Gorges de la Diosaz**, instead of driving back down to the valley.

► Barcelonnette and the Ubaye *208C1*

The 13th-century base of the Count of Barcelona is a rough mountain town, visibly old if not irresistibly charming, beneath modern ski resorts (**Pra Loup** and **Le Sauze**) in one of the most remote valleys of the French Alps. Until a road was cut through the tight Ubaye gorges around **Le Lauzet** in the late 19th century, the area's best connections were with Italy via the **Col de Larche**: Savoy ceded it to France in 1713.

MOUNTAIN ROADS SOUTH

All routes south to the Maritime and Provençal Alps are tortuous, slow and closed for a long winter: the 60km (37-mile) road to St-Etienne-de-Tinée peaks at the Cime de la Bonette, the highest main road in the Alps. The Col de la Cayolle road is even slower and very narrow. The Col d'Allos road is the least arduous. After the pass it follows the Verdon Valley south past the small resort of Allos, good for access to the Mercantour National Park. On the drawing board is a projected *grande route des Alpes* connecting the highest Alpine passes with the Mediterranean.

ST. BERNARD

High above Lake Annecy, the Château de Menthon (*Open* May, Jun, Sep Tue, Thu, Sat, Sun 2–4.30; Jul, Aug daily 2–4.30; Oct–Apr Thu, Sat, Sun 2–4.30) is the birthplace of the 11th-century saint Bernard, who gave his name to a dog.

Elegant Aix-les-Bains, a long-established Alpine spa, dates from the Roman occupation of Gaul

▶ Bourget, Lac du, and Chambéry 208B3

Like Lake Annecy, the slightly larger and deeper Lac du Bourget is long and thin. Much though it was admired by Romantic poets (notably Lamartine), its shoreline and surrounding mountains—long ridges towering above it on either side—are less varied than Annecy's. Its main town, **Aix-les-Bains**, an ancient spa and one of the grand Alpine resorts of the 19th century, is lively enough (as spas go), with a beach, gardens by the lake, plenty of sports on and off the water and boat trips to **Hautecombe Abbey▶▶**, 73310 St-Pierre-de Curtille (*Open* for audio-guide visits, Wed–Mon 10–11.30, 2–5), mausoleum of the Savoyard dynasty. Most of the buildings are in neo-Gothic style. The D914 runs high above the west bank through pretty farmland with views from the **Chapelle de l'Etoile▶**.

Chambéry Now in the busy prefecture of Savoie, Chambéry was the capital of the transalpine kingdom of Savoy until it lost its status and its Holy Shroud to Turin in the mid-16th century. Despite the high reputation of its herby vermouth, it hardly demands a visit, but there is a good regional **museum** not far from the cathedral, a fine arts museum and an amusing 19th-century **elephant fountain** at the central crossroads. The Italianate arcades of **rue de Boigne▶** lead to the ducal **castle▶** and late Gothic **Sainte-Chapelle**. On the southeast edge of town, the home of Madame de Warens (**Les Charmettes**), where Rousseau spent six years (1736–42), has been restored as a museum.

HIGH-ALTITUDE WALK
From St-Véran, drive 6km (4 miles) to the pilgrimage chapel Notre Dame de Clausis, beneath a splendid curtain of frontier peaks. A marked path leads to the border at the Col de St-Véran in about one and three-quarter hours. From here it is about an hour's walk north along the crest to the Col de Chamoussière, skirting the Pic de Caramantran (3,026m/9,928ft). Return to the Clausis Chapel by the GR58 trail. This walk requires sturdy footwear and good weather.

▶ Briançon and the Briançonnais 208C1

The highest town in Europe (1,320m/4,330ft) plugs a strategic junction of valleys at the heart of the Dauphiné Alps. Above the anonymous modern town that sprawls around a tangled road junction, the walled **upper town▶** stands splendidly intact, a gaunt citadel built by Vauban for Louis XIV but subsequently much altered and reinforced with outlying forts on the heights above the town and the Col de Montgenèvre.

Alpine crossroads At 1,850m (6,070ft), the Col de Montgenèvre is the easiest crossing of the western Alps, busy with armies and wayfarers throughout history and still kept open all winter. Since the opening of the Fréjus Road Tunnel the volume of traffic has declined, improving the quality of life at the border village and ski resort of **Montgenèvre**. A more picturesque route to Italy is via the **Névache Valley** and **Col de l'Echelle** (1,766m/5,794ft) to Bardonecchia. There are interesting churches at **Plampinet** (*Open* only in summer) and **Névache**. Along the Guisane Valley to the west of Briançon, a succession of hamlets make up the ski resort of Serre Chevalier, named after a rounded peak (2,483m/8,146ft) accessible by cable car. Lifts from downtown Briançon to **Mont Prorel** (2,572m/8,438ft) have opened up additional skiing and summer walks, with views of the Durance Valley and, from the summit, the peaks of the Ecrins.

Chalets and sun To the south of Briançon, the remote lunar expanse and famously sunny **Queyras▶▶▶** (now a

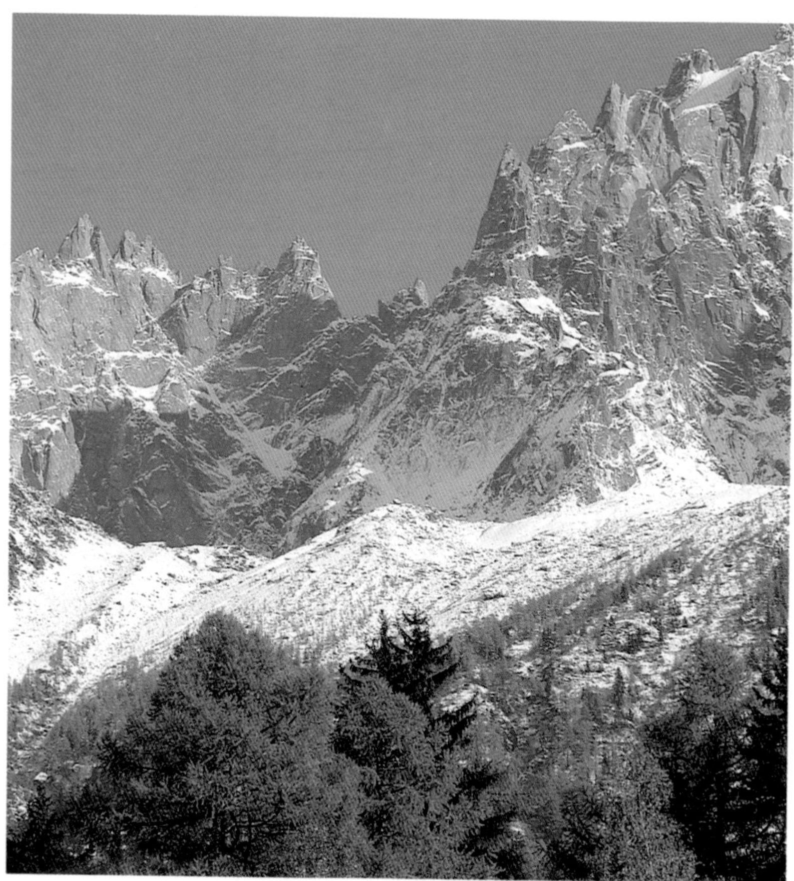

regional park) has a few small resorts. **St-Véran▶** is the most interesting of them, and at 2,000m (6,560ft) is one of the highest villages in Europe. St-Véran's sundials, fountains, crosses and houses crowned by wooden grain-stores, are typical of the region. One house with traditional Queyras interior is preserved as a museum. **Aiguilles** is the other main crafts village. The massive fortress above the village of **Château Queyras▶** and the fortified town of **Mont Dauphin** (above Guillestre) are both mostly Vauban's work.

Autumn tints stop short of the snow-covered 'aiguilles' above Chamonix

High roads Motorists who are neither in a hurry nor put off by hairpins can travel the length of the Alps via the high road: 80km (50 miles) from **Chamonix** to **Bourg St-Maurice** via the **Mont Blanc Tunnel** and **Col du Petit St-Bernard** (2,188m/7,178ft); 120km (75 miles) to **St-Michel-de-Maurienne** via the **Col de l'Iseran** (2,770m/9,100ft); 67km (42 miles) to **Briançon** via the **Col du Galibier** (2,646m/8,680ft) and **Col du Lautaret** (2,058m/6,750ft); 53km (33 miles) to **Guillestre** via the **Col de l'Izoard** (2,360m/7,740ft); 51km (32 miles) to **Jausiers** via the **Col de Vars** (2,111m/6,925ft); and 133km (83 miles) to **Nice** via the **Cime de la Bonette** (2,802m/9,190ft), from which point it is downhill all the way to the sea. All high passes close in winter.

CABLE CAR TO HEAVEN
Chamonix has the most spectacular lifts in the Alps. The most exciting trip is over the Massif Mont Blanc to La Palud in Italy via the Aiguille du Midi, and six stages of cable car and telecabin. On the oppposite side of the valley, the Brévent and Flégère cable cars give the best views of Mont Blanc and the snaking Mer de Glacé glacier respectively.

►►► Chamonix

208C3

Chamonix likes to add Mont Blanc to its name, and throws in 'world capital of Alpinism and skiing' for good measure. If it added that the grandeur of its setting is without rival in Europe, no one would argue. The white dome of the highest Alp (4,807m/15,771ft) officially occupies St-Gervais communal territory, but it was at Chamonix that the pioneers of Alpinism looked for a way to cross the chaotic mass of glaciers descending almost to the valley floor: the Glacier des Bossons drops 3,600m (11,800ft) vertically at a gradient of almost 45 degrees.

Old and new A vibrant, often overcrowded and traffic-plagued town of 10,000 inhabitants, Chamonix is a mixture of modern blocks, old-fashioned villas and bulky hotels. Clientele and population are remarkably diverse: elderly people, rugged mountaineers and sporty holiday-makers who come for the climbing, skiing, hang-gliding, golf and bar crawls. Near the central statue of Mont Blanc's 18th-century conquerors, Balmat and de Saussure, the **Musée Alpin** illustrates the history of the valley and Mont Blanc.

Chamonix now sprawls over the central section of the 15km (9-mile) valley, where heavy traffic (2,000 juggernauts a day) using the road tunnel through Mont Blanc to Italy is an added scourge. The tourist office issues useful maps of summer walks at less polluted altitudes. Above Chamonix, the valley is more peaceful. **Argentière**, skiing focus of the valley, is the main resort, but for peace and quiet the best bases are the hamlet of **Le Lavancher►►** (superb views of Chamonix's 'needle-like' rocky pinnacles, the 'aiguilles', and good walks) and the village of **Le Tour**.

Despite a few lingering traditions, Chamonix has been strongly cosmopolitan ever since a mainly English clientele flocked there more than a century before skiing took off

Long walk The celebrated Tour du Mont Blanc (GRTMB) walk, via Italy, Switzerland and France, takes more than 10 days to complete. It can be cut in half by taking the cable cars or bus between **La Palud** and **Chamonix**, or joined briefly from any resort along the circuit. The best combination of easy walking and spectacular views is the south-facing balcony **walk►** between **Planpraz** and **La Flégère**, both accessible by lift from Chamonix. It takes about two hours, and is nowhere arduous, although sturdy shoes are needed.

Among early mountaineering exploits, one of the most impressive was the conquest of table-topped Mont Aiguille in 1492, by royal command. Curiosity about reported sightings of angels on the summit provoked this expedition, but it was the Enlightenment's spirit of scientific enquiry which gave further impetus to high Alpine exploration.

Interest focused on Mont Blanc, visible from Geneva and increasingly well known for its glaciers. In August 1786, 25 years after Geneva scientist Horace de Saussure offered a reward to the first man to conquer Mont Blanc, the climb was achieved by a local doctor and a guide, **Paccard** and **Balmat**. **De Saussure** went up with 18 guides and no ropes in 1787. On his return, a **Colonel Beaufoy** set off immediately for the summit. This man 'was almost the first of the mountaineering race' wrote the English Alpinist **Edward Whymper**: he climbed to amuse himself.

New explorers Colonel Beaufoy's idea of fun did not catch on until the late 19th century, when the railway brought a new generation of explorers to the Alps. In 1864 and '65, Whymper climbed the Aiguille Verte and the Grandes Jorasses in the Massif Mont Blanc, the highest peak in the southern Alps (the Ecrins) and, in an expedition which killed four of his team, the Matterhorn in Switzerland.

Chamonix With its scores of rocky pinnacles, Chamonix was the mountaineers' headquarters. Hotels in the village had telescopes through which friends watched progress and, at the wave of a hat from on high, cracked a bottle of champagne. A smart advertiser set up a champagne hoarding on the summit, but underestimated the power of the elements, as did **Dr Janssen** of Meudon, who was carried up Mont Blanc in a litter and devoted years to building an observatory on top. Completed in 1893, it registered a minimum temperature of -43°C (-45°F) before sliding off into the valley as part of a glacier.

New tests Climbers have since continued to seek ever greater challenges—most recently, climbing without ropes or nails driven into the rock. At the same time, competitive climbing on indoor walls has become a TV sport. Traditionalists scoff, but dedicated climbers need the sponsorship that celebrity brings. Many mountain resorts now have these artificial climbing walls.

GUIDES
Chamonards formed the first company of mountain guides in 1832.

Every year thousands of people climb Mont Blanc, still thought by most people to be Europe's highest peak; in fact, Mt. Elbruz in the Caucasus tops it by 835m (2,740ft), at 5,642m (18,510ft)

GREEN LIQUEUR

The famous green and less potent yellow Chartreuse liqueurs are based on a secret herbal elixir whose recipe was imparted to the monks in 1605. They are no longer produced at La Grande Chartreuse but at the small town of Voiron (northwest of Grenoble), where the vast cellars are open to visitors. All but the recipe is revealed, and free tasting is offered.

▶ Chartreuse, Massif de la *208B2*

Climbing abruptly from the Isère between **Chambéry** and **Grenoble**, the wettest massif in the Alps is thickly forested, and at its most beautiful in autumn. Roads are narrow and the main resort, **St-Pierre-de-Chartreuse**, is small. A road from the Col de la Porte leads to open pastures near the top of the **Charmant Som▶**, a good viewpoint over **La Grande Chartreuse**, founded by St. Bruno in 1084. The 17th-century buildings are not open to visitors and women are not supposed to enter monastic land; but there is an interesting museum at the entrance (**La Correrie▶**) which also sells Chartreuse. The monks built the road along the gorge of the Guiers Mort from **St-Pierre** to **St-Laurent-du-Pont**.

▶ Die *208A1*

An ancient walled town beside the Drôme, Die has a few fragments of its Roman buildings: a triumphal arch (Porte St-Marcel) and Roman columns in the cathedral porch. The local sparkling wine (Clairette de Die) is a decent champagne substitute.

▶ Evian *208C4*

Evian was transformed from old walled village to grand spa resort after Baron de Blonay gave his lakeside château and park to the town in 1865. Gardens, a domed casino and baths took their place; big hotels have followed. There is plenty to do: boat trips on the lake, exhibitions and a full range of sports.

▶ Grenoble *208B2*

This is a modern university city, with a busy pedestrian area around the places Grenette and St-André. A gondola lift spans the river to the rocktop **Fort de la Bastille**. Paths lead down to the Musée Dauphinois (regional history and crafts) and the church of St. Laurent. The **Musée de Grenoble▶▶**, 5 place de Lavalette, BP 326 38000 Grenoble cedex 01 (*Open* Wed–Mon 10–6.30. *Closed* public holidays. *Admission: inexpensive)*, has an outstanding modern art collection. There is also a museum of the Resistance and Deportation (housed in the Château de Vizille).

▶ Léman, Lac (Lake Geneva) *208C4*

The giant of the Alpine lakes is a 70km (44-mile) bulge in the Rhône's course, which enters in the east near Montreux and exits via Geneva. From the frontier near Geneva, a minor road follows the shore of the narrow part of the lake (Petit Lac) to **Yvoire▶▶**, a medieval village. **Excenevex▶** has the best beach on the lake. **Thonon▶** is the main town of the French bank and Evian's great rival, with a more everyday lifestyle. Surrounded by its arboretum and vineyards to the east of town, the splendid **Château de Ripaille** (*Open* Feb–Oct. Guided tours only) was the retreat of Amadée VIII, first duke of Savoy, who was pulled out of retirement to be anti-pope (Felix V) during the Great Schism. Between Evian and the Swiss border at **St-Gingolph**, mountains climb steeply from the lake's deepest waters. For a bird's-eye view of the lake, take the cable car from **Thollon** (12km/8 miles from Evian by the D24) to the **Pic de Mémise▶** (1,677m/5,502ft). Thonon and Evian are good places for boat trips.

►► Lyon *208A3*

Famous for its trade fairs and bankers in the Renaissance and its silk and gastronomy industries ever since, Lyon spreads over the confluence of the Saône and Rhône. On the narrow peninsula between the two rivers, the place Bellecour and the place des Terreaux are the twin poles of civic life. Between them, the rue de la République is the city's main shopping axis. Nearby are excellent museums: the **Musée Historique des Tissus** and **des Arts Decoratif►**, 34 rue de la Charité, 69002 Lyon (*Open* Tue–Sun 10–5.30. *Admission: moderate;* ticket gives entry to both museums), the **Musée Historique des Tissus►►** and the **Musée des Beaux Arts►►**, 20 place des Terreaux, 69001 Lyon (*Open* Wed–Mon 10.30–6. First floor closed noon–1.15; second floor closed 1.15–2.15. *Admission: moderate).* The restored old quarter on the Saône's right bank is the focus of Lyonnais chic, with Renaissance palaces, designer shops and lively *bouchons* (bistros). There are remains of Roman **Lugdunum►►** near **Fourvière basilica (views►►)** and a good **Musée de la Civilisation Gallo-Romaine (et Parc Fourvière)►►**, 17 rue Cléberg, 69005 Lyon (*Open* Tue–Sun 10–5. *Admission: moderate).* Also worth a visit is **Musée d'Art Contemporain**, Cité Internationale, 81 Quai Charles-de-Gaulle, 69006 Lyon (*Open* during exhibitions, Wed–Sun noon–7. *Closed* Tue. *Admission: moderate).*

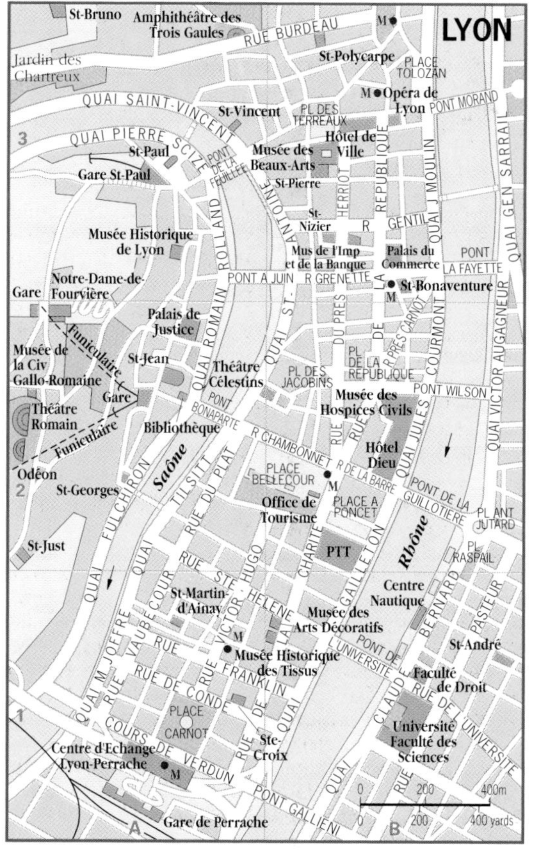

CULTURAL LIONS

Hustling hard to keep up with the Parisians and justify its possession of Europe's largest protected Renaissance quarter after Venice, and now a World Heritage Site, Lyon is culturally very active, with its own Biennale d'Art Contemporain. In 1993, the 1831 opera house was completely revamped by architect Jean Nouvel, sprouting a voluminous glass top floor in the process. In 1995, Renzo Piano designed the new Museum of Contemporary Art to the north of Lyon, in the Cité Internationale. Even the Roman amphitheatre at Fourvière sees rock concerts, and every evening more than 150 monuments are bathed in illuminations.

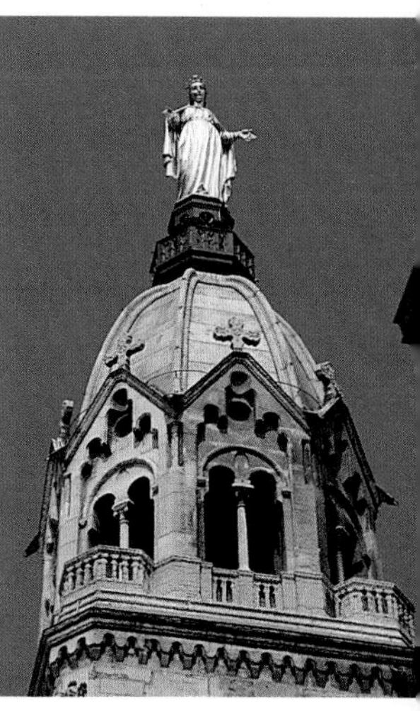

Lyon's Fourvière basilica gives access—via 300 steps—to an observation point with views over the city to the Alps

PENKNIFE PASSSION
Collecting finely crafted penknives is a French 'national sport' and, in the countryside, no self-respecting man sits down to table without his faithful knife. Opinel, the famous Savoyard knifemakers, continue their century-old tradition in Chambéry, while their old factory in St-Jean-de-Maurienne is now the Musée de Opinel.

► La Maurienne *208B2*

The Arc Valley is the southernmost of Savoie's great thoroughfares. The main valley, from the dreary border town of **Modane** to the confluence of Arc and Isère near **Chambéry**, is dull, dark country, punctuated with power stations and factories. **St-Jean-de-Maurienne** (see panel and page 219) is worth a stop for the cathedral, with beautiful 15th-century choir stalls and an alabaster reliquary for three of the Baptist's fingers.

The most developed of the few resorts above the valley is **Valloire►**, on the road to the Galibier Pass, well placed for an overnight stop. It has an ornate baroque church and has not lost all its village charm.

Above Modane, the upper Arc Valley (**Haute Maurienne**) is of greater interest. Apart from **Lanslebourg**, at the foot of the Mont Cenis Pass, the villages have charm and a wealth of baroque art in their churches. The best are at **Avrieux**, **Termignon**, **Lanslevillard** and **Bessans►**, where the carving tradition is maintained. Termignon is the main gateway to the high mountains of the Vanoise. **Bonneval►►**, the last village before the long climb to the lofty Iseran Pass (summer skiing), is a showpiece unspoiled mountain village in a severe setting, with a few simple hotels.

A typical Maurienne chalet

MONT CENIS
For many great armies and Grand Tourists on their way to Rome, the passage of Mont Cenis was the focal point of the journey. Local guides (known as *marrons*) loaded winter voyagers into sleigh-like carriages which they guided downhill at high speed, with frequent capsizes. Napoleon had the sweeping hairpin road built, and for a brief period, before the opening of the Fréjus Tunnel in 1872, there was a railway over the pass. A reservoir now fills much of the broad basin between the pass and the Italian border.

► Mont Aiguille *208C3*

A table-topped tower on the southern flank of the Vercors, Mont Aiguille (2,086m/6,844ft) is not remotely like a needle. Its previous name, Mont Inaccessible, had to go once an intrepid team had scaled the cliffs in 1492 by order of Charles VIII, to check for a colony of angels. All they encountered were flowers, birds and chamois. It is well seen from the N75 south of Grenoble.

► Morzine *208C3*

A large, traditional year-round resort at the heart of the Chablais between Mont Blanc and Lake Geneva, Morzine occupies a complicated junction of narrow valleys and suffers from too much traffic. It does, however, have delightful surroundings, dotted with Alpine chalets and mountain restaurants. This is good walking country, with or without the help of the various lifts above Morzine and the smaller **Les Gets** nearby. A hairpin road and a cable car take you up to the clifftop modern resort of **Avoriaz►**, where cars are prohibited.

Drive

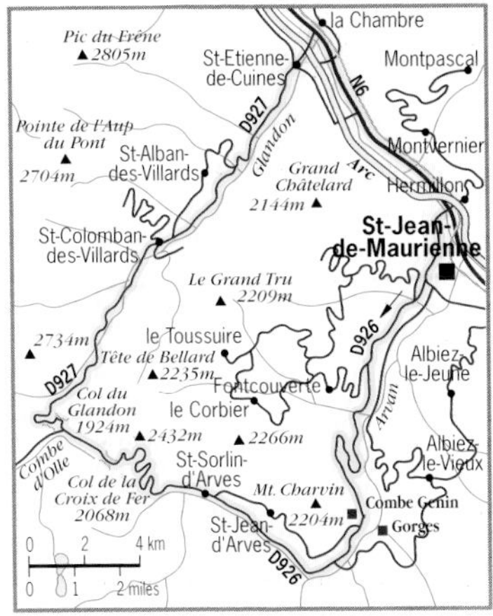

The Croix de Fer and Glandon passes

Start at St-Jean-de-Maurienne.
This splendidly varied 54km (34 miles) of mountain road presents few map-reading difficulties but demands full concentration from the driver at all times, climbing steeply via tunnels and hairpins from the Maurienne up the Arvan Valley before emerging into a beautiful landscape of open high pastures above the modest mountain resort of **St-Sorlin d'Arves**.

D926 as far as Col de la Croix de Fer. D927 to Col du Glandon and La Chambre.
The route switchbacks over the **Croix de Fer** (2,068m/6,785ft) and **Glandon** (1,924m/6,312ft) passes, in close proximity with differing views. To the south of the Croix de Fer, the spiky **Aiguilles d'Arves** (on the left) and the glaciated **Massif Grandes Rousses** together frame the more distant **Meije**.

The **Col du Glandon** gives a good view north to Mont Blanc. The descent to **La Chambre** is also narrow, mostly tortuous and in places steep, requiring careful attention to the road.

Take the N6 for the return journey to St-Jean.

Drive

Over the mountain from Morzine

Start at Morzine. D354 to Samoëns.
From Morzine it is a beautiful drive over the mountain to **Samoëns** (woods and orchards) via the **Col de Joux Plane**, a popular picnic spot with a view of Mont Blanc. At Samoëns, an old village once famous for its stonemasons, a 550-year-old lime tree shades the central square. There are botanical gardens and summer and winter sports facilities, including river rafting and skiing.

D907 to Sixt-Fer-à-Cheval (for excursions to Cirque du Fer à Cheval and Cascade du Rouget).
At **Sixt**, 13th- to 17th-century former abbey buildings surround another fine lime tree. East of Sixt, the road ends beneath a magnificent horseshoe of cliffs and waterfalls (**Fer à Cheval**). To the south, the narrow D29 climbs to the **Cascade du Rouget**; hikers can continue uphill to more waterfalls.

D907 back to Samoëns and Taninges; D902 to Les Gets and Morzine.
The return from Samoëns to Morzine passes the small resort of **Les Gets**, with lifts to **Mont Chéry** (1,829m/6,000ft), a superb viewpoint.

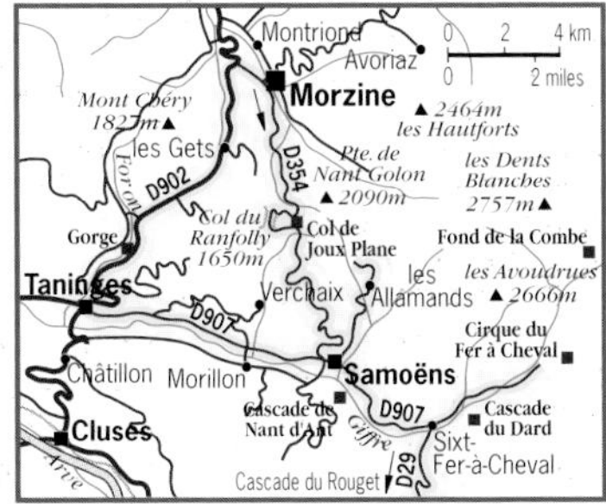

Alpe d'Huez's easy access for today's skiers belies the remoteness of the Oisans, famous in the 19th century for itinerant salesmen, who spent the winter months carrying their village-crafted wares as far afield as the Orient

► L'Oisans 208B2

Facing each other across the dark Romanche Valley, **L'Alpe d'Huez** and **Les Deux Alpes** are the big ugly sisters of Dauphiné skiing, with high open snowfields in easy reach of Grenoble. In summer, both offer plenty of sport, including glacier skiing. L'Alpe d'Huez is reached by a famous hairpin climb (a punishing finale to one stage of the Tour de France) from the mineral-rich town of **Bourg d'Oisans**. A summer road continues over the Col de Sarenne to the picturesque old villages of **Clavans** and **Besse**. The narrow **Vénéon Valley►►►** road, the D530, leads south to the heart of the **Massif des Ecrins**, the highest mountains in the southern Alps and a famous climbing area. At the end of the dark road, **La Bérarde** is an austere village, mainly of interest to climbers. In winter the road is closed beyond **St-Christophe** and its population dwindles to one.

Beside river and main road to the west of the Lautaret Pass, the rough old village of **La Grave** and its Romanesque church are dominated by the mighty pillars and hanging glaciers of the **Meije►►** (3,983m/13,068ft), which is best admired from the road up to **Le Chazelet**, a delightfully rustic village. La Grave has simple hotels, a good cheese shop and a tall, wild ski area.

GLACIER CIRCUIT
A two-stage telecabin climbs from La Grave to the Col des Ruillans (3,200m/10,500ft) for a close-up view of the Meije and a distant one of Mont Blanc. The surroundings are glacier: not for walkers. However, in summer it is about an hour's walk from the mid-station up to the picturesque old Evariste Chancel refuge/restaurant, via the Lac du Puy Vachier, rich in trout. A well-marked path leads down through woods to the river below the village. Stick to the path (cliff danger to the left). The descent from Chancel to La Grave takes about an hour and a half.

► Serre Ponçon, Lac de 208B1

When full, the V-shaped reservoir at the confluence of the Durance and Ubaye rivers is popular for water-sports. **Savines-le-Lac** is the main lakeside resort but is a modern and characterless place. The old town of **Embrun►** makes a more appealing base, with simple hotels and an Italianate 12th-century cathedral, where marble lions support the columns of the main doorway. The tourist office is housed in a chapel with some 15th-century murals.

A geological *spécialité du pays* is the **Demoiselle Coiffée**—a pillar of earth saved from erosion by the boulder on top. The best examples are beside the D453, the road climbing steeply from **Remollon** (on the Sisteron road) to **Mont Colombis**.

The Rhône Valley remains what it has always been: a north–south thoroughfare for travel and trade. Motorway and railway follow the broad river past power stations, cement factories, unlovely towns and vineyards which produce muscular red and white wines. The motorway plunges through the middle of Lyon —a hazardous crossing in view of the speed of the passing traffic.

Lyon (see also page 217) has had a long history of success, since its foundation in 43BC and its subsequent elevation to the status of capital in Roman-occupied Gaul. Its strategic position on the banks of the Saône and Rhône rivers, on the route between Paris and the Mediterranean, has made this a prosperous city, and the focus of busy development. There are plenty of aesthetic attractions for visitors—mainly due to the commercial and industrial (silk and textiles) successes of the past: wealthy merchants and bankers of the 16th century built tall, elegant houses which still stand, some having been extended with an extra floor.

To the south of Lyon the mountains of the Vercors and the eastern wall of the Massif Central enclose the valley before it opens out beyond **Montélimar**, city of nougat and gateway to the land of almonds and honey, Provence.

Valley cuisine Food is the main reason to visit the Rhône Valley, rather than pass swiftly through it. The most famous landmarks on a gastronomic itinerary are **Paul Bocuse** at Collonges, a northern suburb of Lyon; **Pyramide** at Vienne; and **Pic** at Valence. These are not the only outstanding restaurants in the region, and many would say they are no longer the best. But they are generally regarded as holy places in the modern history of French cooking.

Valley sights Sightseeing interest is contrastingly modest: an outstanding vintage vehicle museum at **Rochetaillée-sur-Saône**, north of Lyon; a Roman theatre and well-preserved temple, and several medieval churches (the cathedral and St-André-le-Bas) at **Vienne**; the museum and Roman site across the river at **St-Romain-en-Gal**; a restored Romanesque cathedral at **Valence**, where the museum has a fine collection of Roman drawings by Hubert Robert, leading exponent of this popular 18th-century genre; a comprehensive shoe museum at Romans-sur-Isère; and a few well-sited fortress ruins, notably **Crussol**, near Valence.

Northeast of Lyon, the film-set walled village of **Pérouges** (named after the colony of immigrants from Perugia who settled there in the Middle Ages) has been scrupulously restored and preserved, and its various crafts revived, albeit for tourists.

LOCAL POSTMAN HERO
Often overlooked are the pastoral hills of the Drôme, which rise from the Rhône valley east of Valence and Montélimar. Here, in the village of Hauterives, is an extraordinary monument built by one of France's most celebrated self-taught creators, the Facteur (postman) Cheval. His fantastical Palais Idéal freely mixes Hindu, Buddhist and Islamic temple features with European medieval elements. It took 33 years —from 1879 to 1912— for this determined and inspired man to complete his life's masterwork.

N 7
MONTELIMAR
NOUGAT
LE BOUQUET
Z.I. Nord du Meyrol BP 71
26202 MONTÉLIMAR CEDEX

LA VALLOUISE
La Vallouise is a tributary valley of the Durance to the south of Briançon, and one of many remote areas where Waldensian heretics hid from persecution in the Middle Ages. The village of Puy-St-Vincent, now a ski resort, commemorates the 15th-century visit of St. Vincent Ferrer.

The valley is the main gateway to the Ecrins National Park, with the might of Mont Pelvoux towering above the small resort of Ailefroide. The road continues to a point where two glaciers (Noir and Blanc) once converged. Now they have retreated, and it is a long hike up to the ice. There is a national park exhibition/information point near the village of Vallouise (tel: 04 92 23 32 31).

▶ La Vallouise see panel — *208C1*

▶▶ La Vanoise — *208C2*

The oldest French national park, founded in 1963, is a wilderness of empty high valleys, glaciers and rocky peaks culminating at the 3,855m (12,648ft) **Grande Casse**, and bordering the older Italian Gran Paradiso national park. The peripheral area has seen ski resort development on a scale unmatched elsewhere in the Alps. **Val d'Isère**, **Tignes**, **Les Arcs**, **La Plagne**, **Courchevel**, **Méribel** and **Val Thorens** are the big resorts. More charming alternatives are the old villages of **Pralognan**, **Champagny** and **Peisey-Nancroix** on the Tarentaise side (north) of the park; **Bonneval**, **Termignon** and **Aussois** on the Maurienne side (south). The old village of Champagny-en-Vanoise is famous for traditional Beaufort cheese, the best of hard French Alpine cheeses. Savoie's baroque churches have all undergone extensive restoration. Tours and information are available at the tourist office in Bourg-St-Maurice.

Hiking trails cross the park and refuges offer simple lodgings. At the heart of the park, the **Vallon de la Leisse▶** is rich in wildlife. The car park at Bellecombe, 14km (9 miles) north of Termignon, is the closest access point.

▶▶ Vercors — *208A1*

The unbroken walls of the Vercors rise abruptly to peaks of more than 2,000m (6,560ft). Behind lies a tranquil, thickly forested highland region. Its striking limestone river gorges converge at **Pont-en-Royans▶** before feeding the Isère. **Villard-de-Lans** is the largest of the modest resorts, a good base for impressive drives: along the dark **Gorges de la Bourne▶** and **Grands Goulets▶▶** (very narrow) and the St-Jean-en-Royans to Vassieux road (D76). The Vercors was a Resistance base until 1944, when German forces launched an aerial assault on the region and the villages of **Vassieux**, **La Chapelle** and **St-Nizier** were razed. Vassieux has a Resistance museum, and a museum of prehistory on a Neolithic site discovered in 1970.

Pont-en-Royans, where rivers converge

In 1874, a visiting lawyer recorded his impressions of Bonneval-sur-Arc, at the head of the Haute Maurienne: 'low grey houses, half buried and huddled tightly together for warmth. In winter the inhabitants live in the underground stables warmed by their animals. Wood being rare and coal too expensive, the usual fuel is sun-dried dung. Snow covers the ground for six or seven months a year, often cutting communications and trapping the villagers like marmots in their burrows.'

Sun and shelter Alpine architecture is adapted to the hardships of mountain life. Warmth, exposure to the sun and winter storage space for animals, grain and the staple ingredients of the Alpine diet—long-life cheeses, hams and big disks of dark bread—are the priorities.

In some places villages are widely spread across the steep sunny slope (*adret*) of a valley. **St-Véran**, in the Queyras, is a fine example. Elsewhere, as at **Bonneval**, where the slopes are too steep, the houses are clustered around the church on the valley floor at a safe distance from regular avalanche paths.

Wooden castles Except at high altitude, wood is generally plentiful in the Alps, and widely used in the construction of the chalet (the word is a diminutive of *château*). In the northern Alps, a few old chalets with wooden roofs and chimneys survive. More often, chalet roofs are constructed from rough stone tiles (*lauzes*), gently pitched to support a thick insulating blanket of snow for the winter. In the Vercors, steeper roofs are the custom, and the end walls are traditionally stepped, to facilitate access to the roof. Most chalets have large, sheltered balconies exposed to the sun, for storing firewood and drying things. Grain is either stored under the eaves or in separate buildings, raised on stone stilts to keep the rats out and to allow air to circulate.

BONNEVAL-SUR-ARC
Although modernized, Bonneval has changed remarkably little (externally, anyway). In the absence of local forest, the houses are built almost entirely of stone, wood being reserved for the balconies. The Bonnevalains still dry dung as a fuel.

Alpine architecture at Bonneval

▶▶ REGION HIGHLIGHTS

Arc-et-Senans *page 226*
Autun *page 227*
Auxerre *page 227*
Beaune *page 230*
Brou *page 232*
Flavigny-sur-Ozerain *page 233*
Fontenay Abbey *pages 231, 233*
Tanlay, Château de *page 239*
Tournus and Brancion *page 239*
Vézelay *page 239*

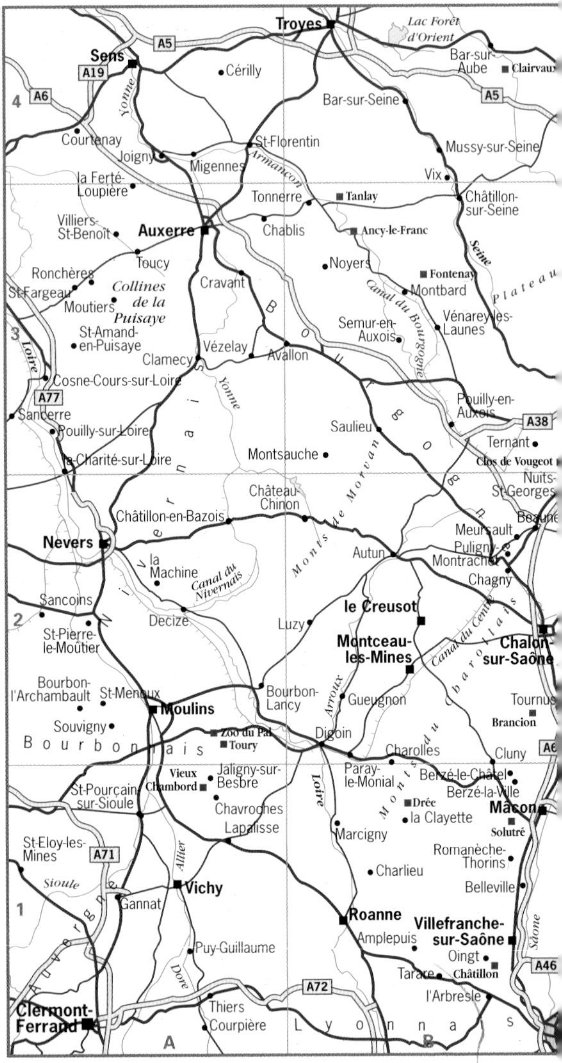

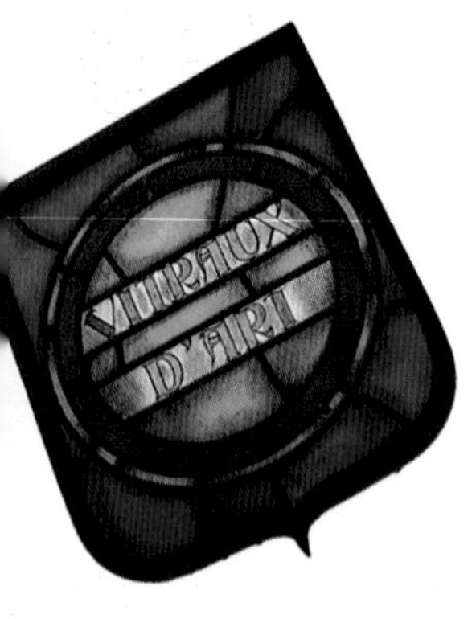

THIS IS THE WARM HEARTLAND of gastronomic France, a welcoming landscape of dazzling mustard fields, rich pastures and golden villages. There are snails (France's finest) and smelly cheeses, best beef from the gleaming white Charolais herds, and the sumptuous wines of the Côte d'Or. The best wine tourism is at Beaune, headquarters of the industry. Great pageantry surrounds the climax of the wine calendar in November: a famous harvest festival and wine auction at Beaune.

The fancy dress and the noble brotherhoods of *vignerons* recall the golden age of Burgundy, when its 14th- and 15th-century Valois dukes lived in luxury appropriate to the Imperial status they craved. In the Hundred Years' War they skilfully switched allegiance between French and English camps. Their real power base was in the Low Countries. Only when the English

Burgundy & the Jura

BURGUNDY AND THE JURA

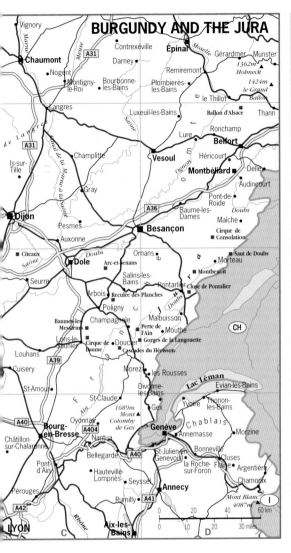

were finally expelled could the French crown turn its attention to the problem of Burgundy. The struggle between the valiant knight, Duke Charles the Bold, and the arch manipulator, King Louis IX, can be seen as the clash of two eras. Charles went down fighting in 1477 and France took control. In an earlier age (10th to 12th centuries), Burgundy saw the foundation of two monastic orders: first at Cluny, later at Cîteaux near Dijon, where Bernard of Clairvaux led the reaction to Cluniac decadence. Burgundy has fine Romanesque churches and abbeys in unadorned Cistercian style.

Franche Comté was named in the 14th century because it was a part of Burgundy, free of the French crown, and is quite different—a remote region of forests and mountains (the Jura). The Jura offers its own unusual wines and an escape to the simple life.

The contents of Louis Pasteur's house in Arbois have been perfectly preserved

PASTEURIZATION
Louis Pasteur (1822–95) was born at Dole and five years later moved with his family to Arbois. Pasteur discovered the causes of fermentation and developed the heat treatment of milk known as pasteurization; his work opened a new era of preventive and curative medicine.

SALTY SPRINGS
The salt springs in Lons-le-Saunier and Salins-les-Bains have been exploited since prehistoric times. At Salins, a handsome old town hemmed in between hills beside the fast-flowing Furieuse river, the salt mine only ceased operating recently, but it is open to visitors (guided tours only). In underground galleries, salty brine was bought up from a depth of 250m (820ft). The brine was then reduced to salt in large cauldrons over a coal fire. Today the salt waters of Salins are used only for medicinal purposes (whence Salins-les-Bains).

► Ain, Vallée de l' *225C1*

The much-dammed River Ain feeds hydroelectric plants as it descends through rapids, gorges and reservoirs on the 190km (118-mile) journey from its source near Champagnole to the Rhône. In and around the upper valley, watery beauty spots include the **Gorges de la Langouette►** and the **Perte de l'Ain►**, where the river disappears into a rocky cleft. But the outstanding attraction is the **Cascades du Hérisson►►**, a series of magnificent waterfalls reached by the D326 (and subsequently on foot) from Doucier. There is fishing and boating on the Lac de Chalain, and a number of watersports stations on the long stretches of reservoir lower down the Ain.

► Ancy-le-Franc, Château de *224B3*

A fine Renaissance château, Ancy-le-Franc was designed in the mid-16th century by the Italian Sebastiano Serlio, in a new classical style. The sobriety of the exterior is quite different from the exuberant ornamentation of earlier Loire châteaux, and contrasts with the more complex design of the inner court. Inside (guided tours), much of the furniture and decoration is original, designed by Primaticcio and the School of Fontainebleau (*Open* Apr–Nov Wed–Mon. *Admission: expensive*).

► Arbois *225C2*

Louis Pasteur's home is an attractive honey-toned small town beside the river Cuisance, close to some of the best Jura scenery. Arbois produces interesting, little-known wines, including one of the best of all rosés, and the exceptionally strong and expensive *vin jaune* (from Château-Chalon and Arbois), which is not bottled for years and keeps for up to a century. *Poularde au vin jaune* is a ubiquitous local variety. *Vin de Paille* is made from overripe grapes traditionally dried on straw. There is a small wine museum near the arcaded central square. Pasteur's house is beside the river on the edge of town (*Open* daily Apr to mid-Oct; guided tours only).

►► Arc-et-Senans *225C2*

Although incomplete, the monumental complex of buildings, **Salines Royales**, 25610 Arc-et-Senans (*Open* Jul, Aug daily 9–7; Apr–Jun, Sep, Oct 9–12, 2–6; Jan–Mar, Nov, Dec 10–12, 2–5. *Admission: expensive),* erected for the royal saltworks near Salins is a rare survivor of late 18th-century industrial architecture by the visionary Claude Nicolas Ledoux (1736–1806). The buildings are used for exhibitions, a museum of Ledoux's work and ideas, and a salt museum (*Open* daily).

►► Autun *224B2*

Autun has interesting survivals from antiquity, but its great treasure is the 12th-century cathedral of **St-Lazare►►**, with outstanding carved tympanum and a wealth of lively carving on the capitals inside. The nearby **Musée Rolin►**, 5 rue des Bancs (*Open* Apr–Sep Wed–Mon 9.30–noon, 1.30–6; Oct–Mar Wed–Sat 10–noon, 2–5, Sun 10–noon, 2.30–5. *Closed* public holidays. *Admission: moderate)*, has a rich collection of Gallo-Roman and Gothic statuary and the 15th-century Master of Moulins' beautiful painting of the Nativity.

► Auxerre *224A3*

An old town of cobbled streets and timbered houses, Auxerre makes a good halt for visitors on the way south. The most central of the three churches turning their backs to the river is the Gothic cathedral of **St-Etienne►**, which took more than three centuries to build. Its elaborate lopsided façade was robbed of much of its decoration during the Wars of Religion. There are beautiful 13th-century windows inside, and 11th-century frescoes in the crypt. The **Musée-Abbaye de St-Germain**, 2 place St-Germain, 89000 Auxerre (*Open* Jun–Sep Wed–Mon 10–6; Oct–May 10–noon, 2–6. *Closed* public holidays except Easter, Pentecost, 14 Jul and 15 Aug. *Admission: moderate)*, has France's oldest crypt, and the museum has a good archaeological collection, with a **Musée des Beaux Arts** in an adjoining wing, with frescoes from the mid-ninth century, depicting scenes from St. Germain's life. The main square (place Leclerc) has a Renaissance gateway with a 17th-century astronomical clock. The **Musée Leblanc-Duvernoy**, 9 bis rue d'Egleny (*Open* Wed–Mon 2–6. *Closed* public holidays except Easter, Pentecost, 14 Jul and 15 Aug. *Admission: inexpensive)*, has a good collection of faïence and tapestries.

► Avallon *224A3*

Old Avallon, a well-preserved walled town, has hotels and restaurants for most pockets. Inside the ramparts, all is convincingly old. A 15th-century watch-tower spans the main street, the old church of St-Lazare has good carvings on the façade doorway and there are gardens outside the walls, looking out over the leafy **Cousin Valley►** (see page 233), which has good secluded hotels.

BURGUNDY CANALS
France's three greatest rivers, the Loire, Seine and Rhône, have added to Burgundy's navigable rivers to create a 1,200km (745-mile) network of waterways, now little used for commercial traffic (except for the Canal du Centre between Digoin and Chalon-sur-Saône) and ideal for slow-moving houseboat holidays. The best choices are the Canal du Bourgogne (at its best in the Auxois, between Tonnerre and Vénarey); and the Canal du Nivernais, which crosses wonderfully peaceful countryside between Decize and Cravant (south of Auxerre). Two of the main hirers are Bâteaux de Bourgogne at Auxerre (tel: 03 86 72 92 10) and Burgundy Cruisers at Cravant (tel: 03 86 81 54 55). Both offer bicycle rental.

The fine Gothic cathedral of St-Etienne in Auxerre, built between the 13th and 16th centuries, beside the River Yomme

The hills of Burgundy produce one of the world's greatest white wines (Montrachet), the most expensive red (Romanée Conti) and everyday Beaujolais by the unpretentious boatload. About four-fifths of all burgundy is red.

The medieval village of Berzé-le-Châtel, in the heart of the Mâconnais

A MONKS' CHATEAU
There are few impressive vineyard châteaux to rival those in the Médoc. Clos de Vougeot is one of the few exceptions to the no-châteaux rule. Originally a Cistercian property, it is now the headquarters of the proud Confrérie des Chevaliers du Tastevin, who hold banquets and initiation ceremonies there. The interior (guided tours) has vaulted cellars and old wine presses.

The wines The greatest vineyards form a long narrow strip (only 4,000ha/9,885 acres in total) along a south-east-facing slope extending south from Dijon and past Beaune. This is the Côte d'Or, of which there are two halves. Between Nuits-St-Georges and Dijon, the Côte de Nuits vineyards (including Gevrey Chambertin, Vosne Romanée and Vougeot) produce red wine. The southern half is the Côte de Beaune, which makes red and white. Villages include Aloxe Corton, Pommard, Meursault and the two Montrachets (Chassagne and Puligny).

Golden-green wines of a different style, but scarcely less prestigious, are produced at Chablis near Auxerre. Geographically and in the taste of its wines, Chablis is closer to Champagne than the Côte d'Or.

The output of the small Côte Chalonnaise, south of the Côte d'Or, is no match for the Grands Crus to the north but is still fine wine. Mercurey and Rully are the best known appellations. South of Tournus, a large area of the Mâconnais and Beaujolais produces excellent everyday wines, mostly white in the Mâconnais, almost all red in Beaujolais. In northwestern Burgundy, Pouilly-sur-Loire's white wines have more in common with those of nearby Sancerre than any burgundy. Pouilly Fumé is its best wine, not to be confused with Pouilly Fuissé, pride of the Mâconnais.

The grapes In Burgundy proper, the Chardonnay grape is used throughout for white wine, Pinot Noir for red. Pouilly Fumé is made from the Sauvignon grape, Pouilly-sur-Loire from the Chasselas. In the Beaujolais, the Gamay thrives on sandy ground, giving light and fruity wine which is drunk young—often within weeks of the harvest (*beaujolais nouveau*).

Vineyards and tasting Many of the finest vineyards belonged to the Church, whose estates were broken up after the Revolution. The high price of the best wines is another reason for fragmentation: prime vineyards cost as much as 750,000 euros a hectare and change hands in tiny lots. The 50ha (125-acre) vineyard of Clos de Vougeot is split between 80 growers, who produce wines of different character and quality all called Clos de Vougeot.

Many of the big *négociants* (Bouchard and Drouhin) are based at Beaune. A few welcome visitors and offer tastings but many charge a fee and there is pressure to buy. Much the best alternative is to pay to visit the Marché Aux Vins in Beaune, an association of private wine-growers, where a fine selection of bottles stand open at your disposal, in tasting order—from white to Beaujolais to the big reds of the Côte d'Or. Tasting at the

16th-century Château de Meursault is organized similarly. A tastevin and spittoons are provided.

Beaujolais is higher and steeper than Burgundy, almost mountainous in places. Driving is slow and many of the villages have great charm, with tastings at wine growers' co-operatives. The best area to explore is southwest of Villefranche, although this is not Grand Cru country. There are picturesque ruins at Châtillon and Oingt, ninth-century murals and capitals in the church at Ternand. A good place to sample Beaujolais wine is the **Hameau de Vins**, La Gare, 71570 Romanèche-Thorins (*Open* daily 9–6; Jan–Mar, Nov–Dec 10–5. *Admission: expensive*), where you can also take in a guided tour giving the history of the wines.

Classification Burgundy production is strictly controlled and classified. On the Côte d'Or, the best vineyards (called *climats*) are designated Grands Crus (32, including Richebourg, Romanée Conti, Chambertin and Montrachet). Next comes a larger number of Premiers Crus, then vineyards entitled to use the communal name (Gevrey Chambertin, Beaune, etc), finally plain Bourgogne. Chablis also has Grands Crus and Premiers Crus, followed by Chablis and Petit Chablis. In the Mâconnais, Pouilly-Fuissé and St-Véran are the best appellations. Mâcon plus the name of a village (Mâcon-Viré, for example) indicates a better wine than Mâcon Villages, which is better than plain Mâcon. Beaujolais also has a superior subsection of Beaujolais-Villages and 10 Grands Crus, of which Moulin à Vent is usually rated the best. Unlike most Beaujolais wines, it keeps.

OENOLOGICAL PATIENCE
The only problem with Burgundy's aromatic Pinot Noir red wines is that they require patience. Unimpressive when young, red burgundies reach their optimum only between five and eight years after harvest and so do not come cheap. The alternative is the fruity Beaujolais whose exaggerated world demand is such that a lot of mixing goes on... Things look up, however, with the whites. These are delicious within two years of harvest, although a fine Chablis Premier Cru peaks at 10 years. Recent exceptional years were 1995, 1996, 1999, 2002 and 2005.

If half a day en route *is all you can afford for the region, devote it to Beaune, capital of burgundy with a small 'b' (the wine), at the heart of the area's most prestigious vineyards. Ducal capital until the 14th century, it remains a medium-size town with its old walls and town gates intact. Its position at a motorway intersection two-and-a-half hours south of Paris is ideal for a break in the journey.*

BEFORE YOU LEAVE
The 12th- to 13th-century church of Notre-Dame has beautiful tapestries (not on show in winter). There is a good wine museum near the church and an unmissable wine-tasting opportunity at the Marché Aux Vins, opposite the Hôtel Dieu. Or visit the Musée du vin de Bourgogne, rue d'Enfer, 21200 Beaune (*Open* Apr–Nov daily 9.30–6; Dec–Mar Wed–Mon 9.30–6. *Admission: moderate*).

On the main square in the old town, the market hall houses the tourist office. Across the street is the **Hôtel Dieu**, rue de l'Hôtel Dieu, 21200 Beaune (*Open* last week in Mar to Oct daily 9–6.30; Nov–Mar daily 9–11.30, 2–5.30; guided visits by appointment. *Admission: moderate*), an outwardly unspectacular charitable hospital founded in 1443 by Nicolas Rolin, Chancellor of Burgundy and great art patron.

A unique survival, the Hôtel Dieu functioned as a hospital until 1971 and is now a residential home for the elderly, partly staffed by a few remaining nuns and funded by the famous annual auction of the produce of its many Côte de Beaune vineyards. The auction (www.beaune.com) sets the annual price level for burgundy and is the focal point of the 'Trois Glorieuses', a three-day wine festival on the third weekend in November. The other two events are banquets at Clos de Vougeot and Meursault.

From the entrance portico, you can glimpse the brilliant hues of the tiled roof of the Hôtel Dieu's beautiful courtyard, the most elaborate roof in Burgundy, but it is well worth entering to see the old pharmacy, the kitchens and, above all, the vaulted 70m (230ft) ward, which remains in its original disposition: beds (with room for two in each), in the nave, curtained off except for services.

Beaune lies in the very heart of Burgundy's most celebrated vineyards

In 910, 12 monks left the Abbey of Baume les Messieurs and founded a new community at Cluny, not far from Mâcon. Under abbots answerable only to Rome, Cluny's influence spread rapidly, and hundreds of dependent houses were founded throughout Europe.

The Abbey of Cluny The mother Abbey's 177m (194yd) third church, built between 1080 and 1130 at the height of Cluniac power, was the largest and most splendid church in Christendom. If the heavenly host could be content with earthly habitation, declared one impressed visitor, this would be the ambulatory of angels. Cluny later fell into decline under absentee abbots and was dismantled after the Revolution; a single tower of the transepts remains standing. The museum is in the former abbey's palace. The **Musée d'Art et d'Archéologie**, Palais Jean-Bourbon, 71250 Cluny (*Open* daily Sep–Apr 9.30–noon, 1.30–5; May–Aug 9.30–6.30. *Closed* public holidays. *Admission: expensive*), houses a collection of Cluny capitals.

Above: Berzé-la-Ville; below: Cluny

Cistercian austerity Cluniac churches were erected to glorify God; the more splendid, the better. In 1098, a new abbey was founded at Cîteaux near Dijon, in a spirit of reaction to the excesses of Cluniac life and art. A local nobleman later founded an abbey at Clairvaux. Preaching a return to the frugal spirit of the Benedictine rule, he condemned the waste of money lavished on vast churches. Life under Cistercian rule was austere, and the architectural style of the monasteries is unadorned simplicity.

The gardens have recently been redesigned and replanted and are not to be missed. There is no better example than the **Abbaye de Fontenay**, 21500 Marmagne (www.abbayedefontenay.com *Open* daily Apr–Oct 10–6; Nov–Mar 10–12, 2–5. Guided visits by appointment. *Admission: expensive*; see page 233).

CLUNIAC ARCHITECTURE

Of many examples of Cluniac architecture in Burgundy (especially in the Brionnais), Paray-le-Monial's church, contemporary with Cluny, is almost a replica of the lost original on reduced scale. A chapel at Berzé-la-Ville (between Mâcon and Cluny) has early frescoes, probably by the artists employed at Cluny itself (*Open* daily 9–12, 2–5).

Besançon lies in a deeply wooded basin, almost enclosed as the River Doubs loops around it. Its old central area is now entirely closed to cars—only buses whisk you around.

CHICKEN EXTRAORDINAIRE

King of chickens, chicken of kings: the *poulet de Bresse* is to the battery-reared oven-ready bird what a Grand Cru burgundy is to *vin ordinaire*. Bresse is in fact a poultry appellation, with limited output and strict production rules. The birds are sold with a seal, a numbered ring and a certificate of origin. In their early months they enjoy the freedom of the farmyard before spending two weeks in a 'finishing room' fed on a mixture of creamy milk and wheat. The result is peerless white meat, firm but succulent, with no fat.

▶ **Beaune** see page 230

▶ Besançon *225D3*

The capital of Franche-Comté, Besançon is a dignified city, with fine façades along the Grande Rue, notably the Renaissance **Palais Granvelle**, 96 Grand Rue, 25000 Besçancon (*Open* May–Sep Wed–Sun 1–7; Oct–Apr 1–6. *Admission; inexpensive; free on Sun and public holidays*), which has been transformed into a 'time museum'. The cathedral dates from many periods, with equally varied contents, including a 19th-century **astronomic clock▶▶**. The **Musée des Beaux Arts et d'Archéologie▶▶**, 1 place de la Révolution (*Open* Wed–Mon 9.30–12, 2–6. *Closed* public holidays. *Admission: moderate)*, has rich collections of paintings, ceramics and sculpture. The **Citadelle▶▶**, rue des Fusillés-de-la-Resistance (*Open* daily Easter–Jun, Sep, Oct 9–6; Nov–Mar 10–5; Jul, Aug 9–7. *Admission: expensive)*, encloses a natural history museum, animal park, aquarium, insectarium and noctarium.

▶ Bresse *225C1*

From the Saône to the Ain at the foot of the Jura, the Bresse plain is rapidly crossed now by motorway from Mâcon to Geneva. The area's busy market town, **Bourg-en-Bresse▶**, is good fun on market day (Wed and Sat morning). The main attraction is the church at Brou (see below).

▶▶ Brou *225C1*

A suburb of Bourg-en-Bresse, Brou contains rare treasures of late Gothic art in the 16th-century monastery church, behind which lies the story of Margaret of Bourbon, her son Philibert and his young widow, Margaret of Austria. The choir contains the three marble tombs of Philibert and both Margarets, painted windows, and carved wood and stonework, all of breathtaking quality. The adjacent monastery is now the **Musée de Brou▶**, 63 boulevard de Brou (*Open* daily Apr–Sep 9–12.30, 2–6; mid-Jun to mid-Sep 9–6; Oct–Mar 9–12, 2–5. *Closed* public holidays. *Admission: expensive)*.

▶ Châtillon-sur-Seine *224B3*

The **Musée du Châtillonnais▶▶**, rue du Bourg, 21400 Châtillon (*Open* Jul, Aug daily 10–6; Sep–Jun Wed–Mon 9.30–12, 2–5. *Admission: moderate)*, of this little town has a huge (1.64m/5.5ft) sixth-century BC bronze vase, found with ornaments in a princess's tomb at Vix, 7km (4 miles) north of Châtillon.

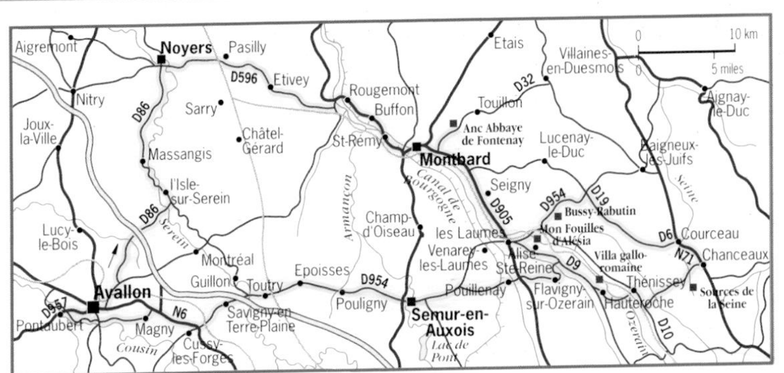

Drive

The Auxois

Start at Avallon. Take the D86 to Noyers.
Noyers is delightful: admire its town gates, timbered houses and towers from the old fortifications.

D956 takes you to Rougemont.
Montbard near Rougemont was the home of 18th-century natural historian Comte de Buffon. The forge he founded near Buffon has been restored (*Open* Apr–Sep).

A detour on D905/D32 takes you to the Abbaye de Fontenay.
This is the outstanding example of Cistercian simplicity and peace.
Back to D905 and on to Venarey-les-Laumes and Alise-Ste-Reine.
Alise-Ste-Reine has a museum with finds from a Gallo-Roman town, thought to be *Alesia,* site of the Gauls' heroic last stand against Rome in 52BC. Vercingetorix's statue looms above.

Timbered house at Noyers

D954 to Bussy-Rabutin.
The Château de Bussy-Rabutin (*Open* Wed–Mon 9.15–12, 2–6; admission: moderate) has an entertaining collection of portraits of warriors and royal mistresses.

Take D19/D6 to Courceau, N71 to Chanceaux and D103C to St-Germain-Source-Seine.
The river issues from a cave 2km (1 mile) south of St-Germain. A Roman temple once stood nearby.

Take D103C/D10 to Thénissey and Hauteroche, then D9 to Flavigny-sur-Ozerain.
Flavigny-sur-Ozerain is a walled village of tumbledown charm, known for its aniseed sweets.

Continue to Semur-en-Auxois.
Admirably set on a rocky spur almost encircled by the Armançon, this old town still bristles with towers. Take the D103B 4km (2.5 miles) south for watersports at the Lac de Pont.

Take the D954 to Cussy-les-Forges via Epoisses, N6 to Magny, D427 to Pontaubert, D957 back to Avallon.
A double row of fortifications encloses the elegant château at Epoisses, a village renowned for its cheese. The rest of the route follows the pretty Cousin Valley, skirting Avallon.

KIR
Bourgogne aligoté (local white wine made from the inferior *aligoté* grape) mixed with Dijonnais *crème de cassis* (blackcurrant liqueur) is a traditional regional aperitif, now named after Canon Kir, Mayor of Dijon during the 1940s. Kir served the drink at all public functions in a bid to boost flagging sales of *cassis*. In what many kirophiles would consider an excess of promotional zeal, the canon's recipe was one-third *cassis* to two-thirds wine; one-fifth to four-fifths is a more palatable mixture.

Part of the Palais des Ducs is sited on top of remains of the walls of the Roman castrum

▶ Dijon

225C3

The first Valois duke, Philip the Bold, made Burgundy a great independent power at the heart of Europe by marrying the heiress of Flanders. Dijon became his capital and here, with the help of Flemish artists, Philip and his successors built themselves a magnificent palace and an equally lavish necropolis, the Chartreuse de Champmol. Both have been transformed and now only hint at their original magnificence. Dijon still has a core of picturesque medieval streets, but it is primarily a busy industrial city, great for gourmets but short on charm.

The **Palais des Etats et des Ducs de Bourgogne▶**, place de la Liberation, 21000 Dijon (*Open* Wed–Mon 10–5. *Admission: free),* overlooks the semicircular colonnade of the 17th-century place de la Libération, at the end of Dijon's main shopping axis, the rue de la Liberté. As well as the town hall, the palace houses the **Musée des Beaux Arts▶▶**, with medieval kitchens and an outstanding collection of sculpture, of which the highlights are two masterpieces of 14th- to 15th-century Burgundo-Flemish art, the tombs of Philip the Bold and John the Fearless (with consort) in the vast Salle des Gardes. Both the tombs and the altarpieces in the same room came from the chartreuse of **Champmol**, 1 boulevard Chanoine Kir, Dijon. (*Open* daily 8–6. *Admission free*), now a mental hospital (in the direction of the A38 motorway). Most of its original buildings and works of art have been destroyed or removed, but it retains the **Puits de Moïse▶** (Moses' Well), a wonderful group of six prophets (Moses is the one with horns) by 15th-century sculptor Claus Sluter. The door and well have recently been restored.

Dijon's churches are of minor interest. The cathedral has a 10th-century crypt, and St-Michel a Renaissance façade. Notre-Dame's Gothic façade has rows of grimacing monsters and a 14th-century Jacquemart (mechanical clock with figures hammering the chimes). The most interesting old streets in the **medieval zone▶** behind the palace are rue des Forges (where the 15th-century Hôtel Chambellan is the tourist office), rue Verrerie and rue de la Chouette.

▶ Doubs, Vallée du *225D2*

From its source in a forest cave near the village of Mouthe, the River Doubs charts an indecisive course, flowing five times as far as a crow would fly on its way to the Saône. The most beautiful stretch of the valley is where the river defines the Franco-Swiss border between the **Saut du Doubs▶▶** (a splendid 30m/98ft waterfall near Morteau) and the village of Goumois: impressive limestone gorges and good canoeing and trout fishing. In the upper valley, Malbuisson is a peaceful lakeside resort, also popular with fishermen. Between Pontarlier and Morteau, **Montbenoît's abbey church▶** has a richly decorated 16th-century choir.

▶ Fontenay see pages 231 and 233

▶ Lons-le-Saunier *225C2*

Lons-le-Saunier, an old Roman salt town, is now the prefecture of the Jura and still functions as a spa. Rouget de Lisle, composer of the *Marseillaise*, was born at No. 24 rue du Commerce in 1760 and the town clock plays a few notes of the tune on the hour.

▶ Moulins *224A2*

The capital of the dukes of Bourbon, big players in the politics of medieval and Renaissance France, Moulins is now a quiet market town. The cathedral has beautiful 15th-century stained-glass windows and the famous **triptych** by the Master of Moulins (1500), with donor portraits by the Duke and Duchess of Bourbon. The **Musée d'Art et d'Archéologie▶** in the old Bourbon château is worth a visit. Mechanical figures hammer the chimes on the 15th-century Jacquemart clock-tower.

▶ Nevers *224A2*

Nevers has been famous for its spun glass and faïence porcelain since the 16th century, when Lodovico Gonzaga of Mantua, Duke of Nevers, imported artists from Italy. The industry survives, and there are collections of both in the town **museum▶**. Other buildings of interest include the cathedral; the turreted 15th- to 16th-century ducal palace (housing the tourist office); the Porte du Croux; and **St-Etienne▶▶**. The tomb of Bernadette Subirous, visionary of Lourdes, is displayed in the convent of St-Gildard.

THEATRICAL VIEWS
In the vineyard hills between Lons-le-Saunier and Arbois, erosion has carved a series of splendid valleys (*reculées*) ending in abrupt amphitheatres (*cirques*) of cliffs with caves, resurgent streams, stalactites and underground lakes. The Cirque de Baume heads a valley occupied by the ancient abbey of Baume les Messieurs. There is a good viewpoint over the valley from the D471 east of Lons-le-Saunier. A similar clifftop belvedere overlooks the Reculée des Planches and Cirque du Fer à Cheval beside the D469 Arbois to Champagnole road.

BACK IN TIME
At the Chantier Médiéval de Guédelon, D 955, 89520 Guédelon-Treigny (*Open* Apr–Jun Thu–Tue 10–6; until 7 Sun and public holidays; Jul, Aug daily 10–7; Sep, Oct Thu–Tue 10–5.30. *Admission: expensive*) the château of Guédelon is being built using entirely medieval methods, tools and even animals.

When in Lons-le-Saunier, don't miss an improvized sandwich of Jura's celebrated hard cheese—Comeé; 500L (110gal) of milk are needed for a 50kg (110lb) cheese

GUSTAVE COURBET
In Parisian café society Courbet posed as a rough peasant, embraced revolutionary politics and professed an anti-everything philosophy of art, conveniently known as Realism. Returning often to Ornans, he painted local landscapes, hunting and village scenes, including the still disturbing *Burial at Ornans* (1850; Musée d'Orsay), executed on a grand scale. His preferred subject, however, was himself. After a spell in jail for helping to pull down Napoleon's column at place Vendôme in 1871, Courbet spent his last years in Swiss exile.

▶ Ornans *225D2*

In this small Jura town old ramshackle houses prettily overhang the waters of the River Loue against a backdrop of wooded escarpments that are instantly recognizable from the work of painter Gustave Courbet (1819–77). His birthplace on the left bank near the bridge has become a museum, where you can see several of his paintings.

▶ La Puisaye *224A3*

Southwest of Auxerrre lies the relatively unexplored region of La Puisaye, familiar to many people through the writings of Colette (whose full name was Sidonie Gabrielle Claudine Colette), who spent her early childhood at St-Sauveur-en-Puisaye (its château is now the **Musée Colette**).

Apart from the quiet beauty of the area, with its woodland, hedgerows, meadows and many lakes, the main reason for coming here is to visit the 20 or so churches decorated with exceptionally fine and unusual murals dating from as early as the 12th-century (see panel).

La Puisaye has also been famous for its pottery since the 14th century, and numerous pottery fairs and markets still abound. Old earthenware is best seen at the **Musée d'Art Régional▶** at Villiers-Saint-Benoît, the **Château de Ratilly** and the **Musée du Grès de Puisaye** in Saint-Amand. At **Moutiers** you can visit the vast 18th-century horizontal kiln (measuring 75sq m/807sq ft) used to fire Puisaye household earthenware, and still operational today. Both the frescoes and the pottery made use of the locally mined ochre, exported in vast quantity throughout the 19th century. Today only one mine remains and can be found at Saint-Amand.

The popular winter and summer resort of Les Rousses

▶ Les Rousses *225D2*

On a high (1,100m/3,610ft) plateau at the foot of the summit ridge of the Jura mountains, Les Rousses is a busy summer and winter resort, with watersports on its **lake▶**, walking and riding in the forest. In winter there are long cross-country ski trails and the Jura's best downhill skiing. Local cheese and butter is made at the dairy, which you can visit. There is more skiing at the Col de la Faucille (1,300m/4,265ft), 18km (11 miles) up the N5 nearer Switzerland. Mont Blanc is visible on a clear day.

PUISAYE'S MURALS
Perhaps the most striking murals are those at La Ferté-Loupière (early 16th century), where a cortège ranging from pope to peasant is escorted by death in a dance that unfurls along 25m (82ft) of the nave. It is preceded by the Dict des Trois Morts et Trois Vifs, a frequently recurring theme in Puisaye (as at Villiers St-Benoit, and the recently discovered version in the Chapelle Sainte-Anne at St-Fargeau). Other outstanding frescoes are found at Moutiers and Ronchères.

▶ Saulieu and the Morvan *224B3*

Saulieu is what the French call an *étape gastronomique*: a punctuation mark on an ancient thoroughfare, with a long-established reputation for good restaurants. The town can also boast beautiful carved capitals in the 12th-century basilica (**St-Andoche▶**), and a bronze statue of a bull. This is the acclaimed masterpiece of the sculptor Pompon, born at Saulieu in 1855.

To the west of Saulieu, the **Morvan hills▶▶** stretch north to Avallon and south to Autun. The Morvan is Burgundy's wilderness and a regional natural park, with fast-flowing rivers for canoeists and fishermen, reservoirs for watersports, rocky escarpments for climbers and forests for walkers. However, its peaks scarcely soar, and the views from its finest belvedere (Mont Beuvray 821m/2,694ft) do not take the breath away.

▶ Sens *224A4*

Northern gateway to Burgundy, Sens is a moderately attractive country town with the first pure **Gothic cathedral▶** to be built in France, begun in the mid-12th century. Sculptures around the main doorway, much damaged in the Revolution, include a statue of St. Stephen, to whom the cathedral is dedicated. The interior has fine medieval and Renaissance stained glass; the oldest windows are on the north side of the choir, and include a depiction of the murder of archbishop Thomas à Becket of Canterbury, who had spent six years at nearby Pontigny hiding from the ill-disposed English king, Henry II. The treasury of the **Musée de Sens▶▶**, place de la Cathédrale (entrance via Palais Synodal) 89100 Sens (*Open* Sep–Jun, Wed–Mon 10–12, 2–6; Jul, Aug daily 10–6. *Admission: moderate)*, is unusually rich in vestments, tapestries and miscellaneous religious objets d'art.

▶ Solutré *224B1*

The great rock of Solutré hangs over the best vineyards in the Mâconnais (Pouilly and Fuissé) like an unfurling wave. The foot of the cliff has been excavated to reveal the bones of 100,000 horses, from the period 15,000 to 12,000BC, now known as the Solutrean age. A few human skeletons and artefacts from earlier and later periods have also been found. These are now housed in the **Musée de la Préhistoire▶**, 71960 Solure-Pouilly (*Open* Apr–Sep daily 10–6; Oct, Nov, Feb, Mar Wed–Mon 10–12, 2–5. *Closed* Dec, Jan. *Admission: moderate)*, at the foot of the rock.

HORSEMEAT

Place of ritual sacrifice or prehistoric knacker's yard? The usual explanation for the hapless horses of Solutré is that the local inhabitants cornered wild horses on top of the rock and scared them with fire into jumping off the cliff. Down below, the dead animals were cooked and eaten, and their bones discarded. An early example of *boucherie chevaline*.

Sens lies on the banks of the Yonne, which joins the Seine to the north, bringing heavy river traffic

Drive

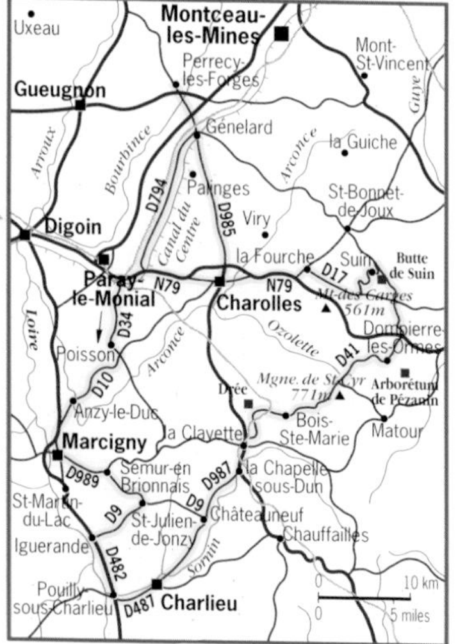

The Charolais and the Brionnais

This is a tour of Burgundy at its most picturesque: pastures dappled with white Charolais cattle; golden churches (keys usually from the *patronne* at the café next door); beret-clad locals with baguettes under their arms riding rusty bicycles.

Start at Paray-le-Monial.
Paray-le-Monial's 12th-century basilica of Sacré-Coeur is no humble village church but a majestic example of Cluniac Romanesque architecture, a smaller version of the demolished abbey church at Cluny itself.

Take D34 then D10 to Marcigny. Continue on D989 to Semur-en-Brionnais and D9 to St-Julien-de-Jonzy and Iguerande.
The tour continues via a series of smaller churches in more rustic surroundings, with octagonal towers and richly carved doorways and capitals. These are at Anzy-le-Duc, Semur-en-Brionnais, St-Julien-de-Jonzy and Iguerande.

Take the D482 to Pouilly-sous-Charlieu, then D487 as far as Charlieu.
Charlieu is a busy little market town with fragments of an old abbey. There are guided tours of the ruins, but the best part is the 12th-century carved doorway of the porch, which is visible from outside.

The route continues along the D987 to La Clayette and D193 as far as Drée.
Both La Clayette and Drée have interesting châteaux to admire from outside, but only Drée can be visited, in summer.

Take D325/D41 to Dompierre-les-Ormes and continue via D41 and D379 to Butte de Suin.
The route threads its way through the wooded hills and farmlands of the Charollais passing Pézanin arboretum, with hundreds of exotic species (near Dompierre-les-Ormes), and offering a choice of panoramic picnic spots—the Montagne de St-Cyr near Montmelard (771m/2,530ft) or the Butte de Suin (593m/1,946ft).

D17 and N79 take you back to Paray-le-Monial via Charolles.
Charolles has given its name to the finest provider of steak to French tables. Apart from this, unless your visit coincides with the weekly Wednesday cattle market, the town is of little interest.

Farther on, Perrecy-les-Forges has an old priory with beautiful carvings in the porch.

▶ Tanlay, Château de *224B3*

A gracious moated Renaissance château near Tonnerre, Tanlay has elegant round towers, bell-shaped domes, and swans in the moat. The interior (guided tours only) has period furniture, sculpted chimney-pieces and a *trompe l'oeil* gallery (*Closed* Tue and Nov–Apr).

The highlight of Tanlay's château is the painted ceiling (School of Fontainebleau) in the Tour de la Ligue depicting courtiers as divinities

▶ Ternant *224B3*

This humble village church, in the middle of nowhere, contains two beautiful wooden **triptychs▶** donated in 1435 by Duke Philip the Good's chamberlain, Philippe de Ternant, who is portrayed in both works.

▶▶ Tournus *224B2*

Tournus is a quiet town sandwiched between the motorway and the Saône, and dominated by the towers of **St-Philibert▶▶**, one of the oldest and finest of France's great Romanesque churches. In the cobbled central area, old houses and former abbey buildings cluster beneath the martial walls and towers of the 11th- to 12th-century church. Inside, massive unadorned pillars of salmon-hued stone support a series of transverse barrel vaults. Oldest of all is the crypt, with several Roman columns and 12th-century frescoes. From Tournus, the D14 west takes you to **Brancion▶▶▶** (15km/9 miles), a picturesque semi-ruined fortified village.

▶▶▶ Vézelay *224A3*

The single street of a picturesque old village with some fine old houses, usually overrun with tourists, climbs a steep hill to a great **pilgrimage church▶▶▶**. By laying false claim to the relics of Mary Magdalen, the abbey at Vézelay became a popular stop on the pilgrimage to Compostela. St. Bernard of Clairvaux launched the Second Crusade there in 1146. The present church, which was rescued from dilapidation by the much-maligned Viollet le Duc in 1840, dates mostly from the 12th century. Its most striking features are the alternation of chocolate and golden stone in the arches and bands of the vault; and beautiful relief carving over the doorway leading from narthex to nave and on the capitals along the nave; as well as the sheer luminosity of the interior. Concerts are held in this magical setting in summer.

RECOMMENDED WALKS

Vézelay is an excellent starting point for walking, both in the countryside under the '*colline eternelle*' and farther afield in the Morvan Regional Park. The tourist office has all the necessary information. A good first stop is the Château de Bazoches, home of France's great founder of civil engineering, Vauban, 10km (6 miles) south of Vézelay (*Open* Apr–Oct).

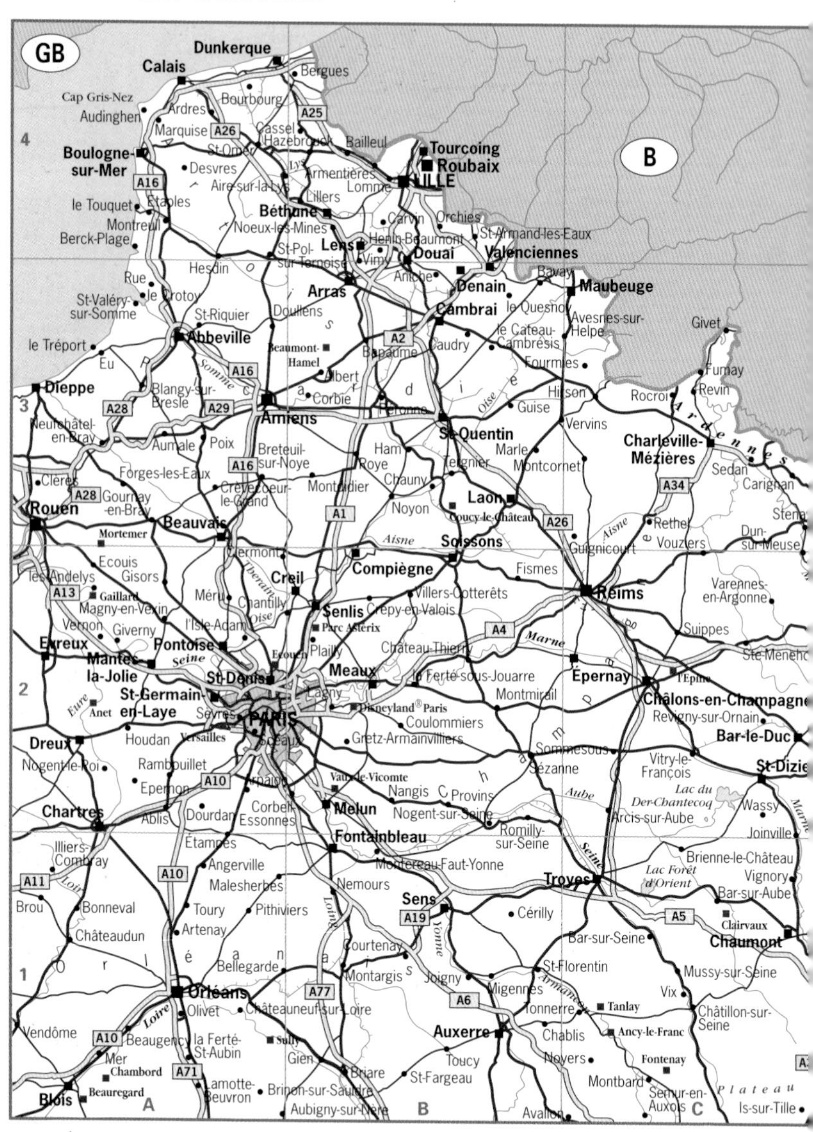

REGION HIGHLIGHTS

THE NORTH PROSPERED in the Middle Ages, and the profits of the great trading towns funded splendid, unsurpassed Gothic buildings in Amiens, Laon and Reims. There is fine building from other periods too, as in the Renaissance squares of Arras and Charleville-Mézières. While the Loire may be the natural habitat of the *château-de-luxe*, this border country is studded with fortress-châteaux of all ages, from fearsome feudal ruins like Coucy to the star-shaped strongholds of Louis XIV and the indestructible remains of Hitler's Atlantic Wall.

The countryside, too, is worth exploring, especially where the bare and spacious plateaux give way to the lush valleys of slow-moving rivers like the Somme. With its superb sandy beaches and high cliffs alternating with

Alsace-Lorraine & the North

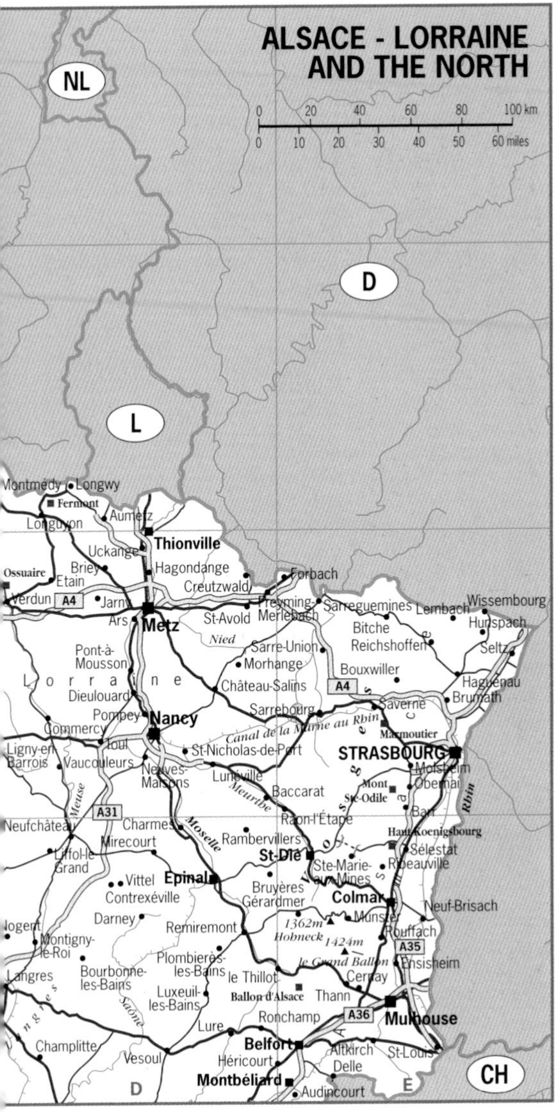

great sweeps of sand-dunes, the Channel coast is one of France's finest. Its ports, Calais, Boulogne and Dunkerque, are among the country's busiest. The chalk hills and escarpments of champagne country around Reims and Epernay lead to Lorraine, with heavy industry in the north and its elegant capital, Nancy, in the south. The wooded Vosges Mountains guard the way to the Rhine Valley and Alsace. Indisputably French, this easternmost province has a Germanic feel expressed in its dialect, its food and wine, and in the utter charm of its half-timbered and flower-bedecked towns and villages, from Strasbourg, one of the capitals of the new Europe, to the humblest wine village along the Route du Vin.

ALSATIAN BEER FAME
Legend has it that France's patron saint of beer, Arnoldus, provided a miraculous draught of the foaming liquid for the pall-bearers at his funeral. Arnoldus was Bishop of Metz in Lorraine, and while his province still brews beers of reputation, it is nearby Alsace that has acquired international fame with Germanic-sounding and tasting brands like Kronenbourg. In the industrial North, as well as lagers the many breweries also make top-fermented ale-like beers in Belgian style, as well as a curious 'red' beer.

▶ Amiens *240A3*

Much battered in two world wars and extensively modernized since, the ancient capital of Picardy on the banks of the Somme has a glorious Gothic **cathedral▶▶▶** with an array of sculpture adorning the west front which captures the visitor's attention. This Bible story in stone focuses on the famous statue of Christ known as *'Le Beau Dieu'*. The serene simplicity of the interior is enhanced by the incredible richness of the 16th-century choir stalls.

The city's other attractions include the **Musée de Picardie▶**, 48 rue de la République (*Open* Tue–Sun 10–12.30, 2–6. *Admission: moderate*), with statues and Greek and Egyptian antiquities, local history at the 17th-century **Hôtel de Berny** (*Open* Apr–Sep Thu–Sun 2–6; Oct–Mar Sun 10–12.30, 2–6. *Admission: inexpensive*), Auguste Perret's extraordinary 1947 skyscraper, and a museum devoted to the author **Jules Verne**, who is buried in a **cemetery▶**. In the flood-plain of the Somme are Amiens' watery **Hortillonnages▶**, a strange area of market gardens threaded by innumerable little channels and in part accessible only by boat.

▶ Ardennes, Les *240C3*

These densely wooded uplands, most of them on Belgian territory, are the abode of deer and wild boar, a paradise for hunters and walkers. They form a high plateau penetrated by the deep valley of the meandering Meuse, best experienced by boat (*bateau-mouche* from Charleville-Mézières or Monthermé) or when viewed from the numerous crags along its course. Industry found an early foothold along the banks of the river; engineering works and quarries are today complemented by a nuclear power station at Chooz. There are fine fortresses at **Rocroi▶** and **Sedan▶▶**, the largest fortified castle in northern Europe and a Protestant stronghold in the 16th century, as well as at **Charleville-Mézières▶**, with its splendid Renaissance square, the **place Ducale**.

▶▶ Arras *240B3*

Arras, the capital of Artois, is renowned for its tapestries of the late Middle Ages. It spent its accumulated wealth on its 16th-century **town hall** and on adorning its two squares, the **Grand' Place** and the **place des Héros**, with the dignified town houses seen today. Flemish gables, harmonious brick and stonework, and continuous arcades combine to form one of the finest urban compositions in northern Europe. Beneath it all run the extensive cellars which sheltered the citizenry during the devastating bombardments of World War I. Many of the town's 16th-century houses that surrounded the squares were destroyed.

The arches in Arras form a pretty backdrop to a cup of coffee

Born in the Ile-de-France, the Gothic style flourished in the prosperous towns and cities of the North. Its liberating effect can be seen, not only in world-famous cathedrals like Laon, Reims and Amiens, but across the whole region, in great abbey churches like St-Riquier and urban basilicas like St-Omer and St-Quentin. There are less well-known cathedrals at Noyon and Soissons, both masterpieces in their own right, though the latter is upstaged by the majestic façade of the great monastery church of St-Jean-des-Vignes.

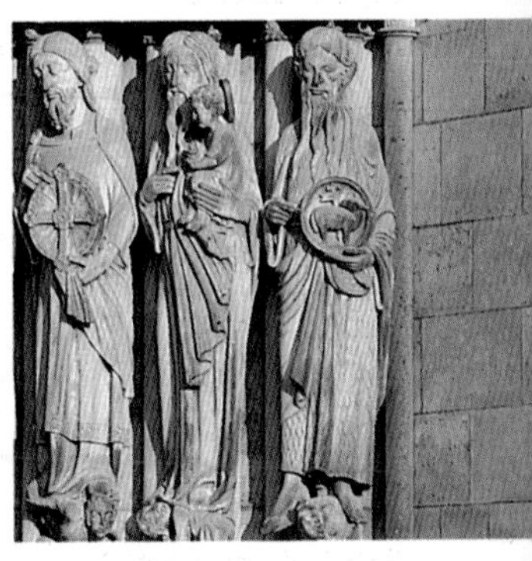

The achievement of the Gothic architects is matched by that of the sculptors and craftsmen who collaborated with them. Fine-grained local limestone lent itself to masterly carving, as in the sculpted figures adorning the west front at Amiens cathedral. At Amiens, too, similar virtuosity is evident in the wood-carving of the splendid choir stalls.

Emergence of Gothic The style underwent constant development as the great master-masons sought to exploit its technical and symbolic possibilities. At 12th-century Laon, we see it still in an early stage of evolution; the cathedral has the many towers typical of earlier churches, and its minimally pointed arches seem to hark back to their rounded Romanesque predecessors, while the intricate west front, with its bold projections, openings and deep shadows, has an extraordinary plastic quality.

Reims Cathedral

Flowering and flamboyance In the 13th century, the style reached its zenith; at Amiens, the use of flying buttresses enables the masonry of the walls to be reduced to an absolute minimum, making way for the great windows through which the daylight streams into the soaring spaces of the interior.

By the time Abbeville's **St-Vulfran** was built in the 15th century, decoration had become more important than structure; in this final, flamboyant phase, window-tracery writhes, flame-like, and the west front carries an overload of ornament.

Occasionally a cooler influence is felt from across the Channel, as in the tall, soberly decorated tower of St-Omer's Notre-Dame, an echo of English Perpendicular style.

CHANNEL TO-ING AND FRO-ING
Boulogne and Calais both have longstanding connections with *la perfide Albion*, visible across the Channel. First was Julius Caesar in 55BC, who used the site of Boulogne to launch his invasion of England; 18 centuries later, Napoleon planned to follow Caesar's example, but was waylaid skirmishing elsewhere. Calais' burghers were principally concerned with defending their town, but today the Channel Tunnel has opened the floodgates to thousands of holidaying Brits. In the other direction go, not the French, but carloads of wine and beer snapped up at Calais' alcohol supermarkets, many of which are British-owned.

▶ Ballon de Guebwiller *241E1*

At 1,424m (4,672ft), this (also called the Grand Ballon) is the highest of the *ballons*, the bare rounded mountain-tops rising impressively from the tree-clad slopes of the southern Vosges. No one should shirk the short walk up from the car park to the summit: at your feet the Alsace plain; beyond the Rhine, the wooded heights of the Black Forest; to the south the Jura and the distant Alps.

▶ Belfort *241E1*

Connoisseurs of station names on the Paris Métro will remember Denfert-Rochereau, named after a hero of the Franco-Prussian War. Besieged in Belfort's citadel by superior force, this doughty colonel and his men withstood the German assault for 103 days, giving up only after the armistice. Their heroism is commemorated by the **Belfort Lion**, a great beast in red sandstone guarding the way up to the **citadel▶▶** and overlooking the workaday town on the banks of the Savoureuse far below.

▶ Bergues *240B4*

Sitting serenely behind its protective walls and elaborate moats, this is one of the prettiest little places in French Flanders. Built in yellow brick, it has resisted many an attacking army.

▶ Boulogne *240A4*

With its old core, the Vieille Ville, still surrounded by medieval ramparts and dominated by its idiosyncratic 19th-century cathedral, Boulogne beats its rivals Calais and Dunkerque for character. **Nausicaà▶▶,** boulevard St-Beuve, Boulogne (*Open* Jul, Aug 9.30–7.30; Sep–Jun 9.30–6.30. *Admission: expensive*), France's second-largest aquarium, makes an additional reason to visit. Its port lands more fish than anywhere else in France. To the north of Boulogne stretch the cliffs, dunes and beaches of the **Côte d'Opale▶▶** (Opal Coast), culminating in the mighty headland of **Cap Gris-Nez**. Farther north still, at Cap Blanc-Nez, is the amusing Musée du Transmanche, relating serious and utopian projects for crossing the Channel.

Old Boulogne's basilica replaced a cathedral destroyed by Revolutionary zeal but still contains a Romanesque crypt

▶ Calais *240A4*

Wrecked in World War II and unstylishly rebuilt, this busy port is a mere 38km (24 miles) from the English coast, whose chalk cliffs are clearly visible on a fine day. The English siege of 1346–47 is commemorated by Rodin's celebrated and moving bronze of the **Burghers of Calais**, at the foot of the tall town hall tower. Nearby, an old German bunker has been converted into a war museum (see page 257).

▶ Cambrai *240B3*

Famed since medieval times for its fine linen known in English as 'cambric', Cambrai suffered terribly during the German retreat of 1918. An industrial town, it is also the focus of a rich agricultural area and is famous for its tripe and sausages, as well as for the minty titbits called *bêtises* ('nonsenses'). Gates and cobbled streets form the old heart of town, with its striking Spanish house and enjoyable Museum of Fine Arts.

▶ Cassel *240B4*

The flat farmlands of French Flanders are relieved by a number of isolated knolls, the 'Monts de Flandres'. On the highest of these (176m/577ft) perches this exquisite little Flemish town, its cobbled **Grande Place** lined with fine old buildings. From the summit of the knoll, with its 18th-century windmill, there are terrific views.

▶▶ Colmar *241E1*

Large numbers of visitors come to Colmar to appreciate the special character of Alsace. High-gabled, timber-framed houses front the old streets and squares of the perfectly preserved central area; outstanding are the galleried **Ancienne Douane▶** (Old Customs House), and the **Maison Pfister▶**. The **Krutenau district▶▶**, Colmar's superbly restored 'Little Venice', is particularly picturesque. Also worth seeing is St. Martin's Cathedral, with its Gothic, Romanesque and Renaissance elements.

But Colmar's greatest treasure is kept indoors, in the chapel in the **Musée d'Unterlinden▶▶▶**, place d'Unterlinden (*Open* Apr–Oct daily 9–6; Nov–Mar Wed–Mon 9–12, 2–5. *Admission: expensive*). Here, in all its terrifying intensity, is the *Issenheim Altarpiece*, the masterwork of Matthias Grünewald. The folding panels of the altarpiece were painted around 1515 for the Prior of the Monastery of St. Anthony at nearby Issenheim. Its visionary evocation of the suffering in the *Redemption of Christ* still has the power to move; seldom has the agony of the dying Christ been more forcefully portrayed. The impact of the altarpiece is such that it is best left to the end of your visit. Apart from the Orlier altarpiece by Grünewald's near-contemporary, Martin Schongauer, and the 24 panels of the *Passion* altarpiece attributed to his workshop, there are local collections of 16th- to 19th-century decorative and traditional arts, and an array of modern French paintings (by Braque, Picasso, Léger, etc). Schongauer's work can be seen again in the **Dominican Church**, where his *Virgin in the Rose Bower* has pride of place.

ALSATIAN DELICACIES

Alsace is one of France's gastronomic provinces, serving Germanic food with a French accent, like *choucroute* (sauerkraut), garnished with Strasbourg sausages or pork chops. From Strasbourg, too, comes *foie gras*, goose liver eaten *au naturel* or as pâté. Pork plays a big role, but so do delicate tasting poultry and trout (from the Vosges) and eel. Munster cheese is renowned, as is *kougelhopf* cake.

Colmar's narrow streets are rich in immaculately restored houses, some dating from the 16th and 17th centuries

Drive

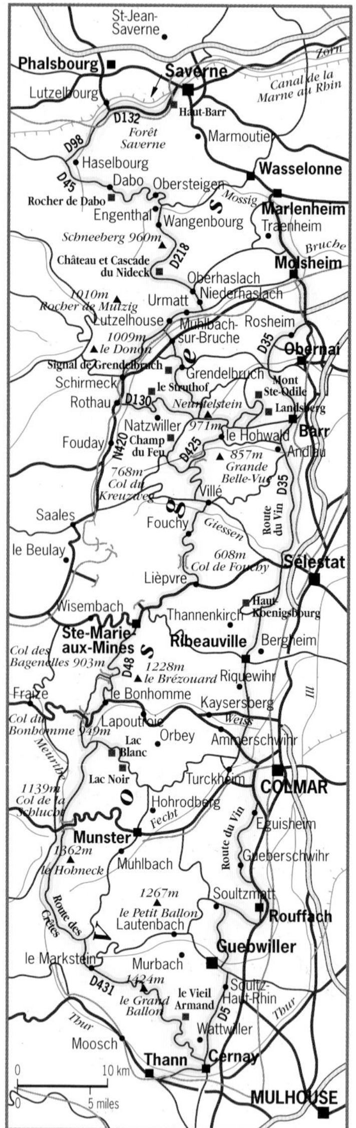

Route des Crêtes

Rising gently to the east from the Lorraine plateau, then dropping abruptly through the vineyards to the broad plain of the Rhine, the wooded Vosges Mountains are among France's most attractive uplands. From rugged sandstone heights in the north to the gently rounded forms of the *ballons* in the south, this superb walking country extends for 170km (105 miles) between the German border and the Belfort Gap. The Route des Crêtes was built during World War I to serve the French front line; it now forms a magnificent drive.

Start at Saverne. Take the D132 southwest and turn left on to the D98 at Lutzelbourg. At Haselbourg follow the D45 and at the little resort of Obersteigen turn right on to the D218.
This part of the Vosges has romantic landscapes of woods, pretty valleys and castle ruins commanding fine views.

Just beyond Niederhaslach, with its great Gothic church, turn right on to the N420 along the picturesque valley of the Bruche. At Lutzelhouse you can either head south via Muhlbach up to the panoramic viewpoint at the Signal de Grendelbruch or continue along the valley past Schirmeck to Rothau and turn left on the D130 to Le Struthof.
The approach road to **Le Struthof** was built by the slave workforce of the Nazi concentration camp. Chilling remains still stand, and there is a museum.

The alternative routes rejoin near the Neuntelstein viewpoint. Head east on D130 and D426 to Mont-Ste-Odile.
Visitors crowd the mountain-top convent dedicated to **Ste-Odile**, above all on her feast day (13 December). Alsace's patron saint lived in the eighth century; the imposing masonry of the great earthwork known as the **Mur Païen** (Pagan Wall) harks back to much earlier times, when Gaul was ruled by the mysterious Celts.

Return westward via D109. Turn left on to D426 to the little upland

resort of Le Hohwald, then go southwest on the D425, turning right after the Col du Kreuzweg to the Champ du Feu.
From the **Champ du Feu** observation tower there are staggering views that can extend as far as the Black Forest, or even as far as the Swiss Alps on a clear day.

Return to D425 and continue south to Villé, then to Fouchy and the pretty Col de Fouchy. Down in the valley again at Lièpvre, turn right to the small industrial settlement of Ste-Marie-aux-Mines. At the Col des Bagenelles, follow signs to Le Bonhomme, where you turn right to travel to the Col du Bonhomme.
The **Col du Bonhomme**, traversed by one of the main routes linking Alsace with Lorraine, marks the northern end of the Route des Crêtes.

The Route winds along for 83km (52 miles) as far as Thann in the south.
Splendid forests alternate with high pastures, while far below are

attractive lakes. All along the route are spectacular viewpoints, the most celebrated being that of the **Grand Ballon** (1,424m/4,672ft). A sombre reminder that the ridgeline was bitterly contested by the opposing armies is the National Memorial at **Vieil-Armand**. The Route descends sinuously to Cernay and then 6km (4 miles) west to Thann.

Drive

Route du Vin d'Alsace

This second tourist route of Alsace, some 180km (112 miles) long between Thann in the south and Marlenheim in the north, is well signposted. Its winding course is best taken at a leisurely pace, with ample time for tasting—details available locally or from the tourist office, 4 rue d'Unterlinden, in Colmar.

From Thann, follow the Route via Eguisheim, past Colmar to Kaysersberg.
The vines grow in a narrow north–south band along the foothills of the Vosges. Here are immaculate villages, whose cobbled streets and squares and high-gabled timber houses epitomize Alsace. Many, like three-towered **Eguisheim** or triangular **Turckheim**, have all the airs of miniature towns. The most popular town is probably Riquewihr, almost unbearably crowded on occasion. Kaysersberg, with its fortified bridge, was the birthplace of the great humanitarian Albert Schweitzer.

Continue north past Sélestat and Obernai to Marlenheim.
Castles abound in this frontier province, most of them in romantic ruin. One exception is **Haut-Koenigsbourg▶▶**, 67600 Orschwiller (*Open* Mar, Oct daily 9.45–5; Apr, May, Sep 9.30–5.30; Jun–Aug 9.30–6.30; Nov–Feb 9–12, 1–5. *Closed* public holidays. *Admission: expensive*), its formidable silhouette rising imperiously over the forested slopes above Sélestat. It was reconstructed for Kaiser Wilhelm II in the early years of the 20th century, when Alsace was ruled from Berlin.

STORK SHORTAGE
One of the emblems of Alsace is the stork's nest atop a chimney stack or steeple. Weighing up to half a ton, these form annually refurbished residences, occupied each summer. Courtship is noisy, with much flapping of wings and clattering of bills. Eggs can number up to half a dozen. Sadly, the stork population has declined dramatically in recent years, though efforts are now being made to augment their numbers by breeding them in captivity.

DUAL IDENTITY
Long-settled by German-speakers, Alsace was assimilated into France as Louis XIV pushed eastward to the 'natural' frontier along the Rhine. While accepting French rule, the population felt uneasy with Paris' centralizing tendencies, and not everyone regretted being reabsorbed into the German Reich after the Franco-Prussian War of 1870–71. Re-annexation by Nazi Germany in 1940 was a less happy experience. Today's Alsatians are content to live in a Europe where Germany and France are partners and where their own identity can flourish.

▶ Coucy-le-Château *240B3*

In the Middle Ages, this ridgetop castle was one of the greatest strongholds in the land. Near the end of World War I, the retreating Germans added to the depredations of the centuries by blowing up the massive keep. But enough remains of walls, towers and huge gateways to enclose completely the modern village of Coucy and to leave an unforgettable memory of medieval might. The usual approach winds up from the south to the Porte de Soissons, with its little museum.

▶ Douai *240B4*

War-damaged in 1914–18 and again in 1940, Douai nevertheless retains a good number of 18th-century buildings, an ensemble of which houses the **Musée de la Chartreuse**, with its collection of 17th- and 18th-century paintings as well as its 64m (210ft) Gothic **Beffroi▶** (bell-tower), one of the finest in the North. In the 17th century, the town became a refuge for English Roman Catholics.

Douai was the administrative hub for France's great northern coalfield; at nearby Lewarde, in an old mine, is the **Centre Historique Minier▶**, which gives a good picture of mining life.

▶▶ Koenigsbourg see page 247

▶ L'Epine *240C2*

Pilgrimages have taken place here ever since shepherds saw an image of the Virgin Mary in the middle of a burning thorn (*épine*) bush. The late-Gothic church erected to commemorate the apparition dominates the humble half-timbered houses of the village huddling at its foot.

▶ Langres *241D1*

The **Plateau de Langres** is a vast rolling upland straddling the headwaters of three of France's great rivers, the Marne, the Meuse and the Seine. Perched on one of its limestone promontories is the ancient town of Langres itself, still intact within its well-preserved walls. The most rewarding walk leads round the ramparts, passing towers and gateways. Within the town are many splendid old houses, some of them of Renaissance date. Important vestiges of the Gallo-Roman town, Andematunum, are housed in the **Musée d'Art et d'Histoire**.

▶▶ Laon *240B3*

This walled and gated city dominates the flatlands all around. The Gothic **cathedral▶▶▶** rises over the rooftops. The west front is a triumph of early Gothic drama and ebullience, while the interior has a simplicity and dignity. The figures of oxen in the towers commemorate the beasts who hauled the heavy stone. Below the bluff lies the new town, linked by an innovative overhead tram, the Poma. A new World War I museum, the **Musée du Caverne du Dragon▶▶**, chemin des Dames, 02160 Laon (*Open* For guided visits only; May, Jun, Sep daily 10–12, 1–4.30; Jul, Aug daily 10–12, 1–5.30; Oct–Dec, Feb–Apr Tue–Sun 10–12, 1–4.30. *Closed* Jan. *Admission: moderate*), is dedicated to the battle of Chemin des Dames, and is housed in the caverns where the Germans had their HQ during the war.

Laon, once the capital of France, is an attractive town surrounded with medieval ramparts and imposing entrance gates

▶ Lille *240B4*

Lille is the capital of the North; an industrial conurbation of more than a million inhabitants. While much of this sprawl lacks allure, the heart of the city is full of style and life, a fascinating mix of French and Flemish influence, though the huge **Citadel** is entirely French, built by Louis XIV's military engineer Vauban. The enlarged, revamped **Palais des Beaux Arts▶▶▶**, place de la République (*Open* Mon 2–6, Wed–Sun 10–6, Fri 10–7. *Admission: moderate*), displays Flemish and Dutch masters through to Impressionists. General de Gaulle's birthplace, **Maison Natale du Général de Gaulle** (*Open* Wed–Sun 10–1, 2–6. *Admission: moderate*) includes his christening robe.

▶ Lunéville *241D2*

In the early 18th century, the Duke of Lorraine built a château here to rival Versailles. His **palace▶** houses a porcelain museum. In January 2003 a fire devastated the château. While restoration is underway only part of the château is open to the public.

▶ Marmoutier *241E2*

Just to the south of Saverne stands the monastery of Marmoutier. Built in red Vosges sandstone, begun in the 11th century, its commanding west front is one of the finest examples of Romanesque architecture in Alsace.

▶ Metz *241D2*

Metz has been a fortress city for most of its long existence. Between 1871 and 1918 it belonged to Germany, and buildings dating from this period, like the huge **railway station**, have a distinctly Germanic air. But the **cathedral▶▶** is characteristically French, with a lofty interior and sumptuous stained glass, including modern work by Marc Chagall. Metz's riverside is worth seeking out, not least for the formidable gateway known as the **Porte des Allemands**. The history museum, the **Musée de la Cour d'Or▶▶**, 2 rue du Haut Poirier (*Open* Wed–Mon 9–5). *Admission: moderate*), is exemplary.

LUNÉVILLE'S SON

Little is known of the life of painter Georges de la Tour, born at Vic-sur-Seille near Lunéville in 1593. It appears that he pursued his career as court painter to both the Duke of Lorraine and King Louis XIII with a worldly and ruthless determination. This is not reflected in his pictures, which have a mystical stillness and peacefulness never since matched. He is master of nocturnal interiors peopled by serene figures whose calm features are lit by the concealed flame of a single candle. Few works survive, but examples can be seen in the Musée Historique Lorraine at Nancy.

VOSGES SPAS
Lorraine is world famous for its water—few can fail to recognize the name Vittel—and any number of spas have grown up in the south of the province. As well as Vittel and nearby Contrexville (both with bottling plants open to the public, Apr–Oct), there are several places (Plombières, Luxeuil, Bourbonne, for instance) tapping the waters springing from the fringe of the Vosges Mountains. Pretty surroundings, parks and gardens, elegant old-fashioned spa architecture and a general atmosphere of leisure and pleasure make these little resorts as attractive to the casual visitor as to those in search of a cure.

HEAVENLY VOICES
Among the Meuse's attractions is the tiny village of Domrémy-la-Pucelle, near Neufchâteau, famed for being the birthplace of Joan of Arc (*la pucelle* in question). Her family home, despite extensive alterations, remains a good example of a 15th-century peasant house and is open to the public. By the woods where the 13-year-old Joan first heard heavenly voices, there now stands a less inspiring 1900s basilica, a magnet for pilgrims. Four years after receiving her divine instructions, Joan left the Vosges, never to return.

▶ Meuse *240C2*

Some 900km (560 miles) long from its source near Bourbonne-les-Bains to its mouth in the North Sea, the Meuse is part of the extensive system of canalized waterways linking France to adjoining countries to the northeast. For nearly 160km (100 miles) between Neufchâteau and Stenay, it flows in a trench-like valley marked to the east by the high limestone hills of the Côtes de Meuse. Fortress-cities like **Verdun▶** guard this section of the river, and some of France's most fateful battles have been fought along its banks, at Sedan in 1871 and again in 1940, and above all at Verdun (see page 259).

▶ Moselle *241D1*

The Moselle starts its life as a mountain stream high in the Vosges. The most attractive part is between here and Epinal, where it flows through rich farmlands. From Neuves-Maisons near Nancy, however, it becomes one of Europe's great industrial waterways.

▶ Mulhouse *241E1*

The dynamic industrial town of Mulhouse attracts visitors for its outstanding museums and its symbol of modernity, the lofty **Tour de l'Europe▶**. The **Musée National de l'Automobile▶▶**, 92 avenue du Colmar (*Open* Jan Mon–Fri 1–5, Sat, Sun 10–5; Feb, Mar, Nov, Dec daily 10–5; Apr–Oct daily 10–6. *Admission: expensive)*, has a superb collection of vehicles, French and foreign, from prototypes to famous racers. The **Cité du Train▶▶**, 2 rue Alfred de Glehn (*Open* Jan Mon–Fri 10–2, Sat, Sun 10–5; Feb, Mar, Nov, Dec daily 10–5; Apr–Oct daily 10–6. *Admission: expensive)*, is the national collection of railwayana and features French steam locomotives of yesteryear. The **Musée de l'Impression sur Etoffes▶▶**, 3 rue des Bonnes Gens (*Open* Tue–Sun 10–12, 2–6. *Admission: expensive*), explains the cotton printing processes, and has a display of fine fabrics. Electropolis is a recent attraction devoted to the story of electricity. At the open-air **Ecomusée d'Alsace**, off the D430 to the north, traditional buildings have been reconstructed to show the domestic life and crafts of the past.

▶ Munster *241E1*

This little resort in the vine-clad and wooded valley of the Fecht in the southern Vosges is famous for the pungent and semi-soft Munster cheese. Nearby is the **Petit Ballon▶**, 1,267m (4,157ft) high and one of the province's most spectacular viewpoints.

Capital city of the Duchy of Lorraine before becoming part of the kingdom of France on the death of its last duke, Stanislas, Nancy prides itself on its classical townscape, product of the urban planning of its enlightened rulers.

Elegance and harmony Stanislas had been king of Poland. When he was deposed in 1736, his son-in-law, Louis XV, managed to engineer him the dukedom of Lorraine. Full of architectural enthusiasm, Stanislas set about linking the rectilinear 'New Town' laid out by his predecessor, Duke Leopold, to the old town around the Ducal Palace. Together with his architect, Héré, he planned an urban composition of unsurpassed elegance and harmony, the place Royale (now **place Stanislas**).

Flanked by lesser buildings in the same richly ornate but dignified style, the monumental **Hôtel de Ville** dominates the square, facing north and an **Arc de Triomphe**. The exits from the square are guarded by Jean Lamour's gilded ironwork grilles of the utmost sumptuousness. The best view of the whole ensemble is from the Hôtel de Ville's upper floor, reached by a splendid staircase, also the work of Héré.

Museums and galleries The lengthy place de la Carrière is terminated by the colonnaded Palais du Gouvernement. Beyond is the austere Ducal Palace containing the fascinating **Musée Historique Lorraine,** Ducal Palace, 64 Grand Rue, 54000 Nancy (*Open* Wed–Mon 10–12, 2–6. *Admission: moderate*), with luminous interiors by the painter Georges de la Tour (see panel page 249).

Nancy's other museums include the **Musée des Beaux Arts**, place Stanislas (*Open* Wed–Sun 10–6. *Admission: moderate*), with collections of European art from medieval to modern times, and the not-to-be-missed **Musée de l'Ecole de Nancy**, 36–38 rue du Sergent BlauBau (*Open* Wed–Sun 10.30–6. *Admission: moderate*). The city was France's most important showcase of art nouveau outside Paris, and the fascinating collections of this museum, housed in an elegant residence of the period, make this one of the best places to experience the heady luxuriance of the decorative arts of the turn of the 20th century.

Gallé Emile Gallé established his glass workshop in Nancy in the early 1870s. He excelled in making exquisite vases in translucent cameo glass, inspired by the motifs and techniques of Japanese art. Gallé was also a designer of extravagant furniture, like the bed inlaid with a huge mother-of-pearl moth that can be seen in the Musée de l'Ecole de Nancy.

THE DAUMS
The Daum brothers, Jean and Antonin, developed complex techniques for giving glass ever greater subtleties of tone and texture.

Guibal's Neptune fountain and Lamour's magnificent gilded ironwork grilles frame the western end of place Stanislas, Nancy's classical architecture showpiece

KIWIS ALOFT!
Le Quesnoy's ingenious design failed to protect its German defenders from the New Zealand Rifle Brigade in 1918; they employed medieval siege tactics and scaled its walls with ladders.

▶ Neuf Brisach *241E1*

In 1697, the French were forced to withdraw from Alt ('old') Breisach, one of the chain of strongholds they had built on the east bank of the Rhine. The fortress-town of Neuf ('new') Brisach was its replacement. It is a perfectly preserved example of the genius of Louis XIV's military engineer, Vauban, who has a museum devoted to him.

▶ Obernai *241E2*

Among the vineyards at the foot of the sacred mountain of Mont-Ste-Odile, Obernai is the epitome of an Alsace wine village. In the place du Marché stand the 15th-century **town hall** and the 16th-century **Corn Hall▶**, over-looked by the tall **Tour de la Chapelle**. A statue of St. Odile graces the fountain in the middle of the square, and not far away stands the pretty **Puits aux Six-Sceaux**, a little Renaissance well.

▶ Le Quesnoy *240B3*

Still intact after more than three centuries, the extensive moats and bastions of this quiet little fortress-city are a masterpiece of baroque military engineering and a reminder of the vulnerability of France's northern frontier. The moats are now a leisure park.

▶▶▶ **Reims** see page 253

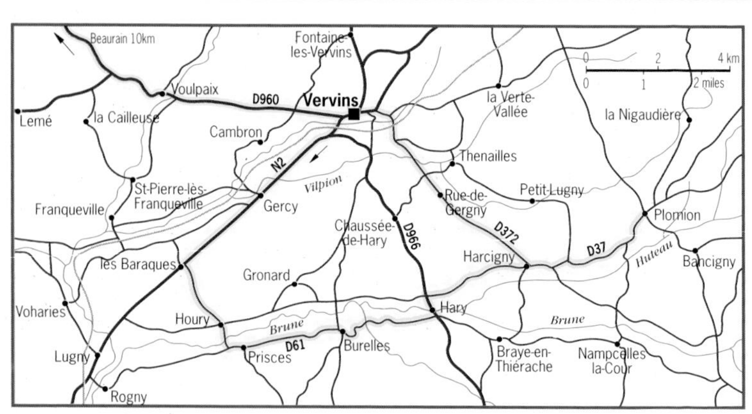

Drive

La Thiérache

This lush green frontier countryside with its rich pastures and cider orchards was always vulnerable to the ravages of invading armies. The harassed locals' response was to fortify their parish churches, many of which still stand.

A drive through La Thiérache can focus on the town of Vervins.

From here a number of fortress churches are within easy reach: brick-built **Burelles**, twin-towered **Plomion**, 12th-century **Prisces** with its massive tower, lonely **Beaurain** on its isolated eminence. The churches' interiors were adapted to withstand a siege, with a well, a bread-oven, and upper floors to house the villagers.

World-famous for its great Gothic cathedral, Reims owes its name to St. Rémi, the saint who, in the year 498, baptized the heathen Clovis, King of the Franks. Later, Reims became France's coronation city, with 25 rulers crowned here.

Treasures of Reims The cathedral was begun in 1211, and all but ruined during World War I. Expertly restored, it has an inspiring west front: high up above the great rose window is the Gallery of Kings; down below, in the left porch, is the Smiling Angel. Inside, the stained glass is among the finest in France. Adjoining the cathedral is the old Bishops Palace, the **Palais du Tau**, 2 place du Cardinal Luçon, 51100 Reims (*Open* mid-May to mid-Sep Tue–Sun 9.30–6.30; mid-Sep to mid-May 9.30–12.30, 2–5.30. *Admission: expensive*), housing the Cathedral Treasury . Not far away is the **Basilica of St-Rémi**, whose monastic buildings are a storehouse of medieval art and arms—**Musée St-Rémi**, 53 rue Simon (*Open* Mon–Fri 2–6.30, Sat, Sun 2–7. *Admission: moderate*).

Champagne The process by which champagne acquires its sparkle is said to have been invented by a 17th-century monk, Dom Perignon. The caves (premises with famous names such as Veuve-Cliquot, Piper-Heidsieck, Taittinger and Pommery) can be visited.

On the flanks of the Montagne de Reims, just to the south of the city, vines give way to a regional park sheltering deer and wild boar. The vines spread out along the valley of the Marne and south of the town are the slopes known as the Côte des Blancs. A sojourn hereabouts may convince you of the justification for the staunch refusal by the French to let any other drink be marketed under the name of champagne, and you are likely to come away convinced that no other sparkling wine can ever match the refinement of the product of France's northernmost vineyard.

REIMS

The chalky rock on which Reims stands is as hollow as a Swiss cheese, with mile upon mile of caves providing ideal conditions for the production and storage of the region's most renowned product.

The Musée des Beaux Arts, Abbaye St-Denis, 8 rue Chancy, 51100 Reims (Open Wed–Mon 10–noon, 2–6. Admission: moderate; free 1st Sun of each month), has some rare Renaissance art. Below: Tête de Brigand, bronze bust by Camille Claudel (Rodin's lover)

Sélestat's Bibliothèque Humaniste is an impressive symbol of the town's educational prowess during the Middle Ages and later was the cradle of Alsatian humanism

►► Ronchamp *241D1*

High up on Ronchamp's hilltop, the pilgrimage chapel of Notre-Dame-du-Haut is an atmospheric modern church (*Open* daily). Designed by Le Corbusier in 1955, it is as much a sculpture as a building, with a billowing roof. The mysterious interior is lit by stained-glass windows deeply set into massive concrete walls. The town has a mining museum, to be found at place de la Mairie (*Open* May–Aug Wed–Mon 10–noon, 2–6; Sep–Apr Wed–Mon 2–6).

► St-Omer *240A4*

Now bypassed by the A26 motorway, this small town was once the first stop for visitors heading inland from Calais. It is a dignified place with fine old 17th- and 18th-century houses and a network of canals, the **watergangs►** (boat trips available). The imposing **Basilica of Notre-Dame►►** has a tall tower in English Perpendicular style and an interior that is a veritable museum of ecclesiastical art.

▶ St-Riquier *240A3*

The village is dominated by its great abbey church, founded by the Benedictines in the seventh century. The present building dates mostly from the 15th and 16th centuries; built in pale local limestone in Flamboyant Gothic style, it has the scale and presence of a cathedral.

▶ Sélestat *241E1*

The cramped network of medieval streets here is contained within Sélestat's ring of long-since demolished walls. It has two good churches, Gothic St-Georges and 12th-century **Ste-Foy▶**; the latter, with its three towers, is one of the finest Romanesque buildings in the province. The **Bibliothèque Humaniste▶▶**, 1 rue de la Bibliothèque (*Open* Jan–Jun, Sep–Dec Mon, Wed–Fri 9–12, 2–6, Sat 9–12; Jul, Aug Mon, Wed–Fri 9–noon, 2–6, Sat, Sun 9–noon, 2–5. *Admission: moderate*), contains collections of books and manuscripts dating back to the seventh century.

▶ Somme *240A3*

Despite witnessing some of the bloodiest battles of World War I, the Somme flows peacefully through a lush valley set among open chalklands. It reaches the sea at the wide Baie de la Somme, an attractive estuary well endowed with crustaceans and other forms of marine life, much of which is consumed by visitors to the little port-resorts of **Le Crotoy** (to the north) and **St-Valéry▶** (to the south). Vintage trains run from Le Crotoy via St-Valéry to the sandy beaches of Cayeux-sur-Mer.

▶▶▶ Strasbourg *241E2*

Seat of the Council of Europe and the European Parliament, Strasbourg is the jewel in the crown of Alsace. Sited between the branches of the River Ill just west of the Rhine, the ancient city is dominated by the single soaring spire of the superb medieval **cathedral▶▶▶**, a building particularly rich in sculptural decoration. Inside, a three-tiered triumph of Gothic carving depicts the drama of the Last Judgement, while close by is a 19th-century astronomical clock, popular for its midday performance; 330 steps lead up the tower.

Strasbourg is well endowed with museums. The **Musée de l'Oeuvre Notre-Dame▶** (*Open* Tue–Sun 10–6. *Admission: moderate*) has original sculpture from the cathedral. Three museums (**Beaux-Arts, Archéologique, Arts Décoratifs/ Musée Archéologique**) are grouped in the **Palais de Rohan▶▶**, 2 place du Château (*Open* Wed–Mon 10–6. *Closed* public holidays. *Admission: moderate*); the ceramics collection is one of the best in France. The **Musée Alsacien▶** (folk culture) spreads over three 16th- and 17th-century dwellings, and the **Musée d'Art Moderne et Contemporain▶**, 1 place Jean Hans-Arp, 67000 Strasbourg (*Open* Tue–Wed, Fri–Sun 11–7, Thu 12–10. *Closed* Mon. *Admission: moderate*), featuring European painting and sculpture from Impressionism to the present day, is now in its new purpose-built home alongside the château.

At the west end of the 'island' formed by the arms of the Ill is **La Petite France▶▶**, with winding streets, half-timbered houses and turreted bridges, best observed from the **Barrage Vauban**, with its viewing terrace.

EUROPEAN CROSSROADS

Strasbourg's Palais de l'Europe houses the Council of Europe; but the European Parliament now has its own home in the same district, the Quartier Européen. Other institutions, like the European Court of Human Rights and the European Science Foundation, have found Strasbourg's location on the border between western and central Europe a congenial place to be.

The cathedral square, Strasbourg, at the heart of a vast pedestrian area served by a mini-train

Many of the most dramatic struggles in the course of French history have taken place in this region, where the gently rolling countryside offers few natural barriers to invasion from the northeast.

HOMAGE TO THE GREAT WAR
At Péronne, south of Arras, the Historial de la Grand Guerre (*Open* May–Sep daily 10–6; Oct to mid-Dec, Feb–Apr Tue–Sun 10–6. *Closed* mid-Dec to mid-Jan. *Admission: expensive*) presents the experiences of the three main contenders. A short film gives archival background to the Commonwealth volunteers, while a free guide to the Circuit du Souvenir (battlefields, memorials and museums of the Somme) shows Britain's contribution.

World War I saw a tenth of France's population dead or missing (1.4 million) and nearly 3 million injured

Early days The English—called *les goddons* (meaning God damn!) for their peculiar habit of continuous swearing—were the perennial enemy, and some of the decisive battles of the Middle Ages were fought here, such as **Crécy** and **Agincourt** (*Azincourt* in French). Later, French anxiety about the exposed frontier incited successful attempts to push the kingdom's border northeast, cementing it in place with chains of fortresses and fortified towns. Many of them designed by Louis XIV's ingenious military engineer, Sebastien Le Prestre de Vauban, these baroque strongholds were the ultimate deterrent of their day, with few financial constraints inhibiting the lavish layout of places like **Le Quesnoy** or the Citadel at **Lille**.

The war to end wars The outcome of the Franco-Prussian War of 1870–71 was decided by Napoleon III's humiliating defeat at Sedan. His successors worked for decades to create an impregnable chain of huge forts along the Meuse. But in 1914, in the opening weeks of World War I, the river was crossed again as the German armies marched southwest. Stalemate followed the successful French counter-attack on the Marne, and for four long years the opposing armies attempted to bleed each other white in a series of lumbering and indecisive offensives. The scenes of greatest devastation, both of landscape and of human life, took place along the Somme (where the British attack in 1916 cost 600,000 casualties before grinding to a halt), in the soggy fields of Flanders, and at Verdun, where relentless German pressure was countered by equally determined French resistance.

Afterwards, memorials arose all over the now silent battlefields to commemorate the unprecedented slaughter. The cemeteries of the British War Graves Commission, much of their classical architecture designed by the great Edwin Lutyens, have a serene, timeless air. They are thickest on the ground in the windswept fields north of the Somme around the rebuilt town of **Albert**, from which a waymarked '*Circuit de Souvenir*' guides the visitor around the killing grounds. A stretch of trenches has been preserved at the Newfoundlanders' Memorial at **Beaumont-Hamel**. Farther north, at **Vimy Ridge**, dramatically visible from the A26 motorway, the Canadian Memorial and museum towers over the hilltop. Here, the land has been given in perpetuity to the Canadian nation, a tribute to the 60,000 sacrificed in its capture. The clash of arms in the titanic struggle which raged for 18 months around **Verdun** finds no echo today in the eerie forest now covering the land scoured by shellfire. Here are some poignant memorials of the war, like the white-towered **Ossuary** of Douaumont, as well as the **Memorial Museum** at nearby Fleury (*Closed* mid-Dec to mid-Jan).

World War II Haunted by memories of the carnage, inter-war French governments sought to protect the nation from a recurrence by building a 20th-century equivalent of Louis XIV's frontier fortresses along the Franco-German border. As in the time of Vauban, no expense was spared, but when the test came in 1940, the ultra-modern fortifications of the Maginot Line were simply outflanked by the Wehrmacht's Blitzkrieg through the 'impenetrable' Ardennes to the coast. Remains of this costly deterrent which failed to deter can be seen at **Fermont** near Longwy or at **Lembach** in Alsace.

Fighting in the North, both in the spring of 1940 and in the Liberation of 1944, was brief compared with the long drawn-out battles of 1914–18. The epic of **Dunkerque** is recalled by exhibits in the town's Musée des Beaux-Arts; the fate of Calais during the war and occupation, by the Musée de la Guerre housed in a bunker in Calais. The most tangible remains from World War II are the formidable concrete coastal fortifications built to repel the Allied invasion which the Wehrmacht had convinced itself would be launched against the beaches of the Pas de Calais rather than in Normandy. One of the blockhouses of this 'Atlantic Wall' at **Audinghen** on the cliffs between Calais and Boulogne has been converted into a private museum (*Open* Easter–Sep daily 9–6). Germanic mastery of reinforced concrete is demonstrated again in what is supposedly the biggest such structure ever built, the bunker rising ominously over the tree-tops at **Wizernes** near St-Omer, now a museum, La Coupole. Constructed by men forced to work on the project, this was to serve as a launching ramp for the V2 rocket bombardment of London, but was put out of action by air attack.

DUNKERQUE'S NEW FACE

Dunkerque was bought back from the English by Louis XIV in 1662. In 1945, 90 per cent of the town was destroyed but since then it has been rebuilt and revitalized to become France's third-largest port. Boat tours of the port leave from the Bassin du Commerce. The walk past the two locks to the lighthouse gives views over the vast docks.

The central area of Toul, much of which was rebuilt after World War II destruction. Toul once had the status of an independent enclave within the duchy of Lorraine

STAINED GLASS
Known as the 'Ville Sainte du Vitrail', Troyes' exceptional heritage of stained-glass windows, dating from the 13th to 19th centuries, provides in-situ restoration laboratories whose methods remain essentially unchanged despite improved techniques (better quality leads, more sophisticated soldering and a 3,000-strong palette as opposed to the original 12 hues). The School of Troyes' last known great master was Linard Gontier (17th century), specialist in *grisaille*, a technique of shading (Eglise St-Martin-ès-Vignes). The 19th century saw a revival of the art.

FLYING CARS
Le Touquet airfield, now used only by the private planes of the prosperous, was busy in the 1950s with the bulky Bristol Freighters of Silver City Airways, whose pioneering attempts to fly passengers' cars across the Channel eventually came to nothing.

▶ Thann 241E1

This little industrial town, southern terminus for both the Route des Crêtes and the Route du Vin (see pages 246–247), is overlooked by the ruins of its medieval castle, the Engelsbourg. The demolition of the fortress in 1673 left a massive cylindrical chunk of the keep lying on its side. Seen from a distance it resembles a huge eye staring down the valley—hence the local name, *L'Oeil de la Sorcière* (Witch's Eye). Thann's imposing Gothic **church▶** is called 'The Cathedral' by locals; beneath its tall spire it has an ornately sculpted porch, while inside, the carving of the choir stalls is equally lively. *The Madonna of the Vineyards* is the name given to the church's painted wooden statue of the Virgin and Child, a reminder of the famous Rangen wine produced here.

▶ Toul 241D2

Long a fortress city, Toul's strategic importance was suddenly reinforced when Alsace-Lorraine was lost following the Franco-Prussian War of 1870–71. Huge sunken forts, like the one open to the public at nearby **Villey-le-Sec**, were hurriedly built to protect France's shrunken eastern frontier. But the star-shaped moats and bastions which still ring the old central area are of much earlier date, as is the Porte de Metz, a creation of Louis XIV's engineer, Vauban. Toul's **cathedral▶** has an ornate west front and pretty cloisters, the latter a feature, too, of the town's other principal church, **St-Gengoult▶**.

▶ Le Touquet 240A4

Known as 'Paris-Plage' (Paris Beach) when first laid out in the 19th century, this seaside resort with its 12km (8-mile) sandy beach soon became popular with wealthy visitors from the far side of the English Channel, and its chic shops, *Club Nautique*, and many other sports and leisure facilities still attract the would-be smart set. Behind the main part of the town, its roads laid out grid-fashion, are villas set among the pine trees of a planted forest.

Past glories are characteristic, too, of enchanting little **Montreuil▶**, a short way inland up the pretty valley of the Canche. Its population may only be a fraction of what it was in the Middle Ages, but its citadel and ramparts still stand, a fascinating mixture of medieval and Renaissance fortifications.

The flower-filled streets of Hunspach, near Wissembourg, one of northern Alsace's most delightful villages. Half-timbered houses, often intricately carved, line the streets

►► Troyes 240C1

Troyes has a wealth of half-timbered houses and medieval streets and passageways. A stroll around the old heart evokes the atmosphere of medieval times, when merchants congregated from all over Europe to attend the great fairs held here. Beyond the elegant Gothic façade of the Basilica of St-Urbain stands the **cathedral**, its interior bathed in the light streaming in through the magnificent stained glass.

Troyes has almost as many museums as churches, all of them housed in venerable buildings. Outstanding among them is the **Musée d'Art Moderne►**, place St-Pierre, 10003 Troyes (*Open* Tue–Sun 11–6. *Admission: moderate)*, which includes work by Soutine, Rodin, Vlaminck, Van Dongen, and above all, Derain.

ALSACE WINES

The white wines of Alsace are some of France's most distinctive. Unlike their mild-mannered cousins from across the German border, they have a dryness and power that makes them ideal companions for the hearty food of the region. And unlike other French wines, they are generally identified by type of grape (everyday Sylvaner, fruity Gewürztraminer, robust Riesling) rather than by locality. Gewürztraminer, Tokay Pinot gris, Riesling and Muscat are all also used for the delectable '*Vendanges Tardives*', harvested several weeks later than usual to allow the famous 'noble rot' (*botrytis cinerea*) to work its magic.

►► Verdun 241D2

The name of Verdun seems fated to be forever associated with the attempt by the German High Command to decide the course of World War I by 'bleeding France to death'. A tour of the battlefield extending along the Meuse to either side of the city is a powerful reminder of the futility of war. The most evocative monuments are on the right bank, among the new-grown forest blanketing the scenes of devastation. There are great fortifications like **Fort de Vaux**, or **Fort Douaumont**, captured almost accidentally in February 1916 by a German platoon in the early stages of the 18-month battle. Nearby is the **Ossuary**, with its tall, white Tower of the Dead rising over the countless graves. The course of the struggle is compellingly re-created in the **Memorial-Musée de la Bataille de Verdun►**, 1 avenue du Corps Européen (*Open* Apr to mid-Dec daily 9–6; Feb, Mar daily 9–12, 2–6. *Closed* mid-Dec to Jan. *Admission: expensive)*, built on the the site of Fleury.

►► Wissembourg 241E2

This is one of the most charming little places in Alsace, with old houses, ancient ramparts and a big Gothic church in red sandstone. It makes a good base from which to explore northern Alsace. Nearby are some of the province's most delightful villages, Oberseebach, Hoffen, and rustic perfection itself, **Hunspach►►►**. To the west is the rugged, wooded country of the northern Vosges, with ruined medieval castles like **Fleckenstein** and **Falkenstein**. A later age contributed one of the key strongholds of the Maginot Line, the fort near Lembach known as the **Ouvrage du Four a Chaux►** (*Open* May–Oct daily; guided tours only, 3–5 per day; Nov–Mar, weekends only. *Admission: moderate)*.

CONVERSION CHARTS

FROM	TO	MULTIPLY BY
Inches	Centimetres	2.54
Centimetres	Inches	0.3937
Feet	Metres	0.3048
Metres	Feet	3.2810
Yards	Metres	0.9144
Metres	Yards	1.0940
Miles	Kilometres	1.6090
Kilometres	Miles	0.6214
Acres	Hectares	0.4047
Hectares	Acres	2.4710
Gallons	Litres	4.5460
Litres	Gallons	0.2200
Ounces	Grams	28.35
Grams	Ounces	0.0353
Pounds	Grams	453.6
Grams	Pounds	0.0022
Pounds	Kilograms	0.4536
Kilograms	Pounds	2.205
Tons	Tonnes	1.0160
Tonnes	Tons	0.9842

MEN'S SUITS

UK	36	38	40	42	44	46	48
Rest of Europe	46	48	50	52	54	56	58
US	36	38	40	42	44	46	48

DRESS SIZES

UK	8	10	12	14	16	18
France	36	38	40	42	44	46
Italy	38	40	42	44	46	48
Rest of Europe	34	36	38	40	42	44
US	6	8	10	12	14	16

MEN'S SHIRTS

UK	14	14.5	15	15.5	16	16.5	17
Rest of Europe	36	37	38	39/40	41	42	43
US	14	14.5	15	15.5	16	16.5	17

MEN'S SHOES

UK	7	7.5	8.5	9.5	10.5	11
Rest of Europe	41	42	43	44	45	46
US	8	8.5	9.5	10.5	11.5	12

WOMEN'S SHOES

UK	4.5	5	5.5	6	6.5	7
Rest of Europe	38	38	39	39	40	41
US	6	6.5	7	7.5	8	8.5

Arriving

All visitors to France must have a valid passport, but only some need a visa. Visas are not necessary for citizens of EU countries, Australia, Canada, New Zealand or the US staying less than three months. Regulations do change, so check with your French Consulate.

Air The national airline is Air France, which operates worldwide. France's largest airport by far is Roissy (Charles de Gaulle) in Paris. Other airports with frequent scheduled international flights include Bordeaux, Lyon, Marseille, Nantes, Nice, Strasbourg, Perpignan, Biarritz, Nîmes and Toulouse. Several budget airlines provide an excellent network of cut-price flights to French airports from the UK.

Coach Eurolines operates services from the UK to more than 60 destinations in France—information from any National Express agency or from 52 Grosvenor Gardens, London SW1 (tel: 0870 514 3219; www.eurolines.co.uk).

Rail Rail Europe, 178 Piccadilly, London W1J 9AL (tel: 0870 837 1371; www.raileurope.co.uk) can give information about services by train from the UK to any station in France. Eurostar (tel: 0870 518 6186; www.eurostar.com), via the Channel Tunnel, connects London with Paris, Gare du Nord in under three hours, and with Lille, Avignon, Disneyland, Calais and other stops. A large number of passes are available offering a wide and complex range of rail travel options in France and Europe. Inter-Rail passes (under and over age 26 versions) and Euro-Domino passes (adult, youth and child versions) are available to European citizens, but must be bought outside France. Eurail passes or Euro Selectpasses (three to five contiguous countries) can be bought from French Railways by non-European residents, while in North America, France Railpass, France Rail'n'Drive and France Senior or Youthpass, and France and Italy/Spain passes offer even more possibilities.

In the US, contact Rail Europe (www.raileurope.com; tel: 888/382-7245); in Canada tel: 800/361-7245.

Travel Facts

Sea Several ferry, hovercraft and catamaran services link France with the UK and Ireland. Current operators include P&O European Ferries (tel: 0870 598 0333; www.poferries.com), Hoverspeed (tel: 0870 164 2114; www.hoverspeed.com), Sea France (tel: 0870 443 1653; www.seafrance.com), Brittany Ferries (tel: 0870 907 6103; www.brittanyferries.com) and Condor Ferries (tel: 0870 243 5140; www.condorferries.co.uk). The cost of crossings varies widely according to the time, day and month of travel, and many special deals are available for car and foot passengers, including package deals with selected hotels or planned routes. Hovercraft and catamaran services, while much faster than conventional car ferries, are more easily disrupted by bad weather.

Eurotunnel The fastest way of crossing the Channel with a car is through the Channel Tunnel on Le Shuttle (tel: 0870 535 3535; www.eurotunnel.com). Cars are loaded onto trains and the journey takes 35 minutes. You stay with your car during the journey, but you can stretch your legs by walking about in the air-conditioned carriage.

Dune du Pilat on the Atlantic Coast is the highest sand dune in Europe at 114m/374ft and great for kids to play on

Camping
There are more than 11,000 campsites in France. They have to be registered and graded (by the Fédération Française de Camping et Caravanning, 78 rue de Rivoli, 75004 Paris, tel: 01 42 72 84 08; www.ffcc.fr or www.campingfrance.com) from one to four stars, depending on the facilities provided. A four-star site will have communal indoor recreation areas, hot water, lock-up for valuables, washing machines and usually a shop; one-star sites are more crowded and sometimes have only cold water. Local farmers often let out their fields to campers—*camping à la ferme*—with basic or non-existent facilities.

A camping *carnet* is useful; some campsites won't let you in without one, and it includes some third-party insurance cover. It is obtainable by members from motoring organizations and affiliated caravan and cycling clubs. One *carnet* covers up to 12 people.

Children
The French tourist industry shows a keen interest in promoting facilities and attractions for children, and several cities provide amusement parks and museums designed to attract them. **Disneyland Paris** (32km/20 miles east of Paris) offers not only a theme park but also hotels, a campsite and a golf course (for parents). **Parc Astérix** (38km/24 miles north of Paris) is a long-established popular attraction. Poitiers' **Futuroscope** is a hit with more technologically aware children and adolescents. The mega **aquarium** at La Rochelle is popular and Boulogne's **Nausicaà aquarium** is also a splendid attraction.

Many large towns have museums, often with hands-on exhibitions, parks, circuses, water parks (*parcs et centres aquatiques*) and zoos. In Paris, **Le Musée en Herbe** (Jardin d'Acclimatation) and **Cité des Sciences**, with its Argonaut, Géode and Techno Cité, will appeal.

In general, children are welcome in restaurants, hotels and bars, and there will often be special rates. Some hotels may provide a baby-listening service.

Climate

The south of France, including the Mediterranean coast, has hot, dry summers and warm, wet winters. Showers are short and sharp, often in the middle of the day. Summer winds are cooling and gentle but the colder and fiercer Mistral, which comes from the north, can swirl around for days in winter.

Northwest France is affected by the Atlantic, often rainy, yet with mild winters and rather cool summers. The southwest area of Aquitaine, including the Dordogne, has hot summers. Eastern France has a more continental climate, with hot summers and cold winters.

In the mountains, altitude is an important factor. While the Vosges are hot in summer, the Massif Central is stormy and the southern Massif very dry. In contrast, the Cévennes get a lot of rain and the northern Massif can become very hot.

As for Paris, late April to early May is the best time for a visit—neither too hot, too wet nor too crowded. In July and August, many restaurants close and the city can be wonderfully quiet, and hotels less expensive.

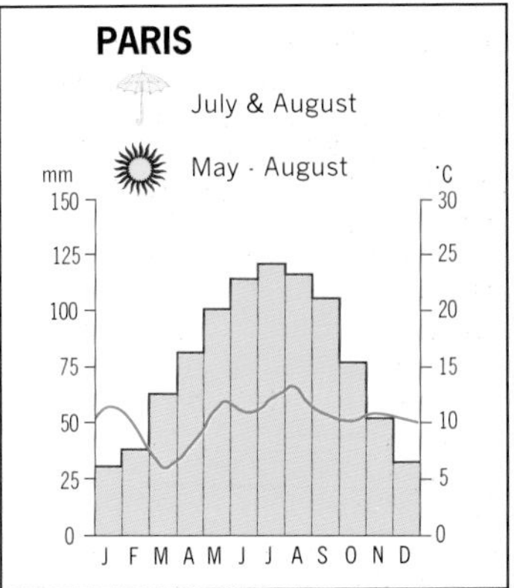

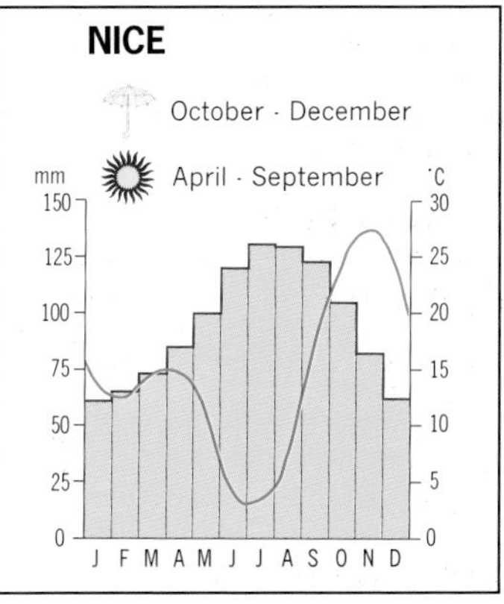

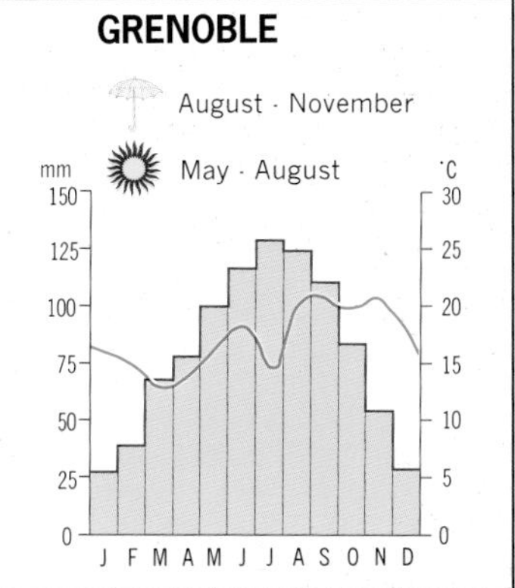

UK Customs regulations

Tax/duty-paid goods: Within the EU, anyone can import or export any reasonable amount of goods for personal use, including gifts. Duty-free allowances ceased in 1999. The following quantities are given as guidance levels only and may be exceeded if you can provide proof of personal consumption:

Tobacco: 800 cigarettes or 400 cigarillos or 200 cigars or 1kg tobacco.

Alcohol: 10 litres of spirits more than 22 per cent vol (38.8 proof); 20 litres of alcohol less than 22 per cent vol; 90 litres of wine, of which no more than 60 litres can be sparkling wine; 110 litres of beer.

People under 18 may not import alcohol or tobacco into the UK. Non-EU visitors should check with their local customs and excise departments as to what they can take home.

Crime

Holidaymakers are often more careless abroad than at home and leave tents open, luggage visible in cars and personal property unattended on beaches, making life easy for the opportunist thief. Pickpockets travel on public transport and visit busy places. If your money or belongings are stolen, contact the police at once (tel: 17). You'll also need to report the theft in person and sign a statement at the nearest police station for insurance purposes.

Cycling
Ride on the right-hand side of the road unless there are cycle paths.

Bicycles can be rented from cycle shops, some tourist offices and also from many SNCF stations. Bicycles can be transported free in the luggage van of some trains and as hand-baggage on TGVs and some other trains. Alternatively, you can send it registered from one station to another, but it will not travel with you so send it a few days in advance. The leaflet *Guide du train et du vélo* lists stations and prices.

Get more information from The Touring Department, Cyclists Touring Club, Parklands, Railton Road, Guildford, Surrey, GU2 9JX, UK (tel: 0870 873 0060; www.ctc.org.uk) or from the Fédération Française de Cyclotourisme, 12 rue Louis Bertrand, 94207 Ivry-sur-Seine (tel: 01 56 20 88 88; www.ffct.org).

Visitors with disabilities
Facilities have improved greatly over the past few years, and now many hotels, public buildings, lavatories, airports and the railway system have been modified to facilitate access.

RADAR in the UK (Royal Association for Disability and Rehabilitation) can provide several useful annual guides, including *European Holidays and Travel Abroad* and *Access in Paris. Paris–Ile de France for Everyone* is available from CNRH—see addresses below.

Concessions and help are available from airlines, railways and ferry companies. The FGTO can provide further details and the SNCF issues a leaflet, *Le Guide du Voyageur à mobilité réduite*, which is helpful for visitors using wheelchairs.

Useful addresses
Australia: NDS, 33 Thesiger Court, Denkin, ACT 2006 (tel: (02) 6283 3200; www.nds.org.au.
Canada: Canadian Abilities Foundation, 340 College Street, Toronto, Ontario M5T 3A9 (tel: 416/923-1885; www.enablelink.org).
France: APF, 17 boulevard Auguste-Blanqui, 75013 Paris (tel: 01 40 78 69 00; www.apf.asso.fr); CNRH, 236 bis rue de Tolbiac, 75013 Paris (tel: 01 53 80 66 66).
Ireland: Irish Wheelchair Association, Blackheath Drive, Clontarf, Dublin 3 (tel: 01 818 6400; www.iwa.ie); National Rehabilitation Board, 25 Clyde Road, Dublin 4 (tel: 01 668 4181); Northern Ireland: Disability Action, Portside Business Park, 189 Airport Rd West, Belfast BT3 9ED (tel: 028 9029 7880; www.disabilityaction.org).
New Zealand: Disabled Persons

Costumes and gifts on display in a central Strasbourg shop

Assembly: PO Box 27–524, Level 4, Wellington Trade Centre, 173–175 Victoria Street, Wellington (tel: 04 801 9100; www.dpa.org.nz).
UK: RADAR, 12 City Forum, 250 City Road, London EC1V 8AF (tel: 020 7250 3222; www.radar.org.uk).
US: Mobility International, 132 E. Broadway, Suite 343, Eugene, Oregon OR 97401 (tel: 541/343-1284; www.miusa.org); SATH (Society for the Advancement of Travel for the Handicapped), 347 Fifth Avenue, Suite 610, New York, NY 10016 (tel: 212/447-7284; www.sath.org).

Driving

Accident Contact the police immediately (tel: 17—this calls the ambulance too), particularly if someone is injured. You and the other parties involved must complete and sign an accident statement form (*constat à l'amiable*) and exchange insurance details. Try to persuade witnesses to stay in order to make statements.

Age You must be at least 18 years of age to drive in France.

Breakdown If your car breaks down, try to move it to the side of the road and flash your hazard-warning lights. Place a red warning triangle on the road 30m (33yd) behind your car (100m/110yd on motorways). Emergency phones (*postes d'appel d'urgence*), linked to a local police station, are placed at 4km (2.5-mile) intervals on main roads and every 2km (1 mile) on motorways.

Children Children aged 10 and under must sit at the back of the car, belted up. If, however, a specially approved, fitted seat facing backward is fixed in the front of the car, a baby may use it.

Documents You must bring with you a full valid national driving licence, the vehicle's original registration document and insurance certificate. If you've borrowed the car, you'll need a letter of authorization from the owner. You'll also need a nationality plate or sticker. You can bring in any vehicle to France for up to six months in a year without customs documents.

Drink Maximum permissible alcohol levels are very low, and it is much wiser not to drink at all. The penalties are high and the French police carry out random breath-testing. Any driver found to be above the legal limit (0.05 per cent) can be fined on the spot, and visitors may be banned from driving in France and have their driving licence confiscated.

Fines Drivers in France can be fined on the spot, although for some infringements the police may accept vouchers from people with insurance cover. If a motorist considers he is innocent, he can pay a deposit (*amende forfaitaire*), and the police will issue a receipt.

Filling stations There are plenty of filling stations: on motorways they are placed about every 24km (15 miles). In some rural areas they may be shut on Sundays. You can usually pay for fuel with a credit card. Garages displaying the *Bison Futé* (wily buffalo) sign give away a free road map of France produced by the French Ministry of Transport. This shows less congested routes and information points and lists restaurants, garages and hotels.

Useful phrases at garages include *faîtes le plein* (fill it up) and *vérifiez l'huile* (check the oil).

Fuel Unleaded fuel is sold in two grades: 95 octane (*essence sans plomb*) and 98 octane (*super sans plomb*). The minimum amount you can buy is 5L (1gal). Diesel (*gazole*) is cheaper and readily available. Fuel is cheapest at hypermarkets and is exorbitant on the motorways.

Insurance Fully comprehensive insurance, which will cover you for some of the expenses incurred after an accident, is advisable; motorists can easily extend their national cover to go abroad with their car. The best policies provide you with a place to stay while your car is being repaired, or replace your vehicle if it's a write-off. Insurance

Setting the world to rights: women in traditional Breton dress

policies are likely to cover spare parts, and fitting charges up to a certain amount.

Lights Drivers taking their own car from the UK and Ireland must adjust their headlights, in order not to dazzle oncoming drivers, by fitting headlight converters (black masking tape in pre-cut shapes) over the headlamps.

If other drivers flash their headlights at you, this can mean that they are claiming priority and that you should give way to them.

Renting a car Car rental may be included in a fly-drive package holiday, or in co-operation with French Railways. Otherwise it is generally cheaper to book with international car rental companies in your own country and pay by credit card than waiting till you arrive in France. Most companies offer weekly rates with unlimited mileage. Although the minimum age of car rental is 18, many companies insist on drivers being 21 or even 25. Cars can be rented from about 200 railway stations and at airports.

Road signs Driving is on the right (*serrez à droite*). Unless otherwise indicated, give way to traffic coming from the right (*priorité à droite*): Take care in towns and on small roads!

Outside built-up areas, traffic on main roads usually has precedence over traffic from side roads. A yellow diamond sign indicates you have priority.

vous n'avez pas la priorité you do not have priority
cédez le passage give way
toutes directions route for through traffic
sens interdit no entry
sens unique one way street
déviation diversion
passage protégé main roads having priority
rappel restriction continues (lower speed limit, for example).

Seat belts It is obligatory to wear these, in the back too. If you are stopped by the police for not wearing them, you can be fined on the spot.

Speed limits In dry weather a higher speed limit applies than in wet weather. Unless otherwise indicated, maximum speed limits are as follows, with wet weather maximums in brackets. Motorways with tolls (*autoroutes à péage*) 130kph/80mph (110kph/68mph); on dual carriageways and motorways without tolls 110kph/68mph (100kph/62mph); other roads, 90kph/56mph (80kph/50mph); in built-up areas, 50kph/30mph or less, under all conditions.

On motorways there is a minimum speed limit of 80kph in the outside (overtaking) lane during daylight on flat roads with good visibility.

For two years after passing their test, new drivers may not drive faster than 80kph on normal roads and 110kph on motorways.

Toll roads Most motorways in France impose tolls. Payment can be made by credit card.

Electricity

In France, the supply is 220 volts and the frequency is 50 Hertz (Hz), including electricity on graded campsites. You will need travel adaptor plugs for gadgets such as hairdryers and shavers. Because of different voltages and frequencies used in Canada and the US, a transformer may also be required.

Embassies and consulates
Only in extreme circumstances do you contact your country's embassy. It is the Consul who issues emergency passports, contacts relatives and advises how to transfer funds.
American Embassy: 2 avenue Gabriel, 75008 Paris (tel: 01 43 12 22 22). There are consulates in Bordeaux, Strasbourg, Lille, Lyon, Nice, Rennes, Toulouse and Marseille.
Australian Embassy: 4 rue Jean-Rey, 75724 Paris Cedex 15 (tel: 01 40 59 33 00).
British Embassy: 35 rue du Faubourg-St-Honoré, 75383 Paris (tel: 01 44 51 31 00). There are also British Consulates in cities throughout France, and many other towns have Honorary Consuls.
Irish Embassy: 4 rue Rude, 75116 Paris (tel: 01 44 17 67 00). There are Honorary Consuls in Antibes, Cherbourg, Lyon and Monaco.
Canadian Embassy: 35 avenue Montaigne, 75008 Paris (tel: 01 44 43 29 00). There are consulates in Lyon, Nice, Strasbourg and Toulouse.
New Zealand Embassy: 7 ter rue Léonard de Vinci, 75116 Paris (tel: 01 45 00 24 11).

Emergency phone numbers
Police/Ambulance—17
Fire (*Pompiers*)—18
Emergency medical aid is available through SAMU (*Service d'aide médicale d'urgence*)—15.
Local numbers are on the first page of local phone directories (*l'annuaire*).

Health
No vaccinations are required for visitors from Europe, the US, Canada, Australia or New Zealand. Visitors from EU countries can receive emergency medical treatment more cheaply if they have the European Health Insurance Card (EHIC). However, reciprocal health agreements do not cover the cost of non-emergency medical treatment. Full health and travel insurance is recommended for visitors from EU countries, and is essential for visitors from outside the EU.

To find a doctor, ask at your hotel or campsite, or enquire at a local pharmacy. For minor problems, you can simply go to a pharmacy to ask for advice (see **Pharmacies**).

Hitch-hiking
It is forbidden to hitch-hike on motorways but permitted on other roads.

Insurance
If you go on a package holiday, the tour operator will offer an insurance policy, but you are under no obligation to buy it, although you may have to buy equivalent cover from another insurer.

A holiday insurance policy should cover (at least) medical expenses; loss of luggage and money; curtailment of your holiday; delayed departure and delayed baggage.

If you are taking your car, you need to be covered for accidents, breakdowns and third party.

Language
Two separate Romance languages evolved within France: in the north, the *langue d'oïl* and in the south, the *langue d'oc*, or Occitanian, which included dialects spoken in Limousin, Auvergne and Gascony, as well as in Provence. Today, many Provençal words survive and the **Institute of Occitanian Studies** strives to promote the language, in which some vowel sounds differ from the French and the last syllable is often pronounced.

Roman influence was felt less in Brittany, which had been invaded by Celts driven out of Britain by the Saxons hundreds of years earlier. The Breton language, closely related

Haras du Pin stud, Normandy

to Welsh, is spoken in the west, and there is a strong movement to promote it.

In the south, the Pyrenees divide two groups of people from their more politically active counterparts in Spain, with whom they would like to form a separatist nation. In the west are about 50,000 Basques; in the east are the Catalans. Both groups speak their own languages: Basque is unlike any other language, while Catalan is similar to Provençal. In Alsace, which for so many years bounced between Germany and France, the local language is more akin to High German.

Meanwhile, the **Académie Française** works hard to preserve the purity of the French language; but speech changes faster than the written word, and, to their great annoyance, many words of English and American derivation (*le parking, le weekend*) are now firmly part of the French language.

Basic phrases
yes oui
no non
thank you merci
please s'il vous plaît
hello bonjour
good evening bonsoir
goodnight bonne nuit
goodbye au revoir
can you show me the way to...? pouvez-vous m'indiquer la direction de...?
where is...? où se trouve...?
I would like/we would like...
je voudrais/on voudrait
how many/much? combien?
this one ceci
that one cela
that's enough ça suffit
left à gauche
right à droite
near près
straight on tout droit
opposite en face de
what time? à quelle heure?
I don't feel well je ne me sens pas bien
Could you call a doctor? (Est-ce que) vous pouvez appeler un médecin/un docteur, s'il vous plaît?
Help! Au secours!

Numbers
one un/une
two deux
three trois
four quatre
five cinq
six six
seven sept
eight huit
nine neuf
10 dix
20 vingt
100 cent

first premier/première
second seconde/deuxième
third troisième
fourth quatrième
fifth cinqième

Days of the week
Monday lundi
Tuesday mardi
Wednesday mercredi
Thursday jeudi
Friday vendredi
Saturday samedi
Sunday dimanche

Lavatories
Usually referred to as W.C. Men are *Messieurs*; women are *Dames*. Public lavatories vary from older, smelly ones to the high-tech self-flushing variety.

In Paris, the large department stores have clean lavatories. It's always a good idea to take your own paper.

Maps
For planning a holiday in France, and when you get there, good maps are essential. Two useful country maps to have are the AA's *Big Easy Read France* atlas, at 3 miles to the inch, or the AA's *Big Road Atlas France*, at 4 miles to the inch.

Once you are in France, you need maps on a larger scale (1:200,000).

The French equivalent of the Ordnance Survey is IGN (*Institut Géographique National*), which publishes a series of large-scale maps of long-distance footpaths (*Grandes Randonnés*): The largest scale maps are the blue ones (*Série Bleue*—1: 25,000). The AA's *Touring Map France* series has 16 sheet maps at 2.8 miles to the inch.

Local information or tourist offices may supply town plans free of charge.

Media

English-language newspapers are on sale in most towns, but the farther south you go, the more likely they are to be a day or two late. *Le Monde* is the most distinguished French newspaper; *Le Figaro* is the longest established, *Libération* the youngest in spirit; several news magazines cover a broad range of emphasis and bias.

Local and regional press is well-developed in France and can be a useful source for local events.

Any type of music can be found on the crowded French airwaves; tune in to France Infos (105.5MHz) for news.

The BBC World Service broadcasts in English on medium wave 648KHz.

For entertainment in Paris, buy the weekly listings magazine *Pariscope*, which has an English section.

Money matters

The unit of currency is the euro. Bank notes are available in denominations of 10, 20, 50, 100, 200 and 500 euros; coins come in denominations of 1, 2, 5, 10, 20 and 50 centimes and 1 and 2 euros.

To change foreign currency into euros, find a bank displaying a *Change* sign or go to a foreign exchange bureau; avoid changing money at hotels, as the rate is poor. There are plenty of ATMs that accept foreign cards.

Major credit cards—Carte Bleue (Visa/Barclaycard) and Eurocard (Access/MasterCard) and charge cards (Diners and American Express)—are widely accepted in larger hotels and restaurants, shops and garages, although smaller establishments may not accept them.

Museums

National museums usually charge an entrance fee but allow free entry to permanent collections for those under 18, reduced price for people between 18 and 25, and free entry for some visitors with disabilities.

Municipal and private museums usually charge an entrance fee. Reductions or free entry are often available for children, students, groups, people over 60, people with disabilities, and for visits on Sundays.

National holidays

Most shops and banks are shut on the days listed below. If any falls on a Sunday, the holiday is taken on the Monday.

New Year's Day—1 January
Easter Monday
Labour Day—1 May
VE Day—8 May
Ascension Day—May (Thu, 40 days after Easter)
Whitsun (Monday)—May/Jun (10 days after Ascension)
Bastille Day—14 July
Assumption Day—15 August
All Saints' Day—1 November
Armistice Day—11 November
Christmas Day—25 December.

Opening hours

Banks Hours vary, but banks are generally open 9–noon and 2–5. They are usually closed Saturday and Sunday. Banks close early the day before a public holiday.

Detail of a fountain in Evreux, Normandy

Museums National and municipal museums usually close on Tuesdays; exceptions include Versailles' Trianon Palace and the Musée d'Orsay, which close on Mondays. Each museum has its own hours; most close on some public holidays.
Shops Hours vary depending on the type of shop, location and season. For example, lunchtime in summer in the south of France may extend to 4pm and the shops then stay open later in the evening.

Food shops are open Tuesday to Friday 7 or 8am–6.30 or 7.30pm. Some close all day Monday but some may open in the afternoon. On Saturday and Sunday they may open mornings only. Smaller shops may close at lunchtime (noon–2). Bakers are open on Sunday mornings. Supermarkets and hypermarkets open from about 9am until 9 or 10pm. They are closed on Sunday and some hypermarkets also close on Monday mornings.

Pharmacies

Easily recognized by the illuminated green cross, pharmacies are mostly privately owned and run by highly trained staff who can give first aid and advice about ailments. They are not allowed to dispense prescriptions from a foreign doctor. Pharmacies are usually open six days a week, and on Sundays at least one pharmacy in a town is open (*pharmacie de garde*). Its name and address will be displayed outside other shops, announced in the local paper and available from the local *gendarmerie*.

The 15th-century Hôtel Dieu in Beaune, founded as a hospital

Places of worship

Every town and village has a Catholic church, though not all of them offer Sunday masses—priests often officiate in more than one village. Protestant churches exist in most large towns, particularly in Paris and the Dordogne, which was once a Huguenot area.

Members of the Jewish community, Buddhists and members of non-conformist churches may have more difficulty in finding out whether there is a place of worship in town.

Muslims are well catered for in most of France because of the large North African population.

Tourist offices, town halls and notice boards can give information on religious services.

Post offices

Open 8–5, 6 or 7 weekdays, 8–noon Saturday. Small offices close for lunch weekdays.

La Poste, the French post office, deals with post and telecommunications. You can buy stamps (*timbres de poste*) and phone cards (*télécartes*) and cash postcheques and send telexes or faxes. You can also buy stamps and phone cards from tobacconists (*tabacs*).

You can collect letters (showing your passport as proof of identity), which should be addressed to yourself, c/o Poste Restante, Poste Centrale, followed by the number of the *département* and the name of the town where you will be staying.

Letter boxes are mustard yellow and often fixed on walls. For posting abroad, use the slot marked *départements étrangers*.

Public transport

Air A comprehensive and frequent air network links all the major French cities with each other. Air France operates daily services to about 50 business and holiday destinations, mostly from Paris. For information, contact Air France (tel: (UK) 0870 142 4343; www.airfrance.com).

Deregulation has spawned numerous smaller operators who compete on the main routes and fill in the gaps on the cross-country routes. Check with local travel agents.

Road Where bus services do exist outside of the main towns, they tend to serve a specific purpose: taking children to and from school, serving a local market—often weekly—or connecting with trains. The timetables are therefore often sporadic, seasonal and inconvenient. There are some long-distance buses, but they are not plentiful.

Tickets are bought on the bus and must be validated (*composté*). If you are in a group or making several journeys, it's worth buying a book of tickets (*carnet*).

Rail Eurostar operates cross-Channel connections from London (tel: (UK) 0870 518 6186; (France) 08 92 35 35 39; www.eurostar.com). French Railways or SNCF (*Société Nationale de Chemins de Fer*) operates throughout France (SNCF information in France (tel: 08 36 35 35 35; English language: 08 36 68 77 14; www.sncf.fr).

The flagship of the rolling stock is the fleet of high-speed **TGV** trains (*trains à grande vitesse*), which holds the world train speed record (574.8kph/357mph); normal passenger services operate at about 300kph (186mph).

The TGV network now extends through much of France: west to Brest, Quimper and Le Croisic; southwest to Bordeaux, Toulouse, Tarbes and Irun; southeast to Lyon, the Alps, Nice, Marseilles and Béziers; north to Reims, Lille, Calais and the Channel Tunnel.

Although all routes converge on Paris, it is now possible to bypass the capital through connections at Lille.

Euro City trains, for which you must make a reservation, are fast, comfortable, international trains that go to more than 200 towns, including 14 European capitals.

Marker flags for oysters, the Atlantic Coast's special delicacy

Within France the *rapide* and *express* trains (first and second class) stop more often, and there are even slower local trains. The RER (*Réseau Express Régional*) rail service runs on suburban routes around Paris.

For longer distances, you may decide to travel at night. Many trains have couchettes holding up to six people, both sexes, second class (four people first class), with washing facilities at the end of the carriage. Two- or three-bedded sleepers are more comfortable, with their own washbasins, but first-class sleepers can cost nearly five times as much as a couchette.

Tickets

TGV: There are three levels of TGV depending on time of day, day of week and time of year. Reservation on these trains is obligatory and there is a small booking fee.

Other: These are divided into white periods (more expensive, normally at weekends and holidays) and blue periods (cheaper, normally weekdays). Reservations are sometimes necessary.

'Train Verts' (Green trains), including some TGVs, offer 15 per cent reductions with, normally, no reservation required.

All tickets must be validated (*composté*) at machines on the platform before boarding the train. Discounts are available for senior citizens, passengers under 26, passengers with children, large families and for advanced reservations. Contact SNCF for more information).

Paris To travel on the Métro (underground) it's cheapest to buy a book (*carnet*) of 10 tickets; one ticket can be used for journeys of any length. Tickets from the same *carnet* can be used on buses, but here, the longer your journey, the more tickets you must use. (Tickets from some *tabacs*, bus terminals or Métros.)

A tourist ticket called *Paris Visite* is valid for one, two, three or five days and allows unlimited first-class train and bus travel; half price for children under 12. The *Mobilis* card, for which a photo is required, is a second-class version but is valid for only one day at a time. The *Carte Orange*—photo also needed—enables you to buy coupons valid for a week (Monday to Sunday) or a calendar month. If you have a *Carte Jeunes* (see below), you can get a Ticket Jeunes, which gives you cheap travel at weekends and public holidays: RATP (tel: 08 36 68 77 14; www.ratp.fr).

Honfleur Harbour

Student and youth travel

Several types of reasonably priced cards are available to people under 26, giving discounts on hotels, meals and travel, as well as to cultural and sporting events. You will need identification and a photo for all of them.

The International Student Card (ISIC), for which you also need a student card, entitles you to cheaper museum entry and beds in university residences (www.isic.org).

The International Youth Travel Card, also known as GO 25 Card, is for under 25s. Buy it from Voyages Wasteels (tel: 01 55 82 32 33; www.wasteels.fr); it is valid in many countries.

The *Carte Jeunes* (Youth Card) is available for those under 26 and can be bought from around 5,000 outlets, including railway stations.

A booklet, *Youth Tourism*, is available from the French Tourist Office.

Accommodation Members of national associations can stay at French hostels if they have a membership card with photo. Write to Fédération Unie des Auberges de Jeunesse, 27 rue Pajol, 75018 Paris (tel: 01 44 89 87 27; www.fuaj.fr) for a list of hostels.

International Accommodation Centres, providing 11,000 beds, give another cheap alternative and offer organized sports and sightseeing. They go by different names in different areas of France. All belong to an organization called UCRIF and a list of them is available, free, from the FGTO or La Maison de l'UCRIF, 27 rue de Turbigo, 75064 Paris (tel: 01 40 26 57 64; www.ucrif.asso.fr).

Other information is available from the Paris Tourist Office, 25–27 rue des Pyramides, 75009 Paris (tel: 08 92 68 30 30; www.parisinfo.com), and from OTU offices, tourist offices and CRIJ (Youth Information Centres) offices throughout France.

Travel There are various rail passes for people under 26 and the SNCF also has discounts available for those

Caen Cathedral

under 25. See **Arriving** under **Rail**, and **Public transport** under **Rail**.

Telephones
Most public phone booths require phone cards; buy them from post offices, tobacconists and stations. You can receive calls in a booth if a blue bell sign is displayed.

All French numbers have 10 digits. The following prefixes have been added to the old 8-digit numbers:
Ile de France: 01
Northwest: 02
Northeast: 03
Southeast: 04
Southwest: 05

To call abroad from France, dial 00 then dial the country code:
Australia: 61
Canada: 1
Ireland: 353
New Zealand: 64
UK: 44
US: 1

Then dial the area code (omitting the first 0), followed by the number.

Time
France is one hour ahead of GMT from October to late March, and two hours ahead of GMT the rest of the year. The time in other countries compared with France, October to March, is:
Australia: Central—eight hours ahead; Western Australia—seven hours ahead; Eastern—nine hours ahead.
Canada: Eastern—six hours behind; Western—nine hours behind.
Ireland: one hour behind.
New Zealand: 11 hours ahead.
UK: one hour behind.
US: Eastern—six hours behind; Western—nine hours behind.

Tourist offices
There are more than 5,000 tourist offices, in France, called either *Offices de Tourisme* or *Syndicats d'Initatives*. Information is also available from the local *Mairie* (town hall). Some tourist offices only open seasonally.

The French Government Tourist Office (FGTO) publishes literature in English, which is available from:
Australia: Level 22, 25 Bligh Street, Sydney NSW 2000 (tel: (02) 9231 5244).
Canada: 1981 Avenue McGill College, Suite 490, Montréal, Québec H3A 2W9 (tel: 514/288-4264).
Ireland: Maison de la France, 10 Suffolk Street, Dublin 2 (tel: 01 635 1008).
UK: Maison de la France, 178 Piccadilly, London W1J 9AL (tel: 09068 244 123; premium rate).
US: Maison de la France, 444 Madison Avenue, New York, NY 10022 (tel: 212/838-7800).

MORE INFORMATION:
For more information, look up the website of the French Tourist Office (www.franceguide.com).

HOTELS

The French Government Tourist Office (FGTO) publishes lists of approved hotels, rated on a scale from one-star to four-star. Some local tourist offices can help with last-minute bookings.

Although it is possible to stay throughout the country in hotels belonging to hotel chains (including Campanile, Ibis, Mercure, Novotel, Sofitel and Formule 1), it is generally the traditional French hotel that offers picturesque charm with a memorable gastronomic experience. Many of the simpler family-run hotels, mainly in rural areas, belong to the Logis de France organization, and can be recognized by a distinctive yellow fireplace logo.

Following inspections, they are classified with one, two or three 'chimneys'. A guide to the 3,700 or so Logis hotels is available from the FGTO, bookshops, or La Fédération Nationale des Logis de France, 83 avenue d'Italie, 75013 Paris (tel: 01 45 84 70 00; reservations: 01 45 84 83 84; www.logis-de-france.fr).

Staying in a château can be more personal, and not necessarily very expensive. Some luxury hotels and châteaux belong to the Relais et Châteaux organization; their brochure is available from the FGTO. A free copy of the guide is available at the French Tourist Office, 178 Piccadilly, London; or send a £5 cheque or postal order to Relais & Chateaux, 5 Dovedale Studios, 465 Battersea Park Road, London SW11 4LR (tel: 0800 200 00002; www.relaischateaux.com).

More modest guest-house rooms are available in thousands of country houses, farms and even châteaux, through Gîtes Chambres d'Hôte/Gîtes Tables d'Hôte, identified by the yellow and green Gîtes de France logo, which features a cockerel and a roof, with a Chambres d'Hôtes sign. Information is available from the Fédération National des Gîtes de France, 59 rue St-Lazare, 75439 Paris (tel: 01 49 70 75 75; www.gites-de-france.fr).

Hotels Abroad offer a bed-and-breakfast booking service, which can include ferry bookings. They will book hotels at either a single destination or various regional stops. Contact: 5 Worlds End Lane, Green Street Green, Orpington, Kent BR6 6AA (tel: 0845 330 2500; international: 00 44 1689 882500; www.hotelsabroad.com).

Loisirs Acceuil Many *departéments* now have a Loisirs Acceuil booking service to reserve local hotels, gîtes and campsites, without charging a fee. Contact the relevant tourist office or send an SAE to the French Tourist Office for a list.

Self-catering France is well-endowed with self-catering facilities. Gîtes de France offers thousands of rural properties; many are converted farm buildings, and may be remote. All are inspected and graded into three categories (tel: 01 49 70 75 75).

Some establishments place the emphasis on their restaurant and offer bedrooms as an ancillary service. The following list of recommended hotels includes a selection of places where restaurants are attached to hotels and the standard of cooking is above average in its category. Restaurants are listed separately for Paris and other cities.

Hotel price bands are based on a double room, with breakfast, per night.
€—up to 120 euros
€€—120–250 euros
€€€—250 euros and above

Restaurants price bands are based on a three-course menu, per person without alcohol.
€—up to 25 euros
€€—25–50 euros
€€€—50 euros and above

PARIS

L'Abbaye St-Germain (€€€)
10 rue Cassette, 75006 tel: 01 45 44 38 11
www.hotel-abbaye.com
A fine 17th-century town house with attractive courtyard and sophisticated décor. No restaurant.

Hôtel Costes (€€€)
239 rue St-Honoré, 75001 tel: 01 42 44 50 00
www.hotelcostes.com
This hotel has a contemporary feel. There are charming nooks facing on to the courtyard. Rooms are equipped with marble-topped basins. The chic bar-restaurant remains popular in the city.

Le Crillon (€€€)
10 place de la Concorde, 75008
tel: 01 44 71 15 00
www.crillon.com
One of the world's great hotels, classical and elegant throughout, has two lavishly decorated restaurants (lunch menus are good value).

Hotel du Cygne (€)
3 & 5 rue du Cygne tel: 01 42 60 14 16
www.hotelducygne.fr
Housed in a 17th-century building in Les Halles. Has small but charmingly furnished rooms.

Les Deux Iles (€€)
59 rue St-Louis-en-l'Ile, 75004
tel: 01 43 26 13 35
www.deuxiles-paris-hotel.com
In a beautiful 18th-century town house on the island, this hotel is well-furnished, with a comfortable bar and elegant sitting room. No restaurant.

Esméralda (€)
4 rue St-Julien-le-Pauvre, 75005
tel: 01 43 54 19 20
Views of Notre Dame, objets d'art, antique furnished rooms and an eccentric style characterize this 17th-century building. No restaurant.

Four Seasons George V (€€€)
31 avenue George V, 75008
tel: 01 49 52 70 00
www.fourseasons.com
Fabulously renovated classic with restaurant run by Taillevent defector Philippe Legendre.

Des Grands Hommes (€€)
17/19 place du Panthéon, 75005
tel: 01 46 34 19 60 fax: 01 43 26 67 32
www.hoteldesgrandshommes.com
Hotel since the 18th century, with glassed-in garden, on quiet (at night) square. Bedrooms are smart with good views from 6th-floor balconies. No restaurant.

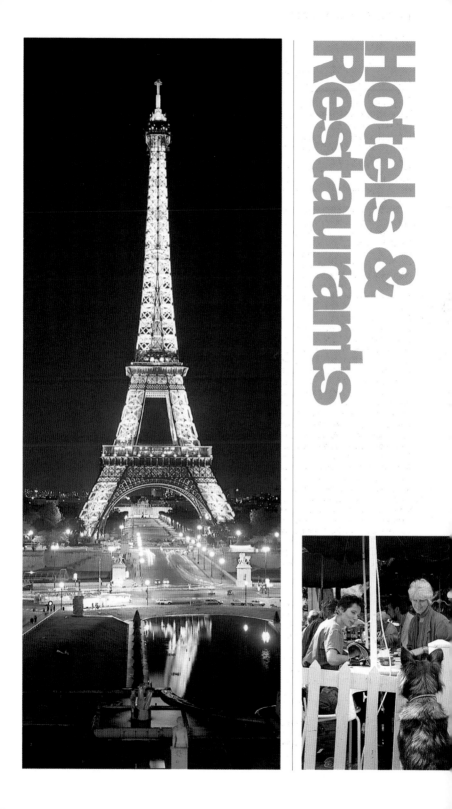

Hotels & Restaurants

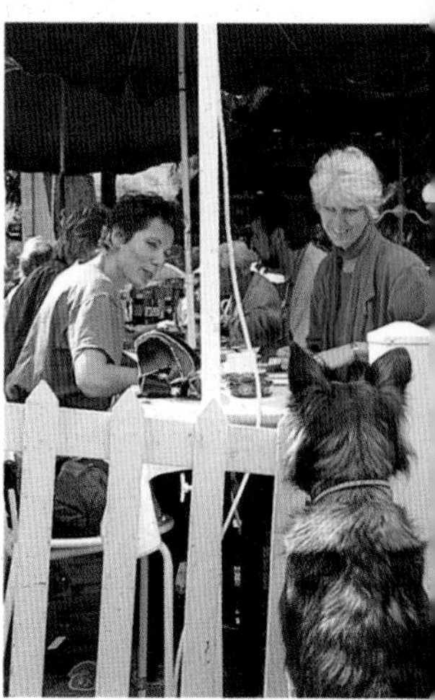

Hôtel des Jardins du Luxembourg (€€)
3–5 impasse Royer Collard 75005
tel: 01 40 46 08 88
www.les-jardins-du-luxembourg.com
This no-frills, comfortable 23-room hotel is in a very quiet street. Some rooms have wonderful views.

Hotel Lenox Saint Germain (€€)
9 rue de l'Université, 75007
tel: 01 42 96 10 95
www.hotellenoxsaintgermain.com
The Lenox is a stylish little hotel with small bedrooms and a chintzy salon. No restaurant.

Des Marronniers (€€)
21 rue Jacob, 75006
tel: 01 43 25 30 60
www.hotel-marronniers.com
Popular hotel with small garden and courtyard in front. No restaurant.

Le Pavillon de la Reine (€€€)
28 place des Vosges, 75003
tel: 01 40 29 19 19
www.pavillon-de-la-reine.com
On Paris's most beautiful old square, this is a comfortable hotel in a 17th-century building, with garden and courtyard. Parking. No restaurant.

Place des Vosges (€)
12 rue de Birague, 75004 tel: 01 42 72 60 46
www.hotelplacedesvosges.com
Just around the corner from the square, a 17th-century house decorated in rustic style, with newly fitted bathrooms and salon. No restaurant.

Prima Lepic (€)
29 rue Lepic, 75018 tel: 01 46 06 44 64
www.hotel-paris-lepic.com
Pretty hotel in the heart of bohemian Montmartre.

Hôtel des Trois Colleges (€)
16 rue Cujas, 75005 tel: 01 43 54 67 30
Picturesque hotel with contemporary furnishings and a view of the Sorbonne and the Panthéon from the beamed attic rooms. *Salon du Thé* afternoons.

NORMANDY

Auberge de l'Abbaye (€€)
Le Bec-Hellouin, 27800 Eure
tel: 02 32 44 86 02
This exceptionally delightful 18th-century inn near the abbey serves resolutely Norman cooking.

Auberge St-Pierre (€€)
rue Principal Intra Muros, Le Mont-St-Michel, 50170 Manche tel: 02 33 60 14 03
www.auberge-st-pierre.fr
Historic rampart building on the way up to the great abbey church. This hotel has modernized bedrooms and a busy restaurant.

Château d'Audrieu (€€€)
Audrieu, 14250 Calvados
tel: 02 31 80 21 52
www.chateaudaudrieu.com
A fine 18th-century château, in large grounds with swimming pool, offers excellent and inventive cooking complemented by an extensive wine list.

Le Dauphin (€€)
place de la Halle, L'Aigle, 61300 Orne
tel: 02 33 84 18 00
This old post house, renovated with care in traditional style, has a fine collection of Calvados (apple brandy) in the restaurant and in a little shop.

Hotel de France (€)
15 rue Emile Demagny, Isigny-sur-Mer 14230 Calvados tel: 02 31 22 00 33
Small friendly hotel in a picturesque fishing port, serving excellent, good-value meals.

France et Fuchsias (€€)
20 rue Maréchal Foch, St-Vaast-La-Hougue, 50550 Manche tel: 02 33 54 42 26
www.france-fuchsias.com
Well-run, simple town hotel with an excellent restaurant serving good fish dishes. It is popular with the yachting fraternity from the nearby marina.

Grand Hôtel (€€€)
Promenade Marcel Proust, Cabourg, 14390 Calvados tel: 02 31 91 01 79
www.grandhotel-cabourg.com
This hotel has an enviable position right on the beach, with a terrace and lots of bustle. Some bedrooms are enormous. A Proust choice with the madeleines of memory still served.

Le Lion d'Or (€€)
71 rue St-Jean, Bayeux, 14400 Calvados
tel: 02 31 92 06 90 www.liondor-bayeux.fr
Still the best-known hotel in town, with bedrooms around a flowery courtyard, and a busy restaurant.

Les Maisons de Lea (€€)
3 place Ste-Catherine, Honfleur, 14600 Calvados tel: 02 31 14 49 49
www.lesmaisonsdelea.com
A hotel right in the bustling heart of town, with a lovely terrace looking out over the church.

Manoir d'Hastings (€€€)
18 avenue de la Côte-de-Nacre, Bénouville, 14970 Calvados tel: 02 31 44 62 43
www.manoirhastings.com
This renowned restaurant now has rooms (though that should not suggest lack of comforts; merely that the bedrooms, in a rather dull modern block in the garden, came after the restaurant). The menu includes a particularly fine *tarte chaude normande*.

Le Manoir du Lys (€€)
route de Juvigny, Bagnoles-de-l'Orne, 61140 Orne tel: 02 33 37 80 69
Set in spacious grounds, this 19th-century hunting lodge has comfortable rooms and Michelin-starred cooking.

Hotel de la Marine (€)
2 Quai du Canada, Arromanches 14117
tel: 02-31 22 34 19
www.hotel-de-la-marine.fr
This classic hotel on the waterfront has a restaurant with fine views. It makes an ideal base for visiting Normandy landing beaches.

La Verte Campagne (€€)
le Hameau au Chevalier, Trelly, 50660 Manche
tel: 02 33 47 65 33
This old farmhouse is peaceful, and the dining and sitting rooms (with log fires) are very comfortable.

BRITTANY

L'Ascott (€€)
35 rue du Chapitre, 35400 St Malo
tel: 02 99 81 89 93
www.ascotthotel.com
Chic little boutique hotel in an 18th-century ship owner's house. B&B only, but there is an excellent restaurant next door.

D'Avaugour (€€)
1 place du Champ Clos, Dinan, 22100 Côtes-d'Armor tel: 02 96 39 07 49
www.avaugourhotel.com
Conveniently placed town-house hotel with rampart gardens and an airy restaurant overlooks place Du Guesclin in the heart of historic Dinan.

Les Bains de Mer (€€)
11 rue de Kerguelen, Bénodet, 29950 Finistère tel: 02 98 57 03 41 www.lesbainsdemer.com
A modern hotel near the sea with a swimming pool, some family rooms and seafood in the restaurant.

Le Bretagne (€€€)
13 rue St-Michel, Questembert, 56230 Morbihan tel: 02 97 26 11 12
www.residence-le-bretagne.com
This ritzy place offers a gastronomic pilgrimage. Alain Orillac is one of the region's best chefs, and meals are served in the stylish salon or winter garden.

Hotel Bricourt Richeux (€€€)
1 rue Duguesclin, Cancale, 35260 Ille-et-Vilaine tel: 02 99 89 64 76
www.maisons-de-bricourt
One of France's top hotel-restaurants. Some rooms are in an elegantly furnished old stone manor house on clifftops with windows overlooking the bay of Mont-St-Michel. The Maisons de Bricourt restaurant, equally elegant, is in a separate building. Known for its gorgeous seafood.

Château de Locguénolé (€€€)
route de Port-Louis, Hennebont, 56700 Morbihan tel: 02 97 76 76 76
www.chateau-de-locguenole.com
This 19th-century château, situated in extensive wooded grounds, is rather formal in parts, and has a restaurant renowned for Breton cuisine.

Chez Pierre (€)
Raguenès Plage, Névez, 29920 Finistère
tel: 02 98 06 81 06
Delightful family hotel in a rural setting close to the beach. The new annexe has duplex rooms. Children can eat early and are well catered for.

Le Goyen (€€)
place J Simon, Audierne, 29770 Finistère
tel: 02 98 70 08 88
www.le-goyen.com
Port-side hotel, impeccably run. Adolphe Bosser, the owner, is one of the best chefs in Brittany.

Hotel Ker-Moor (€€)
avenue de la Plage, Bénodet, 29950 Finistère tel: 02 98 57 05 01 and 02 98 57 04 48
www.kermoor.com
This hotel has a large garden, with a swimming pool and tennis courts, just across the road from the beach resort.

Manoir de Lan-Kerellec (€€€)
Trébeurden, 22560 Côtes-d'Armor
tel: 02 96 15 00 00
www.lankerellec.com
Sophisticated and elegant little manor house with sea views in a leafy residential area with a path down to the beach. Good fish cooking.

Manoir de Moëllien (€€)
Locronan, Plonévez Pozray, 29550 Finistère
tel: 02 98 92 50 40
www.moellien.com
This austere old stone manor stands in an isolated setting 2.5km (1.5 miles) northwest of Locronan. There are 10 ground-floor rooms, which have French windows.

Hotel la Plage (€€€)
Ste-Anne-La-Palud, Plonévez Porzay, 29550 Finistère tel: 02 98 92 50 12
www.plage.com
Isolated at the edge of an enormous expanse of sandy beach, this hotel has a high standard of cooking, with a well-chosen wine list.

Hotel du Port (€)
Port-Manech, Névez, 29920 Finistère
tel: 02 98 06 82 17
Neat, compact hotel/restaurant up a short hill from the port and beach of this bustling little resort.

Le Roche Corneille (€€)
4 rue G Clemenceau. 35800 Dinard
tel: 02 99 46 14 47
www.dinard-hotel-roche-corneille.com
Smart château hotel in the middle of Dinard with highly regarded fish restaurant.

Le Roof (€€)
Presqu'île de Conleau, Vannes, 56000 Morbihan
tel: 02 97 63 47 47
Part of the Best Western group, this hotel is by a small beach on the Morbihan gulf.

La Tarais (€)
Calorguen, Dinan 22100
tel: 02 96 83 50 59
www.latarais.com
Old Breton stone farmhouse *chambres d'hôte* run by English-Dutch couple, within easy reach of Côtes d'Armor. Evening meals available.

Villa Tri-Men (€€)
16 rue du Phare, Sainte-Marine 29120 Combrit tel: 02 98 51 94 94 www.trimen.fr
Attractive little hotel with fresh modern furnishings, a fine restaurant and picture windows overlooking the estuary and marina in a delightful little south-coast resort.

LOIRE

Hotel Balzac (€)
47 rue de la Scellerie, Tours
tel: 02 47 05 40 87
This is a traditional old hotel, right in the heart of Tours, which has an attractive courtyard.

Le Bon Laboureur (€€)
6 rue du Dr. Bretonneau, Chenonceaux, 37150 Indre-et-Loire
tel: 02 47 23 90 02
www.amboise.com/laboureur
An peaceful and attractive establishment, with bedrooms in annexes or around the flowery courtyard.

Le Bussy (€)
Montsoreau, 49730 Maine-et-Loire
tel: 02 41 38 11 11
email: hotel.lebussy@wanadoo.fr
This hotel has fine views of the powerful white château and rustic-style bedrooms.

La Caillère (€€)
36 route des Montils, Candé-sur-Beuvron, 41120 Loir-et-Cher tel: 02 54 44 03 08
www.lacaillere.com
Small country house, with the emphasis on the restaurant—one of the best in the area.

Château d'Artigny (€€€)
Montbazon, 37250 Indre-et-Loire
tel: 02 47 34 30 30
www.artigny.com
Arguably one of the finest château hotels in France, the comfort and facilities cannot be faulted, provided you like the style.

Château de Briottières (€€)
49330 Champigné
tel: 02 41 42 00 02
www.briottieres.com
Beautifully furnished château in huge grounds, with big bedrooms. Meals by arrangement.

Hotel Château des Tertres (€€)
route de Monteaux, Onzain, 41150 Loir-et-Cher
tel: 02 54 20 83 88
www.chateau-tertres.com
This tranquil 19th-century château is set in large grounds. No restaurant, but free bicycle rental.

Domaine des Hauts de Loire (€€€)
Onzain, 41150 Loir-et-Cher
tel: 02 54 20 72 57
www.domainehautsloire.com
Sober and elegant 18th-century mansion, with very large and beautiful rooms and apartments.

Gargantua (€)
73 rue Voltaire, Chinon, 37500 Indre-et-Loire
tel: 02 47 93 04 71
www.hostelleriegargantua.com
Fine restaurant with rooms in 15th-century town mansion in the old part of town.

Grand Hôtel du Lion d'Or (€€€)
69 rue G Clemenceau, Romorantin, 41200 Loir-et-Cher tel: 02 54 94 15 15
www.hotel-liondor.fr
Old coaching inn around courtyard. Didier Clement is one of France's finest chefs.

Grand St-Michel (€€)
103 place St-Michel, Chambord, 41250 Loir-et-Cher tel: 02 54 20 31 31
www.saintmichel-chambord.com
A comfortable hotel with a superb position—at the edge of a forest clearing opposite the château.

Jeanne de Laval (€€)
54 route Nationale, Les Rosiers-sur-Loire, 49350 Maine-et-Loire
tel: 02 41 51 80 17
www.jeannedelaval.com
One of the best-known eating establishments in the Loire. Bedrooms are simple.

Moulin Fleuri (€)
route du Ripault, Veigné, 37250 Indre-et-Loire
tel: 02 47 26 01 12
www.moulin-fleuri.com
Charming family-run, acclaimed restaurant-with-rooms in converted watermill by the Indre.

Hôtel de la Sologne (€)
place St Firmin, Beaugency, 45190 Loiret
tel: 02 38 44 50 27
www.hoteldelasologne.com
Traditional hotel on the main square, overlooking a ruined castle. Breakfast is served in the garden.

Splendid (€)
139 rue du Dr Gaudrez, Montreuil-Bellay, 49260 Maine-et-Loire
tel: 02 41 53 10 00
This hotel has small, pretty bedrooms. The annexe has a swimming pool and garden.

ATLANTIC COAST

Chateau de Mirambeau (€€€)
1 Avenue du Comte Duchatel, 17150 Mirambeau tel: 05 46 04 91 20
www.chateauxmirambeau.com
Beautiful, comfortable 4-star Renaissance-style chateau hotel in 8ha (20 acres) of grounds on the edge of the village of Mirambeau, north of Bordeaux.

L'Etape (€)
2 avenue d'Angoulême, Cognac
tel: 05 45 32 16 15
This comfortable hotel just out of the heart of town has a restaurant and a ground-floor brasserie.

France-Angleterre et Champlain (€€)
20 rue Rambaud, La Rochelle, 17000 Charente-Maritime tel: 05 46 41 23 99
www.france-champlain.com
This fine old town house with a pretty garden, in the heart of the old town, is noisy in the morning but quiet at night. No restaurant.

Hôtel Golf de Chantaco (€€)
route d'Ascain, Saint-Jean-de-Luz, 64500 Pyrénées-Atlantiques tel: 05 59 26 14 76
www.hotel-chantaco.com
A Basque-style house, with gardens looking over the famous golf course.

Logis de la Couperie (€)
La Roche-sur-Yon, 85000 Vendée
tel: 02 51 37 21 19
Romantic hotel in large 19th-century country house with extensive grounds. No restaurant.

Hôtel du Palais (€€€)
1 avenue de l'Impératrice, Biarritz, 64200 Pyrénées–Atlantiques tel: 05 59 41 64 00
www.hotel-du-palais.com
Empress Eugénie's villa, high above the sea, is furnished in appropriate style.

Plaisance (€€€)
place du Clocher, Saint-Emilion, 33330 Gironde
tel: 05 57 55 07 55
www.hostellerie-plaisance.com
Rooms are in a renovated old building alongside the bell tower. The restaurant has an extensive wine list.

DORDOGNE

Auberge du Sombral (€€)
St-Cirq-Lapopie, 46330 Lot tel: 05 65 31 26 08
Very old house, beautifully restored, in high medieval village. Simple country style with cooking to match.

Des Beaux-Arts (€€€)
1 place du Pont Neuf, Toulouse, 31000 Haute-Garonne tel: 05 34 45 42 42
www.hoteldesbeauxarts.com
This well-kept small hotel, with a downstairs brasserie, is open until the small hours.

De Bordeaux (€€)
38 place Gambetta, Bergerac, 24100 Dordogne tel: 05 53 57 12 83
www.hotel-bordeaux-bergerac.com
Situated on the main square, the restaurant has a terrace for eating out.

De la Bouriane (€€)
place du Foirail, Gourdon, 46300 Lot
tel: 04 89 88 40 91
Simple, traditional hostelry in small market town offering above-average cooking.

Au Déjeuner de Sousceyrac (€)
Sousceyrac, 46190 Lot
tel: 05 65 33 00 56
Simple auberge in remote village, with small bedrooms. Excellent cooking and good-value local wines.

A l'Escargot (€)
5 boulevard Gambetta, Cahors
tel: 05 65 35 07 66
www.hotel-escargot.com
Hotel/restaurant with tastefully furnished rooms in an annexe. There are two dining rooms serving generous meals, including snails, of course.

L'Esplanade (€€€)
Domme, 24250 Dordogne tel: 05 53 28 31 41
Traditional old hotel within the fortifications of the village of Domme. The rustic restaurant has been awarded many accolades for its cuisine.

France (€€)
route d'Aurillac, Saint-Céré, 46400 Lot
tel: 05 65 38 02 16
www.lefrance-hotel.com
Modern, rustic-style hotel with a fine garden. Good-value menus.

France (€)
3 rue Marc-Dufraisse, Ribérac, 24600 Dordogne tel: 05 53 90 00 61
www.hoteldefranceriberac.com
Revitalized old building, with small garden and good value menus.

Grand Ecuyer (€€€)
rue Voltaire, Cordes-sur-Ciel, 81170 Tarn
tel: 05 63 53 79 50
www.thuries.fr
Wonderful medieval mansion, sumptuously restored, with renowned patron/chef.

Les Griffons (€€)
Le Pont, Bourdeilles, 24310 Dordogne
tel: 05 53 45 45 35
www.griffons.fr
Fine 16th-century house on the banks of the Dronne, with a popular restaurant.

Hostellerie du Passeur (€)
place de la Mairie, Les Eyzies-de-Tayac, 24620 Dordogne tel: 05 53 06 97 13
Better value than some of its competitors in this major tourist town, with a riverside setting.

Laborderie (€€)
Tamniès, 24620 Dordogne tel: 05 53 29 68 59
http://hotel.laborderie.tamnies.com/restaurant
Converted farm in village has annexe rooms in hillside garden and a celebrated Perigord restaurant.

Moulin de la Beune (€€)
Les Eyzies-de-Tayac, 24620 Dordogne
tel: 05 53 06 94 33
www.moulindelabeune.com
This converted mill has large, comfortable rooms and a restaurant that offers good value in the area.

L'Oustal del Barry (€€)
place du Bourg, Najac, 12270 Aveyron
tel: 05 65 29 74 32
www.hotels-restos.com
A fine old house in a medieval village. The restaurant offers good-value menus.

Relais du Touron (€)
route de Sarlat, Carsac-Aillac, 24200 Dordogne
tel: 05 53 28 16 70
Peaceful 19th-century manor in wooded countryside. The restaurant offers elegantly simple food.

De la Tour (€)
place de l'Eglise, Aubazines, 19190 Corrèze
tel: 05 55 25 71 17
Centrally located, with good-value menus. There is a fine tower room with good views.

L'Univers (€€)
2 place de la République, Villefranche-de-Rouergue, 12200 Aveyron tel: 05 65 45 15 63
Simple, central hotel with views over hills and old town. The restaurant offers good-value menus.

Le Vieux Logis (€€€)
Trémolat, 24510 Dordogne tel: 05 53 22 80 06
www.vieux-logis.com
Very peaceful old buildings set in immaculate gardens (with its own helipad).

PYRENEES

Angleterre (€€)
route Luchon, Arreau, 65240 Haute-Pyrénées
tel: 05 62 98 63 30
www.hotel-angleterre-arreau.com
This 17th-century inn, amid fast-flowing rivers and mountain scenery, offers good rustic cooking.

Arraya (€€)
Sare, 64310 Pyrénées-Atlantiques
tel: 05 59 54 20 46 www.arraya.com
A glorious old Basque village house, beautifully furnished and maintained, with small garden. The restaurant has a good choice of regional dishes.

Auberge Atalaya (€€)
Llo, 66800 Pyrénées-Orientales
tel: 04 68 04 70 04 www.atalaya66.com
Delightful old converted farmhouse in tiny Cerdagne village. The restaurant serves outstanding cuisine.

L'Auberge de Castel-Vielh (€)
Bagnères-de-Luchon tel: 05 61 79 36 79
A typical Pyrenean auberge with a garden and terrace has a popular restaurant. Rooms are available.

Auberge du Poids Public (€)
St-Félix-Lauragais, 31540 Haute-Garonne
tel: 05 62 18 85 00
www.auberge-du-poidspublic.com
Old inn in hill-top village. Local reputation for good cooking and wine list.

Hôtel Chilo (€)
Barcus, 64130 Pyrénées-Atlantiques
tel: 05 59 28 90 79
Old Basque house in the heart of a village surrounded by superb scenery. Individually styled bedrooms, gardens and playground. Good restaurant.

La Devinière (€€)
5 rue Loquin, St-Jean-de-Luz, 64500 Pyrénées-Atlantiques tel: 05 59 26 05 51
www.hotel-la-deviniere.com
Exquisitely furnished, tiny hotel.

Hostellerie des Sept Molles (€€€)
Sauveterre-de-Comminges, 31510 Haute-Garonne tel: 05 61 88 30 87
www.hotel7molles.com
In a secluded rural setting 3km (2 miles) from Sauveterre. Elegant but informal, with large garden.

Lons (€)
6 place G Duthil, Foix, 09000 Ariège
tel: 05 61 65 52 44
www.hotel-lons-foix.com
Comfortably modernized posthouse in heart of town, with spacious rooms and riverside views.

Nivelle (€)
St-Pée-sur-Nivelle, 64310 Pyrénées-Atlantiques tel: 05 59 54 10 27
Little Basque auberge with small, simple bedrooms (plus some in modern annexe across field).

Pic d'Anie (€)
Lescun, 64490 Pyrénées-Atlantiques tel: 05 59 34 71 54
A simple hotel in the middle of a walking village.

Les Prés d'Eugénie (€€€)
Eugénie-les-Bains, 40320 Landes tel: 05 58 05 06 07 www.michelguerard.com
Michel Guérard's luxurious and very expensive restaurant/hotel/health farm has bedrooms in a Second Empire mansion or in a converted convent.

Les Pyrénées (€€€)
19 place Charles de Gaulle, St-Jean-Pied-de-Port, 64220 Pyrénées-Atlantiques tel: 05 59 37 01 01 www.relaischateaux.com/pyrenees
Busy, traditional hostelry in the middle of town. Excellent-value restaurant serves regional cuisine.

Les Sources de la Nive (€)
Béherobie, St-Jean-Pied-de-Port, 64220 Pyrénées-Atlantiques tel: 05 59 37 10 57
A pretty riverside house in an idyllic setting, offering good value and excellent regional cuisine.

PROVENCE COAST

Abbaye Sainte-Croix (€€€)
route du Val-de-Cuech, Salon-de-Provence, 13300 Bouches-du-Rhône tel: 04 90 56 24 55 www.hotels-provence.com
These 12th-century abbey buildings in a rural setting have been beautifully converted.

Arène (€)
place des Langes, Orange, 84100 Vaucluse tel: 04 90 11 40 40 www.hotel-arene.fr
In the old town, on a shady square. No restaurant.

D'Arlatan (€)
26 rue du Sauvage, Arles, 13200 Bouches-du-Rhône tel: 04 90 93 56 66 www.hotel-arlatan.fr
Fine and very old mansion near the place du Forum. Your car is parked for you. No restaurant.

Auberge de la Madone (€€)
Peillon, 06440 Alpes-Maritimes tel: 04 93 79 91 17 www.chateauxhotels.com/madone
Astonishing situation, perched high in an isolated medieval village 18km (11 miles) behind Nice.

Auberge des Seigneurs (€)
place du Frêne, Vence, 06140 Alpes-Maritimes tel: 04 93 58 04 24 www.cote.azur.fr
Simple, inexpensive rooms with character in a 17th-century building, and an excellent restaurant.

Hôtel des Augustins (€€)
3 rue de la Masse, Aix-en-Provence tel: 04 42 27 28 59 www.hotel-augustins.com
A beautifully converted vaulted convent with well-equipped bedrooms. No restaurant.

Le Beffroi (€€)
rue de l'Evêché, Vaison-la-Romaine, 84110 Vaucluse tel: 04 90 36 04 71 www.le-beffroi.com
Wonderful 16th-century building up a steep hill in the town's medieval quarter.

Clair Logis (€–€€)
12 avenue Centrale, St-Jean-Cap-Ferrat, 06230 Alpes-Maritimes tel: 04 93 76 51 81 www.hotel-clair-logis.fr
Very simple establishment in large and lush gardens at the heart of the Cap. No restaurant.

L'Etrier Camarguais (€)
chemin bas des Launes, Les Saintes-Maries-de-la-Mer, 13460 Bouches-du-Rhône tel: 04 90 97 81 14 www.letrier.com
An ideal base to explore the Camargue. Informal, friendly service and good food.

Hotel d'Europe (€€)
12 place Crillon, Avignon, 84000 Vaucluse tel: 04 90 14 76 76 www.hotel-d-europe.fr
Just within the city walls and near the sights, this elegant 16th-century mansion has a formal air.

Les Florets (€)
route des Dentelles-de-Montmirail, Gigondas, 84190 Vaucluse tel: 04 90 65 85 01 www.hotel-lesflorets.com
Located at the foot of the Dentelles de Montmirail in the heart of the famous wine village of Gigondas. Good cooking and quality wine (the patron has his own vineyards).

Les Géraniums (€)
place de la Croix, Le Barroux, 84330 Vaucluse tel: 04 90 62 41 08 www.hotel-lesgeraniums.com
Impeccable hotel in picturesque hamlet, with terrace and views of vineyards and orchards. Comfortable bedrooms and good-value country cooking.

Lou Troupelen (€€)
chemin des Vendanges, St-Tropez, 83990 Var tel: 04 94 97 44 88
Modern, Provençal-style buildings, at the back of town, with garden and views. No restaurant.

Mas d'Aigret (€€)
Les Baux-de-Provence, 13520 Bouches-du-Rhône tel: 04 90 54 20 00 www.masdaigret.com
Good-value renovated hotel beneath the citadel, rooms with balconies and a pool.

Hotel Mignon (€)
12 rue Joseph Vernet, Avignon tel: 04 90 82 17 30 www.hotel-mignon.com
Prettily furnished, good-value hotel on central Avignon street; though the rooms are small, it is popular at Festival time.

La Réserve de Beaulieu (€€€)
boulevard Général Leclerc, Beaulieu-sur-Mer, 06310 Alpes-Maritimes tel: 04 93 01 00 01 www.reservebeaulieu.com
The pre-war atmosphere of this Italianate palace lingers on, despite restoration.

Le Saint Paul (€€€)
86 Rue Grande, 06570 St-Paul-de-Vence tel: 04 93 32 65 25
Exquisite château hotel up in the hills yet close to Nice airport, with an acclaimed gastronomic restaurant and superb views.

La Table du Comtat (€)
Séguret, 84110 Vaucluse tel: 04 90 46 91 49 email: table.comtat@wanadoo.fr
Attractive old house set in pretty hillside village, comfortable and sophisticated. Excellent cooking.

MASSIF CENTRAL

Auberge Fleurie (€)
place du Barry, Montsalvy, 15120 Cantal tel: 04 71 49 20 02 www.auberge-fleurie.com
Ivy-covered auberge at the edge of the village, with cheerful country-style restaurant (excellent value).

Auberge Pré Bossu (€€)
Moudeyres, 43150 Haute-Loire tel: 04 71 05 10 70 www.leprebossu.fr.fm
This former farmhouse, in a remote village, is renowned for its cooking by the patron/chef.

Hôtel Beauséjour (€€)
4 rue Basse, 15800 Vic-sur-Cère tel: 04 71 47 50 27 email: beausejour@wanadoo.fr
Large hotel and garden in an attractive medieval village. The restaurant serves Auvergnat food.

Hôtel Bristol (€)
7–9 avenue Maréchal Foch, Le-Puy-en-Velay tel: 04 71 09 13 38 www.hotelbristol-lepuy.com
Renovated hotel with bedrooms in a modern garden annexe. The restaurant offers good-value menus of classic dishes.

Château d'Ayres (€€)
Meyreuis, 48150 Lozère tel: 04 66 45 60 10
This converted monastery in parkland on the edge of the Causses has elegantly furnished bedrooms. Lavish food is served by the welcoming owners.

Château de Bagnols (€€€)
69620 Bagnols tel: 04 74 71 40 00 www.bagnols.com
This lavish château hotel is surrounded by gardens and has a superb gourmet restaurant.

Château de la Caze (€€€)
La Malène, 48210 Lozère tel: 04 66 48 51 01 www.ila-chateau.com/caze/index.htm
A medieval atmosphere can be enjoyed in this castle set in shady grounds about 5.5km (3.5 miles) from the village. The restaurant and additional apartments are in converted farm buildings.

Château de Codignat (€€€)
Bort-l'Etang, Lezoux, 63190 Puy de Dome tel: 04 73 68 43 03 www.codignat.com
A turreted Renaissance château in a wooded park, with antiques and candlelit dinners.

Grand Hotel du Parc (€€)
47 avenue J Monestier, Florac, 48400 Lozère tel: 04 66 45 03 05 http://hotel-restaurant-florac-lozere.grandhotelduparc.fr
Meals are available in this peaceful, large hotel surrounded by extensive grounds.

Hostellerie de la Maronne (€€)
Le Theil, St-Martin-Valmeroux, 15140 Cantal tel: 04 71 69 20 33 www.maronne.com
19th-century house in an idyllic valley near the hill-village of Salers, with superb food and service. It is ideal for lovers of architecture and culture.

Michel Bras (€€€)
route de l'Aubrac, Laguiole, 12210 Aveyron tel: 05 65 51 18 20 www.michel-bras.com
A restaurant-with-rooms, rather than a hotel—but what a restaurant! Michel Bras, one of France's great chefs, makes dreams come true.

Midi-Papillon (€)
place A Lemasson, St-Jean-du-Bruel, 12230 Aveyron tel: 05 65 62 26 04 www.hotel-midi-papillon.com
Well-run hotel in a picturesque valley amid hills and chestnut trees overlooking River Dourbie, offering excellent-value menus combined with more innovative dishes.

Sainte-Foy (€€)
Conques, 12320 Aveyron tel: 05 65 69 84 03 www.hotelsaintefoy.fr
An 18th-century building in the heart of the village. There are pretty bedrooms and two apartments in a nearby former convent. Meals are available.

THE ALPS & RHONE VALLEY

L'Abbaye (€€€)
Chemin des Moins, Talloires, 74290 Haute-Savoie tel: 04 50 60 77 33 www.abbaye-talloires.com
An elegantly furnished and atmospheric former abbey building on beautiful Lake Annecy.

Auberge du Cucheron (€)
Col du Cucheron, St-Pierre-de-Chartreuse, 38380 Isère tel: 04 76 88 62 06 www.lecucheron.net
Pass-top chalet restaurant-with-rooms, in picturesque hiking country.

Beausoleil (€)
Le Lavancher, Chamonix, 74400 Haute-Savoie tel: 04 50 54 00 78 www.hotelbeausoleil.com
This little hotel, in a mountain village 6km (4 miles) from Chamonix, has a pretty garden and tennis court.

Chalet Croix-Fry (€)
la Croix-Fry, Manigod, 74230 Haute-Savoie tel: 04 50 44 90 16 www.hotelchaletcroixfry.com
Cuckoo-clock chalet and delightful annexes, high on mountain pass.

Château de Coudrée (€€€)
Bonnatrait, 74140 Sciez-sur-Leman (Haute Savoie) tel: 04 50 72 62 33 www.coudree.fr
On shores of Lake Geneva, a 12th-century family-owned château. Meals are available.

Hotel Christiania (€)
Centre, Valloire tel: 04 79 59 00 57 www.christiania-hotel.com
Popular, renovated ski hotel with huge bar and dining room serving classic Alpine fare.

Le Fer à Cheval (€€)
36 route du Crêt-d'Arbois, Megève, 74120 Haute-Savoie tel: 04 50 21 30 39 www.feracheval-megeve.com
Hearty Savoy ambience with dinner round the fireplace.

Grand (€)
60 rue de l'Hôtel de Ville, Crest, 26400 Drôme tel: 04 75 25 08 17
Simple family-run establishment with a popular and good-value restaurant, which serves regional dishes.

Michel Chabran (€€€)
29 avenue du 45e-Parallèle, Pont-de-l'Isère, 26600 Drôme tel: 04 75 84 60 09 www.michelchabran.fr
An acclaimed restaurant-with-rooms.

Ostellerie du Vieux Pérouges (€€)
Place du Tilleul, Pérouges, 01800 Ain
tel: 04 74 61 00 88
www.ostellerie.com
A delightful medieval hostelry.

La Tour Rose (€€)
22 rue du Boeuf, Lyon, 69005 Rhône
tel: 04 78 92 69 10 www.tour-rose.com
An elegant hotel, in a glorious 17th-century former convent in the old town. The guest rooms are exquisitely furnished and offer a high level of comfort. The standard of cooking is as exalted as the surroundings. The restaurant, in the former chapel, with its glass roof, serves an extensive array of imaginative dishes. Reservations are recommended.

BURGUNDY & THE JURA

Le Bourgogne (€€)
place de l'Abbaye, Cluny, 71250 Saône-et-Loire
tel: 03 85 59 00 58 www.hotel-cluny.com
Stylish little hotel where Abbey of Cluny originally stood. Restaurant serves superb, imaginative dishes, complemented by excellent wines.

Les Capucins (€)
6 avenue Paul-Doumer, Avallon, 89200 Yonne
tel: 03 86 34 06 52
email: hotellescapucins@aol.com
This comfortable restaurant-with-rooms on a quiet square offers excellent regional cooking with breakfast served in the garden.

Le Cep (€€€)
27–29 rue Maufoux, Beaune, 21200 Côte-d'Or
tel: 03 80 22 35 48 www.hotel-cep-beaune.com
Beautiful Renaissance mansion with courtyard, in the middle of town (your car is parked for you).

L'Espérance (€€€)
St-Père-sous-Vézelay, 89450 Yonne tel: 03 86 33 33 33 www.marc-meneau-esperence.com
At this restaurant-with-rooms the food is produced by one of France's top chefs, Marc Meneau. There is a cheaper bistro opposite, under the same ownership. Some rooms are in a restored mill.

Hostellerie du Vieux Moulin (€€)
Bouilland, 21420 Côte-d'Or tel: 03 80 21 51 16 www.le-moulin-de-bouilland.com
The restaurant offers gourmet eating and a welcome for families in a romantic setting.

Jean-Paul Jeunet (€)
9 rue de l'Hôtel de Ville, Arbois, 39600 Jura
tel: 03 84 66 05 67
www.jeanpauljeunet.com
A chef in the ascendant, combined with a charming and tasteful hotel, makes this a pretty place to stay in the wine-growing Jura.

Le Parc des Maréchaux (€)
6 avenue Foch, Auxerre, 89000 Yonne
tel: 03 86 51 43 77
www.hotel-parcmarechaux.com
This stylish B&B in a quiet part of the city offers a warm welcome and generous breakfasts.

Hotel de la Poste (€)
Charolles, 71120 Saône-et-Loire
tel: 03 85 24 11 32
www.la-poste-hotel.com
Right in the heart of this small market town, Poste offers very good regional cooking.

Les Récollets (€)
place du Champ de Foire, 71110 Marcigny
tel: 03 85 25 05 16 www.lesrecollets.com
A converted convent, this hotel is comfortable and welcoming with open fires and home-made brioches for breakfast. No restaurant.

Relais Bernard Loiseau (€€€)
2 rue d'Argentine, 21210 Saulieu
tel: 03 80 90 53 53 www.bernard-loiseau.com
Bernard Loiseau's restaurant and hotel is famous for its low-fat cuisine. The adjoining 18th-century building is furnished with antiques and paintings, and has charming gardens and a courtyard.

ALSACE-LORRAINE & THE NORTH

Les Alisiers (€)
Lapoutroie, 68650 Haut-Rhin
tel: 03 89 47 52 82 www.alisiers.com
This small, converted hilltop farmhouse has comfortable bedrooms. The restaurant offers robust cooking.

Aux Armes de Champagne (€–€€€)
place de la Basilique, L'Epine, 51460 Marne
tel: 03 26 69 30 30
www.aux-armes-de-champagne.com
Opposite the basilica, this renowned hostelry offers a warm welcome in an informal atmosphere. The restaurant offers a wide range of local dishes.

Boyers Les Crayères (€€€)
64 boulevard Henri Vasnier, Reims, 51100 Marne
tel: 03 26 82 80 80 www.gerardboyer.com
Gérard Boyer's palatial restaurant and hotel, in a 19th-century château in Reims' suburbs.

Château de Montreuil (€€€)
Montreuil-sur-Mer, 62170 Pas-de-Calais
tel: 03 21 81 53 04
www.chateaudemontreuil.com
Just opposite the Roman citadel within the walled historic town of Montreuil-sur-Mer, this family-run, privately owned country house is English in style, with fine gardens. The food is excellent.

La Chartreuse de Val St-Esprit (€€)
1 rue des Fouquières, Gosnay, 62199 Pas-de-Calais tel: 03 21 62 80 00
www.lachartreuse.com
This 18th-century château, set in peaceful wooded grounds, has original furniture in the rooms and a fine restaurant which specializes in seafood.

Le Cheval Blanc (€€)
Sept-Saulx, 51400 Marne
tel: 03 26 03 90 27
www.hotelrestaurantlechevalblanc.com
Traditional coaching inn in middle of quiet village. The bedrooms (in the annexe) are in rustic style.

Hotel du Dragon (€)
2 rue d'Ecarlate/12 rue du Dragon, 67000 Strasbourg, Bas-Rhin tel: 03 88 35 79 80
www.dragon.fr
An elegant 17th-century former town house, where Louis XIV once stayed, close to La Petite France. Comfortable rooms overlook the quiet, old streets, some with views of the cathedral. There is a garden, but no restaurant.

Grand Hôtel de la Reine (€€€)
place Stanislas, Nancy, 54000 Meurthe-et-Moselle tel: 03 83 35 03 01
www.hoteldelareine.com
An 18th-century palace on the place Stanislas.

RESTAURANTS

PARIS

Alain Ducasse au Plaza Athénée (€€€)
Hôtel Plaza Athénée, 25 avenue Montaigne, 75008 Paris tel: 01 53 67 65 00 www.alainducasse.com
One of the best in the city, if not the world, with three Michelin stars for its unrivalled food.

L'Ambroisie (€€€)
9 place des Vosges, 75004 tel: 01 42 78 51 45
Always booked well ahead, this restaurant is small and exclusive, with superb cooking and décor.

Au C'Amelot (€€)
50 rue Amelot, 75011 Paris tel: 01 43 55 54 04
Intimate and friendly little place, where the chef serves a limited but always fabulous menu.

Brasserie Flo (€€)
7 cour des Petites-Ecuries, 75010 tel: 01 47 70 13 59
Jolly and authentic turn-of-the-20th-century brasserie that serves good food.

Cinq (€€€)
Hôtel George V, 31 avenue George V, 75008 Paris, tel: 01 49 52 71 54 www.fourseasons.com/paris
When the famous George V was renovated its restaurant was transformed into one of the best in the city, quickly winning Michelin stars.

La Closerie des Lilas (€€)
171 boulevard du Montparnasse, 75006 tel: 01 40 51 34 50
Famous old Montparnasse bar/brasserie/restaurant where a piano tinkles in the background, and the atmosphere is sophisticated and bustling.

La Coupole (€€)
102 boulevard du Montparnasse, 75014 tel: 01 43 20 14 20
Famous and noisy brasserie with literary and artistic associations, still atmospheric. Open till 2am.

La Fermette Marbeuf 1900 (€€)
5 rue Marbeuf 75008 tel: 01 53 23 08 00 www.fermettemarbeuf.com
Glorious belle époque décor, a good-value menu and wine list.

Le Grand Véfour (€€€)
17 rue de Beaujolais, 75001 tel: 01 42 96 56 27
A historic monument under the arcades of the Palais Royal: the place to dine in formal elegance.

Le Jules Verne (€€€)
Tour Eiffel, Champ de Mars 75007 tel: 01 45 55 61 44
Enjoy a perfect Paris experience in this luxurious restaurant, halfway up the Eiffel tower, which offers stylish modern cooking.

Au Pied de Cochon (€€)
6 rue de Coquillière, 75001 tel: 01 40 13 77 00
A Parisian institution on the site of the former Halles market, now more popular with tourists than early-morning porters. Open 24 hours a day and still good.

Le Procope (€€)
13 rue de l'Ancienne-Comédie, 75006 tel: 01 40 46 79 00
This is one of the oldest café/restaurants (1686) in the world, with literary associations. Agence France Presse telex, fax; piano and pianola. Open till 2am.

La Régalade (€€)
49 avenue Jean-Moulin 75014 tel: 01 45 45 68 58
Fashionable young chef Yves Camdeborde attracts two sittings a night for his authentically rustic dishes. Duck and rabbit are excellent.

ATLANTIC COAST

André (€)
5 rue Saint Jean du Pérot, La Rochelle tel: 05 46 41 28 24
Hotel at base of ramparts with terrace overlooking port. The restaurant serves a variety of seafood.

Le Chapon Fin (€€€)
5 rue Montesquieu, Bordeaux, 33000 Gironde tel: 05 56 79 10 10 www.chapon-fin.com
Extravagant décor is the hallmark here. Weekday lunch menus offer outstanding value. Popular locally.

Chez Jean (€)
1 place du Parlement, 33000 Bordeaux tel: 05 56 44 44 43
In a lovely little square that buzzes with eating places, the stylish food at Chez Jean really stands out. Try the mouthwatering Café Gourmand Dessert Plate.

L'Entrecote (€)
Cours du 30-Juillet, 33000 Bordeaux tel: 05 56 81 76 10
L'Entrecote serves steak and... well, just steak, but the queues outside tell you how well it does it, with endless plates of fries and inexpensive house red.

Le Vieux Bordeaux (€€)
27 rue Buhan, Bordeaux, 33000 Gironde tel: 05 56 52 94 36
One of the best of Bordeaux's many fine restaurants.

PROVENCE COAST

Chez Fonfon (€€–€€€)
140 rue du Vallon des Auffes, Marseille tel: 04 91 52 14 38 www.chezfonfon.com
Overlooking a pretty fishing port, this is one of the most famous restaurants on the coast. Traditional Provençale, including fabulous *bouillabaisse.*

Don Camillo (€€)
5 rue des Ponchettes, Nice, 06300 Alpes-Maritimes tel: 04 93 85 67 95
This simple restaurant serves great local dishes (raviolis, cheeses and puddings are particularly good).

La Mérenda (€€)
4 rue de la Terrasse, Nice, 06300 Alpes-Maritimes. No telephone
It's pot luck for a table in this tiny, traditional bistro.

Le Moulin de Mougins (€€)
424 chemin du Moulin, Quartier Notre-Dame-de-Vie, Mougins tel: 04 93 75 78 24 www.moulin-mougins.com
This old olive mill is the place to sample new chef Alain Llorca's *cuisine du soleil* (cuisine of the sun); Provençal classics with a twist, good cheese.

Restaurant Miramar (€€€)
12 quai du port, 13002 Marseille tel: 04 91 91 10 40 www.bouillabaisse.com
One of the best eating places by the old port, and the place to try the local specialty, bouillebaisse.

Index

Bold figures denote the main entry of a subject.

C

D

E

F

G

H

I

J

K

L

M

N

Picture Credits

The Automobile Association would like to thank the following photographers, libraries and associations for their assistance in the preparation of this book.

CDT CANTAL 201 Chaines des Puys; CDT CHARENTE 128 Aubeterre; CHAMONIX TOURIST BOARD 209 Walkers, 211 Climbers, 215 Paragliders; CHASTEL & COURTOIS 236 Moutiers; HAUTE SAVOIE 25 Skiing; HULTON PICTURE LIBRARY 47 François Mitterrand; ILLUSTRATED LONDON NEWS 45t de Gaulle. MARY EVANS PICTURE LIBRARY 34 39 Louis XIV, 40 Napoleon, 40/41 Women marching to Versailles; 42 Lafayette; poster, 44 Signing of Treaty of Versailles cartoon 75t Bayeux Tapestry, 75b Bayeux Tapestry; SPECTRUM COLOUR LIBRARY 26 Lyon, 28 Carnac, 47 Lyon, 109 Tapestry, 150 St-Sernin.

All remaining pictures are held in the Automobile Association's own library (© AA Photo Library), with contributions from: P Atterbury, P Bennett, R Day, S Day, J Edmunson, M Jourdan, P Enticknap, P Kenward, R Moore, D Noble, T Oliver, K Paterson, N Ray, B Rieger, D Robertson, C Sawyer, N Setchfield, M Short, B Smith, A Souter, R Strange, R Victor, J Wynand